D1596750

Radicalism
in the States

American Politics and Political Economy Series
Edited by Benjamin I. Page

Radicalism

Richard M. Valelly

in the States

The Minnesota Farmer-Labor Party and the American Political Economy

Foreword by Martin Shefter

The University of Chicago Press   Chicago and London

RICHARD M. VALELLY is assistant professor of political science at the Massachusetts Institute of Technology.

THE UNIVERSITY OF CHICAGO PRESS, CHICAGO 60637
THE UNIVERSITY OF CHICAGO PRESS, LTD., LONDON

∞ The paper used in this publication meets
the minimum requirements of the American National
Standard for Information Sciences—Permanence of
Paper for Printed Library Materials, ANSI Z39.48-1984.

Library of Congress Cataloging-in-Publication Data

Valelly, Richard M.
    Radicalism in the states : the Minnesota Farmer-Labor Party
and the American political economy / Richard M. Valelly.
        p.   cm.—(American politics and political economy series)
    Bibliography: p.
    Includes index.
    ISBN 0-226-84535-4 (alk. paper)
    1. Farmer-Labor Party (Minn.) 2. Minnesota—Politics
and government—1858–1950. 3. United States—Economic
policy—1933–1945. I. Title. II. Series.
TK2391.F32M68   1989
324.2776'02—dc19   88-36843
                                                          CIP

For Nanette and Peter

Contents

	Foreword by Martin Shefter	ix
	Preface	xiii
	Acknowledgments	xvii
ONE	The Possibilities of State-Level Radicalism	1
TWO	The Political Origins of the Minnesota Farmer-Labor Party	17
THREE	Beyond Insurgency	33
FOUR	Party and Patronage	53
FIVE	The Political Economy of State-Level Radicalism	70
SIX	The Limits of State-Level Radicalism	83
SEVEN	New Deal Labor Policy and the Minneapolis Strikes of 1934	103
EIGHT	The Crisis of State-Level Radicalism	119
NINE	The Dynamics of Collapse	139
TEN	State-Level Radicalism and Political Change	157
	Afterword	174
	Notes	179
	Bibliography	215
	Index	239

Foreword

Richard Valelly's study of the Minnesota Farmer-Labor party exemplifies an important recent trend in political science—the rediscovery of the American states.

Valelly's focus on party politics at the state level harks back to a tradition of political analysis initiated by V. O. Key. During the ten to fifteen years following the 1949 publication of Key's masterful *Southern Politics*, the study of politics in the American states was at the heart of the discipline. That tradition, however, largely lay dormant for two decades after the early 1960s.

Changes in American politics and in the discipline of political science help account for the waning of this scholarly tradition in the 1960s and 1970s. State party organizations grew weaker and the federal government stronger, regions of one-party dominance diminished, and a candidate-centered politics spread throughout the nation. As the significance and variety of politics at the state level seemed to be declining, scholars turned their attention elsewhere. Equally important, the growing popularity of survey research within the discipline of political science focused scholarly attention upon individual voters rather than on patterns of political organization in the states.

Though explicable, the decline of interest in state politics was unfortunate. The analysis of party systems in the states enabled students of American politics to engage in comparative research and to address numerous significant questions. What are the conditions facilitating the emergence of systems of competitive and noncompetitive party politics? Under what conditions are strong party organizations likely to develop? When does the quest for patronage predominate in party politics? What conditions enable protest movements to penetrate the electoral arena? What are the consequences of different patterns of party organization and competition for the conduct of public policy?

Radicalism in the States sheds light on these issues. One way it does so is by artfully employing the comparative method. Just as Key and his students provided illuminating comparisons of patterns of state party organization within and across regions, Valelly analyzes the conditions generating state-level radicalism by comparing political patterns in Minnesota with those prevailing both in other midwestern states and elsewhere in the nation.

At the same time, however, Valelly draws upon two more recent trends in American political science—political economy and the "new institutionalism." This leads him in directions that were not explored in earlier studies of party politics in the states.

In seeking to account for the emergence of the Farmer-Labor party, Valelly undertakes to situate Minnesota within both the national and international political economy. He characterizes the American political economy of the post–World War I era as "accumulationist." The Republican party's core constituency lay in the industrial states north of the Ohio and east of the Mississippi, and the GOP sought to promote prosperity by reducing the costs faced by American industry. Republican administrations in Washington reduced taxes and public expenditures, and eschewed policies that might increase the price of raw materials and labor. This commitment to deflation was reinforced by America's adherence to the international gold standard. At the same time, tariffs were enacted to protect domestic manufacturers against foreign competition. These policies benefited northeastern industrialists, their employees, and farmers who sold in the home market.

Accumulationist economic policies imposed heavy burdens, however, on farmers in the South and West, as well as on workers in the extractive industries of those regions. These farmers and workers produced commodities for sale in unprotected international markets, whereas the goods they purchased were subject to the tariff. Moreover, Washington's commitment to maintaining the value of the dollar against gold required that America's real interest rates be kept high, imposing additional burdens upon the heavily indebted farmers of the nation's peripheral regions. Finally, merchants in agricultural marketing towns were squeezed as the disposable income of their customers fell and national mail-order merchandisers grew. These distressed farmers, workers, and members of the small-town middle class made up the constituency for radical third-party politics in the 1920s.

But why did these radical third parties seek solutions for the problems their constituents faced through state governments rather than on the national level? Why did such parties emerge outside the Northeastern metropole and the South? And why did state-level radicalism largely disappear by the 1940s? To answer these questions, Valelly turns to the new institutionalism.

A central insight of the new institutionalism is that governmental institutions and public policies structure the conduct of politics. Institutions and policies shape the views of political actors and at times their very identity, and they influence the strategies individuals and groups pursue in the political arena. The new institutionalists are also hardheaded realists who recognize that, as Valelly puts it, "purposive, spontaneous collective action by ordinary people is exceptional. . . . My working assumption therefore is this: whether radical entrepreneurs—we might call them counterelites—can get into the political game and stay in significantly influences whether government intervenes in the economy and adopts redistributive policies" (p. 16). In seeking to account for the rise and decline of the Farmer-Labor party, then, Valelly looks at not only the grievances of its rank-and-file supporters but also the political and institutional context within which elites and counterelites in Minnesota operated.

Two aspects of the nation's political structure in the 1920s encouraged the emergence of state-level radicalism in the upper Midwest. First, the decentralization of power in the pre–New Deal federal system meant that the benefits that were to be gained by controlling state governments were in many respects as great or greater than could be obtained by exercising influence on the national level. For example, strikes were broken far more frequently by state militia than by the U.S. Army, and hence organized labor had a major stake in how the police power of the state was exercised.

Second, there was "organizational space," as Valelly puts it, for political entrepreneurs to operate successfully in states such as Minnesota in the 1920s and early 1930s. In particular, the Democratic and Republican party organizations were considerably weaker and less broadly based in the peripheral regions of the country than in the nation's industrial metropole. This made it possible for third parties to penetrate the political system and acquire an extensive popular following.

The structure of American politics changed in both these respects in the 1930s, and these changes, Valelly argues, largely account for the disappearance of state-level radicalism. By greatly strengthening the national government, the New Deal encouraged political forces to look to Washington more than to the states for solutions to the problems they faced. Thus the nationalization of policy-making and administrative capacities in the United States fostered a nationalization of politics.

Equally important, the New Deal transformed the constellation of interests contending for power at all levels of the American political system. In particular, the Roosevelt administration's farm policies strengthened an agricultural interest group—the Farm Bureau—that was hostile to the Farmer-Labor party, while undermining agricultural organizations allied with the party. At the same time, tensions at the national level between the American Federation of Labor and the Congress of Industrial Organizations, in conjunction with the administration's labor policies, divided the labor movement in cities and states throughout the country, including Minnesota. These developments seriously weakened the Farmer-Labor party.

The conditions that undermined state-level radicalism in the 1930s still characterize American politics and are likely to endure in the decades to come. Valelly's analysis of the Minnesota Farmer-Labor party is thus not merely of local or historical interest. As Barrington Moore has noted, by learning why the "suppressed alternatives" of history failed, we deepen our knowledge of the conditions shaping the present. In this way, Richard Valelly's study of the rise and fall of state-level radicalism enriches our understanding of contemporary American politics.

Martin Shefter

Preface

This is a study of a political party and of the special significance of its history. The American political economy's development and regional differences in the organization of party politics both shaped the history of that party. The Minnesota Farmer-Labor party (1918–44) is the most successful case of a radical, state-level third party that American politics has seen.

In explaining the Minnesota Farmer-Labor party's history this book treats the dilemmas of building a certain kind of organization. It treats the challenges of organizing voters to back a program of redistributing wealth and power so that ordinary people are less menaced by those anxiety-causing operations of a capitalist economy that they normally do not control.

Such helplessness is the lot of most people. A century and a half of panics, depressions, and recessions underscores its depth. Less visible forms of economic change, generated by continuous reorganization of the world's industrial and agricultural division of labor, also reveal the empire of capitalism. These economic changes hem in people who lack inherited wealth or other class privileges that can help them adjust to the disappearance of a market for their skills. Anyone who has ever pondered these features of capitalism and wondered about the extent to which democratic politics can tame them will find the Minnesota Farmer-Labor party's history at least interesting, and possibly fascinating.

The struggle to build in Minnesota an organization for protecting people from some of capitalism's stresses was extraordinarily creative. Much of its creativity was in building a strong party organization. Much of it lay in politically uniting farmers and workers. Farmers and workers have often mistrusted each other, here in America and elsewhere. Yet early in the Farmer-Labor party's history, farm leaders and labor leaders learned how to work with each other inside their organization, in platform writing, in campaigns and ticket balancing, and in the Minnesota legislature. Cooperation was also important in the electorate. The Farmer-Labor party came to enjoy electoral strength both in urban and rural areas of Minnesota.

These are the heartening features of the story. In time, though, the Minnesota Farmer-Labor party's struggle to redistribute wealth and power to ordinary people became limited. Why? Answering this question illuminates the interaction between American political development and the history of a type of politics, what I call "state-level radicalism." This book is also about broad change in American politics. To understand what came to block the Farmer-Labor party's continued success is also to understand why a type of politics became impossible. It is to understand the disappearance in America of possibilities for handling questions of material welfare and political participation in a decentralized way.

The work of such excellent Minnesota scholars as Hyman Berman, Millard Gieske, George Mayer, Steven Keillor, and Arthur Naftalin, all of whom have written meticulously researched monographs, provides one set of answers to the question of "what limited the Farmer-Labor party?" Their work tends to focus on political culture and leadership. Those factors were important, of course. Despite the presence in Minnesota of Scandinavian immigrants with radical or social democratic ideas, which created a political culture conducive to protest, most Minnesotans, like most other Americans, were not particularly ideologically inclined. Also, organizations that challenge the distribution of power in a capitalist society do very much depend on creative leadership. The historians thus suggest that what really counted in the Farmer-Labor party's history was the extent of the gap between the values of the party's leaders and the moderate-to-conservative "American values" of the people whom they had to mobilize. When the gap was narrow, because of good leadership, all was well; when the gap was wide, because of poor leadership, the party was in trouble. It didn't seem to pay to be radical in America, to challenge fundamentally the distribution of power in American capitalism, especially as an older generation of immigrants died or became more conservative.

There was far more to the Farmer-Labor party's history. To understand the party's history fully, and to see its importance, it has to be placed in a comparative framework. One has to ask, what about other comparable cases, both in and outside the United States? One also has to ask questions about the national political-economic context of a state-level strategy for politically challenging the distribution of American capitalism's rewards.

This study thus moves well beyond the historiography of the Farmer-Labor party which I encountered when I began my research and which has grown since then. The reconstruction of the party's history offered here would not have been possible without this historiography. But in order to capture the distinctive relevance of the Minnesota Farmer-Labor party's history to an understanding of political change in America, this book offers new historiography and new analysis.

First, I place the Farmer-Labor party's history in a regional typology of party organization and pursue the implications of the contrasts that this reveals. Second, I place the party's history in a comparative, national and political-economic context.

This book therefore sheds light on the regional development of party politics in America. It also explores the extent to which national public policies and transformations in the national political economy determine state and local politics.

The hard fact that there is more power in Washington to shape the political economy than in a state capital eventually limited the Farmer-Labor party. When politicians in Washington began to do things similar to what Farmer-Labor politicians in St. Paul would have done if they had possessed national power, they disarranged the politics of state-level radicalism. They organized a type of politics out of the American regime, closing off possibilities for America to handle certain questions of material welfare and political participation in a decentralized way.

In the 1930s national governmental capacities permitted a rising class of national politicians, brought to power by national electoral change, to implement policies that moved the United States closer to a political economy somewhat similar to that which the Farmer-Labor party's politicians had long advocated. Successful implementation of these new policies changed the interest-group politics of rural and industrial society. The New Deal's Agricultural Adjustment Act made it possible for an anti-farmer-labor group, the Farm Bureau, to grow. The Wagner Act institutionalized a split between the Committee for Industrial Organization and the American Federation of Labor. Thus new policies opened up opportunities for political entrepreneurs to expand their group organizations. Yet the change in the interest-group systems of America increasingly posed intractable strategic and tactical dilemmas for politicians in St. Paul and elsewhere. Building and sustaining an elite, policy-making consensus at the state level became in certain states, including Minnesota, much harder. Also, the new groups, and conflicts between old and new groups, had an impact at the state level on public opinion. Finally, as the public became more aware of macroeconomic management, the possibilities for discontent with a new welfare state grew. These possibilities became manifest during the Roosevelt Recession of 1937 and 1938.

Simply by pursuing their own agenda, those in Washington, so to speak, created the conditions for dissensus among a group of political entrepreneurs once firmly united around a consensus for protest. And their actions and policies had a remarkable impact on public opinion. This impact constrained the previously successful politicians of state-level radicalism.

What does a set of politicians do when its room for maneuver becomes smaller and smaller? What can it do? Under what circumstances could matters have turned out differently for it? In treating these questions I show how a universe of political possibilities and limits disappeared and a new one took its place. I show how politicians who practiced their craft within a previous and older dispensation were not even fully aware of the magnitude of the change going on around them.

In this respect the experience of the Farmer-Laborites is truly universal. It is an experience common to cases as diverse as the French and Russian revolutions, the collapse of Weimar Germany, and, less dramatically, the collapse in the late 1960s of the Democratic party's hegemony in American politics. In all these cases a political order that was once possible stops being possible. Some new political order takes its place, changing what politicians can do or what they can even think about doing.

This book, at its most fundamental level, is about *that* kind of political change. It is as much about political change in general as it is about the interaction between state-level radicalism and American political development. To the extent that it treats such a transformation, perhaps it will sharpen our thinking about the kinds of transformations going on today. I hope that it will remind us, if reminder is needed, that questions about the possibilities and limits of American politics are always with us.

Acknowledgments

My wife, Nanette Tobin, has given so much time, patience, and love to the process of writing this book that it is in a sense as much her book as it is mine. With gratitude and love I dedicate it to her. I also dedicate it to our beloved son, Peter, who arrived in the middle of the book's composition. I hope that one day he will read and enjoy this study of American politics in the 1920s and 1930s.

I must also thank academic colleagues and friends for their criticism, comments, and encouragement: Walter Dean Burnham, Mike Lipsky, Charles Stewart, and Don Blackmer, all from my department at MIT; Mike Goldfield, Ken Finegold, Mildred Schwartz, and J. David Greenstone, at other institutions. Two graduate school friends, Harvey Rishikof and Beth Rubenstein, encouraged me at an early stage of the work. My friend Ken Sharpe has helped me to think clearly about my work from the day I began researching the Farmer-Labor party. I also thank again Sid Verba, Amy Bridges, and Harry Hirsch for their encouragement and criticism over the years. Members of an informal study group in Cambridge, Massachusetts, gave me useful feedback on my first chapter in early 1987, and I thank them for it. I thank Harvey Klehr and Lowell Dyson for comments and help with securing quite valuable interviews.

I also thank O. R. Votaw, who as a young radical trade unionist in St. Paul helped to found the Minnesota Farmer-Labor party. He read an earlier result of my research and commented on it usefully.

Tom Sample, an MIT graduate student, did data analysis for chapters 1 and 9, cheerfully performing tedious calculations that resulted in two tables and in useful statistics regarding voter behavior in Duluth in the 1930s, as well as other material that could not be used here. I also thank him for a helpful critique of the first chapter.

For financial support, I thank the dean of the School of Humanities and Social Science at MIT and the MIT Provost's Office. The College of the Holy Cross helped earlier with certain small but important research expenses, and I particularly thank Virginia Raguin of the Holy Cross Visual Studies Department for her confidence in my research.

I must also thank the staffs of the Widener, Hilles, Langdell, and Littauer libraries of the Harvard University Library system. Ned Bunker, Charles Warren Bibliographer of American History, Collection Development Department, Widener Library, and Claire Brown, Specialist in Manpower and Industrial Relations, Slichter Industrial Relations Collection, Littauer Library, were very generous with their time and resources. I thank the staff of Dewey Library at MIT and the staff of the MIT Inter-Library Loan office for their help. The staff of Wilson Library at the University of Minnesota at Minneapolis also helped at an early stage of the research.

The Minnesota Historical Society staff has helped me greatly over the years. I thank it again for its efficiency and courtesy. The Minnesota Historical Society Press provided me with a galley proof of Jerome Tweton's quite interesting book, *The New Deal at the Grass Roots*, and I thank it for this courtesy. Pruda Lood of the Hoover Institution Archives staff professionally researched certain parts of the Ernest Lundeen Papers at the Hoover Institution Archives, permitting a useful treatment of the Lundeen Bill on unemployment insurance in chapter 10.

I thank Mark Heistad of Minnesota Public Radio for providing me with copies of his valuable oral documentaries on farm and labor protest in Minnesota. Patrick Coleman, the Acquisitions Librarian of the Minnesota Historical Society Reference Library, gave generously of his time and knowledge of Farmer-Labor ephemera to the process of designing the dust jacket.

Also, I thank my parents, my late grandmother, and other people whom I have not named who helped me to produce the first result of my research into the Farmer-Labor party's history, my Ph.D. dissertation. Their help is still gratefully remembered.

Last, but truly not least, I thank all the people who consented to interviews about their knowledge of the history I treat, and all those who talked with me on the phone, answered letters, tape-recorded their answers to mailed questionnaires, let me see valuable pieces of paper and photographs, or let me listen to valuable tapes. Many of them I cannot name, for one reason or another (although many are named in the Bibliography). All of them illuminated the past or apprised me of key historical details. A significant part of this book's authority depends on their courtesy and kindness.

ONE   *The Possibilities of*
        State-Level Radicalism

America has had several types of party politics: a partial list includes machine politics; factional, one-party politics; mass movement, third-party politics; fluid, candidate-centered party politics permeable to self-starting politicians; and brokered party politics with candidates selected in closed meetings by experienced vote-getters. Why have some types prospered? And then stopped prospering? What is the relationship between these patterns of success and how a democratic government, responsive to electorates whose behavior is organized by competing teams of party leaders, changes—or does not change—a capitalist economy? What role have governmental capacities for intervention played in shaping these changes? What role have institutional structure and variations in party organization and history played? We are likely to ask these questions about political change and continuity so long as competitive party politics persists, and so long as group and public demands for government intervention in the economy persist.

A type of party politics fruitfully studied in the context of these questions is *state-level radicalism*—radical third-party politics clustered in space and time in several political jurisdictions outside the Deep South and with one exception west of the Mississippi. Its leaders and activists sought to gain power at the state level and to influence Congress. State-level radicalism gathered together ideological strands from populism, Debsian socialism, and middle-class progressivism, and it used third-party or nonpartisan tactics to shape public policy. Parties with this type of politics are the Minnesota Farmer-Labor party (1918–44), the Wisconsin Progressive party (1934–48), the North Dakota Nonpartisan League (1915–56), the Washington Farmer-Labor party (1920–24), the Idaho Progressive party (1920–26), the Oklahoma Farmer-Labor Reconstruction League (1922), and other, more ephemeral organizations (in South Dakota, Montana, Texas, and California) which were, nevertheless, strong enough to run gubernatorial and congressional campaigns.

These organizations placed innovative ideas of political economy on the agendas of several political jurisdictions for periods ranging from several months to nearly a quarter century. For instance, the 1934 plat-

1

form of the governing Minnesota Farmer-Labor party called for the gradual abolition of capitalism, public ownership of key industries, a large-scale public works program to relieve unemployment, a full range of welfare programs to be run by the state, the nationalization of banking or the establishment of a central state bank of Minnesota, and state-run marketing and purchasing agencies for farmers.[1] The Farmer-Labor party immediately pulled back from this platform, issuing "interpretations" of it, fearing that it would lose its hold on state government. Its stance in 1936 and 1938 became more moderate. The party's radicalism went through stages, a pattern common to all the radical parties. But the 1934 Farmer-Labor party platform (which was not any more radical than policies that the party had proposed in the early 1920s) represented the deepest impulses of the Farmer-Labor party's activists.[2] Democracy meant limiting the influence of capital on politics and society as much as possible.

The Farmer-Labor party's scope of influence, that is, its appeal to intellectuals, its policy impact, and its imprint on national party and interest-group politics, was considerable. When the Farmer-Labor governor of Minnesota proclaimed in 1933 that he hoped that "the present system of government goes right down to hell" if it could no longer feed and employ people, politicians and intellectuals throughout America took notice.[3]

As for its policy impact, the party helped to institute collective bargaining in Minnesota two and a half years before the Supreme Court's decision that the National Labor Relations Act of 1935 was constitutional. The party also curbed the power of giant bank groups in the Twin Cities and sought to regulate chain stores. It instigated the legal rescue from mortgage foreclosure of thousands of farms and helped to lay the constitutional foundations of the welfare state in America by successfully defending Minnesota's mortgage moratorium law before the Supreme Court.[4] It reshaped the tax system of Minnesota, making its design more redistributive. The party rather ably handled, within limits, the problems of unemployed people. At the national level it shaped congressional debate on unemployment insurance and social security. Not surprisingly, three of America's most social democratic politicians, Hubert Humphrey, Walter Mondale, and Don Fraser, have come from Minnesota.

The North Dakota Nonpartisan League, to take another example, was in certain ways as radical and as successful as the Minnesota Farmer-Labor party. During the league's heyday, 1915–21, it faced the kinds of institutions that, in other states, have hindered mass electoral choice of new policies and new leaders.[5] These are the long ballot; the multiple executive; elective regulatory commissions insulated from direct electoral control through a variety of procedural devices, and one-party politics. But over the course of four elections, two primaries and two general elections, the Nonpartisan League seized control of North Dakota government to an extent probably unknown in American state politics until or since then. The only parallel may be the heyday of Huey Long, "the Kingfish," in Louisiana.

As a result North Dakota became a virtual laboratory for policy experimentation. By early 1919 sympathetic politicians regularly referred to a "New Day" in North Dakota, taking their cue from a Nonpartisan League pamphlet that employed the slogan. Success generated a lot of confidence and, for a time, a lot of money, enough of both to affect politics as far west as Washington and as far south as Texas.

The league succeeded in creating an agency, the Industrial Commission, empowered to manage the state's business enterprises, as well as creating the Bank of North Dakota, the North Dakota Mill and Elevator Association, and the Home Building Association, which would build homes cheaply, thus beginning a system of public housing decades before it appeared elsewhere in the United States. The league also limited the labor injunction and established an eight-hour day and minimum wages for women. These reforms built on an earlier policy, namely, collective bargaining in 1917 and 1918 with the International Workers of the World (IWW; "the One Big Union"), which then controlled harvest labor in North Dakota. Not surprisingly, given the sharp contrast between how the Nonpartisan League ran North Dakota and how the Republican and Democratic parties ran all the other states in the Union, the Nonpartisan League attracted attention throughout the United States. The headquarters of an offshoot of the North Dakota Nonpartisan League, the National Nonpartisan League, received requests for information from as far away as Tokyo.

All of this is in contrast with contemporary state government. State governments in America handle rather knotty policy problems, but in a low-temperature political context. There are exceptions—California's tax revolt in the late 1970s comes to mind. State-level industrial policies have attracted much attention more recently. Still, the political economy of the states typically centers on quietly attracting or retaining investment or on the allocation of revenues and resources to powerful interest groups, ethnic groups, and, more recently, highly mobilized social-issue groups. The political economy of the states does not revolve—as it did in the jurisdictions I discuss in this book—around large questions of political economy:

Should state government be activist and redistributive? How much power should corporations have to set our political agendas? How much power should other organized groups have, be they farmers, workers, or unemployed men and women?

The political entrepreneurs of state-level radicalism pushed for a certain type of political economy. In ideal, typical terms governments in capitalist democracies have performed either an "accumulation" function or have sought to balance "accumulation" and "reform" functions. Both types of political economy depend on governmental commitment to reinforcing the market as an institution. Where they differ is in *how* government acts to maintain the market.[6]

The name "accumulationist" underscores a stress on private savings and capital formation. In performing the function of accumulation, government grants considerable freedom to domestic or foreign private capital to pursue economic growth. And government does little or nothing to guard citizens from the risks, pressures, and dislocations endemic to capitalism. In a crash or recession, or in a long wave that is a mixture of economic distress and areas of growth such as the crisis of the last third of the nineteenth century, the accumulationist government tends to leave equilibrium to a supposedly self-correcting market.

In the orthodox, accumulationist view, government should assure the allocatively efficient redistribution of resources. Thus government's tendency not to act seems to ignore the socially and psychologically painful aspects of reallocation. But in the long run government preserves the public interest in growth, by not impeding the market's efficient reallocation of resources.

The accumulationist government can intervene in the economy, but government intervention is restricted to a very limited set of actions. If government does anything, it should behave "procyclically": for instance, cutting expenditures and taxes in order to reduce business costs during the downswing of the business cycle. Government may even shield private capital from social reactions to capitalism's natural pressures, for example, through the kind of sweeping labor injunction that the Cleveland administration used against the American Railway Union strike of 1894. Also, it should defend the currency in order to guarantee the predictability of money values that would permit business to invest confidently in new products, processes, and plants. Finally, government may under certain circumstances engage in tariff protection, for which many legitimate arguments about the national interest can be entertained. Tariffs simply change prices but otherwise are compatible with a limited state, which can continue to balance budgets and defend the currency. Other than these actions the accumulationist state should do little else, ceding to businessmen, bankers, and stockbrokers unchallenged control of investment decisions.

In the reform type of political economy, government still guarantees capital's command of the basic investment decisions. Government officials in fact worry about business confidence and promote it, for example, through tax policies, foreign economic policies, or even induced recessions designed to tame inflation. But government also seeks to address problems that the market cannot solve or actually creates, thus enhancing the market's legitimacy and its long-run institutional survival. Government performs "reform" functions, seeking to correct the socially inadequate supply of such goods as credit, decent employment, adequate wages, or old-age income security. Government thus works to balance reform and accumulation functions.

How the balancing occurs, with what particular mix of policies, with what scope of coverage in the public extension of those goods the market does not supply on a large scale—these all vary across space and time. A balancing type of political economy does not spring full blown into permanent existence. It is built over time, can vary in several ways through different mixes of policy, and can be partly dismantled. National governmental capacities strongly shape such variation. They crucially determine the particular mix of public policies that elites advocating a balancing political economy can design and implement.

The real world is different from the two ideal types I have constructed. But distinguishing between such ideal types permits a characterization of the political-economic goals of state-level radicalism. The politicians of such organizations as the Minnesota Farmer-Labor party and the North Dakota Nonpartisan League pushed for a change at both the national and state levels in the accumulationist political economy that existed during the first third of the twentieth century. They pushed for a balancing political economy.

Conditions for State-Level Radicalism

What made state-level radicalism possible? Two conditions had to do with incentives. Between the Panic of 1893 and the Great Crash of 1929 there were incentives for politicians in north central, northwestern, southwestern, and western jurisdictions to invent a new type of party politics—state-level radicalism. Particular features of the accumulationist political economy of America generated economic and social stresses on American society, in the context of a national party

The Possibilities of State-Level Radicalism

politics that favored state-level responses to these stresses. Also, the nature of federalism before the New Deal meant that capturing state-level power could be and was a goal for politicians.

These incentives for state-level radicalism were necessary but not sufficient. Taken alone they would predict the emergence of state-level radicalism throughout the United States, yet it clustered in north central and northwestern states. Two other factors explain the location of state-level radicalism: regional variation in the organization of party politics, and the quality and supply of politicians willing to break with regular party politics.

The Persistence of Social Stress

During the latter half of the nineteenth century the American political economy was, with the exception of the Civil War pension system, famously accumulationist. The Civil War pension system did provide old-age income security to a large fraction of the adult population.[7] But otherwise public power overwhelmingly tended to support the considerable autonomy of private decision makers to decide the uses of land, labor, and capital. Political and economic elites believed that demands for policies to aid people squeezed by economic change would destroy a virtuous and natural order.[8] A prominent lawyer termed it a "superstition" that "legislation is a sovereign cure-all for all social ills," and a Supreme Court justice opined that a congressional curb on interstate commerce in goods produced by child labor meant that the American system of government "would be practically destroyed."[9] Grover Cleveland vowed at the beginning of his second term, "No harm shall come to any business interest as a result of administrative policy so long as I am president."[10]

During the electoral realignment of the 1890s those political and economic elites with a stake in an orthodox, accumulationist political economy acquired a mass constituency that proved enormously loyal. With the help of urban workers and prosperous commercial farmers they defeated a national agrarian protest. Over time several factors contributed to the resilience of this mass-elite linkage forged in the 1890s, despite challenges from Debsian socialism and, to a greater degree, from Wilsonian liberalism. Among those factors were Democratic ineptitude in several elections, timely reforms by the progressive elements of the Republican party, the great size of the internal American market, which helped to make a gold-standard-cum-tariffs economy work, and World War I's stimulation of the American economy. The period between 1896 and 1928 is thus rightly known as the "system of 1896."[11]

Despite the strength of the electoral bases of the accumulationist political economy, its social harshness was considerable. In northeastern industrial areas unemployment and underemployment were pervasive, as well as in states, like Montana and West Virginia, dependent on natural-resource extraction. Often—incomparably more often than today—courts, police, and militias sentenced, enjoined, jailed, and shot workers throughout the country. As for farmers, they faced a new, more difficult world in industrialism. They had lived through the national economic policy of restricting the supply of money as the post–Civil War economy expanded. As farm output shot up, prices dropped. Although farmers on the average had prospered, price deflation in combination with the constant addition of new lands to agriculture had the overall effect of keeping agriculture's productivity growth lower than industry's. Wealth thus flowed from the rural economy to the industrial economy. Not surprisingly this redistribution coincided with a large shift in the economy's division of labor. Farming no longer was the major industry it once had been, a vast change that also saw the emergence of rural poverty. Agriculture, as in every industrializing regime, faced an increasingly subordinate status as a sector of the economy.[12]

A highly sectional division of labor helped to drive the political economy. In the area bounded by Minneapolis, Boston, Norfolk (Virginia), and St. Louis were half of the nation's population, about four-fifths of manufacturing employment, about three-fifths of personal income, and a concentration of capital and of educational institutions. Surrounding this advanced section were less developed areas, including the New England states of New Hampshire, Vermont, and Maine. Perhaps the least developed was the South, which had a large base of poor citizens, a tiny middle class, and an even smaller dominant class. The economies of these less developed areas relied heavily on cash crops and natural-resource extraction. And they were also integrated—due to the dynamism of the northeastern industrial metropole—into the national and international economies. They were vulnerable to the business cycle and concomitant price dislocations in much the same way that contemporary underdeveloped areas of the world are. When advanced areas sneezed, the less developed areas caught colds. They depended heavily on "middleman" institutions and services, such as grain and cotton brokerages, railroads, and bankers. Their dependence was less than it had been in the years immediately following the Civil War, but it was far greater than it is now.[13]

What political options for a large-scale change of the political economy were available to groups squeezed by industrialization and an accumulationist political economy? Populism dwindled into insignificance after the 1896 presidential election, when it had its greatest influence. A successor, the Socialist party, proved much less attractive to the electorate than populism. As for the Progressive movement of the early twentieth century, it was more meliorist than populism or socialism. It is risky to generalize about a phenomenon so complex as progressivism. But it would be safe to say that it was shaped by factions for whom reform "was seen as the outcome not of conflict but of consensus management."[14] Thus a difference between the Populists and the Socialists and the Progressives is that one faction of progressivism had lower expectations of participatory politics and higher expectations of disinterested administrative expertise.

During the system of 1896 the national party system simply was not an agent for rapid movement toward a balancing political economy. The menu of policy choices that the national party system offered to the electorate differed greatly from the grand, polar alternatives that characterized the 1892 presidential campaign and particularly the 1896 campaign. Reform of the political economy did come during the heyday of Progressive influence. But it came on the basis of a consensus between party leaders and individual brokers from the world of business who had developed a reform vision. A national, party-based movement of economic protest that, like populism, could place sweeping reform of the political economy on the national agenda seemed impossible.

In this new political structure there was room for a politics of agitation for a basically different type of political economy: state-level radicalism. State-level politics is not often thought of as a focus of broad-based, movement politics. But movement politics did not have to begin at the national level or aim primarily at national power, even though national forces might stimulate its emergence. It was easier to challenge an accumulationist political economy in the smaller constituency of state politics, and the rewards were not trivial, given the condition of federalism. Federalism and the political economy made it both possible and rational for political entrepreneurs to take seriously a politics of state-level economic protest that would appeal to farmers, workers, and, as industrial concentration grew, small businessmen. America was decentralized. Much of its territory had been politically organized after the Civil War or only shortly before. In these jurisdictions there was "organizational space," as it were, to be "filled up." Within this space state-level radicalism could emerge, a harbinger of a social democratic future awaiting American politics.

Federalism and State-Level Radicalism

A second condition for state-level radicalism, therefore, was the state of American federalism in the early twentieth century. Federalism is an institutional arrangement for distributing sovereignty and policy-making responsibilities. It exists so long as subnational governments cannot unilaterally abolish the central government and the central government cannot unilaterally abolish or reestablish the geographical boundaries of existing subnational governments. Within that framework of coexistence certain political decisions are reserved to the subnational governments. The nature of those decisions can change, but in a federal system there will always be decisions that only the subnational governments can make.

American federalism provides incentives for political organizations oriented toward the statehouse as well as toward the White House and Capitol Hill. This is a rather special fact of American political life. After centuries of state building, Europe's political systems are much more centralized. The different extent and nature of political centralization in the European environment has meant that organizations very often have exclusively national strategies for achieving their policy goals.[15] In contrast, the distribution of sovereignty in the United States does not compel American political organizations to work at capturing national power in order to have a reason for being.

The ambit of state governmental sovereignty was much changed, of course, by the early twentieth century. Following the Civil War, the federal courts went far towards curbing the autonomy of state governments in economic regulation. Federalism in commerce and economic regulation betokened allocative inefficiency, or so it seemed to activist federal judges. Also, national competition among the states for investment further circumscribed state discretion in the area of economic regulation. After the federal courts forced states to abandon statutory protections for these interests, the states adopted a policy of attracting investment. This led to what Brandeis once called a "competition in laxity" of regulation. Perhaps the only limits on this kind of interstate competition were infrastructural and locational. Yet these limits themselves mattered less, as technological advances in communications and transportation facilitated the operation of a national economy. Often the federal government promoted such advances, as in the case of the 1916 Federal Highways Act.[16]

Prior to the 1930s "dual-sovereignty" federalism was much more robust than it was after that decade. Scholarly views of federalism that stress the interactive, cooperative nature of relations among government

The Possibilities of State-Level Radicalism

officials at all levels of the political system, and thus reject the concept of dual sovereignty, are clearly most applicable to the post–New Deal era.[17]

Notable regulatory possibilities were embedded in dual-sovereignty federalism. States constitutionally could establish industries, insurance agencies, banks, and storage facilities in order to regulate the private sector indirectly or to compete with it directly.[18] They could also alter the tax codes to meet social and economic goals, for instance, by exempting certain kinds of property improvements that farmers typically made. They could regulate consumer finance and establish occupational and safety codes. And they could more fairly and neutrally administer those regulatory and executive institutions that federalism's development had made possible, such as railroad and warehouse commissions and state militias.

Regulation of the state militias was an important prospect for a state-level politics of economic protest. America has had a violent labor history. In a more politically centralized regime with an equally violent record, the national military might well have been more active than ours was. State militias and local police were the forces that intervened in strikes.[19]

These examples suggest that there were many things that states could do to amend the largely accumulationist political economy that prevailed before the New Deal.[20] Yet an understanding of the political economy and of the evolution of federalism takes one only part way toward understanding the possibilities for state-level radicalism. By themselves these two variables predict the appearance of state-level radicalism across the United States, when in fact it appeared only in north central, northwestern, southwestern, and western states. Why only in this area?

Regional Patterns of Party Building

Regional patterns of party building shaped the possibilities of state-level radicalism. The language of industrial organization theory is useful here: for political entrepreneurs interested in marketing new brands of party politics, regional patterns of party building created different "barriers to entry" into electoral markets.[21]

Party politicians in several northeastern and midwestern cities and states commanded strong, well-established party organizations. Their organizations were heirs to the first mass vote-getting organizations to appear in the modern world, the antebellum political parties which the rise of Jacksonian democracy stimulated. The organizational space of these states was filled up. New entrants into the electoral marketplace faced long-standing barriers to entry.[22]

As for the South, social relations were partly feudal, based as they were on a "labor-repressive" economy.[23] Despite the variety in nominating, campaign, and patronage practices throughout the South, its party politics reflected its semifeudal social relations. After the collapse of Reconstruction, party elites in the southern states began pushing black citizens out of party politics, back onto the land, as a way of restoring the labor-repressive features of the antebellum economy. Their moment of triumph, if it can be called that, came in the wake of populism's defeat in the 1890s, which removed the last remaining obstacle to black disenfranchisement. In terms of party politics the result was a mix of factions and leaders vying for influence inside a set of white-supremacist parties, the Southern Democratic parties. These cliques of politicians conducted their personalistic politics against the backdrop of a shrunken electorate.

Party organization in north central, northwestern, southwestern, and western states resembled southern politics in the sense that it was also one-party politics. Party politicians in these states, however, did not actively reduce the electorate's size in order to exclude a hated racial minority from political participation. One-partyism in these states resulted from realignment in the 1850s and "colonization" by adjacent Republican party elites or by southern settlers, as territories came into the Union.

One-partyism in these states did not, in other words, spring from long-standing loyalties. North central, northwestern, southwestern, and western populations expanded rapidly after the Civil War, and a significant percentage of the people in certain states were foreign-born. Also the percentage of the population which had fought in the Civil War, and thus the percentage of veterans receiving pensions and having a material stake in loyalty to the Grand Old Party, was smaller than in the Northeast.[24] Party electorates in north central, northwestern, southwestern, and western states were less strongly attached to the regular parties than their counterparts in northeastern and midwestern states. In this almost anti-party environment Progressives succeeded, much more than in the Northeast, in establishing such institutional innovations as the direct primary, the recall, the referendum, and the nonpartisan legislature.

This feature of party politics in north central, northwestern, southwestern, and western states persisted well into the twentieth century. As a congressman from Washington declared in Congress in 1924, "In my district and in my state is developing an increasing body of citizenship, independent, thinking men and women upon whom the bonds of party regularity rest lightly, if at all."[25] A recent effort to calculate just how lightly "the bonds of party regularity" rested on voters in north central, northwestern, southwestern, and western states found that between 1876 and 1895 California's Republican electorate was six times more volatile than Indiana's Republican electorate. (Volatility is defined as "the average absolute change from one election to the next in the percentage of total vote" won by a party's candidates.) Similarly the Minnesota Republican electorate's volatility was over three times that of Indiana's.[26]

Table 1.1 suggests a related way of understanding the behavior of electorates in "nonmetropolitan" states, all of which lacked what Mayhew has called "traditional party organizations." (These were autonomous, hierarchical, long-lasting organizations relying on material incentives, rather than ideology, to get people to work in a wide range of electoral settings.) The table presents the standard deviations of the average Republican presidential vote between 1900 and 1928 of all states outside the South. (The three states that came into the Union after 1900

TABLE 1.1 Regional Differences in the Republican Vote in Presidential Elections from 1900 to 1928

State	Mean Percentage of Republican Vote[a]	Standard Deviation from the Mean	State	Mean Percentage of Republican Vote[a]	Standard Deviation from the Mean
California	57.9	6.2	New Jersey	59.0	4.3
Colorado	51.8	10.1	New York	55.3	4.4
Connecticut	57.4	4.2	North Dakota	60.7	11.4
Delaware	55.6	4.7	Ohio	55.6	6.3
Idaho	55.1	9.4	Oregon	57.6	6.3
Illinois	57.5	4.9	Pennsylvania	62.6	4.5
Indiana	52.9	4.0	Rhode Island	57.9	5.0
Iowa	59.9	5.5	South Dakota	58.2	6.8
Kansas	58.9	8.9	Utah	52.1	6.9
Maine	64.2	6.2	Vermont	73.2	5.6
Massachusetts	57.8	6.1	Washington	57.2	8.3
Michigan	65.8	7.9	Wisconsin	55.6	10.0
Minnesota	59.9	9.1	Wyoming	57.6	8.0
Montana	48.5	8.6	Oklahoma[b]	33.4	22.7
Nebraska	53.7	8.6	Arizona[c]	27.1	24.5
Nevada	47.1	8.6	New Mexico[b]	29.9	26.2
New Hampshire	58.0	3.7			

Source: *Congressional Quarterly's Guide to U.S. Elections*, 2d ed. (Washington, D.C.: Congressional Quarterly Press, 1985), pp. 343–52.
[a]Data for 1912 excluded.
[b]Admitted to the Union in 1907.
[c]Admitted to the Union in 1912.

The Political Origins of the
Minnesota Farmer-Labor Party

The Minnesota Farmer-Labor party might never have emerged without the prior organization of the North Dakota Nonpartisan League. It is appropriate, therefore, to begin the time line of the party's history—and of the history of state-level radicalism as a type of politics—with the league's establishment.

Seeing how the league emerged and spread to Minnesota also highlights my explanatory emphases on political entrepreneurship and on how regional variations in party organization created different barriers to entry into electoral markets. A striking feature of the Nonpartisan League's emergence was its rapidity. Its leaders raced to establish branches of the league as far south as Texas and as far west as Oregon and California. These aspects of the emergence and diffusion of the Nonpartisan League underscore how low were the barriers to the electoral markets of non-metropolitan jurisdictions.[1]

The Origins of the North Dakota
Nonpartisan League

The North Dakota Nonpartisan League was in part an offshoot of the North Dakota Socialist party. In the midteens the North Dakota Socialist party came up with an experiment for expanding its membership, establishing a special organization department. The party intended to enroll voters as supporters of the party's platform. But it would avoid asking them to sign Socialist party membership cards. It gave charge of this department to a bankrupt, angry, flax farmer, Arthur Claude Townley, who proved adept at organization, displaying a rare talent for building membership. But in January 1915 the North Dakota Socialist party decided to shut down Townley's operation. It had grown too quickly and threatened to change the party.

Disgusted, and convinced of the depth of farmer discontent after observing acrimonious disputes between agrarian lobbyists and state legislators during the 1915 session of the North Dakota legislature, Townley turned his energies to building his own organization. Townley had learned enough about agrarian discontent to sense his opportunity. He proposed to exploit the recently established direct primary by boring from within the Republican party. With primary victories these nonpartisan candidates would easily win the general election. The direct primary would become an unexpected source of power in a one-party, Republican state.

Townley adapted the skills he acquired in the Socialist party's organization department to the far more ambitious task of capturing control of North Dakota's government by capturing control of the Republican party. Most of his organizers in what became the Nonpartisan League were former Socialists: "men who had always been in the minority tended to be strong on argument."[2] The North Dakota Socialist party's platform had been simple and by present standards modest: state provision of rural credit, establishment of state-owned grain mills and elevators, state provision of insurance to farmers for disease or hail, and unemployment insurance for labor. Under the league's label these and similar proposals no longer bore the stigma of socialism. Specifically, the Nonpartisan League advocated state ownership of terminal elevators, flour mills, packing houses, and cold-storage plants; state inspection of grain; exemption of farm improvements from taxation; state hail insurance on the basis of taxes paid on acreage; and rural credit banks operated at cost.

The wide appeal of this program resulted from a conjuncture of three factors: farmer experience with the North Dakota economy's institutional structure; considerable publicity about this structure disseminated by academic entrepreneurs from the North Dakota Agricultural College; and the learning process that a quite small, homogeneous electorate had gone through in trying to change the economy's operation. Both the electorate and private groups of farmers had tried collective solutions to what they perceived as economic oppression, but these failed altogether or were only partly successful.

In 1915 North Dakota was like a tiny, one-crop, export-dependent nation that did not own its infrastructure. Its population of about 600,000 was almost entirely rural, busy raising primarily wheat, and at the mercy of oligopolistic and oligopsonistic institutions, railroads, terminal markets, and line elevators, based in St. Paul, Minneapolis, and Duluth. Even as they prospered, North Dakota farmers resented these institutions, which tapped the lion's share of the profits to be made from wheat production. They seemed to block farmers' prospects for achieving freedom from debt and for escaping the many uncertainties of agricultural production.

Solutions to farmers' problems had been tried. If knowledge is power, then a basic prerequisite for change was knowledge: during the early teens the North Dakota Agricultural College publicized estimates of dollar losses to North Dakota farmers due to the economy's institutional biases. The North Dakota branch of the American Society of Equity, made up of better-off farmers, tried private marketing cooperatives. Also, the state legislature authorized the beginnings of a public solution: operation of state-owned elevators on an experimental basis, both inside and outside North Dakota. But each of these solutions proved to have limits.

The Nonpartisan League's success thus grew out of a revolution of rising expectations. North Dakota's wheat economy expanded between 1900 and 1910. Five years later the economic impact of World War I further increased demand. A highly homogeneous, small electorate facing a combination of increased debt and prosperity became better informed about the organization and biases of this expanding economy. And as North Dakota farmers struggled with the obstacles to making farming a more economically secure occupation, they came to define these obstacles as collective problems requiring wide-ranging public solutions. Using a rhetoric of conflict that stressed the rapacity of "Big Biz," the Nonpartisan League tapped and developed this revolution of rising expectations.

Rather than trying to change ingrained voting habits, the league adapted itself to the electorate. League leaders decided that the important election in North Dakota would be the Republican primary, more important than the general election. What the league proposed was widening the scope of conflict between the candidates: it would create broad programmatic differences between two sets of primary candidates.

The politics of boring from within the ruling party in a one-party agrarian state had, however, special requirements, different from those of balanced two-party politics. The league needed to reduce the cost to voters, scattered on farms, of becoming politically informed. Success depended on publicity to distinguish clearly between regular and league candidates, who after all would bear the same party label.

Voters profit from stable competition involving predictable disagreements between parties about what public officials should do. In this context voters are likely to know—as well as voters can know—the programs linked to one party label or the other. In formal economic language, stable party competition reduces voters' "information costs," that is, the time and effort that voters "pay" when they work to learn about candidates and party platforms.[3] Voters are disadvantaged when candidates do not have party labels at all or when candidates from the same party are competing, as in a party primary. There may be programmatic differences between candidates, but these are hard to discern unless a voter invests a lot of time and effort in researching these differences. Voters rarely make such an effort or may decline to make it, given the (correctly) perceived trivial impact on policy making of a few well-informed votes. In such a nonpartisan context voters must either abstain, vote ignorantly, or rely on the information provided either by candidates themselves or by an organization fielding the candidates.[4]

A. C. Townley and his Nonpartisan League colleagues understood the problem of information costs very clearly. Having opted for boring from within, they fashioned ways to distinguish clearly between league and regular candidates. In particular, the league's newspaper and its links to the rural press proved very important. So did membership, that is, creating a large pool of voters within the electorate who paid money to league organizers and thus expected receipt of league publicity.

Publicity and political education cost money.[5] The league concentrated on expanding its membership, using techniques for marketing the league such as running training courses for organizers, setting up a commission system of payment to organizers, and providing cars so that organizers could cover rural territory quickly.

Political education and publicity were crucial. Besides simply needing to distinguish between two sets of candidates in a primary, the league also needed to motivate voters to vote a long ballot. North Dakota had many elective offices: governor, lieutenant governor, secretary of state, attorney general, auditor, treasurer, state superintendent of public instruction, five supreme court justices, commissioner of insurance, commissioner of agriculture and labor, and three railroad commissioners. All were important to the league, and the significance of each required emphasis and explanation.

The Diffusion of State-Level Radicalism

The Nonpartisan League's analysis of how to market a new type of politics in North Dakota proved a success in 1916. The league swept the Republican primaries. Its candidate for governor defeated a progressive whom the Republican regulars once considered too radical. Victory in the primaries led to victory in the general election. With the exception of the North Dakota Senate and the office of state treasurer, the Nonpartisan League found itself in control of the state's government.[6]

Displaying remarkable ambition, the Nonpartisan League's leaders decided to diffuse their new type of politics to other political jurisdictions. This is the second point on the time line of state-level radicalism. In January 1917 the Nonpartisan League moved its headquarters to St. Paul,

Minnesota. The league's leaders decided to direct a "peaceful revolution by means of the ballot" in as many colonial states as possible. Gaining power in North Dakota induced wild optimism about the possibilities for power in other states. League leaders even believed that North Dakota's Nonpartisan League governor might be launched into the White House.

Besides their long-run goals, league leaders also believed that an immediate task was reshaping Minnesota politics. Their analysis of farmers' problems inevitably directed their attention to St. Paul and Minneapolis. The Twin Cities headquartered many of the institutions governing North Dakota's economy. "The greatest interest of the League leadership aside from the mother state centered in Minnesota."[7]

Outside of North Dakota the league exerted its most long-lasting organizational influence in Minnesota. The league's entry into politics there sparked raging political struggles within Minnesota's party system, resulting in the formation of a third party, the Minnesota Farmer-Labor party.

Change in Minnesota's electoral market produced turmoil and often a resort to coercion by ruling party elites. The resort to coercion says much about the permeability of party politics there and in other states. Party elites with a tight hold on an electorate rarely need the level of coercion described below. Violence was in fact an indication of how low the barriers to entry to Minnesota's electoral market were.

Coalitional Possibilities in Minnesota
Minnesota politics heated up in the months after the league moved its headquarters to St. Paul. For the league an important moment on its political timetable was 1918, specifically 17 June 1918, when Minnesota's dominant political party, the Republican party, held its primary. The Twin Cities' economic institutions faced a potentially serious challenge. Comparing the IWW (which was reasonably well organized in Minnesota and North Dakota) to the Nonpartisan League, a prominent Minneapolis lawyer stated that the IWW was "un-American and against all government, but it is not as dangerous as the Nonpartisan League or the Red Socialists."[8]

Perhaps the Nonpartisan League seemed more alarming than it should have. By 1910 Minnesota had a wheat belt only to the west and northwest of the Twin Cities. The state had changed greatly from the days of bonanza wheat production. An iron- and lumber-producing area was located in the state's northeast. A highly complex urban economic area encompassed the Twin Cities. Dairying and livestock farming were concentrated in the southeast among the state's oldest counties, while the southwestern counties were mainly given over to corn-hog farming. Scattered throughout these five zones were small towns and cities that combined retailing, servicing of the state's railroad network, construction, specialty industries (such as granite quarrying or meat packing), and banking. Minnesota was more economically heterogenous than North Dakota; its electorate was inherently less receptive to a movement like the Nonpartisan League. Only twenty-six out of eighty-six counties in 1917 resembled the wheat-producing areas of North Dakota.[9]

Minnesota was more urban than North Dakota, indeed, than all of the states, except Wisconsin, to which the Nonpartisan League exported its politics. The combined population of the Twin Cities was about 615,000, spread out over an area of 150 square miles. Duluth, on Lake Superior, had a population a little under 100,000. About 44 percent of Minnesota's population was urban, compared to 13 percent in North Dakota. Of the approximately 207,100 gainfully employed workers ten years old and over in North Dakota, only .02 percent of them comprised wage earners. In contrast, about 12.7 percent of Minnesota's population of 907,000 gainfully employed workers were wage earners.[10]

In this context the Nonpartisan League's official friendliness toward organized labor, while politically trivial in North Dakota, became far more important. The league needed an alliance with the Minnesota State Federation of Labor and the railroad brotherhoods. It also needed an alliance with the Socialist party, then quite strong in Minneapolis. The league's organizational tasks differed greatly from the original challenges it faced in North Dakota.

America's entry into the European war in April 1917, shortly after the league arrived in Minnesota, added yet another task for the league. It faced a strategic problem: how to adapt its economic protest to the wartime political economy? Because many of the league's officials were Socialists or former Socialists, a propensity toward neutralism was possible. But neutralism would block an alliance with organized labor, which with the exception of its Socialist minority strongly supported the war.

In Minnesota's more complicated political context the Nonpartisan League's prospects depended on several factors. The first was the stance toward the league adopted by the state's governing Republican elites and their allies in business, agriculture, and the professions. One possible option, after all, was stealing the league's thunder. South Dakota's Republican governor Peter Norbeck and the state's legislature adopted the league's program for South Dakota, initiating among other policies a rural credits system, a workmen's compensation law, and a large bond issue for the construction of a system of dams for rural electrification and irrigation. The second factor was how the Republican party managed its relations with organized labor during the wartime political economy. Third was the behavior of Minnesota's large group of Socialist politicians, who, besides influencing organized labor, had succeeded in electing the mayor of Minneapolis in 1916 and in increasing Socialist representation on the Minneapolis city council. Unlike the North Dakota Socialist party, Minnesota's Socialists were well organized.

Republican Efforts to Suppress the League

The crucial factor was the Republican response to the league. Rather than seeking to coopt the Nonpartisan League, the Minnesota Republican party tried to crush it. To reduce a complex and unfolding strategy to its essentials, the Republican party and its economic-elite allies used a wartime national public policy—establishment of state and local councils of defense—to develop two tactics for hampering the league's work in Minnesota.

The first tactic was to label political actions and speech by the Nonpartisan League as disloyal. The league did not lack for arguments with which to deflect these smears. It focused on war profiteers and their allies while also strongly supporting the war effort through collections for the Red Cross and promotion of Liberty bonds. Also, it pointed to the obvious contradiction between the smears it faced and the war's avowed purpose, often referring to the regular Republicans of Minnesota as "Junkers."

But in a sense debate hardly mattered. To paraphrase Max Weber, the league did not monopolize the instruments of coercion in Minnesota. This gets to the second tactic that war made possible for the Minnesota Republican party: to use coercion and intimidation. It sought to limit the league's access to public space, shutting down rallies and arresting league speakers. The league found it had three choices: to accept this type of intimidation; to fight back through the courts, often coping with hostile judges; or to invite federal intervention on its behalf.[11]

In mid-April 1917 the Minnesota legislature established a state council of defense. Its statute fit into a larger national effort to create a system of state and local councils of defense. In Minnesota, however, the effort came under the close and direct influence of a businessmen's group, the Minneapolis Civic and Commerce Association (CCA). Even as Nonpartisan League organizers planned a series of political rallies for June, CCA leaders planned how to staff the Commission of Public Safety and to create military and paramilitary institutions under their control.[12]

Minnesota's Republican governor, J. A. A. Burnquist, appointed railroad attorney and CCA member John McGee to the Military Affairs Committee of the Commission of Public Safety. By 25 April 1917 McGee established the Home Guard, a volunteer force meant to replace for the duration of the war the National Guard, which had been federalized.[13] By the beginning of June 1917, the Commission of Public Safety founded county commissions throughout Minnesota. It also established a corps of constables with wide powers to search private homes. By June 30 the Minnesota commission established an undercover detective bureau supervised by a CCA member and Minneapolis grain dealer. The CCA and Minnesota's governor seemed to prepare for a war at home!

A key event that touched off this domestic war was the Producers and Consumers Convention that the Nonpartisan League held in St. Paul in late September 1917. On its last day Senator Robert La Follette of Wisconsin was misquoted in an Associated Press wire report, with the result that he sounded like a German sympathizer.[14] In the ensuing commotion Governor Burnquist announced that he was considering La Follette's arrest and extradition to Minnesota for trial under the state's espionage law. Minnesota's Republican senator Frank Kellogg offered a motion to expel La Follette from the United States Senate for treason.

In the fall and winter months as the Nonpartisan League continued its schedule of lectures and gatherings it came under the surveillance of the Commission of Public Safety's detective bureau. Its speakers found increasing difficulty in holding meetings in Minnesota's southern tier of counties, which were the most politically conservative rural areas.[15] Permits for public meetings were abruptly cancelled. County sheriffs disbanded league meetings after they got underway. Threatening letters from county commissions of public safety arrived at league headquarters. In Martin County the county attorney prosecuted Arthur Claude Townley and a colleague for circulating seditious matter, namely, the resolutions of the Producers and Consumers Conference of September 1917. Local outstate newspapers published editorials praising acts of violence against the league as expressions of loyalty.

In spring 1918 John McGee of the Commission of Public Safety testified before the Senate on the wisdom of a bill transferring jurisdiction of espionage cases to military tribunals. His remarks convey the recklessness and extremism of the hard-line faction in the Republican party of Minnesota. He stated, "A Non-Partisan League lecturer is a traitor every time . . . no matter what he says or does . . . Where we made a mistake was in not establishing a firing squad in the first days of the war. We should now get busy and have that firing squad working overtime."[16] With some justice, then, league leaders characterized the events of 1917–18 as a "carnival of intimidation and oppression."[17]

Nevertheless, what is most striking about the league's entry into Minnesota politics is how rapidly it occurred. While the league faced intimidation, it also very quickly organized northwestern and central Minnesota. The very extremism of the leading figure in the Commission of Public Safety, John McGee, suggests a keen sense among Minnesota's political elites of how quickly the organizational structures linking them to a mass electorate could be overrun by aspiring counterelites.

The Commission of Public Safety and Labor

Besides organized farmers, organized labor was also an actor capable of vaulting into a position of influence. A sketch of labor's quick transformation into a major political actor in Minnesota emphasizes the permeability of the state's party politics to radical political entrepreneurs.

Not only did the small clique controlling the Commission of Public Safety use its power to inhibit the league's organization in about a quarter of Minnesota's rural areas, but also the Commission of Public Safety became in effect an antilabor agency. The commission's behavior towards labor helped, in fact, to build a coalition between organized farmers and organized labor.

The Minnesota Commission of Public Safety initially functioned more neutrally toward labor than it did toward the Nonpartisan League. Governor Burnquist bargained regularly with labor leaders; he and other members of the Commission of Public Safety did not doubt the American Federation of Labor's (AFL) legitimacy.

But they apparently soon noticed how the war-induced scarcity of labor aided labor organization.[18] During World War I the federal government for the first time incorporated labor into elite bargaining over the economy's management. Between September and December 1917 the President's Mediation Commission was the main agency charged with carrying out the new policy of incorporating labor into war management. In 1918 the federal government also established the National War Labor Board.[19] The NWLB prefigured the National Labor Relations Board of the New Deal. Unlike the NLRB, however, the NWLB was explicitly designed to be temporary. The federal government expected the AFL to contain militance in its ranks and to ignore federal repression of labor radicalism. In return the government would help labor to make the most of a unique opportunity for growth.

But precisely because it was avowedly temporary, federal labor policy could easily encourage intransigent behavior in business. Both the wartime demographic revolution in the labor market and federal labor policy threatened utterly to transform industrial relations in a very short time. Those business leaders hostile to trade unions had great incentives to resist union growth. If they held on until the end of hostilities, they could assure something of an identity between the prewar and postwar political economies.

Among those who followed a policy of intransigence were Minnesota's business leaders. Consequently, as the federal government and the AFL grew closer, an opposite movement occurred at the state level: Minnesota's government, which had close links to Twin Cities business leaders, grew hostile toward the Minnesota State Federation of Labor. This split was a striking instance of how a major initiative in federal public policy can recast the terms of state-level political conflict.[20]

Between October 1917 and winter 1918, labor politics in the Twin Cities, after violence and a threat of a general strike, came to center on the reach of federal labor policy. The threat of a general strike triggered federal involvement by the President's Mediation Commission, which issued an order that advantaged a carmen's union at the private street-railway utility in the Twin Cities. Seeking to curb the reach of federal labor policy, the utility simply ignored the President's Mediation Commission, taking advantage of the stance adopted by the Minnesota Commission of Public Safety, which was far less friendly toward the carmen.

In April the Commission of Public Safety acted legally to nullify the reach of federal labor policy. Governor Burnquist convened a meeting of labor and business officials. Shortly after the meeting Burnquist announced to the press that organized labor had agreed to a "status quo" pact drawn up by the Minnesota Employers Association. The pact provided that business would not interfere with existing unions if unions would not initiate any new organization and if they pledged themselves to a no-strike policy. Disputes would be referred to the state Board of Arbitration.

Labor leaders sharply (but futilely) disagreed that they had consented to a pact. Ignoring the Minnesota State Federation of Labor's stance, the Commission of Public Safety legally codified the status quo idea the day after Burnquist's announcement. The new state code meant that the federal labor policy reached to the state line but no further. Under the provisions of the NWLB's regulations, a state labor-relations policy preempted the federal policy.

The Republican party and organized labor were now as far apart as they could get. Circumstances were ripe for a coalition of the Nonpartisan League and labor organizations.

Even before the status quo order there were foreshadowings of an organizational coalition. When in mid-March 1918 the Nonpartisan League met to nominate its slate for the June 17 Republican primary, it selected an official of the railroad brotherhoods to run for railroad and warehouse commissioner. After the convention, Charles Lindbergh, Sr., the league candidate for the gubernatorial nomination, became known as the "farmer-labor" candidate.[21]

Political Entrepreneurship in the Aftermath of the 1918 Minnesota Republican Primary

As the Republican primary drew near, the state's political elites and the farmer-labor coalition campaigned furiously. Lindbergh was arrested briefly in southern Minnesota nine days before the primary, amid the regular Republican threnody of league disloyalty, while Governor Burnquist appeared at "loyalty" rallies accompanied by units of the Home Guard. Primary day came, and the basic question seemed, would Minnesota's ruling elites be overthrown as their colleagues in North Dakota had been?

The Republican regulars held their ground. Lindbergh won approximately 150,000 votes to Burnquist's 199,000. The league treated the primary's outcome optimistically, congratulating itself on the wisdom of league strategy, for the league had only fifty thousand members. But the fact remained that the outcome represented a new organizational problem. The basic league strategy had not worked. Failure generated new pressures for a farmer-labor organizational coalition; the league now truly needed a coalition. What was the next move for Minnesota's "army of progress"? It was a crucial moment in the overall process of state-level radicalism's growth in colonial political jurisdictions. But the ease of its resolution and the availability of new opportunities for political entrepreneurship convey, again, how low the barriers to entry to Minnesota's electoral market were.

A key actor at this juncture in the reordering of Minnesota politics was the Socialist party. It moved to fashion an alliance with the Nonpartisan League. It also broke from the Socialist party's national stance toward the war, a change that paved the way for use of its influence in the labor movement.

The Socialist party was locally strong in Minneapolis, St. Paul, and the Duluth area. Of the three cities, it was strongest in Minneapolis. In 1910 the Minneapolis Socialist party acquired a trade union base composed of local lodges of the International Association of Machinists (IAM).[22] Minneapolis was a magnet for machinists because it was an important railroad- and farm-equipment manufacturing center. In a context of growing frustration over wages and conditions for machinists the IAM lodges in Minneapolis threw their support behind the Socialist party.[23] In 1910 Thomas Van Lear, an IAM official, first ran for mayor of Minneapolis, launching what amounted to a six-year campaign for office that culminated in his election as mayor in 1916.

Van Lear became strongly interested in the Nonpartisan League in the months after its arrival in Minnesota.[24] A common concern about civil liberties drew the league and Van Lear together, for he also found himself a target of the Commission of Public Safety—the notorious Commissioner McGee hated Van Lear and sought to have him removed from office. Eventually Van Lear adopted league tactics, creating the Labor Municipal Nonpartisan League to boost his candidacy for reelection in 1918.

By midsummer 1918 nothing stood in the way of a grand organizational coalition of Socialist trade union leaders, the Nonpartisan League, and the Minnesota State Federation of Labor. Not only did Minneapolis's Socialists link up with the league, they also removed a major obstacle to constructive work within the State Federation of Labor by adopting a prowar stance. Socialist trade unionists had once been ostracized within the State Federation of Labor because of their antiwar stance.[25] But they were now in a position to set the agenda of the federation.

A major figure in setting the federation's agenda was William Mahoney, a St. Paul pressman. Mahoney, an unknown who ran for Congress as a Socialist in 1914 from the fourth district in St. Paul, winning only 7 percent of the vote, soon would become a rather powerful "organization man," becoming president of the St. Paul Trades and Labor Assembly, editor of the assembly's newspaper, and a member of the State Federation's innermost circle of leaders. At the 1918 federation convention Mahoney succeeded in bringing to a vote a resolution on political action that condemned Governor Burnquist's "autocratic methods," called attention to his lack of "co-operation with the labor policy of the Federal Government," and urged that he be "defeated for reelection." The convention strongly approved the resolution, setting the stage for a conference on political action in late August.[26]

What's in a Name? The Farmer-Labor Ballot and the Move to Third-Party Politics

In late August the State Federation of Labor's political action committee, the Working People's Political League, whose vice-president was William Mahoney, met with the Nonpartisan League to consider a slate for the general election. Besides selection of the gubernatorial candidate a key issue was the name for the independent ballot. Later the name would become controversial, for Minnesota's Farmer-Laborites twice seriously considered changing their party's name to "Progressive party," in 1922 and 1935, fearing that their label was too militant sounding. But since no one expected a permanent third party, least of all the participants in the conference that produced the name, the name "Farmer-Labor" was chosen. It echoed the everyday usage of the politics leading up to the June Republican primary. Many years later William Mahoney remembered the discussion among the conferees. They included Mahoney; Arthur Le Sueur, a league official and former Socialist mayor of Minot, North Dakota; William Lemke, who in a later political incarnation became the Union party candidate for president in 1936 (after Huey Long was assassinated); and two lawyers who handled the Nonpartisan League's growing legal business, James Manahan, a progressive Republican prominent in Minneapolis, and Frederick Pike. "Mr. Mahoney insisted that the name Labor be part of the name and Mr. Lemke took a like position in regard to the farmer . . . it was necessary to have a name that would have an economic appeal to these two great bodies of voters, consequently the name Farmer-Labor was chosen."[27]

The 1918 general election campaign proved to be just as much of a pressure cooker as the primary campaign. Burnquist continued to pose as a patriot staging a defense against the Hun. And a catastrophic fire in northern Minnesota gave him the opportunity to demonstrate gubernatorial competence and compassion. The publicity bureau of the Commission of Public Safety quickly circulated literature praising his relief effort. Burnquist also persuaded Teddy Roosevelt to issue a statement, during a stop in St. Paul, that attacked the Nonpartisan League and endorsed Burnquist. For their part, the farmer-labor forces stressed the value of defeating political and industrial "Kaiserism" at home as well as in

Europe. On election day the state's political elites, both the established and the aspiring, held their breath and waited.

The outcome gave Republicans cause for initial relief and, after reflection, nagging worry. As with the primary, the election was in fact a mixture of defeat and gains for the farmer-labor coalition.

In the June 17 primary Lindbergh gained 43 percent of the vote and carried thirty-one counties in a two-way race with Governor Burnquist. The Farmer-Labor gubernatorial candidate in the general election, an obscure hardware merchant who had run for major office only once before (in 1898, for Congress, as a Populist-Democrat) and who never figured again in Farmer-Labor politics, gained 30 percent of the vote in what was basically a three-way race and carried only twenty of eighty-six counties.[28] The limits of third-party action seemed to confirm the wisdom of the league's nonpartisan tactics.

Also, the Farmer-Labor candidates ran rather poorly in highly urban counties (St. Louis, Ramsey, and Hennepin, locations of Duluth, St. Paul, and Minneapolis). He did more poorly than Lindbergh had in these counties, where the Democratic party was the "second party." Overall the Democratic candidate received only about 21 percent of the vote, but he ran reasonably well in urban areas, such as Ramsey and Hennepin counties, where the Farmer-Labor candidate came in slightly behind the Democratic candidate. In St. Louis County, where Duluth is located, the Farmer-Labor candidate came in well behind the Democrat.

Boring from within the Republican party thus had a high payoff. Lindbergh was only 8 percent shy of the Republican nomination, in contrast with the 13 points separating Burnquist and the Farmer-Labor candidate in the general election.

Yet a focus on the apparent efficiency of nonpartisan tactics in Minnesota ignores the breadth of third-party support. While the Farmer-Labor gubernatorial candidate only carried twenty counties, he came in second in forty-two other counties, ahead of the Democratic candidate. In other words, a political unknown brought to the electorate's attention only two months before the general election succeeded in making the Farmer-Labor ballot the "second party" in most of Minnesota. This was, both by the standards of party politics in our era and by the standards of 1918, an extraordinary political performance.

Also, even as the Democratic gubernatorial candidate edged the Farmer-Labor candidate out in Hennepin County, Thomas Van Lear seemed to unite those who voted as Democrats, Socialists, and Republicans in the statewide contest. Van Lear lost to the Republican mayoral candidate in a close two-way race, 51.2 percent to 48.8 percent, in an election that saw only a very small difference between the total voting for governor and the total voting for mayor.[29] Van Lear ran in an officially nonpartisan race, to be sure. But his performance suggested that a well-known farmer-labor candidate could do very well in an urban area.

The "New Day" in North Dakota

At the same time, the farmer-labor movement's leaders were encouraged by the results of the 1918 general election in North Dakota.[30] By 1918 the Nonpartisan League's electoral success in North Dakota had become truly unusual in its scope. The league seized control of North Dakota government to an extent simply unknown in American state politics before or since then.

In 1917 the league controlled all state institutions except the North Dakota Senate and the position of state treasurer. This gave the league an enormous advantage in setting the state's political agenda, which it did through a tightly controlled caucus based in a Bismarck hotel rented during the legislature's session. The league decided to write a new constitution for the state, permitting North Dakota to own industries and to operate free of any ceiling on state indebtedness. This proposal met defeat in the senate, but it set the agenda of the 1918 election.

In that election, after a complete victory in the Republican primary, the league reelected its governor, its entire state ticket for executive offices and commissions, except the superintendent of public instruction, and all three of North Dakota's congressmen. Its control of the legislature was overwhelming. The legislature was poised to enact the league's proposed North Dakota constitutional amendments, which the league had placed on the ballot in the 1918 general election.

The 1919 legislature, controlled by a league caucus under the direction of Townley and William Lemke, established the Industrial Commission, the Bank of North Dakota, the North Dakota Mill and Elevator Association, and the Home Building Association. The 1919 legislature also limited the labor injunction and established an eight-hour day and minimum wages for women. These reforms built on the earlier Nonpartisan league administration's labor policy, namely, collective bargaining in 1917 and 1918 with the IWW, which then controlled harvest labor in North Dakota.

Ever conscious of the requirements of propaganda, Townley and Lemke also had the 1919 legislature establish a state printing commission with the authority to select a newspaper in each county that would print official business. The league used state government to subsidize its own press. A country press would now complement the two dailies in North Dakota that the league operated, in addition to its own publication, the *Nonpartisan Leader*.[31]

Perhaps with steady propaganda and policy success the "New Day" in North Dakota would last a long time. Continued success would, furthermore, help to sustain the league's political momentum in Minnesota. It would provide a working model of state-level radicalism to which Minnesota's farmer-labor leaders could persuasively point.

The Limits to the League's
Political Entrepreneurship
Bitter defeat soon eclipsed the New Day in North Dakota and set the stage for a tactical and organizational crisis of the Minnesota farmer-labor movement. In 1919 the North Dakota Nonpartisan League's unity broke apart under the stresses of factional conflict and of a boycott of North Dakota bonds in national capital markets, which undermined its policy experiments. Factionalism and fiscal turmoil led to the league's final political defeat, a recall election in 1921 in which the third league administration was thrown out of office. This ended the league's history as a social movement aiming to unite farmers and workers. Also, the national organization that the North Dakota Nonpartisan League's success led to, the National Nonpartisan League, rapidly deteriorated during the severe agricultural recession of the early 1920s. Although it survived as an organization until 1956, the North Dakota Nonpartisan League became after 1921 little more than a progressive club within the North Dakota Republican party, a vehicle for the ambitions of such men as William Lemke and William Langer.[32]

By the early 1920s the Nonpartisan League could not provide the same level of support—money, organizers, and publicity—it earlier provided to the Minnesota farmer-labor movement. The leaders of the movement thus found themselves facing new organizational imperatives. It seemed that a vote-getting structure could be created very quickly, but could it last? Where would the resources for stabilizing it come from? The farmer-labor movement's entrepreneurs needed to move beyond the kind of insurgency that the Nonpartisan League created. Their reactions led to a second phase of political entrepreneurship in the context of regional receptivity to reform.

THREE   *Beyond Insurgency*

The Minnesota Farmer-Labor party's history in the 1920s consisted in large part of a struggle by its radical political entrepreneurs to turn their movement into a strong organization. The history of Minnesota politics—indeed, of the entire north central and north-western region of the United States—was littered with third-party insurgencies. No durable third party had ever emerged. Features of radicalism's regional political environment such as party organizational weakness and electoral volatility posed obstacles over the long run for Minnesota's radical political entrepreneurs. These obstacles cut the chances for the entrepreneurs to play a stable role, year in and year out, in setting political agendas.

A basic challenge facing the political entrepreneurs of 1918, then, was to move beyond insurgency, to create an institution. They would have to develop strong party organization in a state where it was comparatively underdeveloped.

Although the story changed in the latter half of the 1920s, the Minnesota farmer-labor movement's entrepreneurs performed very well in several areas between 1919 and 1924. They eventually established a continuously functioning organization for candidate recruitment, endorsement, and support. They sought to educate the electorate, providing cues to voters through a press that the farmer-labor coalition controlled. They developed the capacity to field candidates in all statewide and congressional district elections. Finally, they achieved some success in stimulating the electorate into voting a full statewide ticket. Thus the Farmer-Labor party was strikingly free from the typical factionalism, individualism, and fluidity of state-level party politics in colonial jurisdictions. Although the party's nonpartisan origins hardly predicted such an outcome, the party developed into something of a special case of strong party organization. It became better organized than most American state political parties at the time, approximating the kind of centralized organization associated with the responsible party model.[1]

The success of the farmer-labor movement's political entrepreneurs in turning their movement into an institution had another unusual feature.

Farm leaders and labor leaders learned how to continue working with each other. This cooperation contrasts with, for instance, the Populist movement, whose politicians never learned how to make appeals to the "plain people" of the cities. The bonds forged in the 1918 campaign between Nonpartisan Leaguers and Minnesota's trade unionists stayed intact through later campaigns, despite very strong tactical disagreements. To be sure, with the collapse and disappearance of the Nonpartisan League by the mid-Twenties, control over the Farmer-Labor party passed to labor leaders and practicing politicians. But most of these politicians came from rural or small-town backgrounds; the cooperation established earlier simply took a new form.

A concomitant of this cooperation at the elite level was cooperation at the electoral level. Between 1918 and 1924 dozens of rural counties realigned with the Farmer-Labor party.[2] Also, the Farmer-Labor party's strength in urban areas grew very rapidly until 1922, when it levelled off. Elite cohesion thus played an important role in laying the foundations of a rural-urban coalition based on economic protest.

Toward a "Political League . . . in Sympathy with the Interests of the Common People"

The movement of the Minnesota farmer-labor coalition beyond insurgency can be dated to 20 July 1919, when the Minnesota State Federation of Labor committed itself at its thirty-seventh convention to permanent political action. Over sixty years later a former vice-president of the federation who had attended the convention referred to it as "the famous one."[3]

In making a commitment to permanent political action the Minnesota State Federation endowed the farmer-labor coalition with formidable resources. The thirty-seventh convention capped a spectacular period of growth for Minnesota's trade unions. Between 1916 and 1919 about 50 percent of the state's industrial work force became unionized. Of course, this work force was only a fraction of the state's adult working population. But relative to contemporary rates of unionization this was a whopping level of "union density." Older labor leaders drily referred to the new unions as "mushroom unions," but they were unions nonetheless.[4]

Between the thirty-sixth and thirty-seventh conventions many of the city centrals in Minnesota had experimented with political action; these experiments paid off. Political victories in many cities during the spring elections were fresh in the delegates' minds. In a southeastern railroad center, the local Trades and Labor Assembly elected a majority of the city council and the mayor. In another railroad center, labor elected a mayor, city treasurer, several aldermen, and three members of the board of education. A federation vice-president won a seat on Duluth's city council. And in St. Paul (a predominantly Irish Catholic city) Julius F. Emme, a far-left Socialist soon to join the Communist movement, ran for mayor in May against a Democrat and won a respectable 32 percent.[5]

After listening to William Mahoney and Thomas Van Lear (respectively, the president of the St. Paul Trades and Labor Assembly and the former Socialist mayor of Minneapolis), the assembled delegates at the 1919 State Federation of Labor convention converted the temporary Working People's Political League into the Working People's Nonpartisan Political League. The WPNPL's purpose was "to unite members of organized and unorganized labor into a political league together with those in sympathy with the interests of the common people in order that representatives may be elected to public office who will enact, interpret, and enforce laws that will serve the general welfare."[6]

The Change in the Rules of Minnesota's Electoral Game

In addition to labor support for political action, a Republican-engineered change in Minnesota's electoral rules played a key role in moving the farmer-labor coalition beyond insurgency toward becoming a strong party. Republican efforts to change the electoral game's rules resulted from alarm at the success of the farmer-labor coalition's nonpartisan tactics.

In 1920 the Republican party presented itself as accommodating to farmer-labor demands. The Republicans adopted key pieces of the state-level program of the farmer-labor coalition: they backed workmen's compensation insurance and promoted agricultural cooperatives. They also forced Governor Burnquist out of politics and replaced him with an apparently more moderate governor, J. A. O. Preus.

Nevertheless, in the 1920 Republican primary the farmer-labor coalition's gubernatorial candidate, Henrik Shipstead, a distinguished-looking dentist who combined Norwegian identity, respectability, and radicalism, got a shade under 41 percent of the vote, only about 2 points behind Lindbergh's 1918 performance.[7] The coalition's campaign was vigorous. A. C. Townley showed the same flair for technologically modern campaigns that he demonstrated in his motorized sign-up campaign in North Dakota in 1915 and 1916. Townley engaged an "aeroplane" to barnstorm Minnesota. Agrarian protest acquired an aura of futuristic dynamism. In the Twin Cities and Duluth the WPNPL leafletted voters with a free newspaper, *The People's Voice*. The day before the Republican primary the milk-wagon drivers in Minneapolis—who were politically conscious and very useful for propaganda work—distributed thousands of ballot cards and campaign literature.[8]

In short, Republican accommodation of some of the farmer-labor coalition's demands did not deflect a very strong repeat of the 1918 effort to take over the Republican party. Nor did it deflect quick regrouping after primary defeat to run a very vigorous general-election campaign, a "sorehead" tactic used in the summer of 1920. This effort included keeping the legal name of the Farmer-Labor party alive by filing candidates under that name, even though Shipstead officially ran as an independent.[9] As a gubernatorial candidate Shipstead gained about 6 points over the 1918 Farmer-Labor performance, coming in at 35.9 percent. And in 1920 the farmer-labor coalition ran, for the first time, candidates for all statewide offices. It also increased its strength in congressional elections. In 1918 there was only one farmer-labor candidate for Congress, an independent from St. Louis County who won with 57.1 percent of the vote. In 1920 the coalition ran five independents, three Farmer-Labor candidates, and two incumbents (the coalition had picked up another seat in a 1919 special election) as Democrat and Republican, competing in all ten races, a 90 percent jump in number of competing candidates. True, only one of these, Oscar Keller, went to Congress, running as a Republican, but the statewide average performance was 34.4 percent, ranging from a low of 19.8 percent (an independent) to a high of 58.6 percent (Keller).[10]

The Republicans reacted to apparently successful sorehead tactics. In 1921 the incoming Republican governor, J. A. O. Preus, requested antisorehead legislation from the Republican-controlled legislature that would make it impossible for the farmer-labor coalition to run in a Republican primary and also run a third party if it lost the primary. Antisorehead legislation in 1921 would force the farmer-labor coalition to choose a permanent label for itself.

The legislature passed a bill requiring candidates for executive office in Minnesota to file in party primaries only after March preprimary endorsing conventions. Convention delegate rules heavily advantaged the regular faction of a party and made nonpartisan tactics impossible.[11]

The farmer-labor team now struggled over the issue of how best to organize. While the leadership of the State Federation of Labor favored a permanent farmer-labor coalition in the form of a third party, the Nonpartisan League leadership feared such a coalition. A debate ensued over whether to establish a third party.

The Debate over Establishing a Permanent Party

That the State Federation of Labor was stronger organizationally and politically than the Nonpartisan League determined this debate's outcome. At its second annual convention—which met just before the thirty-eighth annual convention of the State Federation of Labor—the WPNPL agreed that 1920 had been an experiment that paid off handsomely. Here the delegates thought primarily of Minneapolis. In 1920 the local Minneapolis labor party moved closer to asserting direct control over the city streetcar franchise when Minneapolis voters passed a home-rule amendment to the Minneapolis charter. The amendment changed the Minneapolis electoral rules to a two-step procedure involving an early summer runoff between the top two candidates in a late spring nonpartisan primary. A June 1921 election, only a few months after the charter amendment, seemed to place the city's labor forces on the verge of reelecting former mayor Van Lear and thus seizing control of the negotiations between the city and the streetcar company, the culmination of a ten-year campaign to curb corporate power in Minneapolis.

In fact the labor party in Minneapolis lost its long-sought victory against the streetcar company. The June general election came after the 1921 legislature transferred jurisdiction over the streetcar franchise from the city of Minneapolis to the Minnesota Railroad and Warehouse Commission. The Republican party saved the streetcar company in the nick of time. Minneapolis's conservative forces fielded an especially strong candidate, Colonel George Leach, a war hero decorated for bravery in France. Van Lear lost the Minneapolis general election, 45.1 percent to 54.8 percent, a performance that ended his political career.[12]

Nevertheless—and this is part of why Van Lear told the 1921 WPNPL convention that the league had been a "phenomenal success"—the local WPNPL gained control of ten of the Minneapolis city council's twenty-six seats, enough to give the labor bloc the power to bargain with a swing bloc. At the time of the WPNPL convention in July 1921, the city council was still deadlocked in its voting for president of the city council (who named the council's committees)—101 ballots had been taken. Even if the labor bloc later lost control of the council's committees (which it eventually did), its size still gave it unprecedented control over city resources. Among other things, aldermen controlled street work in their wards, including a "complete and separate outfit of machinery and equipment and a separate ward toolhouse."[13] In St. Paul, meanwhile, labor controlled half of the city's commissions, including parks and public safety. In Duluth, labor also controlled the city's department of public safety.

In this context of growing political strength, labor's preference for a third-party ballot in 1922 proved determining.[14] As the date for a party endorsing convention in March 1922 neared, Townley proposed what he called a "balance-of-power" plan by which the farmer-labor coalition would commit itself to issuing endorsements of regular party candidates a few weeks before an election, thus maximizing its influence on legislation by controlling a "great mobile voting bloc" of value to politicians. Townley was loath to create a third party and issued an open letter to his colleagues in the WPNPL, stressing the weakness of third parties and how, historically, nonpartisan movements were the real agents of policy reform.[15]

Townley's preference did not matter. By this time the once powerful Nonpartisan League was much weaker. In 1921 the National Nonpartisan League found itself in serious financial and political trouble. The financial problems resulted directly from a large overhead—the St. Paul headquarters and the various state headquarters—and the postwar agricultural recession (discussed in greater detail in chapter 5.) Much of the league's assets were in the form of postdated checks from farmers now reluctant or unable to honor their paper commitments. The task of liquidating these assets meant an enormous expenditure of organizational effort far in excess of their value.[16] Also, in North Dakota the league had suddenly collapsed after several years of extraordinary success. Its main leaders had been thrown out of office in a special recall election.

Given the imbalance in strength between the Nonpartisan League and the State Federation of Labor, it is not surprising that Townley was unable to prevent a large bloc of agrarian activists from cooperating with trade unionists to establish a third party. Actually, the important debate within the coalition became whether to change the coalition's name and run under the label of "Progressive party." Some argued that the name "Farmer-Labor" was too radical sounding. But in the end the party builders chose to stick with Farmer-Labor.[17]

Partisan Infrastructure and Competitiveness

By the time the farmer-labor coalition's elites rejected Townley's balance-of-power plan and established a political party under the electoral law of 1921, they had already achieved much in terms of constructing an active partisan infrastructure. (This is suggested in both qualitative data in newspaper and archival sources and fragmentary quantitative data from these sources and elsewhere.) Radical entrepreneurs built organizations that specialized in stimulating a winning plurality in quite diverse jurisdictions. They aided either Farmer-Labor candidates or candidates who ran under other labels but with the endorsement of the farmer-labor coalition. Because radio had not yet become a force in politics, the techniques of stimulus included recruiting new dues-paying members and keeping old dues-paying members of such organizations as the Nonpartisan League and the WPNPL; leafletting, distributing buttons, and postering; paying for and distributing special runs of those newspapers that were in the camp of the farmer-labor coalition; holding meetings; staging large rallies to hear a well-known speaker (sometimes with a musical band); contacting important local figures, known as "live wires" and "boosters," who in turn would raise money and let their approval for a candidate and for the coalition be known, often because they were rich enough to have telephones; hiring automobiles, decorated with political banners, to convey voters to polls; and providing sample ballot cards to voters on election day.[18] Two organizations that specialized in these techniques of stimulus were, of course, the Nonpartisan League and the WPNPL. Other organizations were the two leagues' women's auxiliaries, whose purpose was to create voters from adults who had never voted before. These auxiliaries were more influential than a mere membership count would suggest, for a rising generation of women political activists considered the farmer-labor coalition an avenue into statewide campaigns for such offices as state auditor and clerk of the supreme court. Ideologically the women's auxiliaries were a mixture of religious and political fervor.[19] A fourth element in the Farmer-Labor partisan infrastructure emerged in time for the 1922 elections. When the Farmer-Labor party was established in 1922, its officials established Farmer-Labor party county central committees around the state.

These four structures varied in their financial strength, membership, and size of staff. The records regarding these indicators of strength are poor; only impressionistic estimates of strength can be offered. But the data show that easily the strongest of these organizations was the WPNPL. In 1920 the league had a membership of approximately forty-five thousand, which declined over the next three years, as a result of the postwar decline of trade unions, to a paid-up membership of about seventeen thousand. The WPNPL had centers of activity all around the state, centers sometimes aided by local lodges of the railroad brotherhoods, which were not affiliated with the State Federation of Labor but cooperated with it politically.[20] The Nonpartisan League, which had a somewhat larger membership in 1920 than the WPNPL, declined much more rapidly as a result of the postwar agricultural recession. What size it reached by 1922 or 1923 is hard to say, but it seems not to have been more than six to seven thousand.[21] As for the women's auxiliaries, their size seems to have been about five to six hundred, and the Farmer-Labor county central committees may have numbered in total membership somewhere under a hundred.

In addition to this infrastructure, the farmer-labor coalition developed a daily press and a network of outstate county newspapers. The *Minnesota Daily Star*, a publicly owned newspaper capitalized by Nonpartisan League and WPNPL funds and by well-to-do farmer-labor leaders, began publication on 19 August 1920. The *Star* was a complete newspaper that ran national and international news, a women's section, a sports section, and several comic strips. Its radicalism discreetly showed in how it treated such issues as labor injunctions, crop prices, and events in the Soviet Union, running, for instance, Louise Bryant's report on the Kronstadt Rebellion. On its first day of publication it had a circulation of 35,000, compared to 98,000 for the *Minneapolis Journal* and 60,000 for the *Minneapolis Tribune*. By fall 1922 its circulation was up to 50,000.[22] Two labor newspapers, the *Minneapolis Labor Review* and the St. Paul *Minnesota Union Advocate*, although they listed themselves with the Minnesota secretary of state as nonpartisan, added to the impact of the *Star*. The circulation of the *Union Advocate* was approximately 15,000, and the *Labor Review* probably had a similar circulation.[23] The *Star*'s circulation outside the Twin Cities is unknown, but whatever its size it was complemented by a network of pro-farmer-labor county newspapers. In 1920 there were thirty-one counties with such newspapers, and in 1922 there were thirty-three. Finally, the Duluth *Labor World* can be included in the roster of farmer-labor newspapers, even though it too officially listed itself with the Minnesota secretary of state as nonpartisan.

What difference did the development of a partisan infrastructure and a press make to electoral performance? The increase in the number, and in the spatial density and coverage, of organizations dedicated to stimulating and educating the electorate helped to increase competitiveness. Competitiveness I define as having four capacities: to run candidates for all statewide and congressional offices; to increase the vote for the most highly visible of the statewide offices, the governorship; to narrow the gap between the gubernatorial vote and the average vote for statewide executive offices and regulatory offices that were on the same biennial cycle as the governorship; and to win major offices, that is, the governorship, seats in the House of Representatives, and seats in the United States Senate.

In most of these areas there was improvement between 1920, the year of the second Farmer-Labor ballot and the last election in which the coalition was able to use sorehead tactics, and the special senatorial election of 1923.

In 1922 the farmer-labor coalition again ran candidates for all state-wide executive offices but did not field candidates in all ten congressional districts, as it had in 1920, dropping to eight districts. The coalition increased its performance in the gubernatorial race. The gubernatorial candidate, Magnus Johnson, a Norwegian-born farmer who worked as a union glassblower before moving into farming, lost by surprisingly little, 43.1 percent to 45.2 percent, and perhaps through fraud.[24] Relative to 1920, the coalition narrowed the gap between the gubernatorial vote and the average vote for statewide executive offices and regulatory offices on the same biennial cycle as the governorship. In 1920 there was a gap of 26 percent between the raw gubernatorial vote and the average of the raw vote for the other offices, a gap that dropped to 10 percent in 1922. As for its capacity to win major offices, the election was a startling success for the Farmer-Labor party. Henrik Shipstead, the 1920 gubernatorial candidate, won 47 percent in a three-way senatorial race, piling up a 12-point lead over incumbent Frank Kellogg. He became the first of four Farmer-Labor United States senators. Six of the congressional candidates affiliated with the farmer-labor organizational coalition won election, four Republicans (including Oscar Keller), one independent, and one Farmer-Laborite. The eight candidates competing won an average of 44.6 percent, ranging from a low of 31.6 percent to a high of 80.6 percent.

As luck and old age would have it, Minnesota's senior senator, Republican Knute Nelson, died a few months later. In response, Governor Preus scheduled a rematch of the 1922 gubernatorial campaign by announcing that he would run for the Senate. Preus could have appointed Nelson's replacement for the remainder of his term, which expired in 1924, but seems to have preferred creating an opportunity for what he expected would be a Republican victory. Encouraged by his performance in the 1922 election, farmer-labor activists gave their 1922 gubernatorial candidate, Magnus Johnson, a second chance, endorsing him in a June primary election. Johnson beat Preus in the general election by a very wide margin of nearly 100,000 votes, making the Minnesota delegation in the United States Senate a radical redoubt.

From Farmer-Labor Party to
Farmer-Labor Federation

Up to 1923, the record of Minnesota's political entrepreneurs in moving beyond insurgency was impressive. Between summer 1919 and midsummer 1923, Minnesota's radical political entrepreneurs prospered electorally and established a partisan infrastructure. The two trends reciprocally influenced each other. In building the Farmer-Labor party radical entrepreneurs spent enormous amounts of time and energy on establishing regular routines, designing programmatic appeals, and learning how to get along with each other. They also figured out how to get thousands and thousands of ordinary people first to spend time and energy registering to vote and then actually to vote for the new candidates of a new party or vote-getting organization. Throughout this process, winning office helped to sustain their energy. Thus Shipstead's statewide victory—followed a few months later by Johnson's—provided hope and confidence that four years of party building had been worth the effort. A sense of euphoria prevailed during Johnson's campaign against Preus in 1923; his campaign manager, for instance, wrote another activist that "Johnson is having wonderful meetings . . . it looks like a walk-away for the . . . Glass Blower."[25]

Yet one of the key activists in the farmer-labor coalition, William Mahoney—who was the founder, along with Minneapolis's former Socialist mayor, Thomas Van Lear, of the WPNPL—had a far different response to these victories, and to the movement beyond insurgency, than simply a sense of satisfaction. In watching the events of 1922 he became not only increasingly confident that the farmer-labor coalition was a powerful movement but also alarmed and angry about what he considered its disorganization and its vulnerability to being taken over by opportunists. In March 1922, for instance, a committee of Democrats approached the joint Nonpartisan League/WPNPL conference to propose fusion with the Democrats. Although the conference rejected the Democrats' proposal, the offer and the politics of the response apparently alarmed Mahoney. In spring 1922 he proposed at a high-level meeting of farmer-labor leaders that a single partisan infrastructure be established.[26]

After watching the 1922 campaign, Mahoney decided to push harder within the coalition for a sweeping reform of the Farmer-Labor party's partisan infrastructure. From Mahoney's perspective, the 1922 statewide Minnesota campaign had been a disappointing mixture of enthusiasm, disorganization, and a bit of freebooting. For instance, the Nonpartisan League's executive secretary, Henry Teigan, managed Henrik Shipstead's campaign for the Senate; the money for Shipstead's "Defeat Kellogg" campaign came from an ad hoc businessmen's committee. A Farmer-Labor party campaign headquarters, in contrast, handled the gubernatorial campaign for Magnus Johnson. And the congressional campaign was a patchwork quilt of onetime deals and different labels: one Farmer-Laborite, two Democrats, two independents, and three Republicans, one of them with possible links to the organized crime that Prohibition began to engender in the Twin Cities.

Mahoney's plan for consolidation necessarily irritated leaders of the Nonpartisan League in Minnesota and the hierarchs of the formal Farmer-Labor party, who established a newspaper in 1923, the *Farmer-Labor Advocate* (which eventually came to have a circulation of about five thousand), and a network of county central committees.[27] Mahoney's plan meant an end to their influence for the simple reason that the WPNPL was the most powerful element of the coalition's partisan infrastructure. Any consolidation meant more power for trade union activists such as Mahoney and less power for those in the Nonpartisan League and the formal Farmer-Labor party.

Factional disagreements over Mahoney's plan did not erupt until after Magnus Johnson's victory in the mid-July 1923 special senatorial campaign. But after Magnus Johnson won this campaign, Frederick Pike, the chairman of the Farmer-Labor State Central Committee, began to talk within the coalition against Mahoney's plan. Pike assisted the Nonpartisan League with its legal troubles in 1918 and therefore enjoyed the confidence of old leaguers. He argued that giving organizational control of the coalition to organized labor would alienate segments of the party's electorate: "If the independent progressive voters of the state who comprise the largest percentage of the potential supporters of any successful progressive party come to believe that there is in prospect control of the Farmer-Labor Party by a limited group, no matter how worthy the purposes of that group might be, then further growth of the Farmer-Labor party . . . is at an end."[28]

Pike was concerned with image. His claim to trade union colleagues was that the party already had a problem with its name, which made it seem highly class-based. If the party came to be seen as controlled by trade unionists it was doomed, for that would accentuate its already strong class image.

Further, some of Mahoney's colleagues frightened Pike. Mahoney worked closely with Communist trade unionists, in particular a cluster of articulate Communists who were based in machinists locals in St. Paul and were good at trade union organizing. Mahoney and they had apparently worked out an agreement that when necessary they would reduce their political visibility.[29] But—and this was all that mattered to Pike and others—if Mahoney's power grew, their power would grow.

Mahoney's former colleague, Thomas Van Lear, was also frightened by Communist influence. The newspaper that he controlled, the *Minnesota Daily Star*, began to "red bait" Mahoney. The *Star* predicted that consolidation of the Farmer-Labor partisan infrastructure amounted to Communist control of it.[30]

Mahoney scorned these concerns. His elaborate theory of party organization emphasized the special requirements of working class politics in a capitalist society. That the class-based character of the party and the presence of a handful of Communists were political liabilities struck him as ludicrous. "Many of those in the new party are obsessed with the erroneous idea that it may function successfully as a loose aggregation of well-meaning idealists who are striving for some vague reform, and economic interests of the great toiling masses may be placed in the background." It was time to face up clearly and soberly to the realities of American politics: "government itself is a reflex of the ruling economic interests." Consolidation of the Farmer-Labor party's infrastructure into a tightly centralized organization controlling candidate recruitment and endorsement was an absolute necessity. It would unify the "great toiling masses," who otherwise were often easily stymied by their ignorance of who stood for what. As a *Union Advocate* editorial noted, "It is the commonest occurrence to have people even on election day, and while on their way to the voting booth, ask someone else which is the best candidate." Thus, Pike's plan meant defeat over the long run. The party would inevitably lose its militance, become indistinguishable from the regular parties, and leave the working class and the farmers unrepresented. Those who worried about the party's class character were "completely hypnotized with the idea that it is un-American to sanction the organization of a political party with an avowed class character." Mahoney wanted, instead, a "permanent and reliable political agency." He was deadly serious about his work, as a statement made some years later indicates: "When we speak of party, we would go even further than the term ordinarily implies. We favor a strict militant movement . . . The struggle of the masses against the predatory special interests is no holiday affair."[31]

As the political entrepreneur who controlled most of the Farmer-Labor party's partisan infrastructure, Mahoney succeeded in late 1923 and early 1924 in implementing his reform of that infrastructure. First Mahoney changed the WPNPL's name to "Farmer-Labor Federation." He then pressed for a merger of the Minnesota Nonpartisan League into the federation. On 12 March 1924, shortly before the second Farmer-Labor party convention, the Minnesota Nonpartisan League agreed to fuse with the Farmer-Labor Federation. By then there was significant support within the Nonpartisan League for Mahoney's ideas. As one excited farmer exclaimed at an emotional session in which the league decided to join the federation, "Next in importance to spreading the gospel is the union of the farmers and industrial workers!" Finally, at the Farmer-Labor party convention of 14 March 1924, the delegates accepted the Farmer-Labor Federation as the party's infrastructure.[32]

The federation would be an organization for mustering money and political activists. It would be a hierarchy of ward clubs and county associations. The representatives of these clubs and associations would meet periodically in conventions to make "policy decisions that would be binding upon the party and its candidates." At the same time there would be an executive committee for organization of political campaigns. The federation would give this party hierarchy a monopoly of the farmer-labor coalition's money because of dues-paying unions that had been part of the WPNPL's organizational structure. A high level of union affiliation with the Farmer-Labor Federation would also provide its officers with control of campaign funds. Through that financial control, the party elite would control candidate appeals to the electorate and performance in office.[33]

The Performance of the Farmer-Labor
Federation in 1924

The Farmer-Labor Federation's establishment was yet another step forward by Minnesota's radical political entrepreneurs in moving beyond mere insurgency. Their choice in March 1924 for a more tightly organized party shaped how the Farmer-Labor party presented itself to the electorate in the 1924 elections. For the first time since the party's emergence in 1918, all ten congressional districts had candidates running as Farmer-Laborites.

Of these campaigns the weakest performance was in St. Paul's fourth district, where Julius Emme, a Communist running as a Farmer-Laborite, gained only 15.4 percent of the vote, while the strongest was in the seventh district, 58.5 percent.[34] The party succeeded in sending three Farmer-Laborites to Congress. However, it lost its control of the state's delegation in the United States Senate—Magnus Johnson lost to a Republican, Tom Schall. The party's gubernatorial candidate, Hennepin county attorney

Floyd B. Olson, improved only part of a percentage point on Magnus Johnson's 1922 performance, winning 43.8 percent. As for the gap between the gubernatorial vote and the vote for other executive offices, it stayed roughly the same as in 1922, 10.7 percent.

In short, the main consequence of the Farmer-Labor Federation's establishment was elimination of deals with Republican and Democratic politicians in the congressional campaigns. These deals had proliferated between 1918 and 1922. The party's congressional performance in 1924 showed that it could do reasonably well by instead running Farmer-Labor candidates.

Farmer-Labor Federation, Farmer-Labor Association, 1925–29

How stable was the new partisan infrastructure, the Farmer-Labor Federation? How well did it do over the rest of the decade?

The first test for the federation came in 1924 and 1925, for in building the federation Farmer-Labor leaders linked it to a plan for shaping presidential politics. They consequently set the stage for a struggle over whether to abandon the new partisan infrastructure in favor of a return to the old infrastructure. Yet despite this struggle their handiwork was easily defended against its critics.

In addition to arguing his theory of party organization, Mahoney also argued that the establishment of the Farmer-Labor Federation would help Minnesota's farmer-labor coalition to play a key role in setting the agenda of presidential politics in 1924. With the transformation of the Minnesota delegation in the United States Senate into a Farmer-Labor outpost, it became easy for Farmer-Labor activists to negotiate with Senator Robert La Follette of Wisconsin over launching a third-party candidacy in 1924. Mahoney and several others in the farmer-labor coalition believed that the best way to run such a candidacy was to establish Farmer-Labor parties throughout the country. By persuading La Follette to run for president as the national standard-bearer of a cluster of state-level parties, Mahoney hoped to have La Follette lend his extraordinary prestige to the institutionalization of a national third party. This party would be unveiled at a nominating convention in St. Paul scheduled for 17 June 1924. Mahoney indeed had a daring plan for reshaping national party politics, and the Farmer-Labor Federation's establishment dovetailed with it.[35]

Well before the unfolding of Mahoney's scheme there were deep misgivings among Minnesota's radical politicians.[36] As Mahoney's plan turned into a nightmarish fiasco, these misgivings became the source of bitter disillusionment. In the aftermath of the 1924 campaign Mahoney's reconstruction of the Farmer-Labor party's infrastructure was openly attacked.

Actors quite beyond Mahoney's control killed his plan for reshaping presidential politics and turned it into what is now little more than a fascinating "what if?" of American political evolution. Much of the fiasco had to do with La Follette's ambition and his Progressive antiparty background and instincts. La Follette strongly preferred a onetime candidacy and hesitated to be bound to any group of party politicians. One organization that ended up giving him the freedom he wanted was the Conference for Progressive Political Action—an alliance of the IAM and the railroad brotherhoods established to overturn "normalcy" in 1924. When the conference made it clear that it would nominate La Follette at a convention scheduled for July 4 in Cleveland, he was free to choose their nomination. Until then his well-known ambition to run for president before he became too old had, in effect, made him Mahoney's prisoner, as Mahoney perhaps understood. La Follette lashed back at Mahoney, issuing a stinging rebuke by publicly denouncing Communist participation in his plan as a mischievous effort "to deceive the public." Mahoney doggedly went ahead with the St. Paul convention, hoping that somehow a way to salvage his plan would be found.[37] But at this point Mahoney's Communist allies betrayed him. Their Russian superiors in the Comintern moved to assert control over the political direction of American communism. The Comintern instructed a hero of the 1919 steel strike, William Z. Foster, to stage a takeover by Communist cadres from around the country of the St. Paul convention and to bring it under Communist control. To the deep dismay of Mahoney and other non-Communist radicals at the convention, Communists dominated the St. Paul convention.

The pressures of the 1924 campaign and of mending fences with the La Follette presidential campaign held in check Mahoney's opponents within the farmer-labor coalition. The coalition's activists believed that a maximum effort was now required.[38] But once the election was over, Mahoney's reconstruction of the Farmer-Labor party's infrastructure came under attack. The visibility of the Communist issue in 1924 revived advocates of nonpartisanship, who used the issue to attack the Farmer-Labor Federation. Even the name seemed tainted, for the Communists ran their presidential candidate in 1924 through an organization called the Federated Farmer-Labor party.

Yet it was easy for Mahoney and his allies to preserve the federation. At a special postelection conference of Farmer-Labor leaders in 1925, two cosmetic changes were made. As a sop to those disturbed by the name, the Farmer-Labor Federation became the Farmer-Labor Association, and a constitution was drawn up formally excluding Communist participation. How cosmetic these changes were can be gauged by the fact that Communists quickly rejoined the party's infrastructure and played active roles until 1928, when the Comintern entered a period of complete hostility to organizations such as the Farmer-Labor party.

A far more important challenge than the factional disturbance of 1925 was the deep sense of political exhaustion that came over the Farmer-Labor party's elites in the latter half of the 1920s. Many of them invested sizeable chunks of their personal wealth in the development of the Farmer-Labor infrastructure. The most expensive element of that infrastructure was the *Minnesota Star,* which had been mismanaged from the outset and suffered from an advertisers' boycott. When the *Star* was declared bankrupt in fall 1923, after several efforts to save it, the loss to its stockholders was considerable. Only through careful conduct of the receivership by one of Minneapolis's prominent labor lawyers was financial harm to the Farmer-Labor elite avoided. This experience, in combination with several years of draining, intense activity, the disappointment of La Follette's defeat, and La Follette's death in 1925, generated fatigue. No sooner had Mahoney and his allies established the Farmer-Labor Association, which was built to be a "loyalty-absorbing" organization, than they encountered a weakening of the kind of elan and loyalty that such organizations need.[39]

Another sharp challenge to the Farmer-Labor Association was the decline of political action within the Minneapolis and St. Paul labor movements, despite the ability of a few radical politicians to hang onto local public office in both cities. The decay of political action in Minneapolis resulted, first, from Thomas Van Lear's disillusionment with radical politics and, after his defeat by William Mahoney during the struggle to establish the Farmer-Labor Federation, his retirement to Florida. No successor with comparable charisma or energy took his place. Instead, George Leach, the Republican war hero who defeated Van Lear in 1921, became rather popular in working class wards in Minneapolis. Second, the AFL successfully reorganized the Minneapolis Trades and Labor Assembly to punish it for its radicalism. Its more conservative successor was the Minneapolis Central Labor Union. Finally, there was a long-run, unintended consequence of the change in electoral rules that the labor movement fought for under Van Lear as a way to bring the Minneapolis street-railway company under labor's political control. Because Minneapolis held officially nonpartisan elections in the spring and summer after general statewide elections, radical momentum in city politics became increasingly difficult to sustain.[40]

In St. Paul, labor's political action remained fairly strong through the 1926 election, if one takes the average across-ward strength of the Farmer-Labor party's gubernatorial candidate as an indicator. In 1924 this indicator was 47.6 percent, up a point from 1922; in 1926 it dropped only a few points. In Minneapolis, in contrast, the highest value of this indicator came in 1922—in 1924 it dipped a bit, and in 1926 it dropped nearly 8 points. Yet the average strength of the Farmer-Labor party in the 1928 gubernatorial election across St. Paul's wards dropped very sharply, from 42.7 percent to 24.9 percent, far more than the drop registered in Minneapolis, from 37.2 percent to 30.4 percent. In a city that was roughly 25 percent Catholic this was probably a onetime response to Al Smith's campaign. Still, it was a sharp blow to the Farmer-Labor Association's educational theory of political action.

Much of the association's incapacity to prevent the Farmer-Labor party's drop in strength in the Twin Cities—particularly in local and state legislative contests—was due to the numerical and financial decline of the Minnesota union movement. Unlike the Nonpartisan League, the American and Minnesota union movements did not collapse altogether. But their strength continued to decline—slowly, to be sure, but then there was less to decline from than in 1919 and 1920, when a precipitous drop in strength began.

As the weakness in St. Paul in 1928 of the Farmer-Labor party's gubernatorial candidate suggests, the Farmer-Labor Association's theorists faced a severe challenge during that year's presidential campaign.[41] A large faction openly supported Al Smith for president despite the association's intention of echoing the 1924 La Follette campaign by endorsing Nebraska's Senator George Norris for president. Farmer-Labor senator Henrik Shipstead, running for reelection, repeatedly praised nonpartisanism and hardly referred to his partisan affiliation during the general campaign. In response to these problems Floyd Olson toured the state urging voters to remember the Farmer-Labor ticket. He used, ironically, an old Nonpartisan League slogan, "Stick and Win."[42]

The Farmer-Labor Party's Crisis in Comparative Perspective

In spite of its crisis in the later 1920s, of all the cases of state-level radicalism in the 1920s the Minnesota Farmer-Labor party was easily the most successful. Besides the North Dakota Nonpartisan League, there were six other cases: Washington, Idaho, Montana, South Dakota, Oklahoma, and Texas.

State-level radicalism in South Dakota, Montana, and Texas must be classed as nearly ephemeral. In South Dakota entrepreneurs, perhaps stimulated by the high vote for the 1920 Farmer-Labor presidential candidate (19%), offered statewide Farmer-Labor ballots in 1924 and 1926, but they did poorly, while in Montana a Farmer-Labor party in the middle and late 1920s functioned primarily as a vehicle for a pro-Communist state senator, despite a statewide Farmer-Labor ballot in 1924. In Texas, government use of an open-shop law in the 1922 rail shopmen's strike led Socialists in a Farm-Labor Union that was organized in Texas, Arkansas, and Oklahoma to enter the electoral arena. They worked with Nonpartisan Leaguers left from the original effort to diffuse the league to Texas from North Dakota. Together they staged a strong showing in the 1922 Democratic gubernatorial primary, but their forces then disintegrated.[43]

The other three cases are more impressive, but they too resemble flash-in-the-pan movements. In Oklahoma the remnants of the once powerful Socialist party joined with the Farmers Union and the Farm-Labor Union to form a Farmer-Labor Reconstruction League modelled on the North Dakota Nonpartisan League. The coalition succeeded in 1922 in getting the mayor of Oklahoma City, running as a Democrat, elected as governor of Oklahoma. But it was unable to control him, as he quickly abandoned the league platform and its politics, and he was unable to defend them from the Ku Klux Klan. Indeed, throughout the Southwest the Klan precluded possibilities for state-level radicalism.[44]

In 1920 the Washington Farmer-Labor party ran a campaign for all statewide offices, (rolling up over 30 percent for its gubernatorial candidate); for four out of five House seats; and for the United States Senate, (gaining 25.8 percent). It also rolled up a huge third-party vote (19.4%), relative to the rest of the country (.99%), for the 1920 Farmer-Labor party presidential campaign.[45] Yet the party experienced severe factionalism in 1921. While it continued to offer ballots through 1924, it was badly weakened, and it died after the 1924 elections.[46]

In Idaho in 1918 the Nonpartisan League ran a Democrat for governor, who gained 40.1 percent of the vote. In 1919 the Idaho legislature reformed party law to create strong parties. In 1920 the league ran an independent for governor, who won 20.1 percent, and Progressive party candidates for Congress, who gained 26.5 percent and 23.7 percent. By

1922 the league had given way to the Idaho Progressive party, which became the state's second party. After 1926 it collapsed altogether.[47]

Electoral Concomitants of Elite
Weakness in Minnesota

In a comparative perspective Minnesota Farmer-Labor party's leaders' achievements were substantial. Nevertheless, in the latter half of the 1920s the Farmer-Labor party clearly experienced a deepening crisis. Its organizational elites had far fewer financial resources, less ideological cohesion, and much less self-confidence than they had in the first half of the decade. The electoral concomitants of this weakness and disarray were extraordinary, relative to the surge in both organizational and electoral strength that the Farmer-Labor party experienced earlier. In 1924 the number of counties that voted at a level of 45 percent or greater for the Farmer-Labor party was fifty; in 1928 there were no counties at all that voted at 45 percent or more for the party.

Two other useful indicators of decline are the average of the differences in strength between 1924 and 1928 across the state's counties (-23.2%), and the differences between 1924 and 1929 in roll-off, a statistic that measures the electorate's tendency to cast votes for the most important office at an election and not to cast votes for the lesser offices—in 1924 roll-off was 24 percent; in 1928, which also saw a contest for the United States Senate, roll-off was 73 percent. (Roll-off here is calculated by subtracting the smallest total votes—say for secretary of state—from the greatest total votes—say for United States Senate—and dividing the remainder by the greatest total vote). In addition, the Farmer-Labor party was somewhat less competitive in the 1928 elections to the United States House of Representatives than it was in the 1924 elections. In 1924 the party fielded candidates in all ten districts. Its average competitiveness (measured by the average of the reciprocal of the differences between Republican and Farmer-Labor candidates) was 82.8. In 1928 the party fielded candidates in only eight districts, and its average competitiveness was 74.

Minnesota Farmer-Labor Party in Crisis

The organizational history of the Minnesota Farmer-Labor party during the 1920s underscores how strongly the regional political environment shaped the actions of radical political entrepreneurs. In Minnesota such entrepreneurs struggled for a decade with their antiparty environment, avoiding the disappearance from politics that radical entrepreneurs in other states experienced. Yet by the end of the decade their institution was in deep trouble. Indeed, in 1929 the Minnesota State Federation of Labor formally disbanded its political action committee, ending the experiment in party politics that William Mahoney launched in 1919.[48]

The crisis of the late 1920s strongly shaped the actions of the Farmer-Labor elite in the 1930s. Party building preoccupied the Farmer-Labor party's entrepreneurs in that decade as well. There was a third and final phase of political entrepreneurship in the context of regional receptivity to reform. Their entrepreneurial responses in the 1930s to the tasks of party building were crucial in shaping what eventually happened to the Minnesota Farmer-Labor party.

Party and Patronage

In 1930 the Farmer-Labor party ran for a second time its 1924 candidate for governor, Floyd B. Olson. His victory began a new phase in the party's history. The Farmer-Labor party achieved a goal its leaders had sought for twelve years, but it also faced new organizational problems.

Once in power, the Farmer-Labor party needed to reelect those Farmer-Labor politicians who already held office. A second imperative was to assert greater influence over Minnesota's fragmented institutional structure. If party leaders chose to meet these twin challenges, they would have to expand rapidly the party's organizational strength.

In response to these new imperatives facing the party, Olson and other key figures eventually subjected a large part of the state's civil service to direct Farmer-Labor control, partly turning the party into a machine. This change created long-run problems for the Farmer-Labor party. But transforming the party into a political machine had several immediate advantages. It produced useful political resources; it allowed the party to influence the behavior of a sizeable new group in the electorate, the unemployed; it paid off activists for their loyalty. These advantages of patronage made it easier for the party's top politicians to get on with the business of strengthening their power as Minnesota's rising political class and of changing public policy.

The limits on the power of those elites who dominated Minnesota's politics in the 1920s eased this partial transformation of the Farmer-Labor party into a political machine. Also, good government—that is, the cause of elites anxious to shield their interest in efficient government from the influence of patronage politics—was a nonissue in the early '30s, especially after the 1932 elections. Hence, a sense quickly developed within the party that it could profitably use incentives for patronage built into Minnesota's institutional structure and get away with it.

Minnesota's Institutional Structure

At first, though, the party's room for maneuver seemed narrow.[1] Floyd Olson's election in 1930 as governor with 59.3

53

percent of the vote was a considerable victory for the Farmer-Labor party. Olson carried eighty-two of eighty-seven counties. But Olson's victory over his opponent, former state auditor Ray Chase, who got a mere 35 percent (leaving 3.5% for the Democrats), was in large measure a lonely landslide.

Only one of the ten Farmer-Laborites running for Congress that year was elected. The incumbent Republican senator, Tom Schall, who defeated Magnus Johnson in 1924, was handily reelected—in fact, his main competition was his Democratic opponent, not the Farmer-Labor candidate, who ran third in the race. The Farmer-Labor party did elect the lieutenant governor, but no other statewide officers, and the differences between the gubernatorial vote and the vote for other officers were large. The lieutenant governor's vote was 24 percent smaller than Olson's; the candidate for secretary of state had a vote 56 percent smaller. The total vote for the senatorial candidate was even smaller than the vote for secretary of state; thus the party's roll-off in 1930 was 62 percent if we include the senatorial vote in the calculation. The 1930 elections represented a break from the past, but they could hardly be called a massive repudiation of Republican rule in favor of the "cooperative commonwealth."

It was quite possible that Olson's election would have rather slight consequences for public policy. Gubernatorial terms lasted for only two years, and the rules of Minnesota's legislative game posed especially difficult problems for a programmatic party of economic protest such as the Farmer-Labor party.

The legislature met officially for only ninety days during a gubernatorial term, in odd-numbered years. Governors were permitted to call special sessions of the legislature, yet such sessions could easily produce accusations of fiscal irresponsibility from the press and influential private watchdogs, and damage a governor's prestige.

The consequences for legislative politics of nonpartisan elections (enacted by the 1913 legislature) also handicapped the Farmer-Labor party, even more than a short biennial session did. Because Farmer-Labor voters lacked ballot cues, nonpartisan elections sharply cut the legislature's responsiveness to economic protest voting. Nonpartisan elections rewarded incumbents who had name recognition in their legislative districts and who preferred vague stances or no positions at all on controversial policy issues. As the state legislative board of the railroad brotherhoods sarcastically remarked in a 1927 report, nonpartisan elections favored candidates "who in all campaign speeches spoke on conditions in China."[2] The

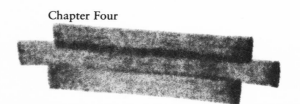

cost, in terms of time, energy, and skill, of educating voters as to who stood for what was very high. Even if in 1930 the Farmer-Labor party had possessed the resources to pay these costs, a special risk would have been attached to using them. For nonpartisan elections also undercut voting discipline within the legislature. Legislators could ignore their caucuses with little fear of electoral sanction. The independence of nonpartisan solons was even greater in the senate, which was elected every four years, when off-year congressional elections were held.

Thus, at the opening of the 1931 session, conservative Republican incumbents dominated the legislature. The small corps of legislators affiliated with the Farmer-Labor party lacked discipline. And after years of being denied access to the legislature's important committees, they lacked self-confidence. In the 1929 session they had not even bothered to put up a candidate for the speakership of the house, and they made only a token effort at the opening of the 1931 session. The rules committees of both houses—especially important in a biennial legislature with a short session—had been off limits to insurgent legislators since the 1923 session. The election of a Farmer-Labor lieutenant governor threatened to change this situation in the senate, since traditionally the lieutenant governor appointed senate committee chairs. But the senate proceeded to organize itself through a committee controlled by conservatives. In short, legislative politics in Minnesota meant special political and organizational problems for the Farmer-Labor party.

These special problems were not the only aspects of Minnesota's institutional structure and its electoral procedures that suggested how far Olson and the Farmer-Labor party were from making any real political progress. Minnesota had several agencies whose work was or could be important to the Farmer-Labor party. One of these was the Department of Agriculture, created in 1919, which encouraged marketing and collected farm statistics. Another was the Industrial Commission, established in 1921, a merger of the Department of Labor and Industries and other bureaucracies. The Industrial Commission handled workmen's compensation claims, administered occupational safety regulations, licensed the qualifications of trades and crafts, and supervised boards of arbitration and mediation. Other relevant agencies were those concerned with conserving Minnesota's natural resources and regulating insurance and banking. Also important were the Tax Commission and the Board of Education. Commissioners, often appointed for staggered terms longer than a single gubernatorial term, governed these agencies. The acquisition of control over Minnesota's semi-independent agencies, the operation of which mattered or could matter to the Farmer-Labor party, would obviously take much longer than Olson's first term.

Besides these semi-independent bureaucracies, there were other important executive offices that could come within the Farmer-Labor party's organizational purview. The auditor leased and sold public lands, timber, and ore. The legal skills of the attorney general and his staff, which acted essentially as general counsel for county attorneys, state departments, and other executive offices, could be used to defend executive policy initiatives. Because the Farmer-Labor party intended an expansion of governmental capacities, control of the attorney general's office had much to recommend it. The attorney general also could influence state-level bureaucratic, fiscal, and regulatory politics, and local fiscal politics, not least welfare and education. The attorney general handled the constitutional defense of statutory policy; if the Farmer-Labor party were to gain controversial legislation that could help its coalition, legal challenges to the changes had to be defeated in the courts.

In addition to the auditor and the attorney general, elected for four- and two-year terms respectively, were the treasurer and the secretary of state, both elected biennially. Control of the treasurer's office would help with policy planning. A Farmer-Labor secretary of state might play a role in pressing the legislature to revise electoral rules. The party wanted to change, for instance, the rule for primary ballots. Once the farmer-labor movement became a party in the 1920s, its leaders began demanding a consolidated open primary ballot. They believed that working class voters on the Minnesota Iron Range did not ask for Farmer-Labor ballots on primary day for fear of losing their jobs.

Then there was the Railroad and Warehouse Commission, consisting of three members elected for periods of six years in biennial rotation. The commission regulated railroad carriers, telephone companies, other public utilities, warehouses, stockyards, and grain storage. The commission's grain inspection service was its largest bureaucracy. The commission mattered to grain and other kinds of farmers, to the railroad brotherhoods, and to machinists engaged in railroad-related work.

Finally, Minnesota's judiciary was also partly subject to party politics, although elections were nonpartisan and decorously conducted. Nevertheless, the Farmer-Labor party could properly seek to exert some influence over judicial elections. The state supreme court had five members. Also, nineteen state district judges were elected. A more liberal judiciary was in the Farmer-Labor party's interest, not least of its trade union wing.

To sum up: Minnesota's institutional structure was unusually resistant to partisan control, and it was highly decentralized. During the long era of Republican hegemony between the end of the Civil War and the rise of the Farmer-Labor party, Minnesota's institutional decentralization was well suited to one-partyism. But an opposition organization such as the Farmer-Labor party faced a great challenge in knitting together such a fragmented structure of government.

No democratic political party could ever fully control Minnesota's institutional structure. A function, intended or not, of its plethora of institutions was removal of an enormous amount of government from party politics.[3] Yet the outcome of the 1932 elections made possible a sweeping change in the Farmer-Labor party's relationship to Minnesota's institutions. Olson easily won reelection in what was essentially a three-way race, getting a little over 50 percent of the vote while his Republican and Democratic opponents got about 32 percent and 16 percent. The Farmer-Labor party also elected the lieutenant governor, the attorney general, and a railroad and warehouse commissioner. This time roll-off was 34 percent, still high, but a distinct improvement over 1930. The party also captured a majority of the state's delegation to Congress: five of the state's nine representatives (Minnesota lost a seat in 1932 through redistricting) would be Farmer-Laborites.

A rise in expectations among Farmer-Labor activists was heightened, of course, by the decisive political defeat that the Republican party suffered at the national level. An action by the new attorney general, Harry H. Peterson, captures the mood within the Farmer-Labor party. Peterson apparently had trouble getting a Republican assistant attorney general to vacate his position. On a day that the man argued a case before the Minnesota Supreme Court, Peterson strode into court, summarily dismissed the man before the justices, and coolly proceeded to finish oral argument for the State of Minnesota.[4]

Pressure mounted sharply within the Farmer-Labor party for Olson to design and implement a strategy that would completely change the party's relationship to the state's bureaucracies. The party wanted patronage throughout the state's bureaucracies, not just those pieces of it that the party colonized during Olson's first term, that is, the oil inspection service, the hotel inspection service, and the game warden division of the Department of Game and Fish.[5] As a member of the Farmer-Labor Association's

Executive Committee told Olson's secretary, "nothing will satisfy the Farmer-Laborites all over Minnesota, but a general housecleaning in all departments."[6]

During his first term Olson made it clear that the party would control state agencies. Olson reversed 122 interim appointments made by his predecessor, Theodore Christianson, including Christianson's appointment of the commissioner of agriculture and the chair of the Industrial Commission, whose antilabor views were strong and well known. Olson also permitted sporadic use of patronage even as he seemed to favor a bipartisan civil service. But Olson allowed in 1933 far greater Farmer-Labor control of Minnesota's bureaucracies. This was an important moment in the Farmer-Labor party's history.[7]

Minnesota did have an elite committed to the autonomy of the state's bureaucracies from party politics. It included, for instance, the League of Women Voters, whose president Olson had made his first budget commissioner, and the social science professoriate of the University of Minnesota. Also, the issue of sound, effective administration figured prominently in both the 1926 and 1928 gubernatorial contests. The Republican governor Christianson, who campaigned on that and related issues such as lowering taxes, had a reputation among the state's political elites as an expert on good government and prudent fiscal policy.

But the 1930 and 1932 elections turned on quite different issues. In 1933 the power of good-government advocates was much weaker. Whether or not parties should control bureaucracies directly did not matter much to voters, even to the usual mass constituency for good government, middle-class voters.

Only one fraction of the electorate focused on issues concerning administration of state government. That fraction—Farmer-Labor activists—wanted direct party control of state bureaucracies. Many were without jobs in a crisis that by then was widely recognized as very severe, and they were highly vocal. Thus, while groups that might veto Olson's decision were weak, a strong group pushed him to take it.

Yet how could Olson possibly succeed without greater strength in the legislature? And where would a party leader begin in bringing such a complex institutional environment under partisan control?

How Prior Administrative Reforms
Helped Patronage

Ironically, Olson's decision to expand patronage was possible, in part, because promoters of good government had once been strong. The executive reorganization of 1925 created the so-called "Big Three": a director of personnel, a commissioner of purchases, and a budget commissioner, all grouped into the Commission of Administration and Finance, subject to unilateral gubernatorial appointment. Following this reorganization, both the Minnesota Supreme Court and the attorney general consolidated this victory for institutional modernization. As the Big Three encroached on the prerogatives of other state officials, the court and the attorney general upheld the legitimacy of central auditing and budget procedures.

In addition Governor Christianson built popular support for the Big Three in 1926 and 1928. His victories legitimated the commission despite conservative Republican opposition. They also overwhelmed Farmer-Labor charges that the commission had antidemocratic implications. In the 1925 session former Socialist state senator Andrew Devold vigorously pressed the Farmer-Labor party's counterproposal—an elective administrative council coupled with Christianson's proposed civil service merit system. But by 1928 this was a dead policy.[8]

However, the commission had a flaw: the 1925 legislature did not enact a proposed civil service merit system. This result had an unintended consequence in 1933. Lack of a civil service merit system, in combination with the Big Three's institutionalization between 1925 and 1930, opened the way for Olson to establish direct partisan control of Minnesota's bureaucracies. Because the governorship controlled job classifications and pay scales through the director of personnel, over the space of a few years many loyal Farmer-Laborites could be spread among the state's bureaucracies. As many as ten to eleven thousand jobs could be awarded to party loyalists.[9]

Another administrative development of the previous decade facilitated Olson's decision to expand patronage.[10] In 1920 the Minnesota electorate approved the trunk highway amendment to the state constitution. This amendment, a response to Congress's authorization in 1916 of a federal role in highway construction, allowed Minnesota to receive public funds for highway construction via the Department of Agriculture's Bureau of Public Roads. Minnesota chose to match federal funds through revenues from motor vehicle registration taxes and gasoline taxes. Collection of both taxes was relatively centralized, efficient, and cheap.

For the Farmer-Labor party the Highway Department was a ripe plum waiting to be picked. During his first term Olson used the Highway Department for his own program of work relief, gaining the enthusiastic cooperation of its Republican commissioner, who had figured in highway administration since 1909. Here President Hoover's emphasis on state, local, and voluntary responses to unemployment helped Olson politically. Olson issued a highway construction code requiring state-financed contractors to pay a minimum wage and overtime on highway work. In 1931 and 1932 the Highway Department paved more miles than it had between 1924 and 1930.[11]

With rural and outstate urban unemployment on the rise, the Highway Department was likely to continue to provide work relief. By putting work relief and patronage together it would be possible to pay off activists and extend Farmer-Labor organization into outstate areas and, perhaps, to secure the loyalty of a sizeable fraction of the unemployed population.

The Strategy of Patronage

Even though the Farmer-Labor party was weak legislatively and Minnesota's institutional structure was quite complex, it was possible for the party's leadership rapidly to assert considerable control over the state's bureaucracies. Further, it was possible to strengthen through patronage the party's infrastructure of political clubs and to incorporate into the Farmer-Labor coalition a new group in the electorate with a very distinct interest in work relief, namely, the unemployed. In turn, these changes would help the party to move toward its policy goals. What made the changes all possible were key administrative developments in the 1920s.

In May 1933 Floyd Olson authorized I. C. "Dutch" Strout, a little-known but quite influential figure in Farmer-Labor history, to draw up a patronage plan. In that month Strout became one of the Big Three, director of personnel for state government. After years of biding his time amid the political gloom of the late '20s, this was Strout's golden chance.[12]

Strout came from Brainerd, a small city in northern Minnesota. Brainerd once was an important railroad point, and it was a center of labor political action in the early 1920s, when it was briefly governed by a WPNPL mayor. Brainerd's WPNPL mayor bravely presided over the city and its police during the 1922 national railroad shopmen's strike, only to be defeated at the next election by a former mayor whose campaign was handled by the Northern Pacific Railroad. This event coincided with the end of the strike and the shopmen's blacklisting.[13] In the late '20s Strout quietly carried on Brainerd's defeated political tradition both as a member of the Socialist party and as a leader in the city's once active Farmer-Labor club.

To his job as state director of personnel Strout brought logistical skills and a detailed knowledge of the state. He was a railroad dispatcher by vocation and had operated a newspaper and magazine delivery service in northern Minnesota. During the first Olson administration he worked as a hotel inspector, touring the state, establishing links with outstate Farmer-Labor clubs, and in general throwing himself wholeheartedly into the patronage politics of the first Olson administration.

As state director of personnel Strout literally rebuilt the Farmer-Labor party's organizational infrastructure. He transformed the Farmer-Labor Association into a clearinghouse for appointments to state government. In order to replace Republican civil servants Strout requested that Farmer-Labor organizations submit lists of prospective appointments. He instructed his two assistants to screen applicants very carefully and, in those many instances where political qualifications appeared equal, to choose the better trained and better educated. Sometimes, though, political qualifications were decisive: as one of the assistants wrote in a memo to Strout concerning a job seeker, "F-L activities while with a CCC camp up north last summer . . . Do not think that he is as yet fully left-wing . . . he may . . . on some bright June morning find that some other group deserved his undivided attention."[14]

As part of his drive to establish direct Farmer-Labor control of the state's bureaucracies, Strout fully used his statutory authority to classify state jobs and establish pay scales, achieving a complete mastery of the details of state personnel administration.[15] Strout, in fact, was obsessive about patronage, going so far as to establish a detective system for ascertaining the loyalties of those who received state jobs, no matter how lowly.[16] Strout encouraged, although he apparently did not require, the new Farmer-Laborites in state government to contribute 3 percent of their monthly income to the Farmer-Labor Association, adding to the association's other sources of revenue. This money went into a special fund that helped to pay for publication of the party's newspaper, the *Farmer-Labor Leader*, later the *Minnesota Leader*. It also paid for a weekly radio broadcast.[17]

More consequential was Strout's assignment of a clearinghouse function to local Farmer-Labor organizations, which meant a rapid expansion in the numbers of campaign and organizational personnel in all areas of the state. The Highway Department became crucial to this outcome once Olson removed its commissioner and replaced him with the former city engineer of Minneapolis, who served under a Farmer-Labor mayoral administration elected in 1931.[18]

The organizational payoff of Strout's strategy can be seen in a letter that

Strout wrote to ninety newly appointed county and area employees. It read, in part,

> You received the appointment as foreman for the State Department of Highways not only because of your ability to perform the services required but more particularly because of the fact that you were given the preferred endorsement of your County Farmer-Labor Association . . . the State Committee of the Farmer-Labor Association on organization and education feels that when you accepted this appointment you also accepted the moral obligation to take the initiative in completing the organization work of the Farmer-Labor organization in your territory . . . With the above in mind we are mailing under separate cover an organizational manual and a supply of membership receipt books, also other miscellaneous organization material.[19]

Strout's planning and top-down pressure, in combination with the material rewards that county- and ward-level Farmer-Labor organizations controlled or could control, had startling results. According to one estimate (in an interview decades later), about four hundred Farmer-Labor clubs emerged around the state. While obviously only a retrospective guess, the impression of sharp expansion is confirmed in the proliferation of organizational notices in the trade union and Farmer-Labor press from that era. Strout thus provided an infrastructure into which both protest and opportunism could be channelled.

The new clubs complemented preexisting clubs. For instance, the two first-class cities had active ward clubs after Mahoney's reorganization of the Farmer-Labor infrastructure in the mid-Twenties. An example is Minneapolis's Third Ward Club, located in the part of Minneapolis where Floyd Olson grew up. It sponsored annual picnics, complete with "races, prizes, entertainment, refreshment, and speakers," held monthly meetings at a neighborhood church, and even established its own newspaper.[20]

In 1930 the Farmer-Labor Association's statewide membership was a mere 7,500. When compared to the approximately 50,000 members that the Minnesota Nonpartisan League had in 1918 and the 45,000 members that the WPNPL had then, too, one sees how small the Farmer-Labor Association was. Up to 1933 the Farmer-Labor Association grew quickly, to 10,000. After 1933, though, the association felt the full impact of the development of a machine. Although there were fluctuations in size after 1933, the association doubled in size to 20,000 and in certain months may even have reached 30,000. So rapid was the association's expansion, and so makeshift were many of the new organizations, that a subunit of the association's state committee, the Farmer-Labor Educational Bureau, distributed a pamphlet on proper procedure for conducting meetings.[21]

A key agency in the new expanded Farmer-Labor Association was this Educational Bureau. Its function was to sustain the ideological and organizational vitality of the new organizations. Strout supported the bureau's staff by arranging for "no-show" clerical positions in state agencies. The bureau's staff comprised several young men who brought journalistic, secretarial, and legal talent to their work. They were the children of Farmer-Labor functionaries, activists, and supporters, such as the editor of the Farmer-Labor newspaper, a trade unionist, and a small-town banker.

The bureau was a centralizing influence within the expanded Farmer-Labor organization. Its staff would research policy issues, monitor the voting records of state legislators affiliated with the Farmer-Labor party, and write, print, and distribute educational pamphlets and bulletins called "Speakers' Notes" to Farmer-Labor organizations. Although the staff was small, it coordinated a far-flung operation, using trucks lent from businesses favored by the Big Three and other agencies to distribute material stored in a St. Paul warehouse. The Farmer-Labor Educational Bureau also arranged for speakers for new Farmer-Labor clubs and wrote speeches for Farmer-Labor leaders.[22]

The final advantage of the decision by the Farmer-Labor party's leadership to establish a political machine was partial incorporation of the unemployed members of the electorate into the Farmer-Labor coalition.[23] Using the Highway Department and federal funding of work relief, the Farmer-Labor party was able to establish a program of party-controlled work relief that lasted the entire time the party was in office.

In 1933 the legislature cooperated with the party by authorizing the addition of over forty-five hundred new miles to the trunk highway system, the part of the highway system that the Highway Department directly controlled. This was a 65 percent enlargement of the system. Because the legislature did not, however, fully pay for the Farmer-Labor party's new use of the Highway Department, the party turned toward federal funding. The legislature issued highway bonds in 1931 and 1932, but in 1933 it did not follow suit, probably because federal funds were available. In 1935 the legislature again issued bonds, in order to comply with provisions of the 1934 Hayden-Cartwright Act, which released money for work relief to state highway departments on condition that the 1935 legislatures appropriate matching funds. Yet the main source of funding for the work-relief program operated by the Highway Department was federal funds. By 1935 large sums of federal work-relief funds were being routed through the Highway Department, in some years (1934 and 1936) on the order of $10 million. Routing work-relief funding through the Highway Department built on Olson's transfer, in December 1933, of the Minnesota branch of the Civil Works Administration from the state Board of Control (whose chair was a Republican) to the state Highway Department. The intermediaries between the governor and the Highway Department were a director of personnel, a position created in 1933, and a special assistant attorney general for the Highway Department.[24]

How many thousands of men received employment on either construction or the maintenance work that construction inevitably engendered is hard to say. Nor is it possible to estimate with any accuracy what percentage of the unemployed was affected by the Highway Department's work-relief program. But the program was explicitly designed to spread work geographically and to generate a large volume of projects. It represented an astute effort to meet both the work needs of the unemployed and the political needs of the Farmer-Labor party.[25]

The Costs of the Farmer-Labor
Party's Reorganization

Let us evaluate not only the benefits of the Farmer-Labor party's reorganization but also its costs. Beginning in 1933 the Farmer-Labor party's leaders exploited the possibilities implicit in the executive reorganization of 1925 and the possibilities for patronage implicit in the administration and finance of Minnesota's highway system. In doing this, the Farmer-Labor leadership transformed the Farmer-Labor Association, generating money and members. The party also paid off longtime activists. It provided, for instance, a job to the daughter of the editor of the *Park Region Echo,* an outstate paper that had long faithfully supported the Farmer-Labor party. In that particular case the party cut a good deal. As the *Echo*'s editor slyly reminded the state's chief oil inspector, an old Nonpartisan Leaguer, "Your Minnesota Leader can take over the duties, no doubt, but I am afraid that it will take more than two years for it to get the coverage of the territory that the Echo's 4350 subscribers give, and radios are getting scarce as hen's teeth in this drouth territory."[26] Finally, the organizational strengthening of the Farmer-Labor party may well have contributed to the party's growing electoral strength. (Details of this growth in electoral strength are provided at the beginning of chapter 8.)

But there was a price for the Farmer-Labor Association's reorganization and expansion. Patronage handed a valuable issue to the party's opponents. Olson had effectively smeared the Republicans during his first term when he launched investigations into Republican mismanagement of the rural credits program of the 1920s and of the state fur farm. Now the Republicans had a chance to counterattack.

The Republicans badly bungled their use of the patronage issue during the 1935 legislative session. A senate committee was formed to investigate Farmer-Labor uses of patronage. Its chair was a conservative Democrat who in the early '20s cooperated with the farmer-labor movement in launching a legislative investigation into the special efforts that the Republican party made to outspend the farmer-labor movement. But he weakened his claim to impartiality by approving blatantly unfair procedures for the conduct of hearings. Olson was able to run rings around the committee, writing an often funny newspaper column lampooning the committee's deliberations. One of the party's publicists also weakened the investigation through witty radio attacks on the influence of money in the legislature. The Farmer-Labor party thus successfully portrayed the investigation as old-fashioned partisan politics, a desperate effort by reactionary conservatives.[27]

Yet patronage was a loaded issue. In time the Republicans would figure out how to use it properly.

Besides permanently changing the party's relationship to its external political environment, patronage created internal problems. Inconsistent systems of participation grew up within the party. During the 1920s ideological reasons for participation predominated within the Farmer-Labor party. Then, with its reorganization in the 1930s, new kinds of participants joined the Farmer-Labor Association, those motivated by material incentives for participation. The material incentive inhered, of course, in job security or the hope of it.

After 1933 the Farmer-Labor Association became unusually complex. Some Farmer-Labor clubs were militant and ideological, while others were not. Older clubs were probably more ideological, and in fact the associations of Hennepin, Ramsey, and St. Louis counties were the most radical. The least ideological are hard to identify. The records of the several dozen county Farmer-Labor Associations have not been collected, but the least ideological were probably established after 1933 and were probably outstate county associations.

The main consequence of this change was that the Farmer-Labor party came to house different groups of activists with very different interests. Sander Genis, the Jewish Socialist leader of the Amalgamated Clothing Workers of Minnesota, eloquently spoke about this division in the party's elite in a speech to the St. Paul Eleventh Ward Farmer-Labor Club in November 1935.

A new movement of this kind calls not for men and women who are ready to jump the band wagon to obtain easy jobs, but rather men and women who are willing to go down the line, who are willing to sacrifice a little of their comforts, so that they may have something to look forward to in the future, so that we may build a better social order where every man and woman will receive their just due, where society will consist of intelligent social planning, where wars will be eliminated . . . where fear, ignorance and uncertainty will be replaced by freedom, intelligence, and a guarantee of the right of liberty in the pursuit of happiness.[28]

Genis thus argued that patronage blocked a collective sense of loyalty to farmer-labor ideas.[29]

This problem of loyalty seems also to have surfaced in highway work relief, if one takes a 1956 study by Frank Sorauf of Pennsylvania highway workers as an indication of worker sentiment. Highway workers were likely to think that "'politics ought not to hurt the working man.' To deprive a man of his livelihood for no other reason than the victory of a gubernatorial candidate" was likely to strike "many of them as unjust, if not immoral."[30] Absent a survey of the Minnesota workers similar to that conducted by Sorauf, one cannot know how much resentment of the Farmer-Labor party's patronage system there was among Minnesota's highway workers. But there is indirect evidence that resentment probably existed. By 1937 state highway employees who were organized into unions demanded civil service merit coverage for their jobs.[31] A Gallup poll found in 1938 that 82 percent of people on relief favored making it a crime for a relief official to influence the vote of a person on relief.[32]

Patronage strongly shaped an internal succession struggle, leaving a bitter legacy that came back to haunt the party.[33] It was widely believed within the party as early as winter 1934 that Floyd Olson would not serve longer than three terms as governor and that he would seek higher office. Thus the choice of Olson's running mate in 1934 was treated as the choice of his successor as governor. The person chosen at the 1934 Farmer-Labor Association convention was state senator Hjalmar Petersen, a small-town newspaper publisher who had steered the party's income tax proposals through the 1933 legislature. He initially had very mixed feelings about becoming governor, but in time he came to believe that he should become governor and took special pride in the fact that his plurality in the 1934 election was greater than Olson's. Yet to his dismay, he watched the patronage chiefs who controlled the party's newspaper, the *Leader,* promote Banking Superintendent Elmer Benson. When Republican United States senator Tom Schall died in office in December 1935, the politics of

Olson's succession became even more charged. Petersen grew bitter when the editors of the *Leader* preempted Olson's choice, running an edition claiming that Olson had decided to appoint Benson to the Senate to fill out Schall's term. Benson now had an enormous edge in becoming the next governor. Further, in 1936 the patronage forces successfully secured Benson's nomination at the 1936 Farmer-Labor Association convention. In public Petersen accepted these results with good grace, and settled for a nomination to the Railroad and Warehouse Commission. But inwardly he seethed with anger, and his supporters within the party were dismayed at the behavior of the "Benson machine."

Alternatives to the Patronage Strategy

Considering the costs of the patronage strategy, one wonders, Were there alternatives to it? Were they acted upon?

One alternative was to push a civil service merit system. This had the advantage of locking several thousand Farmer-Laborites into state jobs while presenting a good-government image to the public. In the 1933 legislative session a Farmer-Labor representative introduced a bill for a civil service merit system. At the 1934 Farmer-Labor Association convention Olson warned his colleagues within the party that a patronage strategy was bad for the party. One of I. C. Strout's assistants pressed for a declaration in favor of a civil service merit system to be made late in the 1934 campaign at a League of Women Voters meeting. Also, at the beginning of the 1935 legislative session Olson called (albeit tepidly) for a civil service merit system. Finally, state senator Henry Teigan introduced a bill for this purpose during the session.[34]

The flaw with this alternative was that the party had a large constituency opposed to it. Olson and others in the party could also have focused the energies of the party's activists early in the 1930s on crusading for control of the legislature. Such a crusade might have rebuilt the Farmer-Labor party on the basis of ideology rather than on a mix of ideology and the prospect of material gain. Olson assigned a skilled political operative to coordinating legislative electoral campaigns, and intended in 1934 to visit key legislative districts personally. At the 1936 Farmer-Labor Association convention Hjalmar Petersen specifically advocated a focus on legislative elections as an alternative to a patronage strategy.

A legislative strategy was, of course, difficult. It essentially asked people in the party to defer immediate pecuniary gain and bureaucratic power in the middle of an economic crisis for the long-run goal of effecting policy change. More to the point, though, was the poverty of the Farmer-Labor

Association in the early 1930s, when a choice of party-building strategies presented itself. Lowering the electorate's high information costs in the context of nonpartisan legislative elections was very, very expensive in terms of time, skills, and money. The Farmer-Labor Association simply did not have enough political resources for a serious legislative campaign—indeed, a major purpose of the patronage strategy was to create such resources. Despite his intentions, in 1934 Olson was unable to campaign in legislative districts because he had to concentrate on his own reelection campaign. That Olson assigned a lone political operative for 198 legislative contests speaks volumes about how little he had to work with.[35]

Reorganization in Retrospect

The patronage strategy, while not a necessary outcome of the long struggle by the Farmer-Labor party's elite to create a strong party organization, was certainly the most likely outcome. What a survey of the entire organizational history of the Farmer-Labor party shows is a constant effort within the party to design strategies for coping with its political environment. We see, first, an effort to transcend the limits to long-run stability posed by the antipartisan habits of entrepreneurs and insurgent politicians. A creative core of leaders in the farmer-labor coalition of 1918–23 understood that the very permeability of Minnesota's electoral markets to radical entrepreneurs created special organizational problems. Their analysis of these problems and of the necessary solution led to the establishment of the Farmer-Labor Association. Second, we see an effort to transcend the limits to party government posed in 1930 by the confluence of trade union weakness, formal disestablishment of labor political action, and the need to assert control over a fragmented institutional structure. On the whole there was creativity and progress: striking success in the early and middle '20s, some decline in the late '20s, and brilliant success again in the '30s. But the final outcome of an effort that lasted fifteen years—that is, the adoption of patronage—undercut the party's future even as the party grew in strength. Patronage was in tension with the good-government issues of the late '20s—the advocates of good government might well recoup the influence over public opinion they once had. Patronage also generated a system of mixed loyalties within the party's organization, and, relatedly, it created a deep split over personalities.

A Changing National Political Economy

Already some of the possibilities and limits of state-level radicalism as a type of politics are rather clear. A historical analysis of how radical political entrepreneurs handled their special environmental problems in building a strong political party has revealed basic limits on this type of politics. A full understanding of the possibilities and limits of state-level radicalism requires placing this type of politics in its national political-economic context. Even as the Minnesota Farmer-Labor party reorganized itself in the 1930s, it faced a rapidly changing national political economy.

In the midst of the most serious crisis of American capitalism, national governmental actors sought to change relationships between the federal government on the one hand and economy and society on the other. Making the most of existing governmental capacities for designing and implementing new public policies, national political elites constructed, step by step, a new political economy. They constructed a balancing political economy that would supplant the accumulationist political economy which the politicians of state-level radicalism themselves sought to change. National political-economic change fundamentally structured the Farmer-Labor party's future and the possibilities of state-level radicalism as a type of politics.

To understand how and why national change did this, let us look back at the political economy of the 1920s. Doing so will provide the background for approaching the Farmer-Labor party's history from another angle.

FIVE

The Political Economy of State-Level Radicalism

During the 1920s the United States government played an accumulationist role in the national political economy. In the 1980s we are more familiar with a different role, in which governmental actors seek to balance reformist and accumulationist public policies. Governmental actors not only protect business confidence and the orderly functioning of market institutions but also, at least rhetorically, respond to demands "to improve the welfare and position of groups that have been neglected or squeezed" by the operation of the market. In an accumulationist political economy governmental actors work to perfect the market while often successfully resisting or only partly accommodating demands for reformist public policies. This type of political economy characterized the 1920s.[1]

After receiving a mandate for a "return to normalcy" in 1920, the Republican party created an accumulationist political economy that supplanted the balancing political economy that the Democratic party briefly created during the First World War. To be sure, the political economy of the 1920s was somewhat more of a balancing political economy than is often recognized. Two examples of reformist public policies are the Railway Labor Act of 1926, establishing an impartial system of collective bargaining for railway labor, and the Sheppard-Towner Act of 1921, which established federal subsidy of educational instruction in the health care of mothers and babies. But the overwhelming direction of public policy in that decade was toward establishment and maintenance of an accumulationist political economy, a direction that began to change only during the Hoover administration. The Harding and the Coolidge administrations promoted efficiency and economy in government, retirement of the war debt, sharp corporate and income tax reductions in order to induce higher levels of business investment, governmental encouragement of more efficient business practices in both industry and agriculture, a moderate level of tariff protection for American industry, and curbing of the regulatory activity of such government agencies as the Federal Trade Commission.[2]

During the Coolidge administration the United States joined European governments in returning to a modified international gold standard. This partial return to the international political-economic arrangements of the prewar years reflected—and reinforced—the Republican party's commitment to engineering an accumulationist political economy. While the gold standard and government intervention in capital markets could and did coexist, neo-orthodoxy created a web of constraints that tended to keep governmental actors within certain basic rules of an accumulationist political economy: keep economic factor costs low, including toleration of moderately high levels of unemployment and a depressed agricultural sector; keep prices steady; defend the currency; balance the budget.[3]

This neo-orthodox political economy appeared to perform very well, at least in the United States. The second half of the 1920s saw moderately high rates of growth and increased mass consumption, based on innovations in the consumer credit markets and improvements in the real wages of workers. Political and economic elites did not envision a balancing role for government and public policy in part because they did not believe that there was any need for such a role. In a statement that reflected this consensus, Lincoln Steffens wrote, "Big business in America is producing what the Socialists held up as their goal; food, shelter and clothing for all."[4]

Notwithstanding a widespread faith in the progressive character of a "business commonwealth," the renowned prosperity of the '20s was unevenly distributed among social groups and regions. Patterns of economic and social dependency established by the late nineteenth century persisted through the 1920s. A "metropole" of dairying agriculture, relatively immune to the business cycle in cash crops, and of industrial and financial institutions existed in the Northeast and in parts of the north central states of Minnesota and Wisconsin. This metropole was surrounded by the midwestern cash crop regions west of Minneapolis and the cash crop regions of the South, composing "the classic underdeveloped region of the country."[5]

The Minnesota Farmer-Labor party sought to provide an organizational home for social groups in Minnesota "neglected or squeezed" by American patterns of capitalist accumulation and their regional aspects. As Magnus Johnson, the party's 1926 candidate for governor, said, "There will be a need for the Farmer-Labor Party so long as the farmers, the wage earners and the small businessmen have economic-political problems to solve."[6] Its leaders sought to speak for groups damaged by the accumulationist political economy of the 1920s. Farmer-Labor leaders and politically active trade unionists and farm organization leaders proposed a different type of political economy, one that balanced accumula-tionist with reformist public policies. A major purpose of the Farmer-Labor party was to push for—and if possible create—new reform func-tions for government.

An Overview of the Farm Crisis

In order to understand the political economy of the Farmer-Labor party's politics, let us turn first to the "economic-political problems" of farmers during the 1920s: reduced national and world de-mand for farm products, incentives for surplus production, and higher production costs.

Between July and December 1920 the demand for grains fell sharply, bottomed out over the winter of 1921–22, and then slowly climbed back up, finally steadying in late 1923. For instance, in June 1920 wheat, on the national average, fetched $2.58 a bushel. By December 1, it dropped to $1.43. The next year, the price of a bushel dropped below a dollar.

The sharp break in prices during the 1920–23 crisis created problems that characterized the entire decade. The postwar farm crisis inaugurated a chronic depression in agriculture that profoundly shaped the problems facing Minnesota farmers for the rest of the 1920s.[7] The average value of a farm in the United States dropped 25 percent between 1920 and 1925. In Minnesota it dropped 31 percent. Agriculture in states outside the metro-politan core of the American economy suffered far more than agriculture within that core.[8]

A proximate cause of the postwar farm crisis was a politically fashioned drop in the foreign demand for American foodstuffs. In time a drop in demand would have occurred anyway, but the actual drop depended on America's unplanned, chaotic war demobilization. Despite a public debate over the need to plan America's "reconstruction," national administrative disarray set in over the winter of 1918–19. President Wilson refused to consider serious reconstruction planning. Also the sixty-fifth Congress in its third session and the sixty-sixth Congress in a special session were unable to plan reconstruction. For farmers these developments signified a possible collapse of the wartime regulatory apparatus geared towards sustaining agriculture. Europe was no longer a booming market, yet the national government would not intervene to manage the shock of collaps-ing markets.[9]

Continued high production exacerbated the consequences of the drop in demand. Expecting a long-term shift to higher output, farmers ex-panded acreage during the war and improved their production techniques.

Thus in the 1920–23 period farmers produced huge crops. The farm crisis of 1921–23, indeed the difficulties of the entire decade, were crises of surplus production. Demand did not change, because demand for foodstuffs is usually price inelastic.

Farmers also faced new and higher costs that were partly due to politics. Because of its "fair-return" clause, the 1920 Esch-Cummins Act's restoration of the railroads to private ownership upped Minnesota farmers' transportation costs during 1921 and 1922. By 1923 "the average freight rates on 50 representative agricultural products in the United States were 159.8 per cent of the 1913 rate. The rate on wheat from Tracy to New Ulm, Minnesota on January 1, 1923 averaged 121.7 percent of the 1913 rate. The rate on oats from McIntosh to Minneapolis, in 1923, was 144.2 percent of the 1913 level."[10]

Farm implements and machinery did not drop in price. If their prices had tumbled as low as grain prices, the structure of production costs might have been less burdensome. But the greater flexibility of industry in cutting production and in keeping prices somewhat stable—a flexibility that stemmed, in part, from oligopoly and wage repression—kept prices for farm inputs high.

Farmers also faced heavier financial and fiscal burdens. They had mortgaged the property that they owned, partly owned, managed, or leased in order to pay for increased wartime production. Between 1910 and 1920 the debt of "full-owner" farmers tripled in Minnesota, yet in the postwar years farmers faced relatively greater fixed interest payments as the economy deflated. And as the value of farmland dropped, mortgage debt increased from a ratio of debt to valuation of a little under a third to a ratio of a little under a half.

Finally, the tax burden grew as farmers began to feel the taxation for highway construction undertaken jointly by the federal and state governments. Farm real estate taxes per acre approximately doubled.[11]

Although the agricultural crisis let up during the second half of the '20s, the economy of grain production in Minnesota never quite recovered from the shock of the 1920–23 farm crisis and the added burdens on farm production. This economy remained vulnerable to recession. By the late 1920s the stagnation of agriculture generated land tenure insecurity, particularly in southwestern Minnesota, which was part of the Corn Belt that extended through much of Iowa, and in the older wheat-farming region, the Red River Valley in central western and northwestern Minnesota. This was a rather bitter pill to swallow, for farmers had succeeded in preventing a large-scale transfer of property out of their hands during the 1920–23

The Political Economy of State-Level Radicalism

crisis. But as time passed tenancy increased and conventional patterns of progress on the "agricultural ladder" slowed down. Farmers were often unable to do little more than service their debt, instead of retiring it.

The Farmer-Labor Party and the Farm Crisis

In the first half of the decade the Farmer-Labor party had a wide array of positions on how best to handle the farmers' "economic-political problems." The party vigorously pushed for solutions on two levels, federal and state. In the early '20s, Farmer-Labor candidates excoriated the postwar deflation as politically engineered at the national level in order to benefit finance capital, thus attacking the operation of the Federal Reserve system. And they campaigned for the repeal of the Esch-Cummins Act.

The farmer-labor coalition also emphasized state-level and regional solutions. State-level solutions included changes in tax law; rural credits provided by the state; state ownership of terminal elevators, warehouses, flour mills, stockyards, packinghouses, and creameries; state hail insurance, and fairer inspections of grain in order to grade it. An example of a regional approach to farmers' problems is the Farmer-Labor party's strong push for increased taxation of Minnesota's iron ore shipping as a way to force eastern industry to move west, thus providing farmers with larger and closer markets, and providing industrial employment. The tonnage tax proposal amounted, indeed, to a regional industrial policy. Consistent with this vision of developing the economies of northwestern and north central states, the Farmer-Labor party also pushed for construction of a Great Lakes–St. Lawrence seaway. These proposals obviously ran counter to the predominant political economic emphases of "normalcy." They envisioned an expanded role for government in the economy, a political economy in which both state government and the federal government balanced reformist and accumulationist public policies.

With the defeat of La Follette in 1924, and the general weakening of insurgency that his death in 1925 symbolized, the Farmer-Labor party no longer played as vigorous an agenda-setting role as it had during the era of the Harding administration, at both state and national levels. It found itself forced to join political bandwagons put together by other groups. It thus joined a broad coalition that (eventually) included Southern Democrats and the western, agrarian wing of the Republican party and that advocated a plan for controlling farm prices known as the McNary-Haugen bill.

Nevertheless, the Farmer-Labor party's alignment with the McNary-

Haugen coalition was quite consistent with its earlier emphasis on an expanded government role in the economy. The plan's name reflected the sponsorship of Republican senator Charles McNary of Oregon, chairman of the Senate Agriculture, Fisheries, and Forestry Committee, and Republican congressman Gilbert Haugen of Iowa, both members of the Republican party's agrarian, progressive wing. They sought to implement ideas first formulated in late 1921 by George N. Peek, a successful farm-equipment executive and a political entrepreneur who provided intellectual, financial, and organizational inspiration for a decade to the McNary-Haugen movement. Peek was a man quite unafraid to have government tamper with agricultural markets on a grand scale; his ideas as expressed in McNary-Haugenism are worth discussing in some detail.[12]

The McNary-Haugen bill was the generic name for a set of five agricultural policy bills that evolved between 1924 and 1928. The McNary-Haugen plan profoundly changed public discussion of agrarian policy. Its ingenuity lay, first, in its identification of surplus production as the aspect of farm economics that caused agricultural depression and, second, in its proposal to control administratively the effects on prices of this surplus production. The plan's premise was the ineffectiveness of existing tariff policy in handling agriculture's problems, since surplus production led to exports heavy enough to depress prices below production costs. The plan's administrative, price-raising solution to surplus production was governmental purchase of commodities and governmental marketing of these commodities abroad at the world price. The plan segregated the surplus from a crop, leaving enough to cover domestic consumption, and dumped the surplus abroad in order to favor farmers with the domestic, protected price. This made the agricultural tariffs that did exist effective for farmers. The agent of this market segregation would be a government board supervising a federal purchasing and dumping corporation. The plan was presented as self-financing—farmers would pay a fee on that part of a crop dumped abroad. This levy would be called the "equalization fee," a name that referred to price equalization.

Critics of the plan expressed shock at the extent of governmental intervention in agriculture. In a veto message of 25 February 1927, President Coolidge emphasized the "almost unlimited control" government would have over agriculture: "The granting of . . . such arbitrary power to a Government board is to run counter to our traditions, the philosophy of our Government, the spirit of our institutions, and all principles of equity."[13] But supporters of the McNary-Haugen plan no longer believed that regulation of marketing and distribution, and liberal credit—the Republican party's responses in the first half of the decade—were enough to help agriculture. McNary-Haugen's advocates did not mind the extent of governmental intervention. They embraced it, for it seemed no different from the extent of governmental intervention on behalf of industry.

The scope of the plan's intervention was great. Under it, all farmers were compelled to receive the protection they desired. This happened through universal payment of the equalization fee, which Coolidge called "the most vicious form of taxation." Payment of the fee constituted a frank admission that the decade's agricultural depression made it impossible for an individual farmer to do what it behooved all farmers to do collectively. No farmer had an incentive to bear the cost of orderly marketing of surplus imposed by any privately administered schemes of surplus control, through private cooperatives, for instance. He obviously benefited by letting someone else bear the costs of such cooperatives. Commercial farmers who supported the McNary-Haugen plan simply wanted an unprecedented degree of administrative, federal intervention into the organization of agriculture.

Much of McNary-Haugenism was based on a perception of deep biases in the American political economy. McNary-Haugenism pointed toward a political economy quite different from the normalcy that characterized the Harding and Coolidge administrations. Government seemed openly to favor eastern financial and industrial capital.

Some supporters of McNary-Haugenism perhaps conceded to themselves that their plan might promote economic disaster. It might well cause more surplus production, compounding the problem, as Coolidge rightly charged, and the foreign dumping would eventually wreak havoc on international trade, as Coolidge also understood. But economics was not the heart of the issue. The issue was equality of economic group power. As Farmer-Labor senator Shipstead put it in a speech in Washington, "We only ask for the same treatment that has been accorded industry, transportation, and banking."[14] The issue was whether or not America would move to a kind of political economy different from the accumulationist political economy it then had.

Supporters of the McNary-Haugen bill believed that there were two Americas, industrial and agricultural, and that those who ran the industrial America wanted to subordinate the other to its interests. Gilbert Fite had captured McNary-Haugenism well. For him, it was "something even deeper than the matter of living standards, incomes, or farm foreclosures. Basically, it was a conflict between agrarian and industrial capitalism. In the 1920's farmers were making a last-ditch stand against industrial and commercial domination."[15] In an important sense, then, the issue was whether an accumulationist political economy turned farmers into second-class citizens.

The Problems of Labor

Organized and unorganized labor also suffered from what seemed a type of second-class citizenship, although for very different reasons.[16] Labor's "economic-political problems," like the farmers', originated in the political economy of the Harding administration. In the early 1920s there occurred a strong open-shop drive that set the tone in industrial relations for the rest of the decade, both nationally and in Minnesota.

For a brief moment after World War I organized business seemed interested in business-labor amity. Soon, however, in reaction to the extraordinarily high level of strike activity in 1919, new open-shop movements sprang up around the country, for instance, in Seattle (which experienced a general strike), Dallas, and Toledo. When they spoke of the open shop these groups meant a shop closed to organized labor rather than a shop for both union and nonunion labor. Over the summer of 1920 the United States Chamber of Commerce further nationalized the movement by holding an organizational referendum on the open shop. And because business-government relations during World War I spurred the formation of trade associations, antilabor plans were quickly diffused from one locale to the next. The movement also gained support from the Republican party.[17]

The national events strengthened the Twin Cities' open-shop organization, the Citizens Alliance. Its origins were in the collapse of the famous Murray Hill agreement between the IAM and the National Civic Federation, which sought voluntary, top-down management of harmonious collective bargaining by employers and unions. In Minnesota, the wreckage of the agreement became the foundation for an open-shop movement. Building on an organization that a former factory worker, A. W. Strong, founded in 1901 (the Employers of Machinists Association of Minneapolis), a determined group of businessmen formed the Citizens Alliance in 1903. Their purpose was to check the organizational and bargaining power of Twin Cities machinists and other unions.[18]

The Citizens Alliance extended the policies that pro-open-shop members of the Twin Cities business community advocated during World War I. The alliance sought to present a united front to labor after the war. Following Governor Preus's election in 1920, the alliance built on a working relationship that antiunion business leaders had with law enforcement officials and with the governor. In St. Paul, for instance, the county sheriff acquiesced in breaking a printers' strike, undermining the utility of the farmer-labor movement's influence over the St. Paul police. In December 1921, at the alliance's request, Governor Preus used the National Guard against South St. Paul packinghouse workers striking against a wage cut, a protest referred to officially as "the usurpation of civil authority by unauthorized persons."[19]

The alliance's behavior even became somewhat sinister. The alliance worked with the Ku Klux Klan. And it employed labor spies and thugs, availing itself of private detective agencies. It was not above using physical violence against labor leaders.[20]

Change in national and state labor law reinforced the alliance's power in the early postwar era. Through a wedding of antitrust law to common-law notions about conspiracies in restraint of trade, the federal courts and the United States Supreme Court developed a body of labor law that facilitated sharp attacks on labor unions. This labor law—which courts in Minnesota began following in 1922—could be used to expand vastly the equity power of courts to issue injunctions against such trade union tactics as boycotts and picketing.[21] Not only was it used in 1922 in St. Paul and South St. Paul, but also in Minneapolis this equity power was used in 1920 and 1921 to halt bannering of an employer by striking workers and support of the strike by the Minneapolis labor press, leading a Minneapolis labor leader to protest that "we are having an epidemic of injunctions the same as we had the 'flu' epidemic." Labor leaders were deeply disturbed by the change in labor law.

> The injunction process is intended to chloroform the workers into insensibility and submission. It carries with it the sanctity of the law, it surrounds itself with a halo which is unfathomable to the uninitiated with the dire results that the onlookers . . . are prone to criticize the motives, as well as the actions of those that dare to resist the injunction process . . . As a matter of fact, there are no innocent bystanders in the labor movement . . . today, the injunction is directed against the Minneapolis Trades and Labor Assembly; tomorrow it may, aye, it will be directed against another labor union, in fact the injunction is used by the employers from coast to coast . . . and the object is all the same . . . namely, to establish the "open shop," to lower the standard of living, drive the workers into submission and thus create a state of involuntary servitude.[22]

Yet a third factor behind the Citizens Alliance's power, operating in conjunction with both the rapid development of a national network of employers' associations committed to the open shop and a changed labor law, was unemployment. During the postwar recession the unemployment rate reached as high as 12 percent of the national labor force, which surely was reflected in the Twin Cities and on the Iron Range. Unemployment continued to be a serious problem in Minnesota throughout the decade.[23] In the latter half of the decade unemployment was surprisingly high. Precise measures are impossible given the lack of comprehensive unemployment statistics for the decade, lack of statistics for unions, and lack of ready data on whether unions responded to the complicated shifts in employment patterns and, if they did, whether they had any success. What we do know is that there were at least three kinds of unemployment in this period. A regular seasonal cycle affected unions, particularly in Duluth, where winter usually stopped port transportation and construction work. There were also recessions in 1924 and 1927. The Minnesota State Federation of Labor took the latter recession so seriously that it advertised unemployment in dozens of country weeklies and among the state federations of Iowa, Wisconsin, North and South Dakota, Montana, and Michigan in order to prevent migration to Minneapolis and St. Paul. Further, there may well have been a secular growth in unemployment. The authors of a study of unemployment trends in St. Paul, Minneapolis, and Duluth at the end of the decade remarked "on the striking fact that the burden of unemployment relief has continued to grow throughout the supposedly prosperous years of 1923–1927."[24]

Capital seemed to be getting the better of labor everywhere in the state. Political despair came to such outstate railroad centers as Brainerd, once a center of labor-political activity. The periodically rebellious Iron Range settled into quiescence, as if the whole region had become like the many Iron Range company towns known as "locations." During the 1920s, the State Federation of Labor considered but then abandoned efforts to organize on the Iron Range, usually citing poor organizing conditions.[25]

In short, several factors combined over the decade to make the Citizens Alliance and antiunion businessmen the dominant force in Minnesota's labor relations. As time passed, the power of these actors fed on itself. It grew out of, even as it caused, labor's weakness and unusual conservatism in the latter half of the decade. During the 1920s, labor's numerical strength at the national level declined from over 5 million members in 1920 to 3.5 million in 1923, a decline that continued, albeit at a slower pace, throughout the rest of the decade. Labor declined not only in terms of the percentage of the work force it organized but also in absolute terms. National trends were mirrored at the state level, enhancing the power of the Citizens Alliance and antiunion businessmen.[26]

The Political Economy of State-Level Radicalism

Given organized labor's increasingly bleak situation during the 1920s, what appeals did the Farmer-Labor party make to labor? As with its approach to the agricultural crisis, the Farmer-Labor party envisioned a mix of state-level and federal solutions. The state-level proposals attacked three aspects of labor's problems: the labor-repressive use of Minnesota's institutions for maintaining public order, the open shop, and unemployment. At the national level the party pushed for congressional curbs on the labor injunction.

The party intended to control Minnesota's means of coercion, particularly the National Guard. The party pledged never to use the National Guard to break strikes, a commitment that became particularly important, as we will see, during the 1934 truckers' strike in Minneapolis. Fearing the institutionalization of the notorious Commission of Public Safety of World War I, Farmer-Labor leaders firmly resisted Republican proposals in the immediate postwar years for establishing a state constabulary. This resistance later played a role in how the legislature established the Minnesota State Highway Patrol in the late '20s and the Bureau of Criminal Apprehension during the first Farmer-Labor administration. Neither agency was intended to be used against labor.

As for the open shop, the party had a somewhat symbolic policy, namely, establishing a state printing plant, a pet policy of the State Federation of Labor. By taking work away from the private sector, a state printing plant would impose a financial penalty on business for its labor policy and, more important, would serve as an opening wedge against the open shop.[27]

The unemployment problem the party addressed by calling for use of the state government's public work for work relief, a policy that was enacted during the 1930s using the state Highway Department. In making this appeal the party picked up on proposals that had been current since the 1921 President's Conference on Unemployment, chaired and organized by Herbert Hoover. The party's support for an otherwise politically dead policy idea illustrates a classic argument for federalism, namely, that state politics is often a laboratory for reform.[28]

At the federal level the party proposed congressional removal of the equity power of federal courts to issue labor injunctions. The party's involvement in promoting what became the Norris-LaGuardia Act is an important detail in the overall sweep of the party's history. Changing policy on labor injunctions got onto the national agenda in 1928 partly as the result of a bill introduced by Farmer-Labor senator Henrik Shipstead. The bill served the useful purpose of getting Congress, under the leadership of Senator George Norris, to begin turning its attention toward a serious problem in public policy.[29]

The Problems of Middle-Class People

Late in the decade—so late that the Farmer-Labor party did little more than promise help for this constituency—a third group joined the Farmer-Labor party's coalition. These were members of the middle class, many living in small towns. About one-fifth of Minnesota's population was in small towns and cities of five thousand or fewer by the end of the decade. One fraction comprised owners of hardware and variety stores and groceries squeezed by competition from larger businesses. Another fraction comprised bankers imperilled by the reorganization of the distribution of credit in the Northwest. These parts of the middle class obviously did not have quite the same perspective on the American political economy that radical farmers and workers did. But they did encounter the economic and psychological menace of Coolidge's "unalterable economic laws," and the experience drove some of them into the Farmer-Labor coalition.

Minnesota's merchants found that the barriers to local and statewide competition dropped steadily through the '20s. Helped by the formulation of new management techniques, national firms such as Sears, Roebuck, and Company and Montgomery Ward competed with the merchants of clothes and variety items for the patronage of Minnesota's rural and urban consumers. When a chain store opened in a regional center such as Mankato, Minnesota it had a dramatic effect on the surrounding towns even though it strengthened business in Mankato itself. Adolph Berle trenchantly characterized the dilemma that these changes posed for independent merchants: "herring do not compete with whales." There were few public policies to protect these herring.[30]

Many local bankers prided themselves on being independent businessmen. And they too were caught in the dilemma of competing as herring with whales.[31] Rural banking suffered badly during the 1920s. Minnesota, like many other states, supported too many banks. State banks often tolerated such poor practices as excessive payment of dividends or excessive lending to bank officers. The nature of the relationship between agriculture and banking was the basic nexus that weakened rural banking over the course of the '20s. The fortunes of rural bankers followed the fortunes of their clients.

At the end of the '20s, the rural banking system experienced a dramatic change in the character of competition. It looked briefly as if giant banks operating out of the Twin Cities, and mimicking a strong national trend toward consolidation in the banking industry, would come to dominate the system. This shift led a small collection of bankers to form a pressure group, the Independent Bankers Association. The IBA joined the Farmer-Labor coalition in 1930 and remained within it through the 1930s.

The IBA's leaders considered the small-town network of church, school, and local bank precious: "a community is better served by local people." This perspective made it possible for some independent businessmen to look to Floyd Olson and the Farmer-Labor party. Ben DuBois, the IBA's leader, once said, "I don't mind a little socialism." There might be too much socialism for the state's independent businessmen, but some of them were willing to take their chances.[32]

The Political Economy of the Farmer-Labor Party
During the 1920s the basic political economy of the Farmer-Labor party was forged. The coalition of interests that the party aggregated resulted from an accumulationist political economy.

During the 1920s farming seemed relegated to second-class status, and small-scale retailing and banking became hostage to giant organizations. As for trade unionism, it barely survived despite further industrialization. William McEwen, editor of the Duluth *Labor World* and the Farmer-Labor party's campaign manager in 1926, worried that the 1920s presaged a kind of slavery for the working man. The "economic control over the lives of workers" represented by the open shop was "no less inhuman than was the property ownership in chattel labor before the civil war." Company unionism had a "deadening effect on the faculties inherent in every manly man," producing a "social cipher" who "takes no part in the civic, industrial, or political affairs of life."[33]

Farmer-Labor leaders wanted to change the limited government associated with Dollar Decade. They wanted a state that would perform "reform" functions. They wanted a balancing political economy. They wanted modern, activist government: the equalization fee, legislative curbing of the "star-chamber methods" with which courts exercised their equity power, a state printing plant, public works, regulation of banking and retailing. This view of government was reflected in other positions that the Farmer-Labor party took: public ownership of utilities, federal operation of Muscle Shoals, construction of a St. Lawrence seaway. Self-help for those squeezed by capitalism would not do; government had to help.

The Limits of State-Level
Radicalism

The Minnesota Farmer-Labor party was founded in a conservative era. But it used power in a liberal, politically centralizing era. Two years after the Farmer-Labor party took on the task of governing Minnesota the Democratic party took on the task of governing the United States. During the "Hundred Days" of the 1933 special session of Congress, the Democratic party gave to the federal government a host of new tasks. The Seventy-third Congress and the president transferred to the federal government primary responsibility for welfare policy. They defined new regulatory tasks in such areas as the supervision of industrial relations, the price levels of the industrial and agrarian economies, and banking. And they redefined the United States' relationship to the international economic orthodoxy that Franklin D. Roosevelt's predecessor, Herbert Hoover, had sought to honor.

The Democratic party inaugurated a balancing political economy, in which the federal government adopted and implemented both accumulationist and reformist public policies. In doing so it radically changed the political environment of the Minnesota Farmer-Labor party. New policies, as we will see, created new politics.

Existing governmental capacities (and efforts to create new capacities) shaped these changes. In order for politicians to create new public policies they must also have bureaucratic tools. Thus the possibilities for political-economic change, and for a recasting of politics, depended on the institutional resources that were available to the Democratic party for implementing public policies.

Contrasts between the Hoover and
Roosevelt Administrations

The political economy of the Hoover administration was considerably less orthodox than a mythmaking view of the past might have it.[1] After the stock market crash of October 1929, Hoover put into high gear a device for economic stimulus that he had carefully developed during the preceding decade—the executive branch conference. During the 1920s Hoover developed a strong interest and some expertise in government management of countercyclical policies through cooperation with business leaders. He held a series of gatherings for business leaders from various major industries, successfully urging them to hold wages up. While 92 percent of firms reporting to the Bureau of Labor Statistics cut wages during the 1921 recession, a recession that sparked the development of countercyclical theory in the 1920s, only 7 percent of reporting firms cut wages in 1930. Hoover also urged state and local governments to increase public works construction. With only a bit of presidential prodding, Congress quickly aided this policy by raising appropriations for public works. Simultaneously, the Federal Farm Board, established by the Agricultural Marketing Act of mid-1929, created grain and cotton stabilization corporations that purchased these commodities in order to sustain their prices. The board was meant to complement private-sector cooperatives, but its design and operation clearly bore the imprint of half a decade of McNary-Haugenism.

As time passed the Hoover administration approached a kind of political-economic Rubicon. Hoover firmly expected that the downturn of 1929 would be as brief as previous downturns in the 1920s. Hoover had considerable economic sophistication. He fashioned during the 1920s a rather elaborate approach to macroeconomic management, the now well-known theory of "associationalism," which stressed governmental collection and diffusion of industrial statistics, federal support for the application of the most advanced science to economic problems, and governmental assistance to private initiatives, for instance, the executive branch conferences which he used to check the impact of the downturn in 1929 and 1930. Hoover considered such macroeconomic management consistent with "what has slowly been built and molded by experience and effort throughout these hundred and fifty years."[2] But despite his sophistication he failed to appreciate that for a variety of reasons the recession could balloon into a very severe, protracted depression. Among these reasons were the growth of debt over the previous decade; the overconstruction of industrial plant, equipment, and housing; the development of labor-saving machinery; and the impact of oligopoly on industrial prices. Hence the Pollyannaish statements about recovery being just around the corner for which he has been ridiculed. And hence a need for political economic innovation that Hoover only partly met in his initial energetic responses. The Great Depression was in a sense beyond Hoover's understanding of political economy, although it should be added that it was beyond any American politician's understanding at the time.

Hoover persistently refused to involve the federal government in directly providing relief to the unemployed. Hoover told Congress that to do so would menace freedom and the "experience of America."[3] Appearing before a Senate committee, Walter Gifford, the business executive whom Hoover recruited to implement the associationalist policy of prodding state and local governments and private charities into providing relief, took pride in his ignorance of relief conditions around the country—it was not the federal government's job to have that kind of synoptic knowledge.[4] Yet unemployment grew markedly worse, approximately tripling during the Hoover administration and reaching perhaps as much as a third of the work force. Equally evocative of Hoover's limits was his insistence in 1932, per the rules of gold-standard orthodoxy, on balancing the budget by raising taxes. Of course, in establishing the Reconstruction Finance Corporation in January 1932 and in recapitalizing it at a much higher level in July 1932, Hoover and Congress did respond quite creatively to the credit crisis which had then reached titanic proportions (and which, in part, accounted for the insistence on balancing the budget). But the Reconstruction Finance Corporation and the other credit innovations of 1932 have to be seen as adding up to a highly accumulationist policy writ large, a case of lending over $2 billion to industry and financial institutions on the assumption that private-sector actors would pick the right strategy for getting the American economy out of its worst economic crisis. In certain key respects the Hoover administration never really went beyond the rules of the political-economic game that Harding and Coolidge reestablished during the 1920s.

In contrast to the outgoing Hoover administration, the incoming Roosevelt administration was more experimental about balancing accumulationist public policies with reformist policies.[5] It immediately established a banking moratorium and then continued to use the Reconstruction Finance Corporation as America's "banker of last resort." The Democratic party also aided government's performance of its accumulation function through the National Industrial Recovery Act, which permitted industry to coordinate investment, price, and wage decisions, a policy accompanied by minimal government supervision and, after Roosevelt issued the President's Re-employment Agreement in summer 1933, an enormous amount of symbolic politics—torchlight parades, the "Blue Eagle," and so forth. But the Roosevelt administration and congressional Democrats also acted very quickly to aid farmers, workers, and the unemployed.

The Agricultural Adjustment Act of 1933 (AAA; the first Farm Relief and Inflation Act) sought to shield farmers from extremely low prices for basic agricultural commodities (wheat, cotton, corn, hogs) by directly controlling their production. In other words, the AAA attempted to raise prices by creating scarcity. The Democratic party, in addition, pumped low-interest money into the agricultural credit markets in order to check the wave of property losses sweeping over rural areas. In time the social limits of these agricultural policies became clearer, for they favored politically powerful commercial farmers at the expense of politically ineffectual tenants and sharecroppers. These policies also burdened already hard-pressed consumers. But in 1933 America's commercial farmers appeared to face immediate and complete economic ruin. These were relief policies, at least in 1933 and 1934.

Another piece of New Deal legislation, the National Industrial Recovery Act, established (under section 7(a) of title 1) federal recognition of collective bargaining outside the railroad industry for the first time since World War I and provided a neutral arena for tripartite bargaining among labor, business, and government. To be sure, this administrative machinery was largely ineffectual. Business respected the principle of collective bargaining by regularly violating it. Section 7(a) stimulated a large-scale attempt at company unionism. But it also stimulated three of the most dramatic strikes in American labor history, the San Francisco general strike, the Minneapolis truckers' strikes, and the Toledo Auto-Lite strike. The organizers of these strikes recognized the change in their political environment. As Roger Baldwin wrote in their aftermath, "The wave of strikes over the year and a half of the New Deal is not to be counted as resistance to it; —it is to be counted as an attempt to enforce by struggle what the New Deal promised on paper."[6] New rights for workers now existed.

The New Deal established a huge program of direct relief and complementary work-relief programs. Following the creation of the Civilian Conservation Corps (CCC), Congress and the president created the Federal Emergency Relief Administration (FERA), which provided enormous sums of direct relief, and the Public Works Administration (PWA), the authorization for which was part of the National Industrial Recovery Act. After the Hundred Days, in November 1933 the Civil Works Administration (CWA) began to operate as a winter job program. In retrospect these programs—which never reduced unemployment rates below levels we would consider very high—seemed inadequate, conditioned as we are by Keynesian macroeconomics to the symbolism of unemployment rates. But in 1933 relief, not the reduction of unemployment to a certain level, was the New Deal's goal. The FERA, CCC, PWA, and CWA amounted to a novel and, for its time, massive effort to help wage earners whose lives capitalism had chewed up.

The New Deal, as its name rightly suggests, was a break from political-economic orthodoxy. Roosevelt's removal of the United States from the gold standard in April 1933—in part a reaction to tremendous congressional pressure to do so during the Hundred Days—was the monetary counterpart of this break. It represented an economic nationalism impatient with the seemingly inhumane prescriptions of a gold-standard, free-trade regime.

The New Deal's initial public policies were an extraordinary, if open-ended, redefinition of American political economy. It was open-ended because Roosevelt and the Democrats stressed the temporary, emergency character of their measures, adopting such symbols of budget balancing as the Economy Act, which slashed federal salaries. But the big bang of the Hundred Days was likely to reverberate in later phases of America's political economic development. Politically, a "new order of possibilities and impossibilities" emerged.[7]

The New Politics of Agriculture and the Farmer-Labor Party

This shift in the American political economy changed the strategic choices available to the Farmer-Labor party's leaders. They sought, often with great cunning, to exploit opportunities opened up by the crisis atmosphere of 1932–34. But a case study of the new politics of agriculture suggests that by the mid-Thirties the party's strategic options had narrowed. Let us turn first to the development of farm protest in Iowa and Minnesota; an understanding of its limits leads to a larger discussion of how the new politics of agriculture placed limits on state-level radicalism.

The Development of Farm Protest

In the early '30s a farm protest organization appeared in Iowa and spread to Minnesota and other states, mimicking the earlier diffusion of the Nonpartisan League from North Dakota. Like the Nonpartisan League before it, radical political entrepreneurs led the Farmers Holiday Association.[8] Most of the farmers who supported it appear to have been commercial farmers. They were not discouraged poor people with lowered expectations. They faced the imminent loss of their homes and recently prosperous livelihoods. As a result, they became radical.

Milo Reno, one of the association's most famous leaders, captured this aspect of the movement well. In a rather moving radio address, "Why the Farmers Holiday?" given in summer 1932, after the association formed in Des Moines, Reno's voice echoed across the plains.

> We are at the parting of the ways. The time is too short to temporize longer. The people of the United States must be saved from the destructive desolation that is due in the coming winter. Therefore, the national Farmers Holiday Association is appealing to the individual farmers, to the cooperative groups, and to all farm organizations to forget all their differences and join in a united effort to correct the situation before it is everlastingly too late to save the farm home, that has been builded by the sweat, the toil, the sacrifice, of those who occupy them.[9]

The association was conservative in the sense that it acted to save a way of life. It was radical in the sense that it was prepared to use protest—to withhold farm products in a holiday that paralleled the withholding of bank services in the bank holidays proclaimed around the country.

The Farmers Holiday Association was an auxiliary of the Farmers Union, an organization with origins in southern populism and historically friendly to organized labor. In Iowa and Minnesota the Farmers Union had a history of reformist politics. Milo Reno, one of the Iowa Farmers Union's founders and its dominant figure in the 1920s, came from a family of Greenbackers. Reno himself worked in the Union Labor party presidential campaign of 1888 and supported the People's party in the 1892 campaign. He claimed to have been deeply influenced by writings on the French Revolution and by Edward Bellamy's socialist novel, *Looking Backward*. The ideas he gleaned from these sources he mixed with an intense love of the Declaration of Independence and with spiritualism. He was self-consciously a farmer-laborite; he worried about "the forces of special privilege" that were slowly undermining "the very foundations of justice and freedom upon which this country was founded."[10]

The Farmers Holiday Association grew out of conditions in the corn-hog and dairy livestock areas of Iowa and Minnesota. These were rich farming lands, areas that weathered the agricultural crisis of the '20s. But the Depression's drop in prices hit them hard.

The Hoover administration's Federal Farm Board did not help them. Its stabilization corporations spent their capital, futilely, on sustaining wheat, cotton, and wool prices. No Farm Board capital was left for buying up corn, hogs, and dairy products.

Debt also burdened these areas. When farm prices dropped, farmers had trouble meeting creditors' demands. Scared creditors enforced their claims. Some large corporate creditors also foreclosed. Because they were not local creditors, their actions seemed ruthless and impersonal, adding to farmers' despair. Farm families faced, to use Reno's terms, the loss of properties "builded by the sweat, the toil, the sacrifice, of those who occupy them." In some cases the original homesteads from the nineteenth century were in peril.[11]

In 1931 Minnesota farms were foreclosed at the rate of 31.2 per thousand; in 1932 they were foreclosed at the rate of 42.0 per thousand; in 1933 they were foreclosed at the rate of 59.1 per thousand. The comparable figures for Iowa were 24.8, 52.5, and 78.3.

In the middle of this drama of dispossession several Iowa farm activists went (in February 1932) to Washington to testify before the Senate Committee on Forestry and Agriculture. There they supported bills for refinancing farm mortgages. More important, they supported a "cost-of-production" bill. Cost-of-production was a concept that Milo Reno had advocated since the mid-Twenties, when he helped to establish the Corn Belt Committee, a nonpartisan political action group that eventually participated in Al Smith's 1928 presidential campaign. Cost-of-production meant administrative calculation of the prices of farmers' inputs in order to set a reasonable profit. The sum of the two—cost of production and profit—would fix the price a farmer received from commodity processors. Like McNary-Haugenism and production control it was a price-raising scheme.

After these hearings in Washington, the Iowans returned home, discouraged about whether Congress would or could solve their problems. They were now prepared for protest.

Protest tactics had been under discussion for some time. In 1931 at the Iowa Farmers Union convention, John Bosch (pronounced "bush") of the Minnesota Farmers Union called for a farm strike, for withholding commodities from farm markets. And as banks closed around the country and cities and states proclaimed bank holidays, Glen Miller, the Iowa Farmers Union president, pushed for a farmers' holiday.

From February until May 1932, the Iowa Farmers Union organized a national convention to be held at Des Moines in order to agree on farm market withholding actions. On May 3 the national Farmers Holiday Association was founded. Its president was Milo Reno and its vice-president was John Bosch.

John Bosch, like Reno, was a political entrepreneur with a radical background. His parents were Populists, and Bosch liked to think of himself as in the Populist tradition. He was well educated and intellectual and worked closely with his brother Richard, who did graduate work at Wisconsin with John R. Commons.

After his election as vice-president of the national Farmers Holiday Association, Bosch set about establishing the Minnesota Farmers Holiday Association. This happened 29 July 1932, at a meeting in St. Cloud. There a gathering of farmers listened to Milo Reno and E. E. Kennedy, secretary of the National Farmers Union, and then voted to make Bosch president of the Minnesota association.

By late summer 1932, the Farmers Holiday Association had become an interest group for national and state politicians to reckon with. In all the states where it emerged it represented commercial farmers galvanized by a crisis into using their time and skills for pressure politics. These farmers were ready for ideas and tactics they would have dismissed a few years earlier.

The association's potential influence very shortly became actual, due to spontaneous actions. Farm pickets blockaded roads leading into Sioux City, Iowa, in August 1932, in order to punish a company that would not negotiate with dairy farmers in the surrounding milk production area.

This action sparked similar actions in Minnesota. There John Bosch expected to concentrate on building an organization, not to preside over highway picketing, but pickets nevertheless took to the roads in southwestern Minnesota, joining the Iowa pickets. Another picket line was thrown up near the Twin Cities in order to prevent shipments to packing yards in South St. Paul.

Although Reno and Bosch did not intend violence, these spontaneous picket lines had the effect for which Reno and Bosch aimed. The pickets enhanced the Farmers Holiday Association's power by gripping national attention. They also caught the attention of midwestern governors, four of whom gathered in Sioux City, Iowa, on September 9 to confer with the Farmers Holiday Association. There, after a parade through downtown Sioux City, farm leaders informed the governors of their demands, including an embargo by each governor, to go into effect September 20 on all commodities selling below cost of production and continuing until a special session of Congress enacted cost-of-production legislation, and a moratorium on farm and chattel mortgage foreclosures. The governors declined to act on these demands and instead declared their interest in tariff revision, currency expansion, orderly marketing, and mortgage moratoria. But merely getting four governors to Sioux City to listen was a victory for the Farmers Holiday Association.[12]

The momentous conflict building between Hoover and Roosevelt in the presidential campaign added to the sense of increased influence among the association's leadership and that of its parent organization, the Farmers Union. On September 14 Roosevelt gave his farm-policy address in Topeka, Kansas, which committed him both to a policy of production control and to general principles that seemed to satisfy all the major farm organizations—the American Farm Bureau Federation, the Farmers Union, and the National Grange. After the speech Roosevelt led the leaders of these farm organizations to believe that they would all play direct and crucial roles in planning his administration's farm policy. As a result, Oklahoma's John Simpson expected Roosevelt to press for cost-of-production in addition to production control. This view among leaders of the Farmers Union and the Farmers Holiday Association, that they would guide the nation's new farm policies, was a vital political force for several more months.

The Farmer-Labor Party and the Farmers Holiday Association

As the rural interest-group politics of the Midwest changed, the leadership of the Farmer-Labor party quickly responded. The party supported the demands of the Farmers Holiday Association, often using highly charged rhetoric. The party avoided using force against farm pickets and rural mobs that gathered to prevent foreclosures. And the party sought to meet the association's policy demands.

In August Governor Floyd Olson laid the foundations for the September 9 meeting in Sioux City by calling for an extraordinarily ambitious regional plan to enforce cost-of-production, proposing declarations of martial law in Wisconsin, the Dakotas, Iowa, Nebraska, Kansas, and Montana. "I would be willing," he stated, "to join with the governors of the other agricultural states in any plan, however arbitrary, which would tend to raise the prices of farm commodities." Olson also proposed combining the several thousand cooperatives in Minnesota into a statewide marketing agency that would "assure the success of the farm holiday." The Farmer-Labor party's candidate for railroad and warehouse commissioner, former Farmer-Labor congressman Knud Wefald, echoed Olson's statement by urging farmers to join the "strike."[13]

After the September 9 conference a rash of picket actions broke out over the Midwest, including Minnesota. Minnesota farmers attempted to stop trucks bound into Minnesota from South Dakota; farmers tried to stop farm products bound through southwestern Minnesota for Sioux City; farmers sought to blockade roads into the Twin Cities. All of these actions posed a law-and-order problem for the Farmer-Labor party, especially in an election year. Yet Olson resisted calls for use of state militia and insisted that law and order was a local responsibility. Eventually the Republican attorney general of Minnesota authorized the state highway patrol, whose chief was running against Olson for governor, to assist county sheriffs in disbanding picket lines thrown up by angry farmers. Despite this rather clever effort to embarrass Olson, he did nothing.

After Olson's reelection, the Farmer-Labor party faced yet another law-and-order challenge posed to it by the Farmers Holiday Association: mob action to prevent foreclosure sales to the creditors of indebted farmers. In addition to demanding legislation that would raise prices for farmers and give them low-cost credit, the Farmers Holiday Association developed two major tactics, the farm market withholding action, intended to raise farm prices, and the prevention of foreclosure sales, intended to save farm properties. In winter of 1933 this second tactic was used extensively in Minnesota.

Actually, there were three variants of the tactic. In addition to breaking up foreclosure sales, angry farmers held "penny sales" and what were called "Sears-Roebuck sales." In a penny sale a farmer repurchased his land from intimidated creditors for very low amounts. In a Sears-Roebuck sale a farmer repurchased his chattel for a nominal sum.

In Minnesota the organizational sponsor of such actions was often a part of the Minnesota Farmers Holiday known as the Tri-County Council of Defense, under the direction of a farmer named Harry Haugland. A Communist organization, the United Farmers League, also played a role in certain locations. The precise incidence of these actions is unknown, but at least twelve such recorded actions occurred in Minnesota. The deterrent effect of these sales is impossible to know, but it may have been considerable.[14]

The respectable counterpart to penny and Sears-Roebuck sales was pushing the legislature for a statutory mortgage moratorium. Beginning in January 1933, as the Minnesota legislature met for the first time since 1931, the Farmers Holiday Association pressed its demand for a moratorium on mortgage foreclosures. On 25 February 1933, Olson issued an executive decree under his supposed police power that provided for a one-year temporary moratorium on farm mortgage foreclosures. Olson may have considered this action illegal, as in fact it proved to be when a court reversed his order. But Olson's decree did move a statutory mortgage moratorium to a prominent place on the Minnesota legislature's agenda.

Iowa had already frozen legal process against mortgage-ridden farmers.

A newly elected Democratic governor signed a mortgage moratorium law on 17 February 1933, eight days before Olson's executive decree. Under this law farmers occupying delinquent realty could hold onto their property by paying for a period of two years a fair rental value to be determined by the courts.

In Minnesota the Farmers Holiday Association staged a march on the state capitol to meet with state legislators. There Olson welcomed them with a speech from a balcony under the capitol's rotunda, as they massed a few dozen feet from the doors of the legislature's chambers. On April 18 Olson signed the Minnesota Mortgage Moratorium Act.

A key actor at this point was the new Farmer-Labor attorney general of Minnesota, Harry H. Peterson.[15] Peterson was an able and active attorney general and established a high-spirited staff of assistants. One of them has remarked that his years in Farmer-Labor government were "the most enjoyable six years of my working life."[16] Several of these assistants had been active Farmer-Labor politicians, for instance, Frederick Pike, who performed legal work for the Nonpartisan League during World War I and acted as chairman of the Farmer-Labor party in the early 1920s. This mix of politics, enthusiasm, and professional pride played a part in the Farmer-Labor party's response to the rise of the Farmers Holiday Association.

Following passage of the Minnesota Mortgage Moratorium Act, Peterson and his staff defended it against constitutional invalidation, first at the state level and then before the Supreme Court. Speaking of *Home Building and Loan Association v. Blaisdell* (290 U.S. 398 [1934]), Peterson bragged, "It undoubtedly is one of the four or five great decisions of all time of the Supreme Court of the United States."[17] The Farmer-Labor party helped to consolidate the gains of state-level agricultural policy making. The constitutionality of the Minnesota Mortgage Moratorium Act established the constitutionality of the entire plethora of moratoria enacted throughout the United States in the early to middle '30s. It also laid an important legal basis for the American welfare state.[18]

Cost-of-Production versus Production Control in Congress

Between Roosevelt's election and his inauguration, state-level agricultural policy making enjoyed a degree of autonomy from national influences. But the creation and implementation of a new national policy in agriculture soon shattered this sphere of autonomy. The Farmers Holiday Association and such allies as Floyd B. Olson and the

Farmer-Labor party's congressional delegation sought to veto the New Deal's agricultural policy and force Congress to enact cost-of-production. Surprisingly, given the strength of Roosevelt's opposition to cost-of-production, they succeeded in keeping the idea on the national agenda for several months, but the "power of the center" was simply greater. Had they succeeded in forcing a choice of cost-of-production on Congress and the president they might well have helped the political and organizational future of the Farmer-Labor party.

Between March and May 1933 two competing approaches to the agricultural crisis were before Congress, the president, and the secretary of agriculture: cost-of-production and an alternative mix that included currency inflation, government control of marketing, and, most importantly, production control. In March 1933 John Simpson, the president of the Farmers Union, appeared before a Senate committee to describe cost-of-production. Given the poverty and distress that the Depression engendered, Simpson rejected the idea of curtailing production. Production would eventually adjust to demand, he argued. In the meantime, the secretary of agriculture should determine the costs of producing the major crops. To calculate cost of production, he should add inputs (seed, fertilizer, hired labor, replacement cost of machinery, taxes, etc.), dental and medical expenses, and educational expenses, deduct gains from cash crop farmers' sidelines, such as eggs and dairy products, and divide the remainder by the average yields of the major crops, thus determining the unit prices that would give to the cash crop farmers cost of production for their crops. The secretary would then license all buyers of major agricultural commodities, requiring each to pay the cost-of-production price for those portions of these crops that were consumed domestically. If farmers produced 800 million bushels of wheat, but Americans only consumed 600 million, a processor paid cost-of-production price for three-fourths of whatever wheat he purchased. The buyer and seller could then agree on any price they wished for the remaining one-fourth.[19]

This scheme clearly recognized that the export market for American crops did not exist. The dumping features of McNary-Haugenism were impossible. But like McNary-Haugenism it sought to raise the price for domestic consumption. The difference between McNary-Haugenism and cost-of-production was the assumption in the latter scheme that the domestic market no longer could sustain a high domestic price—now administrative price fixing was necessary.

The alternative to cost-of-production was production control, although it was coupled with other subsidiary price-raising measures, such as marketing controls and intervention in the commodity options market. The purpose of production control, and of the Roosevelt administration's other approaches, was to create a regulatory structure that would have the effect of raising commodity prices to "parity," that is, to the average ratio between the prices farmers paid for inputs and living costs and the prices they received for their products in the base period of 1910–14. This base period was selected because farmers did well then. The parity concept was initially called the "ratio-price" concept and was invented by George Peek, after studying a Department of Agriculture publication on farm prices, when he proposed in 1921 the ideas that later guided McNary-Haugenism.

The mechanism for indirectly getting the market to deliver parity to farmers was cutting the surplus—at its source. Farmers would be paid to put aside some part of their land. The government would lease it from them. Farm areas would divide up into community committees that would then police farmers' choices of the acreage they would lease to the government. Local democracy, it was hoped, would keep farmers from putting aside unproductive acreage and from claiming a higher figure than they actually idled through the "rentals."

Milburn L. Wilson, of Montana State College, played a key role in formulating this plan. He was one of a group of agricultural economists who acquired great political influence in the late '20s and early '30s, in much the same way that Keynesian economists had political influence in the '50s and '60s. By the end of the 1920s Wilson and other economists, such as W. J. Spillman and John D. Black, repudiated the defining features of McNary-Haugenism—surplus segregation and dumping—because they neglected the problem of overproduction. The time had come to stop encouraging farmers to use as much of the land as possible as intensively as possible. McNary-Haugenism was based on an obsolete view of agriculture, as demonstrated by the failure of the Federal Farm Board to purchase enough farm surplus to raise prices during the early months of the Depression. The solution to farmers' problems was to control how much farmers produced by controlling how they produced. The solution was not for government to buy, store, and market surpluses, but for government to prevent surpluses.[20]

When Roosevelt called the Seventy-third Congress into special session in March 1933, the legislative momentum was with production control for the simple reason that the president favored it, and members of Congress were inclined to take seriously the analogies with war that were in his inaugural address. As the chairman of the House Committee on Agriculture said, "We are at war . . . I am going to follow the man at the other end of the Avenue, who has the flag in his hand."[21] Only six days after receiving the administration's farm bill the House passed it mostly as it had got it. The opposition of Farmer-Labor congressmen did not slow the bill down. Under the rule for the farm bill no amendments could be offered, so in the end four of the five Farmer-Labor congressmen voted for the bill anyway. It was in the Senate that cost-of-production received a hearing, in part because the Farmers Holiday Association threatened Congress with a farm strike in mid-May if it did not enact cost-of-production.

A boom for cost-of-production began to mount. Simpson's testimony appealed to many senators, and many of them were barraged by letters from farmers who favored cost-of-production. On April 12 the Senate amended the farm bill, authorizing the secretary of agriculture to determine cost-of-production prices at his discretion. For a brief moment it looked as if the Farmers Union and the Farmers Holiday Association would get what they wanted.

But Roosevelt and Secretary of Agriculture Henry Wallace categorically refused to accept the Senate's amendment, and on May 9 the House voted not to recede from the administration's stance on cost-of-production. On May 10 Senator Norris of Nebraska was unable to keep together the original cost-of-production coalition of April 12, and the Senate's amendment was deleted, permitting final passage by Congress of the farm bill. It seemed as if the New Deal had buried cost-of-production, especially when Milo Reno called off the mid-May farm strike.

A Second Push for Cost-of-Production

In the months following passage of the AAA of 1933 Milo Reno, Floyd Olson, and others worked to resurrect the cost-of-production concept. A resurgence of farm discontent helped them. The fanfare of the Hundred Days raised expectations that parity prices were just around the corner. But, unsurprisingly, they were not. As the National Recovery Administration (NRA) and the President's Re-Employment Agreement of midsummer 1933 began to have an effect on the economy, the prices of farm inputs stabilized. Anti-NRA feeling among Corn Belt farmers surfaced by late summer, giving radical political entrepreneurs like Reno a chance to capitalize on this discontent.[22]

In early fall, the Farmers Holiday Association met to formulate plans. Taking his cue from the discontent with the NRA, Reno emerged from the session with the proposal that the federal government permit farmers, using cost-of-production prices, to organize price-fixing codes of their own. Reno travelled to Washington to meet with the administration, but failed to get any definite commitment. Afterward, the governor of Iowa agreed to call a governors' conference in Des Moines, and Reno polled the state associations to assess the level of support for a farm market withholding action that would pressure the New Deal into adopting cost-of-production. Merely polling them was itself a way of organizing for a strike.

Reno issued the call for a strike, to begin October 21. Around the Midwest sporadic protests and violence occurred. On October 22 the president went on the air with a fireside chat, announcing that the Reconstruction Finance Corporation would inflate the currency through buying gold. The Department of Agriculture announced that it would furnish loans of 30–35 cents per bushel of corn stored and sealed on farmers' premises. Roosevelt seemed to have won—he could issue checks and inflate the currency; Reno and the Midwest's governors could not.

But the battle was hardly finished. Floyd Olson and four other governors travelled to Washington and met personally with Roosevelt to discuss cost-of-production. After two meetings they thought that they were just about to persuade the president, but the executive palaver ended abruptly when at a third meeting Roosevelt read to them a statement that his administration would not adopt their plan.

In response Reno ordered the farm strike into full gear. As the strike spread, the government counterattacked, liberalizing the corn loan program and announcing a massive program of purchasing pork products for relief. The head of the NRA, Hugh Johnson, prepared for a speaking tour of the Midwest.

This time the power of the center held. Soon, USDA checks "were descending on the land in a gentle, pervasive rain, damping the prairie fire." Johnson found himself speaking to cheering crowds in Minneapolis, Omaha, and Des Moines. The radical attempt to veto the New Deal in agriculture was over. In consequence, state-level radicalism faced a different future than if the October-November thrust for cost-of-production had succeeded.[23]

Governmental Capacities and the New Politics of Agriculture

Roosevelt consciously stole the thunder of the Corn Belt's agrarian radicals. As important as Roosevelt's restoration of the Midwest's political order was the New Deal's reorganization of rural Minnesota's interest-group politics. The AAA was implemented by the agricultural extension service. This system of implementation provided incentives for an organization that was at best ambivalent toward the Farmer-Labor party, the Minnesota Farm Bureau, to grow rapidly. That development, in turn, constrained the Farmer-Labor party's leaders.

Things might have turned out differently. If the Senate had succeeded in May in tacking authority for determining cost-of-production prices onto the 1933 AAA, then the incentives for the Farmers Union to pressure the secretary of agriculture to use this authority would have been overwhelming. The fear that the Farmers Union would indeed pressure him accounted in part for Wallace's opposition to the proposed Senate amendment to the 1933 farm bill. The existence of such administrative authority would have invited the organization of a standing lobby by the Farmers Union and the Farmers Holiday Association for generous cost-of-production prices. As the policy's most vocal proponents, the Farmers Union and the Farmers Holiday Association might well have boosted their influence in Corn Belt states, increasing their membership by taking credit for the policy and its implementation.[24] Between 1917 and 1923 the Nonpartisan League reshaped politics in north central and northwestern states; in the 1930s the Farmers Holiday Association might have played a similar role. Such influence, in turn, would have benefited an ally of the Farmers Union and the Farmers Holiday Association, the Farmer-Labor party, helping it with its effort to develop clubs and county Farmer-Labor associations.

What in fact happened was that the American Farm Bureau Federation and the various state federations took credit for production control. How the AAA was implemented made it easy for the Farm Bureau to do this.

The AAA provided for the participation of local farmers' committees in signing up farmers for acreage reduction contracts with the government. In order to organize these committees the Department of Agriculture used the extension system of county agricultural agents. The extension service was (and is) a system of rural adult vocational education. It built on the rise of applied agricultural economics in the land grant colleges. Initially, it was a privately supported system. In 1914, with the Smith-Lever Act, Congress instituted private support of rural education for farmers by providing for federal, state, and county funding of county instructors in applied agricultural economics. Stimulated by federal pressure on farmers to aid the war effort, by 1918 the extension service encompassed more than 80 percent of United States agricultural counties. When the New Deal was established, the main bureaucratic tool available to the federal government for implementing agricultural policy was the extension service.

Time was short in 1933; Roosevelt had promised not to create a new bureaucracy for handling the farm crisis. And the Cotton Belt, a key base of the Democratic party, wanted action fast—hence the choice of an existing bureaucracy.

This choice advantaged the Farm Bureau. County agents worked closely with local networks of farmers and businessmen during World War I, creating a host of new farm bureaus that then organized themselves into a bloc for pressuring Congress during the postwar recession, the American Farm Bureau Federation. As a result, county agents and county farm bureaus were closely connected to each other.[25] There was a keen consciousness within the Farm Bureau of the organizational consequences of seemingly neutral administrative choices. Because the Farm Bureau was, in a sense, a child of the state, its leaders knew how to exploit state action. The Farm Bureau's national leadership, which included the president of the Minnesota Farm Bureau, recognized the decision by the secretary of agriculture to use the extension system for implementing the AAA as a golden opportunity to increase membership.[26] As Gladys Baker noted in 1939, "In states where the Farm Bureau had an active program it claimed considerable credit for the enactment of the A.A.A. In these states non-farm-bureau members often felt a moral obligation to become members and promoters of the county farm bureau organization."[27]

There were other features of the AAA that further advantaged the Farm Bureau. First, county extension agents were responsible for disseminating information about the New Deal's various farm credit programs. This may have facilitated Farm Bureau credit claiming. Second, certain types of federal credit were not available to farmers unless they cooperated with the AAA. This may have been a direct incentive to join the Farm Bureau or to accept Farm Bureau credit claiming at face value. Third, AAA compliance officers and committeemen received compensation for their work, which in 1933 and 1934 surely proved extremely valuable. These sources of income may also have helped to build the Farm Bureau. Indeed, all of these factors may help to explain why farmers felt a "moral obligation to become members and promoters of the county farm bureau organization."[28]

As for the specifics of the Minnesota situation, the case is admittedly circumstantial but strong. Circumstance one is that the Minnesota Farm Bureau leadership during the 1920s was obsessed with building membership, adopting as its slogan, "There is No Substitute for Membership," and after 1925 participating in Midwest Farm Bureau training schools, whose purpose was to teach methods "for developing a loyal, informed and inspired membership."[29] Circumstance two is the Minnesota Farm

Bureau's jealous guardianship of the county agent system. In the 1933 legislature an effort was made to cut state appropriations for county agents. "It was necessary for the Farm Bureau to exert the full force of its influence in heading off this abortive attempt."[30] Circumstance three is that a large number of AAA contracts were signed in Minnesota in 1933 and 1934. Sixty-one percent of Minnesota's wheat acreage was "signed up"—not a lot of acreage when compared to, say, North Dakota, but about 840,000 acres were involved. In 1934, 79,574 corn-hog contracts were negotiated. One doubts that radical, pro-cost-of-production farmers played key roles in the organization of the temporary committees that worked with county agents to sign and administer these contracts.[31] Circumstance four is the jump in the Farm Bureau's membership. In 1933 it was 5,215, down from 10,062 in 1930. By 1935 it was up to 17,840, spread out over more than seventy of the eighty-seven counties. The Farm Bureau claimed by fall 1935, "There is no anti–Farm Bureau sentiment in the state any more . . . Industrial and processor groups that have always helped to finance subversive groups . . . have seen their efforts nullified." In December, it stated, "The Minnesota Farm Bureau . . . rated above all other states in the national federation in the membership building contest."[32]

In the absence of a county-by-county reconstruction of the implementation of the AAA, perhaps impossible at this late date, no other conclusion seems possible than that the implementation in Minnesota of the New Deal in agriculture helped rapidly to build the Minnesota Farm Bureau. The implementation process was not similarly kind to the Minnesota Farmers Union—its membership actually declined between 1933 and 1938, from 5,486 to 4,880.[33]

What was the meaning of these outcomes for the Minnesota Farmer-Labor party?

The Limits of Farmer-Labor Leadership
In the portrait gallery of the Minnesota capital in St. Paul is a painting of Floyd B. Olson, the Farmer-Labor party's most famous politician. It shows him holding a radio microphone; he looks straight at you, confident, almost smiling, "a true champion of the people."[34] Olson was a great political leader: intelligent, a gifted speaker, and charismatic. He revelled in political combat and had an instinctive cunning about what he could accomplish with his innate radicalism, which stretched back to his youth, when he briefly joined the IWW. It was not

without reason that his admirers seriously believed that he would one day become the first really radical president of the United States.[35]

But despite his best efforts, and those of Milo Reno, Olson was unable to block a national agricultural policy with which he disagreed. The New Deal's use of existing governmental capacities was crucial to this outcome. Their existence also contributed to the continuity of New Deal farm policy after the Supreme Court invalidated the AAA in January 1936. Congress was able quickly to pass the Soil Conservation and Domestic Allotment Act in February 1936, in part because its members knew that the administrative machinery for a slightly revised farm policy was already in place.

By 1935 New Deal farm policy strengthened a basically conservative rural interest group, one that, with its close ties to county bankers' associations, played a role of opinion leadership in rural areas. The process of implementing the New Deal in agriculture evidently enabled the Farm Bureau to take credit for saving Minnesota agriculture.

The Minnesota Farm Bureau was not out-and-out hostile to the Minnesota Farmer-Labor party. Farmer-Labor politicians from rural areas had close contacts with the Farm Bureau, such as Farmer-Labor congressman R. T. Buckler. And Olson did enjoy a rather warm relationship with the bureau, gaining its support, for instance, for his policy of pushing for a state income tax law, which the Farm Bureau saw as a way to relieve farmers of oppressive property taxes. But the party and the bureau did have a history of friction going back to the early 1920s. The bureau also despised policies that benefited other groups in the Farmer-Labor coalition, attacking the highway relief program, for instance, and proposals for giving organized labor collective bargaining rights. This stance was accompanied by some ballyhoo about communism. The Farm Bureau thus differed from the Farmers Union and the Farmers Holiday Association. They, like the Nonpartisan League, were avowedly farmer-labor in their ideology. Their agrarianism emphasized the importance of political alliances among all producers victimized by big business. In contrast, the Farm Bureau adopted a narrow, interest-group ideology. Politics was a game for dividing up public resources among shifting coalitions of small, organized groups, not a conflict between the masses and the privileged few.

The Farm Bureau's ideology and its policy positions constrained the Farmer-Labor party. Much more than those who lead a presidential party, state-level party leaders must worry about hostile or potentially hostile interest groups. The size of the presidential constituency is so great that it tends to diminish the influence of pressure groups with narrow constituencies. A state-level party leader deals with a far smaller constituency. The influence of interest groups grows in rough proportion to the difference between the size of a presidential constituency and the size of a gubernatorial constituency. Consequently, the Farmer-Labor party faced a different strategic environment once the New Deal in agriculture so rapidly strengthened the Minnesota Farm Bureau. For much of the party's history its leaders had thrived on a consensus for protest among rural and urban interest-group leaders. Farm leaders and labor leaders trusted and worked with each other, particularly during the heyday of the Nonpartisan League. A repeat of that heyday seemed possible in 1933. But with the collapse of the Farmers Holiday Association, the weakness of the Farmers Union, and the strengthening of the Farm Bureau, a farmer-labor split instead became possible.

There is an irony here. During the 1920s the Farmer-Labor party's leaders envisioned and pushed for a balancing political economy at the national level. Yet the Farmer-Labor party now found itself constrained by the particular ways in which the Democratic party developed such a political economy. The Democratic party used the governmental capacities available to it for implementing new policies, recasting rural politics and the possibilities of farmer-labor cooperation.

Of course, the development of new policies also helped the Farmer-Labor party. The party's leaders exploited the banking crisis of 1933 and the New Deal's bank policies to consolidate their relations with the Independent Bankers Association, the pressure group that emerged shortly before the 1930 gubernatorial election in Minnesota and was described in chapter 5.[36] Also, the nationalization of protest against chain stores (the chain-store phenomenon was described in chapter 5) and the Seventy-fourth Congress's processing of this protest eventually led to the Robinson-Patman Fair Trade Practice Bill. This process permitted party leaders to continue presenting the party as a cross-class, majoritarian coalition battling the "interests" through its delegation in Congress.[37]

But the state-level organizational consequences of the New Deal in agriculture suggest that how the Democratic party constructed a new political economy, and how particular governmental capacities shaped this change, could limit the Farmer-Labor party's future. As we will see, the impact of New Deal labor policies added to the Farmer-Labor party's strategic difficulties.

SEVEN   *New Deal Labor Policy and the Minneapolis Strikes of 1934*

When Franklin D. Roosevelt signed the National Industrial Recovery Act on 16 June 1933, he signed a bill emblematic of the Democratic party's effort to create a balancing political economy. Title 1 of the NIRA met a key demand of business: industrial self-government, backed by force of law. Yet in order to pass a bill that organized business and organized labor both supported, the president and the congressional Democrats provided in title 2 for a public works program. And they provided in title 1, section 7(a), a guarantee of collective bargaining.

Section 7(a) of the NIRA states "that employees shall have the right to organize and bargain collectively through representatives of their own choosing, and shall be free from the interference, restraint, or coercion of employers of labor, or their agents, in the designation of such representatives or in self-organization or in other concerted activities for the purpose of collective bargaining or other mutual aid or protection." This statement of federal policy overjoyed labor leaders. Daniel Tobin, president of the teamsters, confided a few months later to a White House assistant that "the Bill went through about as good, and even better, than we expected it would go." William Green, president of the AFL, and John L. Lewis, president of the United Mine Workers, compared section 7(a) to the Magna Charta and the Emancipation Proclamation.[1]

Organized labor's experience with section 7(a) was, however, more prosaic than this rhetoric suggests. Passage of the NIRA stimulated an upsurge of gritty, often violent class conflict: a strike wave washed over the United States in 1933 and 1934, much of it moved along by workers' discontent over employer refusal to recognize trade unions.[2]

The year 1934 saw three explosive strikes that gripped national attention — the San Francisco general strike (July 16–19), the first general strike in America since the 1919 Seattle general strike; the Toledo Edison and Toledo Auto-Lite strikes (April 13–June 1); and the Minneapolis truckers' strikes (February–August).

Minneapolis had a ferocious industrial war in 1934. On one side the protagonists, before other actors entered in efforts to settle it, were a Trotskyist group (the Minneapolis branch of the Communist League of

America) and its allies in a teamsters local, General Drivers Local 574, and the Minneapolis labor movement. The cohesion of this trade union coalition had many sources, but one of them was blood kinship: three of the Trotskyist leaders were brothers, Vincent, Miles, and Grant Dunne. On the other side of the struggle was the Citizens Alliance, which was the open-shop group of employers described in chapter 5. Thousands of workers served picket duty. Dozens of businessmen took to the streets as police deputies to engage the pickets. When the war was over, before Labor Day of 1934, two workers were dead and several dozen wounded from police gunfire. Two businessmen, including a member of the Citizens Alliance executive board, had been clubbed to death in a street melee.

As the war progressed, the league and its labor allies insisted on direct bargaining between employers and General Drivers Local 574 — in other words, recognition of the union calling the strike. This was a radical demand. If employers accepted it in the context of a strike that affected the entire city of Minneapolis and had gained national attention, they would shatter the open-shop discipline that governed so much industry in the Twin Cities. The Citizens Alliance maintained a solid front of employer refusal to deal with unions, through credit discipline: local banks threatened firms that recognized unions with shutoffs of credit. The banks proved crucial to the outcome of the war.[3]

The settlement of the strikes changed Minnesota's interest-group structure in ways that constrained the strategic choices of the Minnesota Farmer-Labor party's leaders. It also may have fed the growing rural-urban split that New Deal farm policy made possible.

Organizing an Industrial Union:
The February Strike

There were three strikes. The first was local, encouraged in part by the new national labor policy and the growing electoral strength of the Farmer-Labor party. It was mainly about wages and hours. In the second, the strikers insisted on employer recognition of the union. The third strike, the longest and bloodiest of the three, was again about employer recognition of the union.[4]

The first of the three strikes, in February 1934, resulted from a decision by Trotskyist trade unionists in Minneapolis to organize an industrial union. These were former Communists, and before that Socialists and Wobblies, who during the 1920s were also active in the Farmer-Labor party. In the early '30s, with apparently very little coordination from New

York City, national headquarters of their organization, the Communist League of America, these trade unionists carefully picked trucking as the general industry they could work in.

They were political entrepreneurs, just like Milo Reno and John Bosch and, before them, A. C. Townley and William Mahoney. They decided to begin with coal trucking, which two of them, Karl Skoglund and Vincent Dunne, knew well. The smooth distribution of coal was vital to Minneapolis's population during the harsh winters.

The particular union they chose was teamsters Local 574, a sleepy union of about seventy-five members that was part of a small set of small locals gathered into a grand-sounding Teamsters Joint Council. Local 574 was supposed to be a catchall organization of "general drivers." It was, therefore, the teamsters local that could most easily be turned into an industrial union.

The political context for their effort improved after passage of the NIRA. Now both the national government and the government of Minnesota were officially prolabor.

These political entrepreneurs had recent firsthand experience with organizing the difficult Hormel strike. In 1933 a meatpackers' strike occurred in Austin, Minnesota, due south of Minneapolis near the Iowa border, at one end of the corn-hog belt stretching from eastern Minnesota into Nebraska. It was the first sit-down strike in American labor history.

In a sit-down workers refuse to vacate a plant, thus avoiding the picket-line violence and scabbing that can quickly undermine a strike. In a sit-down workers also place tremendous economic pressure on the employers and political pressure on local and state officials, who must assault unarmed workers in their workplace if they wish to meet employer demands to get a plant running again.[5]

The 1933 Hormel strike was settled in favor of the workers. This settlement encouraged the Communist League's leaders, one of whom, Karl Skoglund, had involved himself in the strike. But they also knew that Minneapolis was not Austin — organization meant a direct challenge to the Minneapolis economic elite and to the city's Republican mayor, who supplanted the Farmer-Labor mayor who served from 1931 to 1933. Communist League leaders believed, in fact, that there would be class war.

Their expectations were a little premature, for the first strike was an easy affair. It came on 7 February 1934, when Local 574 called a strike of the city's coal yards, demanding higher wages, shorter hours, a seniority system, extra pay for overtime, improved work conditions, and direct bargaining between employers and the union. Luck would have it that Local 574 called the strike the day an extreme cold spell hit Minneapolis. The cold snap dealt Local 574 a trump card.

Besides luck, Local 574's strike pickets were extremely well run. A key figure in manning them was Harry DeBoer, son of a Farmer-Labor independent businessman from an outstate city, Crookston. DeBoer's father had employed men blacklisted after the railroad shopmen's strike of the early '20s; DeBoer grew up in a home sympathetic to unionism. His avocation in the late '20s was boxing, but in the winters he worked in coal yards. There he got to know Communist League leaders. A tall, imposing man, he coordinated a system of cruising picket cars volunteered by the strikers, similar to the flying squads used in other famous strikes of the 1930s, the textile strikes of early fall 1934 and the General Motors sitdown. These cruising pickets policed a scattered set of sixty-seven coal yards.

Freezing temperatures and cruising pickets notwithstanding, the coal yard owners refused to deal directly with the union. They negotiated instead with the regional labor board, one of nineteen regional boards established under the National Labor Board (NLB). As the 1933–34 strike wave swelled, the Roosevelt administration hastily built administrative machinery for settling disputes. In August 1933, after the hoopla of the government's campaign to get employers to sign the President's Reemployment Agreement (PRA), the president established the NLB. In December 1933 he extended its jurisdiction to cover disputes under NIRA codes — which were separate from disputes under the bilateral PRA — and by the end of February 1934 the NLB was given certain enforcement tools.

In referring their dispute to the regional labor board the coal yard owners sidestepped the question of employer recognition of unions and asked the federal government to do their bargaining for them. By "bringing the state in" they set a precedent that had fateful consequences for industrial relations in Minneapolis.

Bargaining through the regional board, the coal yard owners agreed to Local 574's wage and overtime demands. A conservative faction in Local 574 argued that this was victory enough, an argument that local politicians endorsed at an open meeting with the local's membership. The rank and file voted to accept the yard owners' offer. But a Communist League organizer warned that the key issue was employer recognition of the union. It seemed as if business had used government to deflect a federal policy, namely, guaranteeing the right to organize.

The February strike, in short, was a brief, quickly negotiated conflict that contrasted with a national trend. During 1933 and 1934 much of the violence and collective action that fueled strikes, and resulted from them, was as much about employer recognition of legitimate trade unions as it was about wages and hours. There was a kind of dialectic: the AFL's organization campaign, on the one hand, and on the other, the response of industry leaders who simultaneously sought, by organizing company unions, to shut organized labor out of the workplace.[6] All of this seemed to pass Minneapolis by. Yet the February strike's wages-and-hours settlement sowed the seeds for a far different conflict over union recognition, the May strike.

Class Warfare and the May Strike

With the advent of spring came layoffs in the coal yards, and many of the first to be laid off were union activists. In response, the Communist League established in Local 574 a voluntary organizing committee that aimed not only to stop the layoffs but also to organize new workers. It sought to organize an industrial union based on all the kinds of work associated with street transportation in Minneapolis: fruit and vegetable trucking, taxi cab driving, delivery work in the furniture and department stores, and various types of warehouse and dispatching work in the city's market district, known as "inside work."

An April 15 mass meeting at a downtown theater culminated the organizing drive conducted by coal yard truckers. The theme was the right to organize. To highlight it, Governor Olson had been persuaded to speak on this right. Olson was at the last minute unable to attend but sent his secretary, Vince Day, who in his youth had been a member of the inner circle of the North Dakota Nonpartisan League when the league governed North Dakota.[7] Day delivered his own rather radical speech and then read a message from Olson, which praised the "union idea" and "the network of unions that forms the most powerful single organization in our country." Olson's message then stated, "It is my counsel, if you wish to accept it, that you should follow the sensible course and band together for your own protection and welfare."[8]

The union recessed the meeting after this speech and signed on new members — Olson's message helped build its membership to three thousand! Then Karl Skoglund reconvened the meeting. The membership voted to strike if employers would not meet their demand for recognition.

On May 7, after fruitless negotiation under the regional labor board's auspices, the employers rejected the demand for what it termed a "closed-shop" agreement. On May 11 the Citizens Alliance's front, the Employers Advisory Committee, opened a headquarters in a downtown hotel and issued notice that a massive strike impended. Local 574 had set up its own headquarters. A local newspaper reported,

> The strike headquarters that the General Drivers union has established at 1900 Chicago are everything but a fort . . . A huge garage that chanced to be vacant has been rented until further notice . . . The garage offices have been converted into the strike office, with desks, typewriters, and stenographers. The space alongside the office is to be equipped as a commissary, in which the union members on picket duty will be fed. Much of the garage space will be needed for the fleet of cars that the union is mobilizing to carry officials and members about the city on strike business . . . At the rear of the building, room has been set aside for mass meetings. A stage has been erected and scores of benches installed.[9]

On the evening of May 15, a Tuesday, Local 574 held the kind of mass meeting for which its headquarters was built. At 11:30 p.m. a strike was declared. On the morning of May 16, all transportation in the city of Minneapolis was struck.

The May strike lasted from the sixteenth to the twenty-fifth. Throughout the strike Local 574 and the Minneapolis police clashed often. Their fight was about who controlled the city's streets, Local 574's pickets or the police. They fought each other on Saturday, May 19, Monday, May 21, and Tuesday, May 22. Of these engagements the third was the most important.

On that morning, fifteen hundred police and deputies gathered in the market district on the city's near north side. The fighting began when someone pitched a crate through a window — no truck had moved. The sound of breaking glass signalled the battle's beginning. Bystanders joined the pickets. The pickets concentrated first on the deputies, who were local businessmen and citizens sworn in for the engagement. The police held back, perhaps a bit of their own class revenge. Many deputies tried to run, ripping off their badges. Pickets killed Peter Erath and Arthur Lyman, a member of the Citizens Alliance's executive board. Then the police line broke and retreated. For hours pickets chased and beat deputies and policemen foolish enough to straggle behind the retreat.

By noon, the Central Labor Union, the Building Trades Council, the Teamsters Joint Council, Minneapolis police chief Michael Johannes, the Hennepin County sheriff, Governor Olson, and General Ellard Walsh, the adjutant general of Minnesota, effected a truce. Bargaining began at a hotel. It nearly ended when police tried to arrest strike leaders. But by May

25 there was an agreement, in part because Olson devised language acceptable to both sides. The agreement included pay increases, protection of prestrike pay increases, and arbitration of grievances under the regional labor board's aegis.

At the outskirts of Local 574's meeting to discuss the settlement a Citizens Alliance spy watched in disguise. As he later told a journalist who came to Minnesota to research a book on the strikes, "There were thousands and thousands of hoodlums and Communists there. Agitators worked the crowd up to the highest pitch of mob fury. They shouted, sang, and yelled. It was really horrible. I felt like slipping away, getting out of Minneapolis onto a farm somewhere."[10]

But the Citizens Alliance did not "slip away." In mid-June it pressured employers into reneging on the May agreement by exploiting ambiguities in Olson's formulations. A spate of wage cuts and layoffs occurred, some seven hundred grievances in all. Employers referred these grievances to the regional labor board but then refused to cooperate in arbitrating them, perhaps aware of how little enforcement power the NLB really had. Again, business seemed to use the federal government to deflect federal policy. Negotiations over whether employers would recognize Local 574's representation of inside workers broke down, despite efforts by Governor Olson to sustain the process. A lot was at stake; there were about twenty-two hundred such workers — "platform men, chicken pickers, banana handlers, etc."[11]

These actions set the stage for the July–August strike.

The July–August Strike

On July 6 Local 574 held a parade in conjunction with the Farmers Holiday Association, with which it worked closely in order to counter a rural backlash. In striking, the workers were keeping farmers from selling their goods in the market district, so the Farmers Holiday Association arranged for a special market.

The crowd, several thousand strong, carried banners and placards with such slogans as "Bosses Do Not Want a Union, We Workers Do," "In a Land of Plenty, We Want Our Share," "Down Depression by Cutting Hours and Raising Wages," and "Smash the Citizens Alliance." Two airplanes carrying the insignia of Local 574 flew in circles over the parade. It was an early evening parade up Minneapolis's Nicollet Avenue toward the Municipal Auditorium. There the "red-and-white banner of the Farm Holidayers" decorated the stage. The climax of the meeting came when Bill Brown, president of Local 574, read a resolution that concluded "that as a united body the unions accept the challenge of the Citizens Alliance, prepare for decisive action, and proceed to a common victory!" The crowd rose to their feet and roared their approval.[12]

Ten days later, after a round of negotiations with employers broke down, Local 574's rank and file voted a strike. A new strike headquarters had been rented, equipped with a hospital. Arrangements had been made for putting unemployed men on picket duty. A ladies auxiliary had been established. A newspaper was printed, the first strike daily in American labor history, *The Organizer*.

The turning point in the strike came soon, in four days, when the police tried to terrorize the union on a day known as "Bloody Friday." The police had a former FBI agent for a chief, whom the mayor had rapidly moved up only days after the February strike. In reaction to the May strike he laid in a new stock of weapons and purged the officer corps.[13] Bloody Friday triggered the intervention of Governor Olson, who implemented a plan for seizing control of the streets of Minneapolis from both the union and the police.

On Friday, July 20, officers placed around the Minneapolis market district on the near north side became quite tense shortly before two. At two a truck began to move from a grocery company at Third Street and Sixth Avenue North, heavily convoyed by police and carrying a few small cartons. Word had reached strike headquarters of the convoy. Strike leaders sent a picket truck into the market district. When it arrived it raced up to the truck the police were convoying and cut it off.

Police opened fire on the pickets standing in the back of the picket truck. Other police fired on bystanders and pickets in the area. Sixty-seven people were wounded, forty-seven in the back, as Governor Olson's commission of investigation later revealed. Harry DeBoer, the picket commander in the area, with five thousand men under his command that day, charged the police, taking buckshot in one of his legs. He managed, along with several other men, to get the wounded pickets in the truck to strike headquarters. There union doctors arranged for transfer of the worst cases to a regular hospital.

Four days later one of the wounded pickets died — the first of two who died. Twenty thousand marchers escorted his body. Bill Brown, a Farmer-Labor activist of long standing who was president of Local 574, ended his brief and choked funeral eulogy with these words: "Deep in the mind and heart of every worker the name of Henry Ness shall live forever. I feel so bad about this thing, this brutal murder, but I want to call upon every worker, man and woman, to protest against it."[14] A detachment from

Fort Snelling, in St. Paul, buried Henry Ness, a veteran of World War I, with military honors.

The Struggle to Settle

Galvanized by the events of Bloody Friday, Governor Olson moved to control public order. He sought, in effect, to link one of his more valuable powers — the capacity to declare martial law — to the federal government's jerry-built capacity to regulate industrial conflict. He was aided by the presence of Father Francis Haas, a top federal labor official who had arrived in Minneapolis on July 17 by airplane to work with E. H. Dunnigan, a staffer from the Federal Mediation Service who had just been in Toledo negotiating the Auto-Lite settlement. Haas had just settled a violent street-railway strike in Milwaukee.

Haas was a confidant of several national labor leaders and directed the National Catholic School of Social Service, in Washington, D. C. He was a student and friend of Father John Ryan, the leader of the liberal Catholic social justice movement. In 1933 and 1934 Haas played a key role in building the NLB and in using its staff to mediate disputes. In July 1934 Haas served as an advisor to the members of the National Labor Relations Board, established under Public Resolution Number 44, which abolished the NLB. But he cut short his work: the New Deal appointed him its ambassador to the Minneapolis strikes.

Haas and Dunnigan quickly worked up and published a plan for ending the strike. It stressed (1) government-supervised elections of bargaining representatives and (2) Local 574's right to represent the workers on strike if it won the elections. Governor Olson then announced that he would take control of the streets of Minneapolis and regulate traffic through issue of National Guard permits, if a settlement was not reached under the Haas-Dunnigan plan. He already had deployed the guard once, on Bloody Friday, to prevent a worker riot after the shootings. Olson set a deadline of noon, July 26, for agreement to the Haas-Dunnigan plan. Olson also published a letter sharply attacking the Citizens Alliance for its bloody-mindedness and its refusal to obey federal labor policy. Referring to the alliance, it stated that the "responsibility for what occurs in the City of Minneapolis, if this strike continues, is entirely upon your shoulders." Conscious of rural and middle-class opinion, Olson noted in the letter that he would use his power on behalf of "all the people of the city of Minneapolis and all people outside the city, including farmers, who desire to do business within the city."[15] Finally, to ease a settlement and placate the Citizens Alliance, Olson arrested two top leaders of the Communist

League of America, James Cannon and Max Schachtman, and removed them to St. Paul. They had come to the Twin Cities to advise Local 574 and to manage the editorial content of *The Organizer.*

All parties to the conflict waited as the deadline approached. On July 26, at noon sharp, Local 574 agreed to the Haas-Dunnigan plan, despite the arrests of Schachtman and Cannon. But the Employers Advisory Committee, the Citizens Alliance front, refused to sign. The governor deployed the National Guard.

Olson soon encountered obstacles in implementing his plan to institutionalize federal labor policy. The prior history and social sympathies of the guard's officer corps meant laxity in issuing permits. Soon traffic returned to about 65 percent of its normal load. Local 574, in response, demanded a role in the permit system, but Olson refused. Local 574 then decided to defy martial law and reimplemented its own permit system for controlling traffic in Minneapolis.

Olson ordered the National Guard to raid Local 574's strike headquarters. On August 1 at 4 a.m. the guard surrounded strike headquarters, and an arresting officer entered under cover of machine-gun emplacements. Inside strike headquarters he detained Bill Brown, Miles Dunne, and Vincent Dunne and arranged for their transfer to a stockade in St. Paul.

Union leaders who escaped from headquarters during the raid re-organized Local 574's picket system. They established a travelling command post. It operated out of filling stations, using pay telephones. Local 574's pickets skirmished, so to speak, all day and the next with guardsmen who tried to arrest them.

Olson sent word that he would meet with Local 574 leaders. Two of them came, including the man who designed the union's permit system, but they refused to negotiate. Olson then sent word that he specifically wanted to meet with one of the Dunne brothers, who was still at large, Grant Dunne, and a young leader, Farrell Dobbs (who in the late '30s would play a vital role in expanding the strength in western states of the teamsters). Dobbs and Dunne refused to negotiate unless the governor released Bill Brown and the other two Dunne brothers. Olson met their requests and evacuated strike headquarters.

His next move was to lean on the Citizens Alliance. On August 3 he ordered National Guard lieutenant Kenneth Haycraft, a Farmer-Laborite, to raid the Citizens Alliance headquarters and seize its files. Other guard officers got wind of the raid, however, shortly before Haycraft's unit moved. They tipped off the alliance, which removed most of its files.

There was now nothing for Olson to do, if he wanted to impose federal labor policy, except to start over. On August 5 Olson reformed the permit system and stipulated that only signatories to the Haas-Dunnigan plan could move trucks. He also appeared in federal district court and successfully argued that his emergency power superseded a petition from the Employers Advisory Committee that asked the court to enjoin, under its equity power, Olson's declaration of martial law.

By August it seemed that Governor Olson's plan to impose section 7(a) on the Citizens Alliance had failed. The National Guard was a recalcitrant instrument of executive power. Earlier in the strikes Olson removed an insubordinate officer, but the foiled raid on the Citizens Alliance showed how deeply political insubordination ran in the guard. As for the federal government, its capacity to regulate industrial relations — through such devices as holding secret elections for bargaining representatives — depended on business's conceding this capacity. Yet the NIRA was a temporary measure. In addition to the antiunionism of the previous decade this helped to arouse intransigence, much as President Wilson's labor policy, which was avowedly temporary, had done. Intransigence might maintain the pre-NIRA status quo. "Capital" might curb the political-economic impact of government recognition of trade unions.

On August 8 Governor Olson and President Roosevelt met. Roosevelt had travelled to Minnesota for a ceremony at the Mayo Clinic, in Rochester, where he stayed for two days.

In Minneapolis the Citizens Alliance bought radio time to denounce the Communist League. Haas and Dunnigan seemed, also, to back away from their original plan. Although the retreat was more apparent than real, designed to open up negotiations, it embittered trade union leaders. At strike headquarters conditions were nightmarish. The strike leaders held a painful discussion about whether they were on the verge of failure.

They did not yet know it, but Governor Olson had devised a way to gain employer recognition of trade unions. In late July a staffer on the NLRB had, at the request of Father Haas, learned an important fact about Twin Cities banks. He informed Haas that the Reconstruction Finance Corporation had $25 million in these banks. Haas, in turn, relayed this fact to Governor Olson, who may well have impressed on Haas that bankers were the generals in the Citizens Alliance. In Rochester, during his discussion with the president about the strike situation, Olson suggested to Roosevelt that the Reconstruction Finance Corporation recall its loans on the ground that, through the intransigence of the Citizens Alliance, the strike was harming the soundness of the collateral for the loans. In fact the strike did cause a lot of damage to the regional and local economy, costing it, in the end, $50 million and drastically reducing bank clearings in Minneapolis.

There was one problem with Olson's ingenious suggestion. In fall 1933 Jesse Jones, the director of the Reconstruction Finance Corporation, reassured banks that the infusion of federal money that he wished to pump into the national banking system would not become an opening wedge for governmental control of banks. What Olson proposed was precisely what Jones promised bankers would never happen. But Olson's idea was consistent with the New Deal's larger aim of establishing a balancing political economy. Would the president agree to use the club of the loans against the Citizens Alliance?

The president did agree, immediately telephoning Jesse Jones. By August 15 the Employers Advisory Committee seemed to agree to a plan for NLRB-supervised elections at 166 Minneapolis firms struck by Local 574. Yet even as the Citizens Alliance seemed to agree, it sought to undermine the spirit of section 7(a), sending out a letter to employers that advised them how to pressure workers into voting the right way.

The letter wound up in the hands of Local 574, which published it in *The Organizer*. The Communist League leaders invested enormous time and energy during the July-August strike in *The Organizer*, keeping it going despite alliance efforts to prevent local printers from doing business with the union. Their efforts paid off in many ways, including the unanticipated benefit at the last minute of keeping the alliance and the federal government honest.

There was, by August 21, a decent agreement between workers and employers. Workers would be rehired without discrimination, and wages above minimums demanded by the union would be arbitrated. Fair elections would be held.

The grand old man and founder of the Citizens Alliance, A. W. Strong, played a key role in brokering the final settlement. This was one of his last acts as a Citizens Alliance leader, for he was quite old. He founded the open-shop movement in Minneapolis to fight the influence of Thomas Van Lear, the Socialist leader of the IAM lodges in Minneapolis, who later became mayor of Minneapolis and a founder of the WPNPL. And he lived to see the president of the United States side with a Trotskyist-led labor union.

Governmental Capacities and the July-August Strike

By 21 August 1934 a great change had come over Minnesota politics. The power of antiunion capital had been drastically weakened. Though the Citizens Alliance found a vigorous rearguard action in 1935 in Minneapolis, the balance of class power in Minneapolis and Minnesota changed decisively in 1934. The capacities of the Minnesota and federal governments to implement a new public policy played a key role in making this change possible.[16]

In using the National Guard as he had, Governor Olson did something completely novel. During the 1920s state national guards were the instrument of last resort for implementing antistrike injunctions and for breaking strikes.[17] Olson used the guard to break the open-shop system that had thrived in Minneapolis for two decades. He showed that threatening to deploy and actually deploying the National Guard were tools that a governor could use to establish new public policies toward labor. He thus set a precedent that he followed in 1935, when he used the guard to affect the outcome of a bitter strike in Minneapolis, and that the other two Farmer-Labor governors, Hjalmar Petersen (August 1936–January 1937) and Elmer Benson (1937–39), also followed.[18]

As political insubordination within the Minnesota National Guard revealed, however, there were limits to the policy that Olson pursued. The establishment of collective bargaining in Minnesota also depended on Roosevelt's intervention. Here the president was just as inventive as the governor. The key to implementing a new federal labor policy was forcing the Citizens Alliance to obey the policy. The key to that, in turn, was threatening the economic health of the Twin Cities banks that monopolized the credit lines of nonunion employers. Governor Olson was able to persuade President Roosevelt to do just this. But it was not enough for Roosevelt to be persuaded; he also had to be *able* to do what Olson suggested. The prior development of a federal capacity to act as banker of last resort, a process that began during the Hoover administration and that Jesse Jones further developed, gave Roosevelt the power to intervene as he did in Minneapolis and to coerce the Citizens Alliance into compliance with section 7(a) of the NIRA.

Change in the Farmer-Labor Party's
Interest-Group Environment

Together Olson and Roosevelt richly rewarded the political entreneurship and exemplary organizational skills of the Trotskyist labor leaders who planned and led the 1934 strikes. General Drivers Local 574 now enjoyed both employer and government recognition, setting the stage for efforts to expand its membership and influence.

There was a cost to the Farmer-Labor party of what Olson and Roosevelt had done to enforce federal labor policy. The creativity of their effort to implement a new public policy also paved the way for a reorganization of the interest-group basis of Minnesota politics. The Minnesota State Federation of Labor was keenly aware of the change: it "red-baited" Local 574, picking up on the public denunciations that Daniel Tobin, president of the teamsters, hurled at Local 574 during the strikes.

For Olson, this change in the interest-group basis of Minnesota politics posed little threat. The Dunne brothers and Karl Skoglund, the core of the Twin Cities branch of the Communist League of America, had known Olson for many years. They respected him even as they criticized him, and found that they had easy access to the inner circles of the Farmer-Labor party.[19]

Two of Minneapolis's Farmer-Labor aldermen were very close to the Trotskyists. Also, Olson appointed to the position of director of personnel in the state Highway Department someone with whom Local 574 was close. This was Joseph Poirier, who was a founder of the Farmer-Labor party in the early 1920s and who worked with Vincent Dunne in the late '20s when Dunne was still a member of the Communist party and an activist in one of the Farmer-Labor ward clubs in Minneapolis.[20] Also, Carlos Hudson, who helped to edit *The Organizer,* drafted speeches for Farmer-Labor congressman (and later United States senator) Ernest Lundeen. And some of the more intellectual Trotskyists in the Twin Cities were friends of Olson's commissioner of education, John Rockwell.[21]

Even though the Trotskyist leadership of Local 574 and Governor Olson knew how to get along with each other, in the long run the empowerment of Trotskyist political entrepreneurs constrained the Farmer-Labor leadership. The leaders of Local 574 had an ideology that meant, ultimately, they were hostile to the Farmer-Labor party. They would always find the Farmer-Labor party too class collaborationist and too conservative. They would always find the party's historic ally, the State Federation of Labor, hidebound and unimaginative. As a result, they had no particular loyalty to the Farmer-Labor party per se and under certain circumstances might easily withdraw their support for the Farmer-Labor leadership.

Electoral Concomitants of the 1934 Strikes
The 1934 strikes not only changed the Farmer-Labor party's interest-group environment in ways that could constrain it, but also seem to have accelerated a decline in Floyd Olson's electoral strength that had been underway since 1930. As the Farmer-Labor party became

far more closely identified with the cause of radical organized labor, a rural backlash against Olson seems to have occurred.

Without survey data it is hard to know just why rural support for Olson declined. Several factors could explain the decline: a reaction to the notoriously radical 1934 platform of the Farmer-Labor party; circulation in rural areas of charges that Olson corrupted the office of Hennepin County attorney in the late 1920s in a criminal case involving a Lutheran minister; anger over farmers' lack of easy access to Twin Cities markets during the strikes; the growth of the Minnesota Farm Bureau.[22]

Olson's reelection in 1934, an outcome that did depend in part on rural support, was in a special sense a considerable accomplishment. Most state electorates have punished governors when they side with labor in "high-temperature" strikes. In 1938, for instance, liberal Democrat Philip Murray lost the governorship of Michigan in large measure because of his role in the Flint sit-down strike. Olson's reelection should thus be seen as an unusual exception to one of the rules of American politics.

Still, the numbers could not have been comforting for Olson. In 1930 Olson won 59.3 percent of the statewide vote; in 1932 he slipped to 50.6 percent; in 1934 he slipped even further to a plurality victory of 44.6 percent. Over the course of these three elections Olson slipped slightly in the three urban counties in which Minneapolis, St. Paul, and Duluth were located. Yet his performance by 1934 was still very strong in these densely populated urban counties, winning an outright majority with an average performance of 52.9 percent. Where Olson lost strength was in rural counties.

That Olson grew weaker in rural counties is not surprising given the scope of his 1930 landslide. But the rate at which he lost strength picked up between 1932 and 1934. In 1930 Olson lost 5.7 percent of the state's counties; in 1932 he lost 16 percent of the state's counties; in 1934 he lost 44 percent of the state's counties. In 1932 Olson carried forty-six of eighty-four rural counties with an outright majority. In 1934 Olson lost strength in 95 percent of these same counties, the average drop being 11.7 percent. The average gain for the Republican party among them was 8.6 percent, and for the Democrats was 2.4 percent.

Especially interesting was the jump in the number of people voting in these counties. This jump strongly suggests the occurrence of rural backlash, particularly since it contrasts with an average decline of 3.6 percent in the number of people voting in the three large urban counties. Typically off-year elections are less dramatic affairs than presidential-year elections, leading to a drop in the number of people voting. The urban counties

New Deal Labor Policy and the Minneapolis Strikes of 1934

followed this pattern of surge in presidential years and decline in off years. But in 1934 only ten of the eighty-four rural counties followed the typical pattern. In the forty-six counties where Olson lost strength the average increase over 1932 in the total number of voters was 7.9 percent. Increases occurred in 93 percent of these counties. Not only did voters in most rural counties, stimulated by the events of 1934, go to the polls in larger numbers than they had in 1932, but also more of this expanded electorate voted Republican than in 1932.

The Limits of Farmer-Labor Leadership

National New Dealers did not intend to harm the Farmer-Labor party. To the contrary, FDR sought consciously to help the party.[23] Yet national New Dealers, in building a new political economy, created obstacles for Minnesota's highly successful case of state-level radicalism.

Simply because people in the New Deal wanted to build a new political economy did not mean that one would come into existence. The implementation of new public policies depended on preexisting governmental capacities, as in the case of the federal extension service, or on the inventive use of governmental capacities, as in Minneapolis in summer 1934. The capacities for building a new political economy were in fact there, and use of them thus reorganized the interest-group bases of American politics, with consequences as well for state electoral politics. These changes constrained the strategic choices of Farmer-Labor leaders.

Their problems differed from those facing the New Deal. Presidential parties have considerable leverage over the national interest-group system. The limits to the power of presidential parties often come instead from the special development of congressional party politics and from the congressional wings of the presidential party. Harding, Coolidge, and Hoover all found this to be true; so, soon enough, would Roosevelt.[24] In contrast, state-level party leaders have, structurally, less leverage vis-à-vis interest groups. The constituencies of gubernatorial parties are smaller. Changes in a gubernatorial party's interest-group environment necessarily constrain the party more, at best merely complicating its strategic options and at worst narrowing them.

EIGHT

*The Crisis of State-Level
Radicalism*

For the Farmer-Labor party 1936 was a year of
contrasts. Floyd Olson, the party's charismatic leader, died in late August,
the victim of stomach cancer. The party lost one of its major resources.
Despite Olson's death the Farmer-Labor party seemed strong. The party's
candidate for governor was a political novice, Elmer Benson. A small-
town bank cashier and clothing merchant, between 1933 and 1935 he
regulated securities and banks in Minnesota and then served in the second
session of the Seventy-fourth Congress, appointed by Olson to serve out
the term of a deceased Republican senator. Despite his political inex-
perience, Benson gained a landslide vote in the 1936 gubernatorial
election. The Farmer-Labor party also captured a record majority of six of
the nine Minnesota seats in the House of Representatives, and it sent a
second senator, Ernest Lundeen, to accompany the party's senior public
official, Henrik Shipstead. It was the third time that the party controlled
the Senate delegation and, more importantly, the first time that both of the
Farmer-Laborites serving as senators were elected to full six-year terms.[1]
The party had near complete control of the state's bureaucracy. Finally,
although Minnesota's legislative elections were officially nonpartisan, the
1936 elections awarded the party control of the state house of representatives for the 1937 session of the legislature. The last time the "Liberal
caucus" constituted a majority of the Minnesota house was during the
1933 session. So strong was the Farmer-Labor party in the house that the
Speaker of the House shut Republicans out of the rules committee and cut
down Republican committee assignments.[2]

Table 8.1 summarizes certain contrasts between the strength of the
Farmer-Labor party's performance in 1936 and its performance in earlier
elections. It shows that Benson far outperformed his distinguished predecessor, whose electoral strength steadily declined between 1930 and 1934.
It also shows that even without the advantage of an election at large of
United States representatives, held in 1932 because of a dispute between
Olson and the legislature over redistricting, the party could do very well in
congressional elections. The two columns on the right suggest growth in
the strength of the Farmer-Labor statewide nongubernatorial executive

TABLE 8.1 Farmer-Labor Electoral Strength, 1930–36

Year	Farmer-Labor Vote for Governor (%)	U.S. House Seats Won by Farmer-Labor Party (%)	Districts Where Farmer-Labor Party Ran (%)	Change in Average, Vote for All Executive Offices	
				All Parties (%)	Farmer-Labor (%)
1930	59.3	10	80		
1932	50.6	55	—ᵃ	+33.6	+33.1
1934	44.6	33.3	100	+2.0	+5.5
1936	60.7	66.6	100	+9.5	+25.0

Source: Bruce M. White et al., comps., *Minnesota Votes: Election Returns by County for Presidents, Senators, Congressmen, and Governors, 1857–1977* (St. Paul: Minnesota Historical Society, 1977), pp. 110–24, 191–96; Millard Gieske, *Minnesota Farmer-Laborism: The Third Party Alternative* (Minneapolis: University of Minnesota Press, 1979), pp. 140, 171, 200, 230. Calculations by the author.
ᵃElection at large.

ticket. The increase between the average number of all parties' votes for executive offices besides the governorship was less than the increase in Farmer-Labor votes for these offices.

Even as the party reached its electoral zenith in 1936, it faced hidden, endogenous weaknesses and strategic difficulties. Its leadership's struggle to create a strong political party through use of patronage generated both the potential for petty factionalism and a decline in internal ideological vitality. Also, the New Deal's effort to construct a balancing political economy altered the organizational bases of American politics. Its public policies recast the interest-group bases of both Minnesota and national politics. This restructuring of American politics began to hem in the Farmer-Labor party's leaders, changing and complicating their strategic and tactical choices.

Between 1936 and 1938 the Farmer-Labor party became even more hemmed in. In 1935 the United States adopted a new national labor policy, the Wagner Act. This policy went considerably beyond section 7(a) of title 1 of the NIRA in its intention to shift national government in a reformist direction. In mid-April 1937 the Supreme Court validated the Wagner Act. It accepted the argument offered by the NLRB that federal supervision of industrial relations would preempt industrial warfare and thus facilitate industrial commerce, consistent with federal responsibility under the commerce clause of the Constitution. The impact on interest-group politics reverberated across Minnesota's political landscape like a thunderclap on a hot summer day.

The New Federal Labor Policy

The Wagner Act and its validation were turning points in American political history.[3] The Wagner Act protected workers' right to organize into unions of their own choosing. It also meant to end the coercion or intimidation of workers by their employers. This emphasis grew in large measure out of labor's painful experience with company unions in 1933 and 1934, when company unionism outpaced regular unionism. Hence the act specifically proscribed certain common unfair labor practices among employers.[4]

The Wagner Act legislated a macroinstitutional change. During the '20s, federal judges behaved as de facto formulators and administrators of American labor policy. But between 1933 and 1935 a hodgepodge system of administrative labor courts sprang up, partly supplanting the federal courts. The Wagner Act expanded and reorganized this ad hoc system into a new institution for administering American labor policy. It established a quasi-judicial agency, the National Labor Relations Board, whose orders were reviewable only in circuit courts of appeals. The function of defending the board's orders in the court system fell to the NLRB's general counsel, not the attorney general. This avoided the dependence on the attorney general that crippled the National Labor Board, the NLRB's predecessor during the NRA period. NLRB election orders were nonreviewable. It had power of subpoena. Its findings of fact were conclusive and nonreviewable. Not judges, but experts on labor relations would enforce labor law.

The Wagner Act and its constitutional validation unleashed a burst of activist administrative behavior. For a series of reasons, a deeply felt sense of social and political purpose guided the board's staff in its early years. Political ideology, a belief in legal realism, and eagerness to apply institutional labor economics to the real world all played a role. There was a heady atmosphere at the board. Its staff possessed a sense of mission, a psychology common among the staffs of independent regulatory commissions in their early years.

New Labor Policy Coincides with a Split in Labor

Through historical coincidence the Supreme Court handed down *NLRB vs. Jones & Laughlin* just as organized labor experienced an internal split.[5] The split emerged in 1935, shortly after the AFL's national convention at Atlantic City, New Jersey. The convention witnessed, and left unresolved, a bitter dispute over how best to organize labor. Afterwards, John L. Lewis of the United Mine Workers, David Dubinsky of the International Ladies' Garment Workers, Sidney Hillman of the Amalgamated Clothing Workers, and other less powerful leaders formed the Committee for Industrial Organization (CIO). They hoped to pressure the federation, the leaders of its various departments, and its hegemonic bloc of such key international unions as the United Brotherhood of Joiners and Carpenters, the teamsters, and the IAM (among others) into changing their organizing policies. The existing policies continued the general AFL strategy of organizing only "strategic workers" in the economy (i.e., those workers whose replacement cost more to a company's productivity than their demands did) and expending none of the federation's scarce resources (time, money, skills) on predominantly unskilled or semiskilled mass production workers. The CIO, in contrast, pushed for the expenditure of such resources on this previously ignored stratum within the work force.[6]

By late 1936 and early 1937 relations between the CIO and the AFL were bad. Yet quite possibly the split in labor was resolvable. As late as September 1937 a Gallup poll found that 75 percent of union members wanted differences between the AFL and the CIO settled.[7]

State labor politics mirrored the open-endedness of labor's split. At the Minnesota State Federation of Labor's September 1936 convention, the delegates voted down a mild proposal merely to ask the AFL to reconcile the split. Instead they adopted a far stronger proposal put forth by Sander Genis of the Amalgamated Clothing Workers and a colleague from the Twin Cities Ladies' Garment Workers. This stronger proposal stated that the CIO was "carrying out the mandates of the 54th and 55th conventions of the A. F. of L. to organize the steel industry" and requested that the "12 national and international unions" in the CIO be reinstated pending a reconciliation of differences. This was a strong prounity position.[8]

Shortly, however, the CIO began rapidly to change. The Wagner Act's validation in April 1937 contributed, at a critical moment in organized labor's history, to the long-run forces behind labor's split. The symbolic aspects of *Jones & Laughlin* created a remarkable opportunity for a fledgling and radical labor movement. The most important tribunal in the land sharply undercut the legitimacy of a system of antiunionism that had flourished for seventeen years, since the dismantling of President Wilson's labor policy. A new, relatively benign governmental machinery for supervising industrial relations was now available. Before *Jones & Laughlin* the upstart CIO really enjoyed legitimacy only among the workers in its unions, among some groups of workers discontented with the AFL because of earlier contacts with it, and among a few political and intellectual elites. After *Jones & Laughlin* the CIO profited from the intersection of both governmental recognition and the employer recognition that became increasingly common. The CIO's leadership made the most of this conjuncture, linking together the various little insurgencies all across America that loosely grouped themselves on the CIO's side.

Up until April 1937, very few CIO unions used the NLRB's election machinery. The CIO grew primarily through organizational confrontation, as in the auto sit-downs, or through secret dealing, as with U.S. Steel. Between October 1935, when the NLRB began operations, and April 1937, when the Court handed down *Jones & Laughlin,* the CIO participated in only ten NLRB-conducted elections. The AFL, in contrast, participated in forty-two elections out of a total of seventy-six for the period, which reflected its position as an established labor federation. However, between April and December 1937, the CIO won hundreds of NLRB-run elections, 445 out of a total of 665 elections conducted by the board involving independent labor unions, or 67 percent. The majority of these wins were in "consent elections," in which the NLRB secured "from all parties concerned an agreement, first, that there shall be an election, and second, as to the proper bargaining unit, the form of the ballot, the polling place, the time of the election and other necessary details."[9]

Increased employer recognition not only allowed CIO unions to develop stronger links to workers but also encouraged formal bureaucratic organization. New CIO bureaucracies handled grievances or shaped management planning. CIO unions often gained written agreements assuring their stability for periods from one year to several years.[10]

The CIO wasted little time in securing hundreds of stable niches in plants all across the country. Between April and December of 1937, about 288,000 workers participated in board-conducted elections involving the CIO. About 81 percent of these workers participated in elections in which the CIO won the election. During that time the elections in which the CIO sought to gain the loyalty of workers involved approximately 136 percent more workers than the elections in which the AFL appeared on the NLRB ballot.[11]

Collateral Effects of the CIO's Institutionalization
As the CIO expanded and grew more bureaucratically stable during 1937, a process that interacted with the activism of the

NLRB's staff, a new set of political and organizational side effects occurred. First, as the CIO became more of a national institution, a problem that had emerged first in 1936 worsened: the proper jurisdiction of the two labor movements. "Jurisdiction" means a union's territory. It is a claim to "exclusive control over a craft or an industrial function" and a claim to the right to organize all the individual workers in that craft or industrial function and to collect dues and fees from those workers. The CIO's institutionalization raised the threat of "dual unionism," that is, of two unions occupying the same jurisdiction. Because two national labor movements existed, two unions, one AFL and another CIO, could and at the time often did make the same claim to "exclusive control over a craft or an industrial function."[12]

Jurisdictional disputes always troubled American labor. The AFL, acting as labor's "private government," had contained the organizational tensions of jurisdictional disputes. Now, however, the CIO's institutionalization heightened labor's centrifugal tendencies, and no private government was available to handle these conflicting claims.[13]

The obstacles to reconciliation between the AFL and the CIO grew over the course of 1937, paralleling the CIO's institutionalization. The mere passage of time meant that the only basis for reconciliation could be either (1) an agreement by the leadership of one of the two labor movements to settle jurisdictional claims on the opposing labor movement's terms or (2) a decision temporarily to stop using the unique opportunity to grow that the Wagner Act's validation created. Both were impossible conditions.

Stable new unions flocked into the CIO and the AFL via the gateway of NLRB elections. It was impossible for both leaderships even to know what all the potential or actual jurisdictional tensions in American labor were. Table 8.2 shows that 1937 saw the greatest burst of organizing activity in American labor history, both within the CIO and the AFL.

The resulting chaos made bargaining between the AFL's and CIO's leaders fruitless. They needed to know clearly what they would be giving up or gaining through negotiation.

The structural impossibility of negotiation strengthened the hands of intransigents in both labor federations. John L. Lewis, who tended towards an autocratic flamboyance, grew more defiant in his attitude toward the AFL. Many "Old Guard" leaders of AFL internationals, such as Bill Hutcheson of the carpenters, Arthur Wharton of the machinists, and Dan Tracy of the International Brotherhood of Electrical Workers, assumed a central role in AFL policy making. They considered industrial unionism little more than a fancy excuse for raiding their jurisdictions.

TABLE 8.2 Union Membership of Nonagricultural Employees, 1900–40

Year	Employees in Union (%)	Year	Employees in Union (%)
1900	6.1	1934	11.9
1910	10.2	1935	13.2
1920	18.5	1936	13.7
1930	11.5	1937	22.6
1931	12.4	1938	27.5
1932	12.9	1939	28.6
1933	11.3	1940	26.9

Sources: Leo Troy, *Trade Union Membership, 1897–1962*, Occasional Paper 92 (New York: National Bureau of Economic Research, 1965), p. 2; Michael Goldfield, *The Decline of Organized Labor in the United States* (Chicago: University of Chicago Press, 1987), pp. 10–11. Goldfield cautions that pre-1930 data are mainly estimates.

Once it developed into something of a competitive threat, they became prepared to protect their interests aggressively.[14]

Many AFL leaders concluded that the CIO was only a rebellious faction. It would not bend to the self-discipline that labor's private government required. There were no valid disagreements over policy—the split simply was power politics. The CIO's argument against crafts organization was "a false issue set up to conceal and obscure the real motives and objectives of the CIO leadership." Its radical organizing tactics, such as the sit-down, "fanned the spirit of unbridled unrest" and showed just how unprincipled the CIO's leaders were. In short, the CIO was little more than an unnatural aggregation of workers. A power-hungry elite duped these workers into challenging the true and historic representative of American labor, the American Federation.[15]

A sense developed among the AFL's national leaders that the federation should strike back at the CIO as hard as possible, for many CIO organizers were Communists. In helping to institutionalize the CIO, the NLRB helped the Communist party to acquire significant new links to the American labor movement.[16] This was because John L. Lewis chose to use seasoned Communist organizers to build parts of the CIO, such as the steelworkers unions. Also, before the NLRB began operating, many Communist organizers had already worked to build the nuclei of various industrial unions. Either way, an unprecedented level of Communist influence among the trade unions emerged, to the AFL's considerable alarm. As far as the AFL was concerned, the CIO's institutionalization not only implied dual unionism but also meant Red unionism.

Minnesota Labor's Response to the National Split

By mid-1937 the political and organizational climate within the national labor movement was quite different from what it was when Floyd Olson died. A chaotic but far-reaching reorganization of the labor movement generated a strong right wing within the AFL prepared to protect both the interests and the values of the federation. This faction had an unbeatable argument for its hostility to the CIO: unless the federation acted decisively against the CIO, those Communists whom the federation defeated in the '20s would have their revenge in the '30s. The AFL would lose the war against Communist influence. Two beliefs guided the actions of federation leaders: the CIO threatened the federation's legitimate institutional interests, and the CIO was an entering wedge in the labor movement for the Communist party.[17]

These beliefs played a critical role in changing the Farmer-Labor party's labor base. Beginning in mid-1937, the AFL's national leaders actively sought to involve state federations and city centrals in the federation's national fight against the CIO. The policy actually began in March 1937, in the 1936 convention's aftermath. But the Executive Council took it more seriously once the full impact of *Jones & Laughlin* began to be felt within labor. It worked hard to export its views to its state and local counterparts, including those in Minnesota. The Minnesota State Federation of Labor, for its part, responded.

New CIO unions emerged in several Minnesota industries: meat packing, lumbering, textiles, machine assembly and electrical work, iron mining, office work, and newspaper work. The increments in organizational strength appear to have been greatest in textiles, lumbering, mining, and machine assembly and electrical work. The gains in this last industry were dramatic, involving large locals in Minneapolis and its suburbs.[18]

The CIO in Minnesota was aggressive and pro-Communist. The various unions within the CIO rapidly linked themselves at the state level, establishing the Minnesota Industrial Union Council in December 1937. This was among the first state CIO organizations to emerge in America. It predated the establishment of similar councils in Michigan, Indiana, and New Jersey, all more industrialized states. The council boasted fifteen vice-presidents, exactly the same number as the State Federation's, not a subtle statement of the council's ambitions. The council also built itself on an axis of Communist union power linking the Iron Range, in St. Louis County, and Minneapolis, Hennepin County. Its executive officers were Communists.[19]

Particular ways in which the CIO grew in Minnesota engaged the worst fears of the State Federation's executive officers. For instance, the way United Electrical, Radio, and Machine Workers (UE) was established in Minnesota enraged the IAM's national and state leadership. Over the summer of 1937 an ambitious and articulate Communist, who helped to found the Farmer-Labor Federation in the early 1920s, led a raid of five machinists locals to establish two large UE locals under Communist control. His timing was excellent, for he swung these locals into UE just as the union's numerical growth and its linking up with midwestern locals outside the historic heartland of UE (Lynn, Mass., Camden, N.J., Philadelphia, and Schenectady, N.Y.) gathered force in the aftermath of *Jones & Laughlin*. He cabled an elated message to the September 1937 UE convention with the news that he had just captured five to six thousand workers for UE: this news made the Minneapolis locals among the largest UE locals outside the northeastern core of the union.[20]

These factors—the anti-Communism of the State Federation of Labor's leadership, the pro-Communist character of the Minnesota CIO and its organizational aggressiveness, including a willingness to raid well-established jurisdictions—had a strong effect on the Minnesota State Federation of Labor's internal politics. In late September 1937, when the State Federation held its fifty-fifth annual convention at Hibbing, on the Iron Range, its internal politics revealed a change in opinion. The delegates chose to adopt the Resolutions Committee's hard anti-CIO line in its report on the AFL/CIO resolutions it considered. They also voted to prevent a Farmer-Labor congressman, John Bernard of the eighth district, who served on the staff of the CIO's Steel Workers Organizing Committee in Minnesota, from speaking at the convention.[21]

Political Consequences of Minnesota Labor's Reorganization

By late 1937, the Minnesota labor movement changed in response to tensions in the national labor movement. How did this nationally rooted change in the Farmer-Labor party's base affect the party? It now faced strategic constraints on how to position itself with the new and old actors in the Minnesota labor movement. By no later than September 1937, as the vote taken to prevent Farmer-Labor congressman Bernard from speaking showed, it was impossible for Farmer-Labor leaders to favor the CIO, wittingly or unwittingly, without earning the State Federation of Labor's hostility. If they did favor the CIO, they would be aligning themselves with the weaker of the two organizations. The State Federation was numerically much larger than the Minnesota CIO.[22]

What complicated the new political situation was that the Communist party and the CIO had interests in allying with the Farmer-Labor party. The Communist party was now in its Popular Front stage. This involved working with and organizationally reinforcing existing left-wing organizations, such as the Farmer-Labor party and the CIO. The Popular Front also promoted new "mass" organizations, such as the American Youth Congress, Unemployed Councils, and the League against War and Fascism.

Through links to existing organizations and through new organizations the Popular Front would advance its domestic political goals. These deliberately resembled the goals of existing reformist and non-Communist left-wing organizations. Such a resemblance—and portrayals of communism as simply a variant of "Americanism"[23]—would legitimate a mass Communist presence in American society. According to the theory of the Popular Front, a significant Communist presence would consolidate American democracy's achievements, most notably the New Deal. This would prevent fascism in the United States. Also, a mass Communist presence would enhance the Comintern's ability to influence American foreign policy, an ability that served the Soviet Union's geopolitical interest in curbing Nazi expansionism.

The Minnesota CIO's organizational and political interests were congruent with the Communist party's. The Minnesota CIO strongly favored political action in order to hang onto gains like the Wagner Act, to which the CIO owed so much, and to extend the New Deal. The Minnesota CIO also actively supported the Farmer-Labor party, in keeping with its strong emphasis on political action.

The Farmer-Labor party thus faced demands for political alliances from two important actors. The Communist party was an old actor in Minnesota politics, but for two reasons it was now more important: (1) it boasted links to the labor movement, and (2) it had a revisionist enthusiasm for providing hard-working and dedicated cadres to liberal and reformist organizations. The Minnesota CIO was part of an apparently dynamic and progressive new labor federation that had a program for moving the American political system to the left and for institutionalizing hard-won reforms.

If the Farmer-Labor party responded to demands for an alliance with these two organizations, it then risked the enmity of the Minnesota State Federation of Labor and the Trotskyist leadership of an increasingly powerful union, teamsters Local 544 (previously Local 574).[24] The Farmer-Labor party and the State Federation of Labor were historically close allies. Despite the formal disruption of 1929, when the State Federation of Labor disbanded the political action committee it established in 1919 under the direction of William Mahoney, the same basic relationship between the Farmer-Labor party and the State Federation existed from 1919 to 1936. In 1936 the Federation endorsed the entire Farmer-Labor ticket. Also, the party and Local 544 reached a truce after 1934 despite Trotskyist ideological hostility to a political formation with a strong middle-class component. Reaching a truce was difficult—after all, Floyd Olson temporarily jailed Local 544's leaders in 1934 after raiding strike headquarters. Eventually, though, a network of elite links between Local 544 and the Farmer-Labor party was formed.

The general reorganization of labor in 1937 gave both the State Federation of Labor and Local 544 new interests. The federation's growth could mean new political demands with antipartisan implications, such as demanding a civil service merit system for state and highway-repair employees. As for the leaders of Local 544, they were increasingly successful at large-scale union organization and thus increasingly self-confident. One of them, Farrell Dobbs, pioneered the development of a key institutional innovation for the teamsters, the area conference, establishing the Central States Drivers Council. Gaining the support of teamster president Daniel Tobin, Dobbs used teamster power in Minneapolis to force unionization on key intercity lines and found ways to appeal to over-the-road drivers, developing a network of locals in North and South Dakota, Iowa, Minnesota, Wisconsin, Michigan, Ohio, Indiana, Illinois, Missouri, and Nebraska.[25] The leaders of Local 544 had new organizational interests that might take priority over political loyalties.

Local 544 also faced a new political conjuncture: first, the competition of the late '30s between the Third International and Trotskyism, in the process of organizing itself into the new Fourth International; and second, a new link between the Communist party and the Minnesota labor movement. This confluence of political circumstances invited an ideological response from Local 544's leaders. Now the Socialist movement needed uncompromising revolutionary leadership. Certainly Local 544's Trotskyist leaders had to confront the geopolitically tainted, almost cynical revisionism of the Popular Front. The front was one of the ways in which Stalinism—which already was responsible for so much damage to the "honor of socialism"—further perverted socialism.[26] Also, Local 544's leaders saw that the Popular Front was a facade behind which Communists assaulted the Trotskyist movement. In the cases of the Moscow trials and the Stalinist liquidation of the POUM in the Spanish civil war, these assumed a particularly ugly form. The alliance between the Farmer-Labor party and Local 544 thus required reassessment if the Farmer-Laborites linked themselves to the Popular Front. As the Communist party entered a new political phase in the mid-thirties, so too the American Trotskyist movement had new dynamics that impinged on the movement's state-level and local alliances.[27]

By the end of 1937 the Farmer-Labor party faced a different political environment than it did in 1936, when Elmer Benson won a landslide vote. National events created by national actors, including the aggressively interventionist NLRB, generated pressures on the party's labor base to reorganize itself. The party's labor base quickly responded. New interests—reinforced by sectarian tensions peculiar to Minnesota—cut across the old interests of labor and old loyalties to the Farmer-Labor party. The party's leadership faced a new, difficult set of strategic and tactical problems.

The Counterattack on the New Deal

Several other factors—also rooted in national policy change—worsened these new strategic and tactical problems of the Farmer-Labor party's leadership. The turmoil in industrial relations in 1937 and 1938 created an incentive, and an opportunity, for capitalist elites opposed to the New Deal to expand their public influence.[28] In and of itself such turmoil would have aroused business alarm. But business reaction to this turmoil was framed by the increasing distance between the New Deal and business elites, a distance that had been building for two years. Before the 1936 election a host of policies—the Social Security Act of 1935, the establishment of the Works Progress Administration (WPA), which portended an expanded role for government in the labor market, the Public Utilities Holding Company Act, and the tax measures of 1935 and 1936—contrasted with business demands for a "breathing spell" from the New Deal. Of these measures perhaps the Revenue Act of 1936 generated the most intense opposition. Its tax on a corporation's undistributed profits encroached on the key business prerogative, autonomy over the disposition of profits, in a fundamental way. In addition to these measures there was Roosevelt's leftward movement in the 1936 campaign. He capped off attacks on wealth and privilege with a rousing speech at Madison Square Garden on 31 October 1936, defiantly stating, "I should like to have it said of my first Administration that in it the forces of selfishness and of lust for power met their match. I should like to have it said of my second Administration that in it these forces met their master."[29] The scope of conflict between the New Deal and its economic and political opposition was thus unusually wide at the outset of Roosevelt's second administration.

Roosevelt's confrontational stance had potentially serious implications for a state-level, radical third party. Because it invited a counterattack that had to focus in the short run on the 1938 congressional and state elections, the autonomy of state-level political elites from national political conflict could easily be reduced. A confluence of other political, institutional, and policy changes added to the incentives and opportunities for counterattack against the New Deal.

The Supreme Court's *Jones & Laughlin* decision of April 1937 was a major social and political event. *Jones & Laughlin* took an important first step toward institutionalizing the social vision behind the Wagner Act. A fundamental social purpose of the act was redistribution of wealth and power to labor. When Senator Wagner explained that the act meant to enlarge freedom, he meant exactly that. For him and for other enlightened politicians the facts of industrial life in America were disturbing, even shocking. They detested company towns, labor espionage, and the para-military groups that did the bidding of corporate executives.

Thus *Jones & Laughlin* administered a huge defeat to antiunionism. True, the bloody "Little Steel" strikes proved that antiunionism was still kicking. *Jones & Laughlin* was nevertheless a critical juncture in American social and political history.[30]

After *Jones & Laughlin* there was a jump in union strength, as table 8.2 shows, during a "strike wave," and a remarkable leap in the number of sit-downs—1937 was the high point in American labor history for sit-down strikes.[31] These events and trends raised worrisome prospects for economic and political elites opposed to or ambivalent toward the New Deal. How much power would labor in general and labor radicals in particular acquire under the aegis of a now constitutional NLRB? How far left would America go? For all business could tell, labor might continue to acquire power under federal protection. In a few years the entire landscape of American politics might be completely different.[32]

Particular aspects of the NLRB's behavior in 1937 and 1938 sharpened such issues: (1) the board's activist effort to shape industrial relations on terms favorable to labor, (2) the rapid growth of its staff, and (3) its unusually successful record after *Jones & Laughlin* in the courts. These touched on both the political and economic interests of American economic elites.

In 1937, and much more effectively in 1938, prominent spokesmen for business interests—journalists, senators, legal counsel of major corporations, business executives—began talking up the need for a fairer approach to industrial relations, for "equalizing" the Wagner Act. Amendments for this purpose began appearing in Congress.[33]

If economic elites were to push for reforms of the Wagner Act in the 1938 elections, or for state-level labor-relations acts, they could do worse than to appeal for help from the AFL and the state federations. These organizations developed an interest in amending the Wagner Act and in establishing state labor-relations statutes tailored to their needs.

Aspects of both the Wagner Act and the NLRB's behavior not only troubled business but also the AFL. In 1937 and 1938 the NLRB strictly interpreted the Wagner Act's clear prohibition of employer influence over workers' choice of unions. This strictness led the board to disestablish AFL unions set up through collusion with an employer. Sometimes the board acted at the CIO's request, since both employers and the AFL often hoped to preempt the establishment of a CIO union. Obviously the board's disestablishment of AFL unions infuriated the federation. It demonstrated that the Wagner Act could harm the federation's organizational interests.

Differences between the NLRB and the AFL broke out into the open in fall 1937. The federation's general counsel, Joseph Padway, warned the board that if it continued to damage the federation's interests, "either the law will be changed to conform with the Railway Labor Act [which explicitly protected craft organization] or labor will work vigorously for the abolition of the Board and we will get along as we did before the Wagner Act was in existence."[34]

This rift between the AFL and the NLRB had a serious political consequence: it led the federation to develop a political alliance with capital and the Republican party in order to push for the Wagner Act's reform. There was a convergence of interests. Both business elites and the AFL shared an interest in amendment of the Wagner Act. In 1938 Republican leaders, sensing an opportunity and responsive to a new generation of politicians, openly bid for labor's support. The AFL, for its part, came out against the undistributed-profits tax in the Revenue Act of 1936. As the elections approached, the movement against the Wagner Act and its supposed maladministration, and against the political influence of apparently ubiquitous radicals, gathered strength. Here the press played a role. National magazines, radio commentators, and important newspapers attacked the NLRB for its pro-CIO and leftist biases, a charge that first emerged as early as summer 1937.[35]

Other aspects of national politics provided incentives and opportunities for the New Deal's opposition to solidify and to extend a rightward trend in public opinion in preparation for the 1938 state-level and congressional elections. In 1937 Roosevelt unveiled a court-packing plan, a plan to reorganize the executive branch, and a plan to establish seven regional authorities for planning use of natural resources. These events and proposals implied a sharp expansion of presidential power and an introduction of planning and bureaucracy. With the dissipation in early 1937 of a sense of crisis—both elite and public opinion agreed that "the emergency was over"—Roosevelt's actions brought to the fore an issue that had simmered since 1933: whether Roosevelt was a would-be dictator. Roosevelt now could plausibly be pictured as such, hostile both to the Supreme Court and to Congress's rightful place in government.[36] This was likely to cost him support in rural areas and small towns, the constituencies advantaged by congressional elections.[37]

Given the approach of midterm elections and the potential for anti–New Deal, antiradicalism issues to emerge in these elections, the Roosevelt Recession of 1937–38 became more than just an economic event. It became a test of the political gains registered in the 1936 elections. It was perhaps possible for the recession to become an occasion for the administration to stage a repeat of the Hundred Days. How the administration actually handled the recession instead reinforced the impact on public opinion both of other events in 1937 and of the efforts of Republican and business elites to shape opinion.

The Roosevelt Recession began in August 1937. At first, the Roosevelt administration sought to retain business confidence by adopting the orthodox, accumulationist response of balancing the budget. But business cared less about the budget than it cared about taxes. Roosevelt's orthodoxy was greeted with hostility and derision. When the recession deepened, Roosevelt decided on a deliberate policy of deficit spending. That policy response of course deepened the gulf between the administration and business, which Roosevelt unsuccessfully sought to bridge through orthodoxy. Roosevelt's eventual Keynesian response underscored that the New Deal was not a temporary, emergency phenomenon and that its tax policies might truly recast government-business relations in America. Roosevelt perhaps hoped to recapture the mystique of crisis and emergency of spring 1933 by calling Congress into a special session for handling the recession. But Congress proved far more recalcitrant in fall 1937 than in spring 1933. The possibilities for a grand consensus between the presidency and Congress faded quickly. Roosevelt could not mask the political-economic significance of the Keynesian response he eventually adopted. His decision to spend signalled that the administration, far from turning back from the balancing political economy it had done so much to establish, intended to deepen it.

The administration's reactions to the recession cost it support in another way. Because it initially sought orthodoxy, it lost valuable time, and as a result the recession hit the country harder than it might have otherwise. Industrial production fell by a third, and unemployment rose by nearly four million. Farm income dropped by 23 percent, the income of farm proprietors by 27 percent.[38] The recession created the potential for an early case of mass discontent with the welfare state, especially since Roosevelt had publicly claimed credit for the recovery that registered by 1935 and 1936. Also, when welfare-state services are first rapidly expanded, their average quality seems likely to drop and to generate voter disappointment with the welfare state. The implementation of old-age assistance and unemployment insurance in 1938 was shaped by federalism and state politics, leading to disarray in their implementation. In addition, there was a considerable residue of anti-WPA feeling that had built up in 1936.[39]

Public opinion seemed responsive to Congress's sympathy with business and to the claim that the energizing powers of business needed to be released by government's stepping back from economic intervention.[40] Suddenly business regained the political high ground. Roosevelt was sensitive to its claims, but because taxes, not budget balancing, were a key focus of business opposition to the New Deal, his effort to narrow the scope of conflict between the New Deal and business failed.[41]

In this political economic context, in the context of the campaign to revise the Wagner Act, in the context of the 1937 strike wave and the outbreak of sit-downs, public opinion shifted to the right rather easily. In 1937 and 1938 public opinion polls revealed considerable hostility to, among other things, sit-downs and the CIO.[42] Of that percentage of the public that had an opinion about the NLRB (34%), the overwhelming majority (92%) believed it to be partial to the CIO.[43] In May 1938, 62 percent of the public thought that the Wagner Act should be either revised or repealed. By November 1938 that figure increased to 70 percent.[44] In June 1937 the Gallup poll found that 50 percent of the public had changed its attitude toward unions. Of this 50 percent, 71 percent said they were "less in favor" of unions.

The Gallup poll found in mid-June 1938 that 72 percent of the public wanted the Roosevelt administration to become more conservative in the next two years.[45] It also found an increase in the percentage of people saying that they intended to vote Republican in the midterm elections.[46]

Newspapers around the country carried extensive coverage of the Dies Committee, the House investigating committee that sought to expose radicalism in American political life, particularly left-wing radicalism. It is perhaps no accident that Orson Welles's "War of the Worlds" radio broadcast of October 1938 sparked a national panic despite the clear announcement that it was a fictional radio play. By then, 77 percent of the public owned radios.[47] Fear of subversion was literally in the air.

The Crisis of State-Level Radicalism

The Farmer-Labor party faced a crisis in 1937 and 1938 that seems odd in two respects. By 1936 the party had achieved political success in several areas of public policy, and in 1936 it reached a new level of electoral power.

Governor Olson guided the 1933 session of the Minnesota legislature through a burst of activist policy making. The legislature adopted an income tax and a tax on chain stores, reduced the property taxes of farmers (producing the "homestead exemption"), passed a moratorium on farm mortgage foreclosure proceedings, established a state old-age pension system, and created a consolidated open primary ballot, long a Farmer-Labor demand. Also, during an extra session of the 1933 legislature, additional monies for public relief were appropriated. While Olson and the conservative faction that dominated the 1935 session of the legislature did not produce major new initiatives, Olson did block this faction from adding a regressive sales tax to the tax system, which he had worked so hard in 1933 to make more progressive, and he successfully pressed the legislature to reform and improve the administration of the state's old-age pension system. Finally, in 1934 Olson turned the Minnesota National Guard into a pro-labor instrument.

However, despite their electoral and policy achievements the Farmer-Labor party's leaders found themselves increasingly hemmed in by changes in their political environment. New Dealers in Washington successfully pushed the American political economy toward becoming a balancing political economy. Electoral realignment, in part, gave them the power to do this. In the 1934 off-year elections the Democrats gained even more strength in Congress than in 1932. This was the only time during the twentieth century that the party of a presidential administration gained during off-year elections. In 1936 Roosevelt won reelection in a landslide.

But the power that the New Dealers had to change the American political economy also came from governmental capacities. New Dealers successfully used existing governmental capacities, and, as in the case of the NLRB, they rapidly created new capacities.

The successful implementation of new public policies created new forms of politics. New policies found new clients within the interest-group systems of rural and industrial society. The AAA, for instance, empowered the Minnesota Farm Bureau and other state farm bureaus. As John L. Lewis recognized at the founding convention of the Congress of Industrial Organizations, the Wagner Act empowered the CIO.[48] These changes in the pressure system of American politics created special problems for the Farmer-Labor party.

The positive short-run impact of the Wagner Act on labor's strength in and of itself created a problem for the Farmer-labor party. Once the Farm Bureau became the dominant interest-group actor in rural Minnesota, rather than a group with an explicitly farmer-labor ideology such as the Farmers Union or the Farmers Holiday Association, any expansion of labor's strength in 1937 and 1938 probably meant rural-urban electoral tensions. Floyd Olson's performance in rural areas in the 1934 elections was a harbinger of such tensions.

The impact of the Wagner Act also complicated the party's relationships with organized labor. The party's labor base reorganized itself in 1937, splitting into left and right wings. Left-sectarian tensions within Minnesota labor exacerbated this split. Two revolutionary socialist factions, Communists and Trotskyists, enjoyed significant levels of strength in the Minnesota labor movement. Yet international ideological dynamics made them increasingly bitter enemies.

Because the Farmer-Labor party controlled the governorship, its actions in any labor dispute or in matters affecting the labor movement were likely to become the focus of intense scrutiny by labor leaders and to provoke sharp disapproval somewhere within the labor movement. The difficulty of maintaining good relations with the feuding leaders of a divided labor movement came at a time when the party needed as much electoral strength in urban areas as it could get, because of the likelihood of rural-urban tensions.

We know that in presidential elections labor leaders do not strongly influence the electoral behavior of voters who belong to trade unions, much less voters who do not belong. But the degree of unity and enthusiasm among labor leaders for a state or local slate of candidates, or a congressional candidate, has far more influence on the outcome of a nonpresidential election, simply because the constituency is smaller and the marginal cost of stimulating the electorate to vote a certain way is thus lower.

If the Farmer-Labor party had been a presidential party, the changes in its interest-group environment might not have been as constraining as pictured. But in the smaller constituency of state politics the proportionately greater capacity of interest groups to shape voter behavior and public opinion necessarily posed special strategic and tactical problems for the electoral and policy-making strategies of Farmer-Labor politicians.

The change at the national level to a balancing political economy also created in 1937 and 1938 what might be called a capitalist backlash. Throughout America the previous balance of power between capital and labor changed. Economic elites mobilized to check the course of this change. This mobilization established an ad hoc alliance with the conservative faction of the AFL and tightened links with the Republican party in preparation for the upcoming state-level and congressional elections in 1938. As a state-level party with a tenuous hold on the Minnesota legislature and lacking the greater administrative and fiscal resources of the national government, the Farmer-Labor party was not in a very good position to face firm, united opposition from economic elites and to counter their investment in state-level electoral contests.

America's first experience with welfare-state discontent during the Roosevelt Recession also posed problems for the Farmer-Labor party. To the extent that the national climate of public opinion created by the New Deal's problems shaped state-level opinion, questions of image and competence became acutely important for the party's leaders. Polls suggested that the public was in a conservative mood, dissatisfied, it seemed, with policy experimentation and political change. Yet policy experimentation and political change were the essence of the Farmer-Labor party's ideology and politics.

Not only the New Deal created problems for the Farmer-Labor party, but also the party's leaders had created problems. Environmental constraints converged at a moment when internally the Farmer-Labor party was prone to petty factionalism. This weakness was a legacy of the party's reorganization in the 1930s, which also left the party vulnerable to a good-government consensus against it.

Further, the Farmer-Labor party needed to adapt itself to new, inexperienced leadership, the result of poor handling, by the party's middle-level leaders and Floyd Olson, of the task of finding a successor for Olson. Despite his landslide victory in 1936 Elmer Benson had yet to define his relationship to middle-level leaders in the Farmer-Labor party. He was an unknown quantity to labor leaders and farm-group leaders. Nor did he have a network of friendships—as Olson had—joining him to prominent businessmen in the Twin Cities. To be sure, Benson was well connected with outstate small-town bankers. But links to the Twin Cities business community were probably crucial for the Farmer-Labor party, if only because they tended to keep the party's elite opposition somewhat disunited.

In short, the Farmer-Labor party's leadership faced quite new and very demanding strategic and tactical problems in 1937 and 1938.

NINE

The Dynamics of Collapse

Between January 1937 and November 1938, the Farmer-Labor party's top leadership somewhat successfully pushed the Farmer-Labor program forward. Governor Elmer Benson, however, worsened the problems that the national political environment posed for the party. The result was crippling factionalism. The disarray among the Farmer-Labor leadership, coupled with a rightward drift in public opinion, created opportunities for Republican political entrepreneurship. A new Republican candidate for governor, Harold Stassen, upstaged the Republican Old Guard and fashioned electorally useful alliances with discontented Farmer-Labor elites. As if following the Hotelling-Downs model of party politics, Stassen adopted Farmer-Labor issues while also developing potent campaign themes and symbols for tapping the public's apparently conservative mood.[1] The results of this strategy were disastrous for the Farmer-Labor party.

One consequence of the party's troubles has been that secondary accounts of Elmer Benson's governorship regularly treat him as an inept politician, yet his good qualities and policy successes should not be overlooked. He had a distinctive, "moralist" style of leadership, resembling Woodrow Wilson or Adlai Stevenson. Indeed, Benson acquired a national reputation as a crusading progressive. For instance, he got the University of Minnesota Board of Regents to reopen the case of William Schaper, a supposedly disloyal professor of political science removed from his position as chairman of the University of Minnesota Political Science Department during World War I. Benson adopted other similar causes during his term in office.[2]

Benson learned quickly how to do things that had symbolic value to labor, such as denying to Pinkerton's its license to operate in Minnesota because it conducted labor espionage. He worked hard as a labor strike conciliator and did not hesitate to use his control of the National Guard on labor's behalf.

Benson sought to build support for the Farmer-Labor party in politically conservative dairy-farming areas by pushing for a tax on butter substitutes. He pushed for and won legislative relief on the property-tax burden through amendment of the Homestead Exemption Act. He projected alternatives to national farm programs, calling the Minnesota Farm Conference and lobbying Roosevelt for new farm policies. The Minnesota Farm Conference proposed farmer-labor cooperation, cost-of-production, attention to tenant farmers, and a national policy of handling mortgage indebtedness based on a revision of the Frazier-Lemke Act, earlier invalidated by the Supreme Court.

When the Roosevelt Recession began, Benson travelled to Washington to urge Roosevelt to embark quickly on a fiscally expansionist policy. He had a shrewd analysis to offer. He sensed that Roosevelt stood a good chance of saving the New Deal's forward momentum if he boldly embraced Keynesianism.

Finally, Benson successfully pushed forward Floyd Olson's program for making Minnesota's tax system more progressive and for using it to curb chain stores and mail order houses. Benson's tax program amounted to the sharpest, most politically controversial attack on corporate and personal wealth in Minnesota that the Farmer-Labor party ever made.

Benson made real progress on delivering or lobbying for substantive policies that would benefit the constituencies for whom the Farmer-Labor party spoke.

Benson also made a decision with enormous negative consequences for the Farmer-Labor party. He turned his administration into a Popular Front government, somewhat like Leon Blum's Popular Front government in France. He built on a significant agreement that his predecessor, Floyd Olson, made with the Communist party. Before he died, Olson allied the Farmer-Labor party with the Popular Front policy of the Comintern.[3] His immediate successor in office, Lieutenant Governor Hjalmar Petersen, continued the agreement.

Benson built on Floyd Olson's policy in four ways. It is not hard to guess why Benson extended the Popular Front agreement. Several of the Communists and Popular Fronters with whom Benson worked were witty, well educated, young, and gifted. They evidently provided a sense of political camaraderie. Also, Benson's extension of the Popular Front agreement may well have served key needs for an inexperienced politician commanding a complex organization. Through appointment policies over three administrations, Floyd Olson dried up his successor's opportunities for placing his own loyalists throughout state government. Having a special set of loyalists may have helped Benson to keep tabs on the organizations and agencies he led.

First, Benson let Communists and Popular Fronters into the Farmer-

Labor administration, giving them bureaucratic power. Also, his executive secretary was quite sympathetic to the Communist party. Second, Communists had considerable influence in designing the Benson administration's strategy toward the state legislature. Third, Benson showed sympathy for the strong relationship between the CIO and the Communist party in Minnesota. Finally, he supported the Communist party's foreign policy. In particular Benson allied himself with Congressman John Bernard of Minnesota's eighth district, who deeply involved himself in aiding the Loyalist side in the Spanish civil war.[4]

Benson's use of the Communist party proved enormously divisive within the Farmer-Labor party just when it most needed elite unity. Benson's policy deepened the new splits in the Farmer-Labor party's labor base and generated intense factionalism. The party's elite cohesion deteriorated, in a staccato succession of crises described below. Eventually, the cohesion of the Farmer-Labor elite shattered completely.

The People's Lobby

A turning point in Benson's administration came in early April 1937, amid a constitutional stalemate. The issue behind the deadlock was whether the Minnesota senate would approve Benson's progressive tax program. It was elected in 1934 and therefore was unchanged by the 1936 electoral tides. Also, its constituency was mainly rural. As a result of how the conflict played itself out, Benson faced hostility among the senate's Farmer-Laborites, not to mention its Republicans.

In his inaugural address to the Minnesota legislature, Benson told it that it must reshape state-level relief programs: "The new obligations which government must assume require additional expenditures. We may as well face the issue frankly."[5] Benson ruled out two sources of revenue, bond issue and property taxation. Circumstances confined Benson to the course he chose. The property tax burden was already excessive in rural Minnesota. In addition, Minnesota was highly indebted, in part the product of the Republican bailout of the state banking system in the early '20s through the establishment of the Rural Credits Bureau, an agency that acquired millions of dollars' worth of poor farm loans. Highway construction and relief expenditures also indebted the state during the Olson administration.[6] Minnesota faced a fiscal crisis if it planned to meet its relief needs. The only way out was politically very difficult: taxation of iron ore. Here Benson reiterated one of the key demands of the Farmer-Labor coalition, a demand it had first articulated with some political success in the early 1920s.

In suggesting a "substantial increase in iron ore taxation" Benson proposed political regulation of an institution that the legislature historically hesitated to regulate. This was U.S. Steel, whose subsidiary Oliver Mining Company ran Minnesota's production of iron ore. The legislature previously taxed iron ore in the early 1920s, in response to farmer-labor strength in the legislature. Now Benson asked the legislature to tax iron ore again, but he faced a likely constitutional obstacle. The house would follow him, but the senate (elected in 1934, before the 1936 pro-Farmer-Labor swing) would not. Also, the postelection illness of the Farmer-Labor lieutenant governor further reduced Benson's potential influence over the senate.[7]

In order to get out of this dilemma Benson and several Farmer-Labor leaders decided to stage a mass protest at the state capitol. This was the People's Lobby. In the early '30s, at the height of the agrarian protest in the Midwest, a farm demonstration played a role in the passage of the Minnesota Mortgage Moratorium Act. A repeat of this type of protest, it was hoped, would pressure the senate to act favorably on the administration's tax program. An important influence in the planning of the People's Lobby was the Communist party.[8]

Unfortunately for Benson, the confrontation between the senate and the People's Lobby on April 5 was raucous, leading to an overnight sit-down in the senate chamber. This sit-down enraged Minnesota's political and journalistic elites. There were calls for Benson's impeachment, and the senate brought criminal charges against four People's Lobbyists. On April 6 the senate prevented the capitol custodial staff from cleaning the chamber, in order to display its disorder. Benson, characteristically, held his ground and attacked criticism of the incident. The People's Lobby assured the senate's intransigence for the rest of the regular session and guaranteed a special session bound both to be acrimonious and to focus public attention on Benson's executive style. Benson's apparent recklessness also startled a bloc of Farmer-Labor senators.[9]

Battles in the Minneapolis Farmer-Labor Party

A second major crisis was shaped by the local impact of national divisions in the labor movement. It exploded even as the Benson administration planned and staged the People's Lobby. Left-sectarian splits emerged within the Minneapolis Farmer-Labor party in winter and spring 1937, in anticipation of the June Minneapolis mayoral contest.[10] Over the weekend of February 27 and 28 the Hennepin County

Farmer-Labor Association met to select a slate for Minneapolis's mayoralty and the city council. A squabble erupted over whom to nominate for mayor. Local 544 and several Farmer-Laborites faced off against Communist delegates on whether to renominate Thomas Latimer, the incumbent Farmer-Labor mayor. His jumpy, violent use of police against pickets during the strikes of summer 1935 made him unpopular among many trade unionists, facilitating a Communist-led revolt. In response to this Communist success, the AFL and Trotskyist leaders held a rump convention on March 14 to protest Communist influence in the nominating process. The convention nominated Latimer, a case of "the enemy of our enemy is our friend," since the Trotskyists had heaped scorn on Latimer in 1935, holding a mock trial of his actions.[11]

Benson intervened, pleading for unity and establishing a negotiating team to bring the two conventions together. Nothing happened. The state Farmer-Labor Association then ruled Latimer the officially endorsed candidate, only to reverse itself in favor of the "regular" nominee, Kenneth Haycraft.[12]

Soon Haycraft and Latimer staged a bitter primary battle. During their bout the Trotskyists attacked Haycraft as a tool of Stalinist influence. They also sought to label him a strike breaker for having served in the National Guard during the 1934 truckers' strike.[13] Haycraft won the primary, but little time remained for regrouping the Farmer-Laborites. His Republican opponent, George Leach (a former mayor who entered politics by defeating Minneapolis's Socialist mayor, Thomas Van Lear), adopted Latimer's charge that "Reds" dominated the Farmer-Labor party. The Communists staged a get-out-the-vote effort for Haycraft as the campaign wound up, but by this time Haycraft was leery of Communist support and publicly repudiated it. Haycraft lost the election.[14]

Leach, in any case, was a particularly dangerous candidate for the Minneapolis Farmer-Labor party. In the middle and late 1920s he enjoyed support in working class wards. A residue of good will and name recognition surely helped him. The Minneapolis mayoral contest in 1937 thus showed how a combination of the AFL-CIO split and left sectarianism could damage the Farmer-Labor party. AFL and CIO unionists, Trotskyists, and Stalinists carried their dispute into the Minneapolis Farmer-Labor party. They did bury their differences to unite behind Haycraft in the general campaign. The factionalism nevertheless made it easier for Leach to win. Throughout this entire process the Farmer-Labor party's top leadership proved unable to control labor's divisions and left-sectarian disputes in Minneapolis.

The Split within the Minneapolis Machinists

Soon another crisis—structured by the massive reorganization of the labor movement underway in 1937—tested the Farmer-Labor leadership. In late August 1937 the Communist leadership of three Minneapolis machinists locals took their membership into the CIO, joining UE, an event referred to in chapter 8.[15] The AFL insisted in July that the Minneapolis Central Labor Union expel its CIO delegates. This order provided the occasion for the bolt to UE. How did the Benson administration react to this new split?

At the end of September Trotskyist leaders joined the State Federation of Labor leadership in sending a delegation to Governor Benson to discuss the split. Benson met with over seventy trade union leaders in the chamber of the Minnesota senate, now out of session. Patrick Corcoran of the Teamsters Joint Council, William F. Wright, general organizer of the AFL in Minnesota, and George Lawson, secretary of the State Federation, officiated. Benson suggested negotiation between the IAM and UE; the labor leaders rejected this suggestion out of hand, following an outburst by Robert Olson, head of the Duluth Federated Trades and Labor Assembly, that the Communist leadership of the UE locals could not be trusted. The meeting ended with Benson unable to satisfy the conference completely.[16]

On October 1 a rally was held at the Minneapolis Armory to attack the Communist leadership of UE. In the aftermath of this rally relations between Governor Benson and the Trotskyists soured. The *Minnesota Leader*, the Farmer-Labor newspaper, attacked Vincent Dunne in an October 9 editorial. It called him an "apostle of mob violence" and demanded from him proper gratitude to the Farmer-Labor party. The party made his career as a labor organizer possible through the restraint it showed during the 1934 truckers' strikes. In response, the Trotskyist-edited *Northwest Organizer* called Benson "irascible" and "sore," eager "to run to his paper and petulantly scribble an editorial."[17]

Soon the *Minnesota Union Advocate*—which during the '20s, when it was edited by William Mahoney, supported the Farmer-Labor party—issued steady criticism of Benson's Popular Front policy. It ran a series of slashing articles by O. R. Votaw, secretary-treasurer of District 77 of the IAM, a former Communist and founder of the Farmer-Labor Federation who became sympathetic to the Trotskyism that his former colleagues, the Dunne brothers, adopted after they all left the Communist party in 1928.[18] Votaw, a talented polemicist, warned that the CIO and the Communist party were already in control of the Hennepin County Farmer-

Labor Association and soon would control the entire Farmer-Labor party. "The blight of Stalinism is attacking the Farmer-Labor Party from above and below . . . The ward clubs are being stuffed with communists and their sympathizers . . . Already there is disaffection among trade unionists throughout the state; and it is not to be forgotten that these are the people who built the party along with the oppressed farmers."[19]

Votaw argued that the Communists cared nothing at all for the Farmer-Labor party: in the '20s they attacked the Farmer-Labor party, now they supported it, and tomorrow, if it suited Stalin, they would attack the Farmer-Labor party again. Votaw also contended that the Communist party hoped to capture the Farmer-Labor party in order to build the CIO and "to break up the established labor movement as represented by the American Federation of Labor."[20] Here Votaw referred to his discovery that the director of personnel of the state Highway Department rented the office next to his to a CIO organizer, a discovery he brought to the attention of the Executive Council of the State Federation of Labor.[21] The presence of a CIO organizer in the state Department of Highways offices coincided with the CIO's effort to raid a machinists local (of garage mechanics) working in the Highway Department. Votaw warned trade unionists "to be on guard against the super-militants, loud-shouters, and super-progressives who gnaw out the 'innards' of every organization where they get a footing."[22]

Factionalism was emerging among Farmer-Labor elites, induced by the state and local impact of the New Deal's labor policies. New ideologies and organizational struggles hardly mixed well with the labor movement's historic ties to the Farmer-Labor party. The events of September and October 1937 indicated that the Farmer-Labor leadership either could not or would not transcend splits in the labor movement.

The Politics of an Assassination

Overlapping the fall 1937 crisis over UE's raid of the IAM was yet another crisis. Shortly before midnight on November 17 Patrick Corcoran of the Teamsters Joint Council was found dead outside his home.[23] An anonymous assailant assassinated him about an hour and a half before.

Suspicion and fear spun through the labor movement. The *Minnesota Union Advocate* went so far as to imply that "a lot of ordinary hoodlums who have been trying to propagate the John L. Lewis brand of unionism in the Twin Cities" were responsible for Corcoran's assassination.[24] James Cannon, the leader of the American Trotskyist movement, hinted that the

Soviet secret police had a role in the murder or at least in the political capital being made of the murder.[25] Communist trade unionists, showing an appetite for left sectarianism, rapidly moved to exploit Corcoran's murder for political purposes and circulated broadsides claiming that "Trotskyite inspired gangsterism" was responsible for Corcoran's assassination.

In order to clear up the charges of gangsterism, a delegation of Trotsky-ists and other AFL unionists met with the Farmer-Labor attorney general, William Ervin. It requested that he appoint a special investigator. Ervin pleaded a lack of funds and steered the delegation toward the Bureau of Criminal Apprehension.

Governor Benson did post a reward of $500 for information leading to the killer's apprehension and later claimed that he sought to prevent the murder when a fearful Corcoran approached him shortly before it.[26] Within Local 544 some may have felt that the Benson administration approved of the Communist effort to exploit the gangsterism issue.[27] And the administration reward was a fraction of the Teamsters Joint Council reward.

State Federation of Labor leaders became concerned over how Twin Cities elites used the issue to discredit the labor movement. Off in Chicago, the *Chicago Tribune*, which had a history of attacks on Farmer-Labor leaders, responded to Corcoran's assassination by attacking the "radical government of Minnesota" for tolerating lawlessness. In St. Paul an indus-try group, the Committee on Industrial Relations, sought to focus public attention on "labor racketeering."[28] Elite reactions to such problems in the farmer-labor coalition were somewhat ominous, in part because by this time Benson had soured relations with elite supporters of the Farmer-Labor party, such as Floyd Olson's friend, Richard Lilly of the First Na-tional Bank of St. Paul. Benson permitted a break-up of an informal semitruce that Floyd Olson had managed to achieve with Twin Cities elites.

By the end of 1937 Benson had exacerbated basic problems facing the Farmer-Labor party. Benson seemed hot, radical, and pro-Communist just when the party needed cool pragmatism. He deepened labor's political disunity just when he and the party most needed a united labor movement.

The Revolt of Hjalmar Petersen

The Benson administration's troubles were tailor-made for an electoral challenge to Benson. While serving out the rest of Olson's term Hjalmar Petersen, Floyd Olson's lieutenant governor, skirmished often with Benson forces in the party.[29] In January 1938, after several months of "respectable gentlemen muttering that Hjalmar Petersen is the man who will save us," Petersen announced his candidacy, despite efforts within the party to coax him out of a fight with Benson.[30] His battle cry was his intention to fight Red influence in the Farmer-Labor party.

Petersen's challenge initially attracted the Trotskyists, not so much because they liked Petersen but because it permitted criticism of Benson.[31] The St. Paul trade union press was more circumspect. Nevertheless, the *Minnesota Union Advocate* continued to run O. R. Votaw's editorials.[32]

The St. Paul faction and the Trotskyists perhaps expected that their support for Petersen would give them influence at the convention of the Farmer-Labor Association. It was scheduled to meet in March in Duluth, a stronghold of the Minnesota CIO. The 1938 Duluth convention was the first time that the Farmer-Labor Association ever met outside the Twin Cities.

The Benson administration and Popular Front forces within the Farmer-Labor party had complete control of the Duluth convention, seeming to leave Benson's critics with no place to go but Petersen's campaign for winning the postconvention Farmer-Labor primary in June.[33] As time passed, however, Petersen's candidacy became much less attractive. One cannot say that Petersen himself was anti-Semitic, but he did allow his campaign to acquire anti-Semitic overtones. The Farmer-Labor party was full of disgruntled job seekers, the fruit of many struggles over patronage. It seemed significant to some of these malcontents that there were Jews in positions of influence within the party and in state government, such as the editor of the party newspaper and Benson's executive secretary.[34]

A second feature of Petersen's campaign was its corporate support. Benson alleged that money from U.S. Steel went to Petersen, via Arthur C. Townley, the former leader of the Nonpartisan League. Petersen himself solicited corporate money.[35]

Thus for a brief period it looked as if Petersen would assemble a coalition of business, anti-Semitic grumblers and agrarians, and Trotskyists and AFL trade unionists who distrusted Benson's alliance with the Communist party. By May, shortly after Petersen's keynote address, labor bolted from his coalition. The *Northwest Organizer* accused Petersen of deepening tensions between farmers and the party's labor base. In St. Paul a special labor committee for Benson became quite active. Previously quarrelling factions in organized labor closed ranks behind Benson against Petersen, helping Benson to win a narrow victory on June 20—Benson defeated Petersen 51.9 percent to 48.1 percent. Turnout was 117 percent greater than in the 1936 primary. As an open primary the Farmer-Labor primary saw Republican crossover voting—Petersen enjoyed an enormous amount of support within the Republican hierarchy.

Although the AFL, the CIO, Communists, and Trotskyists united behind Benson, the experience did not mend divisions in the Farmer-Labor party. The Communists, through their curious logic, came away from the campaign believing that the Trotskyists' support for Benson was really intended "to injure Benson . . . it is they who have by their terroristic methods alienated farmers, cooperators, and small merchants from the labor and Farmer-Labor movement." This was part of the Trotskyist plan to promote fascism.[36] The Communists' argument seems also to have echoed the politics of the Corcoran assassination, for in May 1938 Bill Brown, one of the heroes of the 1934 truckers' strikes, was gunned down by an insane member of Local 544. The Twin Cities press seized on the Brown murder as further evidence that labor needed to clean up its house.[37] The Communist attack on the Trotskyists was based on the correct assessment that the Brown murder had a sharp effect on public opinion, but the Communists apparently implied that the event was part of a deliberate plan to undermine Benson.

For their part, the Trotskyists scorned the platform adopted at the Duluth convention. They considered it insufficiently radical—an outcome they attributed to the requirements of the Popular Front. They also asserted that Communist "paper" organizations wielded disproportionate influence at the Duluth convention, partly disfranchising the Trotskyist and AFL labor base of the party.[38] The State Federation of Labor, too, saw the issue as one of disfranchisement. And it was keenly aware of Benson's growing lack of popularity among rank-and-file trade unionists.[39]

Even as the primary heightened splits in labor, businessmen enraged by the Benson administration had the satisfaction of having practiced an electoral mobilization against the Benson administration. Their effort paralleled the counteroffensive against the New Deal all across the country. In Minnesota this mobilization had an unusual level of ideological cohesion. Major figures in the Twin Cities economic elite became attracted to native fascist movements, such as the Silver Shirts. There seems to have been a sense among a small but somewhat influential clique of businessmen and highly conservative Republicans that "Commie Jews" were threatening to take over Minnesota. Such paranoia first emerged in the wake of the 1934 truckers' strikes; far from dissipating, it became stronger.[40]

Worse for the Farmer-Laborites, business's trial run against Benson in the Farmer-Labor primary taught business that his grasp on power was tenuous. Benson's command of his party did seem rather weak, for Benson and Petersen could not effect a rapprochement. The anti-Semitic overtones of Petersen's campaign deeply wounded the editor of the *Minnesota Leader*, Abe Harris, who already hated Petersen for other reasons, and he refused to retract anti-Petersen statements. Petersen, for his part, would not compromise or apologize for the tone of his campaign. He may have suspected that Benson supporters plotted to assault him one night as he came home to his apartment.[41] During the campaign he made a point of travelling with an armed guard, supposedly to protect himself from members of the Communist-led relief-workers organization, the Workers Alliance.[42] In any case, Petersen refused to endorse Benson, although he did not disavow the party. His attitude was "let the people decide."[43]

Small wonder that the *Minnesota Union Advocate,* looking ahead to the general election in November, warned Benson that the "Farmer-Labor Party has the fight of its political life."[44]

Stassen and Farmer-Labor Factionalism

No sooner did Benson best Petersen in the primary than he faced another challenger just beginning his remarkable political career, Harold Stassen.[45] Stassen developed a campaign for the governorship that relied on and exploited tensions among the Farmer-Labor party's elites.[46] His campaign also made the most of the electorate's apparently conservative mood.

Stassen profited from the Petersen-Benson split that remained after the June 20 Farmer-Labor primary. A bloc of Petersen supporters, led by Petersen's campaign treasurer (who was the Farmer-Labor senator most offended by the People's Lobby), formed a special election committee. This committee voted an endorsement of Stassen. Petersen encouraged these supporters—he appeared at their convention and left it as if on cue moments before its endorsement of Stassen.

Besides benefitting from the splits among Farmer-Labor elites, Stassen deepened Farmer-Labor factionalism. He adopted a labor program strikingly close to the policy preferences of AFL leaders. He promised never to use the National Guard against striking workers, adopting Farmer-Labor policy as his own. He also claimed that he was serious about a merit system for the state civil service. During the 1937 legislative session Benson ignored the State Federation of Labor civil service bill and promoted his own unsuccessful bill.[47] A civil service policy was in the interests of the increasingly powerful state employees and highway employees organizations. Stassen claimed that he would implement a state labor-relations law modelled on the Railway Labor Act of 1926. In 1938 AFL leaders around the country tended to find the act appealing. Unlike the Wagner Act, it had the signal virtue of explicitly recognizing craft jurisdiction. Thus Stassen built a version of the AFL-Republican alliance that appeared elsewhere in America.[48]

In an obvious reference to the State Federation of Labor—which disavowed the Michigan sit-down strikes of 1937—Stassen spoke admiringly of the "responsible" labor leaders of Minnesota. He offered his labor policy as a way to promote labor peace and to protect labor's best interests. Stassen obviously meant to tap the now visible rift between the State Federation and the Benson administration. In 1936 the Minnesota State Federation of Labor endorsed the entire Farmer-Labor slate; in 1938 it endorsed only Benson. At its Mankato convention in September, which Stassen attended and addressed, "there was a visible undercurrent of resentment against using the State Federation as a vehicle for partisan tactics."[49] William Green, president of the AFL, publicly endorsed the Republican opponents of four Farmer-Labor congressmen.

Stassen also knew that the State Federation of Labor worried about the strike wave that coursed through Minnesota in 1937. By 1938 there was public concern in Minnesota about the business climate: there were highly publicized industry decisions during Benson's term to locate new plants outside of Minnesota. These were instances of the classic capital flight or threat of capital flight that has always constrained efforts to design redistributive tax policies. Labor leaders seemed to share the public's concern about capital flight, for obvious reasons.[50]

The keystone of Stassen's strategy for deepening the splits in the Farmer-Labor elite was keeping the Red issue on the public agenda. Was Benson a Communist? Were there really Communists in the Farmer-Labor party? The Red issue had been around for over a decade, but it popped up more and more during the campaign. Often it acquired an ugly and anti-Semitic tone, as in a booklet, *Are They Communists or Catspaws?*, which had a circulation of about thirteen thousand and was produced by Ray Chase, a former state auditor and congressman who was Floyd Olson's opponent for the governorship in 1930. Chase circulated the pamphlet to every candidate for the state legislature and to most of Minnesota's Catholic and Protestant religious leaders.[51]

The culmination of this strategy for exploiting Farmer-Labor factionalism occurred in Washington, D.C., on 17 October 1938. At 10:30 in the morning Congressman Martin Dies gavelled to order a hearing, according to an arrangement Dies worked out with a figure in the Stassen campaign, former Republican mayor of St. Paul, Mark Gehan. Several Farmer-Laborites were there to testify about Communist influence in the Farmer-Labor party. The Farmer-Labor delegation was a living museum of the party's factionalism. By mid-October 1938, shortly before the election, the elite cohesion of the Farmer-Labor party had literally dropped to zero in a highly visible setting, a congressional investigation that captured public attention.[52]

Stassen and the Electorate

Elite disarray within the Farmer-Labor party, in the larger context of the Roosevelt Recession and the apparent disorder of public life in 1937 and 1938, alone would have weighted the outcome of the 1938 elections toward Stassen. But Stassen also developed an electoral strategy that deserves detailed discussion.

Stassen made the most of the increased strength of the Minnesota Farm Bureau. He promised to promote those state programs especially attractive to prosperous commercial farmers, 4-H Clubs, agricultural research, and the like. And his labor policy certainly appealed to farmers alarmed at labor's growth, which included reaching out from the Twin Cities to organize farm-cooperative personnel in 1937 and 1938.[53]

By adopting key Farmer-Labor policies, such as the party's National Guard policy, and by campaigning in industrial workplaces, Stassen moved to his left to attract discontented or not particularly ideological voters who under other circumstances might well have voted Farmer-Labor. He reinforced this movement with, among other themes, his "labor peace" theme, which probably attracted voters on both the left and right of Minnesota's ideological spectrum. In July 1937 a national poll found that 89 percent of the public favored legislation that provided for cooling-off periods before strikes could be called.[54]

Taking advantage of well-publicized contracting scandals, Stassen also developed a rich, "throw the rascals out" theme with a strong good-government component. Stassen thus tapped the potential for an anti-Farmer-Labor, good-government issue, which the Farmer-Labor party itself created. The Republicans had mishandled the issue in 1935, but in 1938 they handled it well. Stassen called for a revolt of the "reasonable middle." "The time has come when the voters of the state must take a temporary vacation from their party and unite in a crusade to bring about a wholesale and necessary change in our state government."[55]

Stassen promised a civil service merit system and an end to the bossism of the Farmer-Labor party's leaders: "These selfish masters of the machine will stop at nothing to deny the voice of the people . . . They will crack the whip like Simon Legree over the employees of the public payrolls."[56] Although not explicitly tied to attacking the New Deal, this "throw the rascals out" theme probably profited from the recent and general discontent with the welfare state.

Finally, Stassen tailored specific appeals for use in urban and rural areas that were historically Farmer-Labor or contested ground. For one thing, he appealed to the mix between politics and Catholicism in such areas as St. Paul, whose population was roughly one-quarter Irish Catholic, and certain rural counties with German Catholic populations. He attacked the pro-Loyalist foreign policy of two Farmer-Labor congressmen, thereby reflecting the growing alarm of the Archdiocese of St. Paul over Communism and events in Spain.[57]

In short, a figure whose only previous electoral experience involved running for county attorney in Dakota County, next door to St. Paul, mounted a truly formidable campaign. Yet in 1937 many Republican politicians assumed that it would be impossible to unseat the Farmer-Labor party and therefore backed Petersen in the 1938 Farmer-Labor primary![58]

Ironically, the Benson campaign only reinforced the unanticipated strengths of the Stassen campaign. Benson mishandled the Red issue, although there is probably little he could have done. In one particularly dramatic incident on the eve of the election, the Stassen campaign was able to disprove a Benson denial that he had been standing next to a youth wearing insignia of the Young Communist League while he participated in a New York City "peace parade." That the Minnesota CIO endorsed the full Farmer-Labor slate and that the Communist party clearly supported his campaign only added to Benson's difficulty. A national poll found in September 1938 that a CIO endorsement would turn 55 percent of the public away from a candidate, while an AFL endorsement made no difference to 53 percent of the public. Benson had the endorsement of both labor federations, but the public probably perceived him as having only CIO backing and Stassen as having AFL backing.[59]

One of the bigger mistakes of the campaign was Benson's obvious use of the WPA for electoral purposes. Benson's effort to politicize the WPA had a certain logic to it. He strongly believed in the political mobilization of the unemployed, seeing them as a potentially very radical group in politics, and thanks to the Roosevelt Recession, there were more unemployed in 1937 and 1938 than there had been in some time. But there were grave difficulties with the strategy. First, the unemployed resented being used for partisan purposes, as a 1938 poll of their opinion showed. Second, the rural unemployed were very difficult to mobilize where local relief officials went out of their way to stigmatize them publicly. Third, public opinion, particularly rural opinion, was deeply hostile to the politicization of relief.[60]

Relief, in any case, was associated in Minnesota with threats to public order and had been since 1934, when several thousand men on work relief staged a riot in Minneapolis to protest the shutdown of the Civil Works Administration (CWA). This threat to public order seemed to worsen. The People's Lobby was part of a tide of protest by the unemployed that swept through the country in the 1930s and peaked in 1937, when relief workers all across the country protested relief cutbacks undertaken by the New Deal in the name of economy.[61]

As with New Deal farm and labor policies, which created new political dynamics, new public policies for the unemployed generated patterns of protest politics that, in turn, created tactical and strategic problems for state-level politicians. During the Roosevelt Recession relief recipients could easily be pictured as pushy, politically exploitive people. There was very little political capital in championing or mobilizing those on relief, and a lot to lose by doing so.

The 1938 Election: A Critical Experience

On election day the Republicans routed the Farmer-Labor party. As one Farmer-Labor county campaign worker reported, "Hurricane! struck here."[62] Stassen won 678,839 votes, matching Benson's presidential-year tally of 680,342; Stassen won 59.9 percent of the vote. The Farmer-Labor party won 59.3 percent of the statewide gubernatorial vote in 1930, 50.6 percent in 1932, 44.6 percent in 1934 (a plurality victory), and 60.7 percent in 1936; it won only 34.2 percent in 1938.

Table 9.1 presents aspects of the Farmer-Labor party's county-level performance in gubernatorial contests in the 1930s. Two figures for each election measure central tendencies of the electorate. The table also presents the standard deviation of the average, county-level differences. The dispersion around the mean in each case was relatively low, suggesting uniform movement in the counties toward or away from the Farmer-Labor party. The figures for 1938 show a great deal of uniform movement away from the Farmer-Labor party across all counties.

Seven out of the nine congressional races went Republican, and one to a

TABLE 9.1 Farmer-Labor Party Performance in Gubernatorial Elections, At Count-Level 1930–38

Year	Mean of Farmer-Labor Vote across Counties (%)	Mean of Differences, One Election to Next, per County (%)	Standard Deviations from Mean of Percentage Difference
1930	60.9		
1932	51.6	−9.4	12.1
1934	42.1	−9.5	6.9
1936	59.9	+17.8	7.4
1938	31.7	−28.1	5.7

Source: Bruce M. White et al., comps., *Minnesota Votes: Election Returns by County for Presidents, Senators, Congressmen, and Governors, 1857–1977* (St. Paul: Minnesota Historical Society, 1977), pp. 191–97. Calculations by the author.

Democratic incumbent. Only one Farmer-Labor incumbent, out of eight running, won reelection. Every single state executive office up for reelection went Republican. This resulted in a rich irony, the election to the office of attorney general of J. A. A. Burnquist, whose use of the Commission of Public Safety during World War I did so much to forge the farmer-labor coalition in 1918. The legislature was overwhelmingly Republican after the election.

The election of 1938 was a realignment away from the Farmer-Labor party toward the Republican party.[63] With the exception of St. Louis County, where the CIO was strong and Benson did rather well in comparison to his performance elsewhere, turnout dropped in urban areas. But in 80 percent of the rural counties it jumped.[64] As in 1934 there was a rural backlash against the Farmer-Labor party, but it was much stronger in 1938.

Rural areas that were historically loyal to Farmer-Labor gubernatorial candidates went Republican. Zingale has identified twenty-seven rural counties that in 1918 became more loyal to the Farmer-Labor party. In 1932, 100 percent of these counties stayed in the Farmer-Labor camp; in 1934, 78 percent of them stayed Farmer-Labor; in 1936, 96 percent of them voted Farmer-Labor; and in 1938, all of them, 100 percent, voted for Stassen. Of the ten additional counties that Zingale identifies as developing loyalties towards the Farmer-Labor party in 1918 and renewing them in 1932, 80 percent voted for Stassen. Of the eight other counties that

Zingale identifies as having become more pro-Farmer-Labor party in 1932, 87 percent voted for Stassen in 1938.[65]

Urban wards and precincts historically loyal to the Farmer-Labor party voted for Stassen. Of Minneapolis's thirteen wards, nine were generally loyal to Farmer-Labor gubernatorial candidates earlier in the 1930s. Of these 44 percent voted for Stassen in 1938. In St. Paul, ten of the twelve wards tended to be loyal to Farmer-Labor gubernatorial candidates in the 1930s. Of these ten 30 percent voted for Stassen. In Austin, site of the 1933 Hormel sit-down, 37 percent of the previously loyal precincts voted for Stassen; in South St. Paul, previously strongly Farmer-Labor, 60 percent of the loyal precincts voted for Stassen; in Albert Lea, where half the precincts were loyal earlier in the 1930s, 83 percent of the historically loyal precincts voted for Stassen. Even in Duluth support for the Farmer-Labor party dropped. St. Louis County, where Duluth is located, was strongly pro-Benson in 1938. Between 1930 and 1936 71 percent of Duluth's voting precincts were pro-Farmer-Labor; of those, 65 percent remained pro-Farmer-Labor in 1938.[66]

The origins of the realignment away from the Farmer-Labor party were in the crisis that the New Deal created for the party. Between 1933 and 1936 the New Deal changed the interest-group organization of rural and industrial society. An anti-Farmer-Labor agrarian group, the Farm Bureau, grew stronger, facilitating a turn toward conservatism in rural opinion. That turn first became manifest in Minnesota in 1934. Also, the Minnesota labor movement acquired a faction somewhat hostile to the Farmer-Labor party. Then institutional and policy changes after Roosevelt's reelection in 1936 prompted new patterns of interest-group and party organization. The Wagner Act solidified the AFL-CIO split. The strike wave of 1937 and relief demonstrations deepened rural-urban tensions. The administration's mishandling of the Roosevelt Recession promoted an early case of mass discontent with the welfare state. Amid this discontent the Republican party, as the party of opposition, reconstructed itself in preparation for the 1938 elections. All of these changes posed very difficult problems for an inexperienced Farmer-Labor leadership, problems it either worsened or could not handle.

To gauge from the collapse of such coalitions as Frank Murphy's in Michigan and Governor Earle's in Pennsylvania, both industrial states with farm populations, it appears that a common set of forces was at work. The Michigan Democratic party as a gubernatorial coalition was a one-man operation between 1936 and 1938—Murphy was very vulnerable to splits in labor, to growing rural discontent with labor, relief, and the

New Deal, and to public ambivalence about his courageous handling of the Flint sit-down. The disruptive impact of the transition to a new political economy felled him. In Pennsylvania, severe tensions between the AFL and the CIO and public debate over the politicization of work relief badly undermined the Democratic party just when it had reached its peak of strength.[67]

The 1938 election was a critical experience that had long-lasting effects on Minnesota politics. Following the 1938 election the Minnesota Farmer-Labor party was unable to capitalize on the small lift in its percentage of the gubernatorial vote. Nor did interest in a national Farmer-Labor party for the 1940 presidential contest help it. In 1938 several other farmer-labor parties, including the only other electorally powerful state-level third party, the Wisconsin Progressive party (whose history I discuss briefly in chapter 10), also collapsed. The Minnesota Farmer-Labor party thus lacked "effective reserves outside the state to call upon for help."[68]

The Farmer-Labor party died in 1944 after several years of continuing factionalism, within the party itself and in the labor movement. Shortly before the 1944 election, the party merged with the Democratic party, creating the antecedent of today's Democratic Farmer-Labor party. The merger resulted from processes unleashed by the Farmer-Labor party's collapse between 1936 and 1938. The collapse was like a railroad switchman, tracking the party toward eventual disappearance.[69]

From 1938 on, the Republican party dominated Minnesota politics. It elected the governors until 1954, and until 1946 it controlled by a wide margin the state's congressional delegation, since Henrik Shipstead converted to the Republican party in 1940, along with the sole surviving Farmer-Labor congressman. The remaining Farmer-Labor senator, Ernest Lundeen, died in a plane crash in August 1940.

Not until 1954 did the Democratic Farmer-Labor party reduce the Republican contingent in the House of Representatives to a minority of four. Hubert Humphrey was elected to the Senate in 1948, but it was not until 1958, when Eugene McCarthy was elected to the Senate, that the Democratic Farmer-Labor party came to control the state's senatorial delegation.

Thus, as the national Democratic party brought a new political order into being, Stassen and the Minnesota Republican leadership brilliantly exploited the tensions that the birth of a new political order generated. They delayed Democratic realignment in Minnesota. Not until the 1950s were Democratic politicians able to establish the hegemony that in many state and local jurisdictions came with the new political order of the 1930s.

TEN

State-Level Radicalism and Political Change

State-level radicalism, as a type of politics, foundered because there was more power in Washington to shape the political economy than in a state capital. What happened in Washington changed what could and could not be done among the states, the counties, and the cities. What was once possible—including state-level radicalism—became impossible, or at least very difficult.

A basic source of the power that national politicians possessed in the 1930s for shaping the political economy was national electoral change, which permitted Democratic control of both the presidency and Congress. In 1934 the Democrats increased their strength in Congress rather than following the more typical pattern of losing strength in midterm elections, and in 1936 Roosevelt won a second term with a landslide vote. Such national electoral change also emboldened New Deal Democrats to pressure the Supreme Court into validating the constitutionality of New Deal legislation.

Power to shape the political economy also came from governmental capacities for implementing public policies. These capacities were crucial to the policy impact of electoral change and resulted from "state-building" processes in the late nineteenth and early twentieth century, during World War I, and during the Hoover administration, most notably the establishment of the Reconstruction Finance Corporation. Their existence made it possible for New Deal Democrats to design, among other policies, relief for agriculture and regulation of industrial relations.

The prior development in America of a relatively densely populated system of interest groups mediated the impact of the New Deal's public policies on politics at the state and local levels. Political entrepreneurs in the interest-group systems of rural and industrial society responded to the opportunities for organizational growth presented by new public policies and shaped the development of the party systems of state and local jurisdictions. New groups with new interests and ideologies emerged, complicating the governing and consensus-building strategies of established party politicians. The relatively smaller size of the constituencies of these jurisdictions enhanced the influence of interest-group entrepreneurs on public opinion and electoral behavior. The new and successfully implemented national policies created at the state and local levels new patterns of competition for power, new organizations, new institutions, even new political attitudes. They disorganized and scrambled older patterns of conflict, older organizations, older institutions, older attitudes.

A factor that added to these constraints was national awareness of the strains of macroeconomic management and political change. The Roosevelt Recession, the administration's vacillation in reacting to it, and the eventual response it chose all created political opportunities for the Republican party. So too did sit-downs, relief protests, court-packing, and executive reorganization. In response a younger generation of Republican politicians willing to adapt to the New Deal was able to mount formidable challenges, in Minnesota and elsewhere, to the politicians who rose to power earlier in the 1930s.[1]

State-Level Radicalism in Canadian Perspective

To test my analysis of how and why state-level radicalism became limited, let us place the Minnesota Farmer-Labor party's history in cross-national, comparative perspective. As a type of politics state-level radicalism was not unique to the United States. There were nearly a dozen cases of similar organizations on both sides of the United States–Canadian border.[2]

In the late Teens and early Twenties radical agrarian movements and farmer-labor coalitions formed and won power in three of the (then) nine Canadian provinces, Alberta, Manitoba, and Ontario, serving as the base for a national Progressive movement. Although they grew much weaker in the late 1920s, they laid the basis for a second wave of province-level radicalism in the 1930s.

In 1932 a Farmer-Labour party emerged in Saskatchewan and in 1934 affiliated with a national protest movement that grouped several small parties and interest groups together, the Cooperative Commonwealth Federation (CCF). The Saskatchewan Farmer-Labour party became the Canadian Cooperative Commonwealth Federation–Saskatchewan Section.

The CCF acquired power in 1944 and governed Saskatchewan for two decades. In 1961 it participated in a national reorganization of left-radical politics in Canada, sponsored by the trade unions, which led to the establishment of the New Democratic Party (NDP). The NDP's founders aimed to create a nationally competitive party. By 1987 the NDP had won, at different times, power in three of the ten provinces. In 1987 and 1988 it seemed within striking distance of forming a federal government.[3]

These Canadian patterns are so different from the American patterns that one may wonder whether province-level and state-level radicalism are really comparable types of politics. There are major differences between the political histories of Canada and the United States—differences in constitutional forms, political culture (Americans are more individualistic and less communitarian in their attitudes), number of jurisdictions in the system of dual sovereignties, size of the electoral universe, the political salience of linguistic minorities, the impact of racial conflict on political development, and involvement in world military and political conflict.

There are also relevant similarities. Both Canada and the United States are social and political fragments of British society and politics. In both cases elites in eastern metropolitan regions guided the development of "colonial" regions geared toward cash crop production and natural-resource extraction. In both cases the diffusion of political parties from east to west meant weaker parties in the west. Finally, federalism is highly developed in both Canada and the United States.

Given these relevant similarities, a question emerges: why did the CCF's leaders solve the tasks of political entrepreneurship better than the Minnesota Farmer-Labor party's leaders? The answer is: in the Canadian context they could.

Political change in America closed off the possibilities of state-level radicalism. Political change in Canada kept open the possibilities of province-level radicalism. The differences between the national context of the CCF and that of the Minnesota Farmer-Labor party were critically important to the differences in outcome of these two similar cases.

The National Context of Province-Level Radicalism
The national context for CCF politics in the 1930s and 1940s was the establishment of Canada as a nation and the Great Depression. In 1867, under the British North America Act (BNA Act), Canada achieved a combination of autonomy from Britain and actual nationhood. This act provided for a strong central government, yet by the 1930s this feature of Canadian institutions had changed. Reflecting a strongly centrifugal economic regionalism that the tariff and railroad policies of the federal government exacerbated in the late nineteenth century, the provincial governments became much stronger vis-à-vis the Dominion than the drafters of the BNA Act intended.

The BNA Act intended strong central government in part out of economic nationalism and in part because its framers feared United States "manifest destiny" and the political consequences of American railroad building. They worried also about the extent of United States militarization during the Civil War. Three institutions or devices permitted central control of provincial governments: federal disallowance of provincial legislation; federal appointment of the lieutenant governor of a province, who had the power to withhold assent to provincial legislation and to "reserve" legislation for the federal government's approval; federal appointment of the judges of provincial superior courts.

To assure provincial political weakness the BNA Act also curtailed the fiscal base of provincial governments by reserving to them only the power to levy direct taxes, then the most unpopular and least used tax. In contrast, the Parliament of Canada was permitted to raise "Money by any Mode or System of Taxation."[4]

By 1930 a major shift in the federal distribution of power occurred, despite Canadian involvement in World War I, which exercised a brief centralizing effect. Provincial governments achieved a nearly coequal status with the federal government. Their tax powers grew considerably through judicial interpretation of the BNA Act. Even though one of the purposes of the BNA Act was to make the federal government the principal institutional framework for economic growth, provincial government achieved parity in this area. The Dominion-Provincial Conference of 1927 symbolized the new state of affairs. At it, the premiers of two of the wealthiest provinces, Ontario and Quebec, jointly proclaimed their belief in a "compact" theory of federalism.[5]

Political responses in Canada to the Great Depression did not alter this federal distribution of power. The Depression hit Canada nearly as hard as it hit the United States, and harder than several already ailing western European economies. But with the exception of certain pieces of federal agricultural legislation, the Dominion did not become an activist government.

Between 1929 and 1933, gross national product in Canada fell 42 percent in current dollars, 29 percent in constant dollars. Industrial activity dropped to almost half the average between 1925 and 1929. Unemployment rose to about 23 percent from a low of 3 percent in 1929. Because of Canada's dependence on exports, the Depression battered agriculture. Income from agriculture in the three prairie provinces dropped nearly 100 percent.[6]

The Conservative government that came to power in the 1930 federal elections, when the incumbent Liberal government was turned out, reacted to these problems quite late during its administration. In 1930 the Conservative candidate for prime minister, R. B. Bennett, campaigned against his Liberal opponent, Mackenzie King, by attacking the Liberals for "timidity and vacillation." But apart from establishing work-relief camps and subsidizing provincial relief expenditures, the Bennett administration did rather little for four years. The Dominion's preoccupations were defense of the currency, budget balancing, and maintenance of public order, through often illiberal use of the army and the Royal Canadian Mounted Police against unions and the organized unemployed.[7]

Still, in 1934 the Bennett administration passed several important measures for regulating agriculture: the Natural Products Marketing Act, for stabilizing agricultural prices; the Farmers' Creditors Arrangement Act, which permitted farmers to enter into compromise arrangements with creditors under the supervision of a government board; the Farm Loan Act, for easing agricultural credit; and the Prairie Farm Rehabilitation Act, intended to help in the reclamation of abandoned farmlands by providing funds for experiment stations.

On the eve of the 1935 federal election the Conservatives turned their attention to workers. In a series of radio addresses to the nation in January 1935, an unprecedented use of the medium, the prime minister called for a new and activist role for the federal government. His party enacted a series of measures that included the Employment and Social Insurance Act, the Minimum Wage Act, the Limitation of Hours of Work Act, and the Weekly Rest in Industrial Undertakings Act. Rounding out this activism was the establishment of a Wheat Board for the orderly marketing of Canada's most important agricultural export.[8]

The Bennett New Deal was rejected in the federal elections of 1935. Making a comeback, Mackenzie King charged Bennett with assuming dictatorial powers and with enacting a program that he knew would be ruled unconstitutional. Whatever support Bennett might have gained from his program was apparently lost to protest parties on his left. The Liberal party, then more conservative (in American, New Deal terms) than the Conservative party, won control of Parliament with a vote of 1,955,727 to the 1,311,459 that the Conservatives won, the remaining 1,139,668 being divided up among other smaller parties. When Mackenzie King became prime minister, he referred the Bennett New Deal to the Supreme Court of Canada for an advisory opinion. The Supreme Court held most of it unconstitutional, except for the farm mortgage adjustment legislation. (The Wheat Board and other farm legislation was not submitted to the Supreme Court.) Its holdings were sustained by the final court of appeal, the Judicial Committee of the Privy Council, a kind of imperial supercourt based in London. The main basis for these holdings was that the Dominion had invaded the powers of the provinces and exceeded its powers. Although the Judicial Committee of the Privy Council during World War I had upheld centralizing Dominion legislation on the basis of emergency power, it held that no extraordinary circumstance justified the legislation of the Bennett New Deal. With that, the weak impulses toward Dominion activism died out until the late 1940s.[9]

There may have been power in Ottawa to shape the political economy, but national political elites did not find it or expand it. History shaped their options: there was no sustained history of national political elites doing anything activist beyond tariff and railroad policies. In contrast, a national center of power based on such institutions as independent regulatory commissions and cabinet agencies staffed by civil servants with a "will to intervene" had been slowly built in Washington since the Civil War. American political elites had a history of using power in Washington to shape the political economy, and this made a critical difference to the possibilities of the reformist coalition that we call the New Deal.[10]

Consequences of National Context for CCF's Politics

In a sense it is not surprising that "no full-length scholarly study of Canada during the Depression exists."[11] Unlike the New Deal, fed by a stream of young technocrats trained by specialists in administrative law at the elite law schools, no cluster of modernizing politicians and bureaucrats descended on Ottawa during the 1930s.

What were the consequences of Dominion inactivity for the CCF in Saskatchewan? The constraints on and inactivity of the federal government meant that the basic tasks facing the CCF's leaders were winning province-level power and parliamentary representation. The rewards of solving these tasks were great. If they won province-level power, they reaped the considerable policy-making advantages of a parliamentary system. Also, because there were only nine provinces, even a small amount of parliamentary representation gave them agenda-setting power in Ottawa.

Here, of course, the CCF enjoyed structural advantages that the Minnesota Farmer-Labor party lacked during the 1930s. The fragmented institutions characteristic of state government and the sheer size of Congress made it harder to implement policies at the state level and to set the national agenda. But how important would the CCF's structural advantages have been if the Bennett New Deal had succeeded?

One task that faced the Minnesota Farmer-Laborites did not face the CCF's leaders: reacting to a shifting national political environment. Because there was no move toward a balancing political economy, based on public policies designed and implemented at the political center, the interest-group politics of Canada's rural and industrial society were not changed in ways that might have complicated the tasks facing the CCF's political entrepreneurs. They enjoyed a degree of stability in their political environment.

In the 1940s, during Canada's involvement in World War II, some centralization did occur. For instance, the provinces delegated tax powers to the federal government through temporary "tax-rental" agreements between the Dominion and the provinces. Dominion-provincial diplomacy also yielded agreement that the Dominion should undertake a national policy of unemployment insurance. But the tax rentals were temporary. And in addition to Parliament's legislative processes, Dominion-provincial diplomacy was (and still is) a key federal policy-making process.[12]

When the CCF came to power in Saskatchewan in 1944, it was able quickly to do concrete things for its constituencies.[13] As Seymour Martin Lipset stressed in his magisterial case study of the CCF, the CCF did things for which there was already a rough consensus among all party elites in Saskatchewan. The CCF did not fundamentally challenge the power of already organized groups. Rather, it acted to entrench their power. What is striking about the CCF's actions in office is how much a provincial government was able to do, unconstrained by the national government or by the unintended consequences at the province level of federal public policies. The main constraints facing the CCF were internal to Saskatchewan society and politics, not external to it.

The CCF passed collective-bargaining legislation that Lipset rightly called "the most pro-union legislation in the democratic capitalist world."[14] Among other provisions it included the right to expropriate the property of companies that refused collective bargaining. It promoted trade union organization in the Saskatchewan civil service. Trade union strength in Saskatchewan advanced rapidly, at a pace over four times the national average for Canada as a whole between 1943 and 1947. The CCF protected farmers against foreclosure and eviction. It promoted health insurance. It increased old-age benefits. It established a series of publicly owned businesses, acting on the power of provinces to set up crown corporations. Although primarily tokens of the possibilities of public ownership, these crown corporations provided jobs in poor areas of Saskatchewan.

Federalism placed certain limits on the CCF. The Mackenzie King administration sought to embarrass the CCF by demanding immediate and full payment on a category of provincial debt owed to the Dominion, refusing interest-bearing provincial treasury bills as payment. This demand was particularly clever because the CCF government very much wanted to avoid alienating rural opinion by raising taxes. Disallowance was another way in which federalism constrained the CCF. Petitions for disallowance of the farm security legislation and other legislation were filed in Ottawa. Yet most of the CCF's activism survived intact, including the basic features of the farm security legislation. And the debt payment crisis was resolved satisfactorily.

The main short-run and medium-run constraints on the CCF were internal to Saskatchewan. For example, because the CCF could not afford to alienate organized farmers, it did not counteract the effects of its farm security legislation on the rural class structure. The legislation made it more difficult for tenants to acquire property, since no farmer could lose his land under the legislation. More radical members of the CCF favored cooperative farming, but their plans received short shrift from their party. To the extent that the CCF promoted cooperatives it, like the Minnesota Farmer-Labor party, promoted the marketing cooperatives of well-to-do, propertied farmers.

CCF leaders also faced tensions between farmers and workers. Its labor legislation was so advanced that a rural backlash set in. Also, pressure on the province to operate crown corporations efficiently—pressure that came in part from the fiscally conservative agrarian side of the CCF coalition—led to conflicts between CCF-appointed managers and the work forces that they managed.

But these were problems and tensions in the CCF coalition *that the CCF itself created* and that it could resolve or paper over in various ways if it chose to. The CCF was as constrained as the Minnesota Farmer-Labor party by organized interests. Interest groups constrained the Farmer-Labor party because of the small size of its constituency. So too they constrained the CCF. In both cases groups were more powerful as jurisdictions grew smaller, but the CCF could shape and react to these interests on its own. Continuous exogenous change of the behavior of these interests did not confront the CCF with constantly shifting strategic and tactical choices and dilemmas.

As a result in large part of a national context very different from the

Minnesota Farmer-Labor party's, the CCF was able to survive and to play a continuing role in setting provincial and national policy agendas. The survival of the CCF, later the NDP, is one of the most important reasons why Canada has more prounion labor legislation than the United States. The CCF's advanced labor legislation in Saskatchewan has slowly been diffused to other provinces and to the federal level. That legislation, in turn, is a major (although by no means the only) factor in the greater strength of trade unions in Canada than in the United States. This development has helped social democratic politics in Canada to weather the 1980s rather well, even as this type of politics has become weaker in many other advanced industrial democracies. The CCF's survival and transformation into the NDP has thus also played an important role in setting provincial and national agendas on welfare policy and government ownership of key industries. "Contagion from the left"—the partial or complete adoption by more conservative politicians of left programs in order to overcome electoral insecurity—has been for some time an important factor in Canadian politics, while it has played at best a trivial role in American politics since 1935 and 1936.[15]

The Case of the Wisconsin Progressive Party

The state-level impact of the American political economy's transformation not only undercut the Farmer-Labor party's strength in 1937 and 1938 but also disorganized, as we saw, governing Democratic farmer-labor coalitions in such states as Michigan and Pennsylvania. What about other cases of state-level radicalism, in particular, the Wisconsin Progressive party?[16] Like the Minnesota Farmer-Labor party, it stressed aid to agriculture, including making milk distribution a public utility, abolition of the labor injunction and regulation of labor based on the Wagner Act, social security, and liberal provisions for welfare and relief. One faction of the party pressed for public ownership of industries and organization of the economy around the principle of "production for use."

Although the Minnesota Farmer-Labor party inspired the formation of the Progressive party, the special importance of the La Follette family in organizing Wisconsin's politics during the first third of the twentieth century meant that the Wisconsin Progressive party differed from the Minnesota Farmer-Labor party. The Progressive party, formed in March 1934, was actually a hybrid of two organizations: the La Follette organization and a coalition patterned after the Minnesota model.

The La Follette family created and maintained its own organization during the first third of the twentieth century. It was a loose collection of local notables, often young liberal lawyers. The La Follettes maintained it through their special method of campaigning, that is, delivering long speeches to gatherings throughout the state and eschewing the use of radio; through keeping a secret list of their supporters; and through publication of the *Capital Times* and the *Progressive*.

The second organization housed within the Progressive party was the Farmer-Labor Progressive Federation. The federation, which strongly resembled the Minnesota Farmer-Labor Federation founded by William Mahoney in the 1920s, was a coalition of the Milwaukee Socialist party, the Wisconsin State Federation of Labor, and liberal farm groups.

These two organizations did not coexist easily. The federation's leaders disliked the primary, that hallmark of progressivism. They sought to get the party's professional politicians to abide by a convention-created platform and to live with the principle of preprimary endorsements. They also sought to establish a statewide organization. Philip La Follette vigorously resisted these innovations. He restricted the federation to its local bases of strength, Milwaukee and smaller industrial cities. He also controlled the platform-writing process in order to maximize his chances of election.

The behavior of Philip La Follette thus played a determining role in the party's history. When he launched a national third party in 1938, National Progressives of America, he split his own organization down the middle, weakening the party during its 1938 campaign.

Nevertheless, the national context also played a key role in the collapse of the Wisconsin Progressive party in 1937 and 1938. The split between the AFL and the CIO damaged a labor-supported party. It weakened the Farmer-Labor Progressive Federation. In the changed environment for labor its leaders in Wisconsin focused more on their new organizational interests than on political campaigning.

The AAA did not affect Wisconsin directly, because few farmers signed up for milk-production control. But the national failure of the cost-of-production alternative to the agricultural crisis of 1933–34 meant that the Wisconsin Farmers Holiday Association quickly weakened, as it did elsewhere. By 1937 and 1938, the Wisconsin Agriculture Council, which represented conservative farmers, was roughly twice as strong as the Farmers Equity Union, a pro-Progressive group. The council was hostile to the wave of labor organization that swept through Wisconsin as elsewhere.

Finally, Wisconsin Republicans connected Governor La Follette to the dictatorship issue that began sticking to Roosevelt in 1937 and 1938. The tactics that the Progressive-dominated bloc in the Wisconsin legislature adopted in the 1937 special session in order to meet Governor La Follette's agenda led to a dramatic revolt at the close of the session. Opposition legislators staged a walkout in which they mockingly gave the La Follette bloc that defeated them the Nazi salute.

Republican charges of dictatorship marked the 1938 campaign. Julius Heil, the millionaire-turned-politician who captured the Republican nomination in a surprise primary win, also campaigned on an "economy" plank. The impact on public opinion of Roosevelt's court-packing plan and of other aspects of the dictatorship issue, in combination with the Roosevelt Recession, gave Heil the power with which to turn the Progressive burst of activism during the 1937 legislative session into a political liability. Earlier in the 1930s the Progressives' tactics in the special session might not have had the same impact on public opinion.

On election day Heil won 55.4 percent of the vote, while La Follette won only 36 percent. The Democratic candidate gained 8 percent. In 1934 and 1936 La Follette was elected with votes of 39.1 percent and 46.4 percent in three-way races. In both 1934 and 1936 Progressives competed in all ten of Wisconsin's congressional districts, and in both years seven Progressives won. In 1938 only two Progressive candidates for Congress won election, out of ten competing.

After the 1938 elections the Farmer-Labor Progressive Federation collapsed. The Progressive party continued to compete until 1946, even electing a governor in 1942, Orland Loomis. Loomis died shortly after the election, leaving the term to his Republican lieutenant governor. He intended, in any case, to merge the Progressive party with the Republican party. Just as in Minnesota, the events of 1937 and 1938 added up to a critical experience that permanently weakened the Progressive party.

Adapting to National Political Change

In May 1935 the *New York Times* published a report on Minnesota and Wisconsin politics. "The American State sometimes seems to be an artificial thing, whose political boundaries become increasingly meaningless. In Wisconsin and Minnesota one sees that this conception is not wholly sound." State-level radicalism in the 1930s revealed that the states possessed political and policy-making capacities that had been underestimated.[17]

Even as the Minnesota Farmer-Labor party and the Wisconsin Progressive party unearthed new possibilities in the structure of American politics, that structure changed. A regime change occurred, in the sense that the mix of possibilities for types of politics and types of political strategies changed.

As a previous and older political order changes, what can the politicians created by that order do to delay, guide, or adjust to change? What could the Minnesota Farmer-Laborites or the Wisconsin Progressives have done?

In the case of the Minnesota Farmer-Labor party, one thing that might have helped was better planning for Floyd Olson's succession. The party's inner circle could have planned leadership recruitment, over and above the Farmer-Labor youth clubs it established. But bad luck played a role here, since Olson did not discover that he was seriously ill until late December 1935. In any case, Olson "refused to groom a successor, partly for fear of creating a rival."[18]

Farmer-Labor and Progressive leaders could have developed a strategy for shaping their national political environment. Here they had two options: Congress and the party system.

A bloc of Minnesota Farmer-Labor, Wisconsin Progressive, and other legislators formed in Congress, prefiguring the caucuses and study groups of today's Congress. As James Lorence has shown, it was a very active bloc. It clashed often with the House leadership over House procedure, committee assignments, and domestic and foreign policy.[19]

The history of the Lundeen Bill captures some of the uses of Congress for the politicians of state-level radicalism. In early 1935 the institution was a useful forum for Farmer-Labor congressman Ernest Lundeen, who astutely used his assignment to the subcommittee on unemployment insurance of the House Labor Committee to publicize his plan for unemployment compensation. By calling for government- and employer-funded compensation to workers equal to wages lost through unemployment, whatever figure that might be, the Lundeen Bill, the "Workers' Bill for Unemployment and Social Insurance," directly challenged the budget-balancing orthodoxy to which Roosevelt paid lip service. Lundeen thus proposed a policy that was highly countercyclical, generous, and fiscally open-ended. And in a boldly decentralizing stroke the Lundeen Bill provided that local workers' and farmers' councils would administer these unemployment compensation funds to unemployed workers.

At the time the bill was actually a chip used by the chairman of the House Labor Committee to maximize his influence in the House. Also, the Townsend Plan was seen as the alternative to the New Deal's social security plan. But the Lundeen Bill did play a role in casting the terms of debate on social security. Hearings were held on the bill, the House Labor Committee reported it out of committee favorably, and it served as the basis for a defeated amendment to the Social Security Act when Congress voted on the act.[20]

The basic limits of the House of Representatives for the politicians of state-level radicalism are revealed by the history of the Lundeen Bill. While the House Labor Committee reported it favorably, the bill never received a rule, and a discharge petition to give it a rule received few signatures. In any case, the Democratic leadership of the House had raised the number of signatures needed for a successful discharge petition. In short, power was in numbers and in the committees, especially the rules committee, and Democrats monopolized both types of power.[21]

In the Senate matters were no better for the Farmer-Labor party and the Wisconsin Progressive party, even though it was and is an institution better designed for bloc politics. Farmer-Labor senator Shipstead was essentially a nonpartisan politician, suited to the antipartisanship of the north central and northwestern states.[22] His allies and friends were other nonpartisan progressives, George Norris of Nebraska and Gerald Nye of North Dakota, for instance. Elmer Benson did speak up for the Farmer-Labor party's national agenda, during his brief stint as Minnesota senator, but of course he had little influence in the Senate, as an interim appointment. The other Farmer-Labor senator, Ernest Lundeen, was both radical and a veteran of Capitol Hill. But he began serving in the Senate in 1937, well after the Farmer-Labor party needed a national strategy.

There was only one Wisconsin Progressive, Robert La Follette, Jr., to add to the Farmer-Labor party's influence. La Follette had considerable influence in the Senate, having been, in a sense, born to serve in it. La Follette played an enormously important role in setting the national agenda in 1937 through the revelations of his committee investigating abuse of civil liberties in the workplace.

To the extent that the La Follette Committee aided the organization of workers it deepened farmer-labor tensions in Wisconsin and Minnesota. To the extent that it aided the CIO's growth it deepened tensions within labor. Finally, its success perhaps encouraged conservative Democratic entrepreneurs in the House to offset labor's influence through the Dies Committee, which helped to crush the Farmer-Labor party and to oust liberal New Dealers from power. The stresses and strains caused by efforts to build a balancing political economy meant that La Follette's influence unintentionally exacerbated the problems facing the Farmer-Labor party and the Progressive party.

As for the party system, the disastrous results of William Mahoney's effort to launch a national third party in 1924 with Robert La Follette, Sr., as its standard bearer undercut the power of the faction in the Farmer-Labor party that argued for forming a national third party. Still, between 1932 and 1935 Farmer-Labor leaders did speak of establishing a national third party. The "radical" 1934 platform of the Farmer-Labor party was written in large part to distinguish the Farmer-Labor party from the New Deal.[23] As the 1936 election approached, the very newness of the New Deal's effort to establish a balancing political economy changed the calculations of those leaders who earlier intended to start a third party. They feared costing Roosevelt the election.

The national labor movement and independent-left critics flocked to the Roosevelt campaign.[24] Roosevelt himself actively reached out toward them, creating a new kind of presidential campaign in the process: "The basis of the campaign would be mobilization *beyond* the Democratic party of all the elements in the New Deal coalition—liberals, labor, farmers, women, minorities. To do this required the elaborate structure of subsidiary organizations and committees which Roosevelt began urging on Farley as early as January 1936."[25]

The collapse of a third-party thrust was so complete that the New Deal and the Minnesota Farmer-Labor party arranged a deal whereby the Democratic party withdrew its candidates for congressional offices and for governor in return for Farmer-Labor support of Roosevelt's ticket. The Farmer-Laborites also received a hefty chunk of campaign funds from Labor's Nonpartisan League, one of the national committees campaigning for Roosevelt.[26]

Roosevelt was so willing to move beyond his own party to assure his reelection that he was instrumental in creating a new state-level third party, the American Labor Party of New York. Its purpose was to mobilize Socialist trade unionists into his coalition. Unlike the Farmer-Labor party and the Progressive party, the American Labor Party, which for this reason is not a case of state-level radicalism, had its origins in the New Deal, indeed, in the White House.[27]

From the perspective of those leaders who previously talked of a third party, the future of the balancing political economy—the Wagner Act, social security, the tax measures—required such unity. Otherwise the Republican party might reestablish the accumulationist political economy of the 1920s.

This experience undercut the possibilities for coordination between the Farmer-Labor party and the Progressive party after the 1936 election. In

Minnesota Benson sought to trade on the obligations incurred in 1936, while in Wisconsin Philip La Follette launched a national third party.

As the 1938 elections approached, Benson mounted a frantic effort to secure help from the New Deal. He travelled to Hyde Park. His secretary appealed for aid to Sidney Hillman and proposed withdrawal of a Farmer-Labor candidate in the first congressional district, where the Farmer-Labor party was historically weak. The withdrawal occurred, and Roosevelt did, rather weakly, endorse Benson. Roosevelt also cooperated in ousting the state administrator of the WPA. But these reciprocal actions did not strengthen Benson, and Roosevelt's intervention in the WPA helped Benson to hurt himself.[28]

In Wisconsin, Philip La Follette unveiled a national third party, National Progressives of America. The bizarre fascist symbolism planned by La Follette dissipated whatever interest the Farmer-Laborites had. A meeting between Benson and La Follette left Benson cold. Benson seemed to prefer relying on the New Deal, and he was committed to the Popular Front. These preferences meant that the Farmer-Laborites did not fully consider whether an attractive third-party alternative could in fact be created, for instance, by working past La Follette to establish links with the Wisconsin Farmer-Labor Progressive Federation.[29]

Although public opinion was hostile to La Follette's National Progressives of America, opinion polls between December 1936 and January 1938 "found that between 14 and 16% of those polled said they 'would join,' not merely vote for, a Farmer-Labor party if one were organized."[30] A 1936 poll found that something like half of the public supported public ownership of various utilities, and a 1937 poll found that 41 percent of the public supported government ownership of banks, both demands advanced by the Minnesota Farmer-Labor party.[31] To be sure, a strategy for tapping these aspects of public opinion was quite likely impossible, and it is hard to see how such a strategy, in any case, could have prevented the disaster of the 1938 elections. But this was the only national option left for the Farmer-Labor party and the Progressive party in 1938.

Their problems were national in origin. Only a national strategy that distinguished them from the New Deal could have saved them. By 1938 the New Deal was a source of weakness, not strength. Yet in addition to Benson's involvement in the Popular Front, the experience of the 1936 campaign so strongly shaped the calculations of the Farmer-Labor leaders that they dismissed this strategy out of hand.

In short, by 1938 there was very little room for maneuver, and it was easily overlooked.

The New Deal Watershed

The possibilities and limits of American politics had changed. The New Deal organized out of American politics a type of politics that flourished in nonmetropolitan, colonial jurisdictions and that had several province-level counterparts in Canada. Certain possibilities for instituting "contagion from the left" via subnational third parties disappeared from American politics, even as such possibilities remained strong in Canada.

In the 1920s a type of economic protest politics emerged in several nonmetropolitan jurisdictions. The political entrepreneurs who established it in Minnesota were highly creative. So too were the entrepreneurs who founded the Wisconsin Progressive Party in the 1930s. But the transition between one type of political economy (that which defined American politics for the first third of the twentieth century) to a new political economy (that which the New Deal began to create) disorganized their politics. A new political class thrown into power by economic crisis, the New Deal Democrats, redefined the relationship between democracy and capitalism in America. The New Deal's redefinition of this relationship shattered the future of the political entrepreneurs who marketed state-level radicalism. New policies created new politics at the state and local levels.

A change also occurred in American political thought. The New Deal—its policy accomplishments, its public philosophy, the presidential style associated with it—defined how citizens and politicians were likely in the future to understand the possibilities of social and economic policy in America. Other ways of thinking associated with other political responses to capitalism that America had tried, were either discredited or not well remembered after the 1930s.

State-level radicalism offered one of several possible ways for understanding the proper relationship between democracy and capitalism in America. Other types of politics that offered alternative visions were populism, Debsian socialism, and the 1924 La Follette candidacy. During the electoral and policy realignment of the 1930s, the New Deal and the Democratic party filled up not only America's organizational space but its conceptual space. The New Deal organized out of American politics—for a time—other ways of thinking about how citizens should politically respond to the social, economic, and cultural problems that capitalism poses as it reorganizes how people treat each other.

The "consensus" view of American political development—which rose to intellectual hegemony in the 1950s—became the most compelling view of our past. Indeed, one of the most sophisticated expressions of this view, Louis Hartz's classic essay, *The Liberal Tradition in America,* argued that the strength of our national consensus about the purposes of our politics made us a nation of amnesiacs, forever ignoring whatever unusual institutional and philosophical variety there was in American political history.

The decline in the 1970s of Great Society liberalism—which can be seen as the New Deal's second wind—and the Reagan Revolution have permanently altered how Americans understand the New Deal and earlier events. Also, the organizational forms of American party politics have changed. The New Deal revived many traditional party organizations. With one or two exceptions, such as Chicago's Democratic traditional party organization, however, these all collapsed in the 1960s. By the 1970s even the Chicago organization was in disarray. The other organizational support of the New Deal Democratic party, the labor political action committee, has weakened and was only slightly revived during the 1984 presidential campaign. As a result of these changes the possibilities for new types of party politics and policy experimentation at the state level now seem greater than they have been for some time, with likely consequences for national politics.[32]

The consensus view that grew out of the New Deal's success in dampening the class conflict of the 1930s is now seen as interesting but not conclusive. A new generation of historians and historically inclined social scientists has either attacked or simply ignored the consensus view of American political development. It has reconstructed a past peopled by men and women with more elaborate social imaginations than the utility-maximizing individualists of the consensus view.

Both history and intellectual change have conspired to widen our collective political imagination. It is open once more for fully appreciating the variety of party organizations that America has had, a variety that includes such organizations as the North Dakota Nonpartisan League, the Wisconsin Progressive party, and the Minnesota Farmer-Labor party.

Afterword

Is state-level radicalism possible today? At least three types of change during the past decade or two make new growth of radicalism plausible: institutional and policy change, change in the role of the states, and intellectual change.

The structural weakness of the Democratic party, only partly reversed by the Dukakis campaign; the decline in turnout in presidential and congressional electoral contests; and the partial dismantling of the balancing political economy that the New Deal fashioned all suggest a collapse of the institutions and policies that the New Deal erected and, more ominously, of the sense of political involvement that both generated and was nurtured by activist government at the federal level. Indeed, much policy activism has shifted to the states. State-level policy activism in the areas of welfare and industrial policy was one of the more interesting developments of the Reagan era. Despite this development state-level politics did not become an arena for heightened political involvement.

By now there is—outside the conservative political movement begun in the 1950s—considerable intellectual discontent with the New Deal and its legacies. Simply to describe the various themes in the revisionist scholarship of the New Deal would be a major scholarly undertaking. But certainly a major theme in this revisionism is ambivalence toward the centralized, bureaucratic character of the New Deal's policies and institutions.

It has recently been argued that the New Deal, paradoxically, laid the basis for discontent with welfare policies by establishing impersonal bureaucratic delivery of welfare services. In this view a promising approach for reinvigorating the sense of social solidarity and the altruism that a welfare state is meant to represent would be genuinely involving welfare recipients in the design and delivery of welfare services. Civil servants and middle-class, private-sector providers of welfare services would no longer monopolize the design and delivery of welfare. This view of the welfare state may well prompt a revisionist appreciation of Farmer-Labor congressman Ernest Lundeen's bill for unemployment insurance, which envisioned precisely this type of decentralization.[1]

174

The New Deal has also been criticized from the perspective of public-law analysis. A major recent restatement of these criticisms reconsiders the New Deal's constitutional vision—its adoption and extension of the major state-building achievements of the late nineteenth and early twentieth century, that is, the independent regulatory commission and enhanced presidential power. It argues that while "New Deal constitutionalism" is understandable and to a degree defensible, there were several costs attached to it. This recent public-law critique of New Deal constitutionalism argues that, among other things, the attack on dual-sovereignty federalism was too great and too damaging to the ideal of local civic self-determination often associated with federalism. Reinvigorating federalism should now be a priority for American politics, along with creatively blending three different modes of oversight of the administrative state; presidential, congressional, and judicial. These checks and balances may well enhance the effectiveness of activist government. From this perspective, state-level radicalism as a type of politics becomes desirable.[2]

The changed structure of American politics, the impact of the Reagan era on state-level policy activism, and the extent and nature of intellectual discontent with the New Deal's legacies would all seem to invite entrepreneurship and protest at the state level. Also, an unusually strong case can be made that the Democratic party's politicians do not care to and do not know how to forge a coalition of the middle class and the lower class, as their reluctance to mobilize nonvoters demonstrates in part.[3] The rapprochement in 1988 between Dukakis and Jesse Jackson grew out of the Democrats' desire to avoid a messy convention, not a real appreciation by the dominant wing of the Democratic party for Jackson's emphasis on mobilization. The organizational space for state-level radicalism would seem quite large. And there is obviously more room for economic equality in America. Even as income inequality grows, however, there have been calls among many respectable analysts for deliberately cheapening wages and lowering social investment in order to make America "more competitive."

Could not state-level radicalism serve as a model for renewing political involvement? Could it not help fight growing inequality? Could it not lead to popularly controlled state-level industrial policies, as distinct from the technocratically designed and implemented state-level industrial policies that proliferated after the 1982–83 recession? If it involved a focus on registering nonvoters, is it not likely that it would have some success?

Prudence requires a somewhat deflating answer to these questions. State-level radicalism might well accomplish these goals, and indeed a focus on registration might be politically very rewarding. But for several reasons I cannot confidently predict the rebirth of state-level radicalism. Redistributive politics has for so long been a federal responsibility that it is hard to imagine any set of talented politicians spending its scarce energies and money on a strategy similar to that which the Minnesota Farmer-Laborites and Wisconsin Progressives chose. In addition, the diffusion of presidential primaries, the openness of the Democratic party to the influence of reform activists, and the development of the presidency since the 1930s all serve to focus reformist entrepreneurship on presidential politics. Political entrepreneurs who seek to place social justice on our agendas are likely to turn their attention to national agendas, at least in the short run. The clock of the American political economy's history would have to be turned very far back for them to focus on state-level power. That seems perhaps more likely than it once did, but "more likely" and "likely" are hardly the same thing.

Let me propose, though, that state-level radicalism is relevant today as more than a model for politics. It might at some time serve that function as Americans search their past for usable institutions that they can adapt to the present, something that they seem to be doing more and more, at least at the level of scholarship. Thinking about state-level radicalism can also lead to useful insights about contemporary American politics.

By showing how American politics was restructured between 1915 and 1940, this account of state-level radicalism may sensitize one to thinking about contemporary politics in a *structural and historical* way. If we break down the study of American politics into small pieces and ask questions about those pieces we may miss the larger and ultimately more consequential patterns that surely are shaping our common life today.

The United States is tightly integrated into a world political economy and into a world system of geopolitical competition. Because of the collapse of the Bretton Woods system and, relatedly, the increased importance of monetarist policy instruments for regulating the economy, domestic American politics now interacts with decisions taken in the financial and industrial markets of Japan and Europe and by Japanese and German central bankers. Also, it is shaped by, even as it shapes, domestic Soviet decisions. Central American insurgencies and civil wars have left strong imprints on domestic attitudes and institutions. A final example: over the past decade two successive presidents have become deeply involved in and discredited or partly discredited by events in the Middle East and the Persian Gulf. These patterns of interaction between domestic American politics and international economic and geopolitical systems all have changed presidential style, presidential campaigns, legislative-executive patterns of conflict, the extent and nature of policy experimentation in the states, and the attitudinal bases of American politics. Just as the national political environment shaped state-level radicalism, the international political environment is surely shaping American democracy and the American political economy.

The analogy is far from perfect, of course. The world has no political center as the United States has, shaping state-level politics. The relative autonomy of American politics from the international system is much greater today than the relative autonomy of state-level politics from the national system between 1915 and 1940.

There are, though, transnational institutions, actors, and political patterns, and they lead to economic and geopolitical policies that in turn strongly influence domestic political patterns. They constrain or shape the behavior of actors who, from a perspective that is solely domestic, seem quite powerful. This account of state-level radicalism stresses how party, policy, and institutions changed politics from the top down, from the outside in. That emphasis may, I think, unlock much of what is shaping American politics today. That emphasis may help one to see another aspect of the relevance of state-level radicalism to today's political dilemmas.

The politicians of state-level radicalism faced a new order, the dynamics of which became increasingly difficult for them to grasp, let alone shape. So too the politicians of the Republican and Democratic parties are facing a new order as the postwar international political economy slowly unravels and as superpower rivalry enters new phases. They, and those who observe them, could do worse than to reflect on what state-level radicalism's history suggests about the nature of political change. In that sense, too, state-level radicalism might well become a part of our usable past.

Notes

Chapter One

1. *Farmer-Labor Leader,* 30 March 1934, p. 5; Steven J. Keillor, *Hjalmar Petersen of Minnesota: The Politics of Provincial Independence* (St. Paul: Minnesota Historical Society Press, 1987), pp. 104–9.

2. Cf. Minnesota, Governor, *Third Inaugural Message of Governor Floyd B. Olson to the Legislature of Minnesota,* St. Paul, 9 January 1935, pp. 3–4, 22–24.

3. Keillor, *Petersen,* p. 96.

4. See the discussion of *Home Building and Loan Association v. Blaisdell,* 290 U. S. 398 (1934) in Sanford Levinson, "Clashes of Taste in Constitutional Interpretation," *Dissent,* Summer 1988, pp. 304–5.

5. Cf. V. O. Key, Jr., *American State Politics: An Introduction* (New York: Alfred A. Knopf, 1956; reprint Westport, Conn.: Greenwood Press, 1983).

6. Cf. Albert O. Hirschman, *Essays in Trespassing: Economics to Politics and Beyond* (Cambridge: Cambridge University Press, 1981), pp. 123–34. See also Peter Gourevitch, *Politics in Hard Times: Comparative Responses to International Economic Crises* (Ithaca, N.Y.: Cornell University Press, 1986), pp. 3–123.

7. Cf. Theda Skocpol and John Ikenberry, "The Political Formation of the American Welfare State in Historical and Comparative Perspective," in Richard F. Tomasson, ed., *Comparative Social Research* (Greenwich, Conn.: JAI Press, 1983), 6:87–148.

8. David Vogel, "Why American Businessmen Distrust Their State: The Political Consciousness of American Corporate Executives," *British Journal of Political Science* 8 (January 1978): 45–78.

9. Michael Paul Rogin, *The Intellectuals and McCarthy: The Radical Specter* (Cambridge: MIT Press, 1967), p. 53.

10. Quoted in Russell B. Nye, *Midwestern Progressive Politics* (East Lansing: Michigan State College Press, 1951), p. 81.

11. Cf. Walter Dean Burnham, "The System of 1896: An Analysis," in Paul Kleppner, Walter Dean Burnham, Ronald P. Formisano, Samuel P. Hays, Richard Jensen, and William G. Shade, *The Evolution of American Electoral Systems,* Contributions in American History, no. 95 (Westport, Conn.: Greenwood Press, 1981), pp. 147–202; Elmer Eric Schattschneider, "United States: The Functional Approach to Party Government," in Sigmund Neumann, ed., *Modern Political Parties: Approaches to Comparative Politics* (Chicago: University of Chicago Press, 1956), pp. 194–215.

12. Alexander Keyssar, *Out of Work: The First Century of Unemployment in*

Massachusetts (Cambridge: Cambridge University Press, 1986), chaps. 1–3, 7, 9, 10, and appendix B; Daniel R. Fusfeld, "Government and the Suppression of Radical Labor, 1877–1918," in Charles Bright and Susan Harding, eds., *State-making and Social Movements: Essays in History and Theory* (Ann Arbor: University of Michigan Press, 1984), pp. 159–92; Robert Justin Goldstein, *Political Repression in Modern America, 1870 to the Present* (Cambridge, Mass.: Schenkman Publishing Co.; New York: Two Continents Publishing Group, 1978), pp. 9–19; Susan Previant Lee and Peter Passell, *A New Economic View of American History* (New York: W. W. Norton & Co., 1979), pp. 292–301; Sidney Baldwin, *Poverty and Politics: The Rise and Decline of the Farm Security Administration* (Chapel Hill: University of North Carolina Press, 1968), pp. 3–31.

13. W. D. Burnham, "System of 1896."

14. Rogin, *Intellectuals and McCarthy,* p. 195.

15. Cf. Bertrand Badie and Pierre Birnbaum, *The Sociology of the State,* trans. Arthur Goldhammer (Chicago: University of Chicago Press, 1983), pp. 77–78.

16. Tony Freyer, "The Federal Courts, Localism, and the National Economy, 1865–1900," *Business History Review* 53 (1979): 344–63; Charles W. McCurdy, "American Law and the Marketing Structure of the Large Corporation, 1875–1890," *Journal of Economic History* 38 (September 1978): 631–49; William Wiecek, "The Reconstruction of Federal Judicial Power, 1863–1876," in Lawrence Friedman and Harry N. Scheiber, eds., *American Law and the Constitutional Order* (Cambridge: Harvard University Press, 1978; reprinted and abridged from *American Journal of Legal History* 13 [1969]: 333–59), pp. 237–45; Paul Peterson, *City Limits* (Chicago: University of Chicago Press, 1981).

17. On this point, see Harry N. Scheiber, "American Federalism and the Diffusion of Power: Historical and Contemporary Perspectives," *University of Toledo Law Review* 9 (Summer 1978): 619–90. See also idem, "Law and American Agricultural Development," *Agricultural History* 52 (October 1978): 439–57; idem, "Federalism and Legal Process: Historical and Contemporary Analysis of the American System," *Law and Society Review* 14 (Spring 1980): 663–722.

18. State constitutions are easily amended and often very long. Cf. Grant McConnell, *Private Power and American Democracy* (New York: Alfred A. Knopf, 1966; Vintage Books, 1970), chap. 6, "The States."

19. Howard M. Gitelman, "Perspectives on American Industrial Violence," *Business History Review* 47 (1973): 1–23. See also Stephen Skowronek, *Building a New American State: The Expansion of National Administrative Capacities, 1877–1920* (Cambridge: Cambridge University Press, 1982), chap. 4.

20. For a measure of how much this has changed see Paul Peterson, *City Limits,* especially his chapter "A Theory of Federalism."

21. Cf. also David R. Mayhew, *Placing Parties in American Politics: Organization, Electoral Settings, and Government Activity in the Twentieth Century* (Princeton: Princeton University Press, 1986).

22. Ibid., chap. 8.

23. See Barrington Moore, Jr., *The Social Origins of Dictatorship and Democracy: Lord and Peasant in the Making of the Modern World* (Boston: Beacon Press, 1966), pp. 115, 152, 553.

24. Map 3.1, "Persons Receiving Military Pensions as Percentage of County Population, 1887," in Richard Bensel, *Sectionalism and American Political Development, 1880–1980* (Madison: University of Wisconsin Press, 1984), p. 68.

25. Representative Sam Hill (D-Washington), quoted in Daniel Ogden, Jr., and Hugh A. Bone, *Washington Politics* (New York: New York University Press, 1960), pp. 3–4. See also Mayhew, *Placing Parties,* chaps. 7–8.

26. Martin Shefter, "Regional Receptivity to Reform: The Legacy of the Progressive Era," *Political Science Quarterly* 98 (Fall 1983): 459–84; quote found on page 462.

27. Interestingly, Mayhew places Massachusetts in the nontraditional-party-organization category, which perhaps accounts for its higher standard deviation in table 1.1. While Mayhew also presents New Hampshire as a nontraditional-party-organization state, its lower standard deviation would seem to be accounted for by the extent to which the Boston and Maine Railroad filled up its organizational space. See *Placing Parties,* pp. 221–22. Mayhew defines "traditional party organizations" in chapter 1.

28. See Daniel Bell, "Marxian Socialism in the United States," in Donald Drew Egbert and Stow Persons, eds., *Socialism and American Life* (Princeton: Princeton University Press, 1952; reprinted separately, 1967).

29. See James Weinstein, *The Decline of Socialism in America, 1912–1925* (New Brunswick, N.J.: Rutgers University Press, 1984), pp. 116–18; Garin Burbank, "Agrarian Radicals and Their Opponents: Political Conflict in Southern Oklahoma, 1910–1924," *Journal of American History* 58 (June 1971): 5–23. See also *Congressional Quarterly's Guide to U.S. Elections,* 2d ed., (Washington, D.C.: Congressional Quarterly Press, 1985), p. 522.

Chapter Two

1. This account of the Nonpartisan League's origins and development is an interpretation using the material presented in Robert Morlan's classic account, *Political Prairie Fire: The Nonpartisan League, 1915–1922* (Minneapolis: University of Minnesota Press, 1955; reprint, St. Paul: Minnesota Historical Society Press, 1985). I also rely on the relevant chapters of Elwyn B. Robinson, *History of North Dakota* (Lincoln: University of Nebraska Press, 1966); on Edward Blackorby, *Prairie Rebel: The Public Life of William Lemke* (Lincoln: University of Nebraska Press, 1963); and on the microfilm edition of the National Nonpartisan League Papers and later microfilm supplements to the papers, published by the Minnesota Historical Society.

2. Morlan, *Prairie Fire,* p. 31.

3. For path-breaking treatments of information costs, see Thomas Ferguson, "Party Realignment and American Industrial Structure: The Investment Theory of

Political Parties in Historical Perspective," in Paul Zarembka, ed., *Research in Political Economy: A Research Annual* (Greenwich, Conn.: JAI Press, 1983), 6:1–82, especially the formal discussion, pp. 8–20; and Benjamin Page, *Who Gets What from Government* (Berkeley: University of California Press, 1983), a theory of the role of information costs in policy making. The basic discussion of voter information costs is in Anthony Downs, *An Economic Theory of Democracy* (New York: Harper & Row, 1957).

4. Cf. Key, *American State Politics,* especially chaps. 4–6.

5. Cf. National Nonpartisan League, *Why Should Farmers Pay Dues?* (n.p., n.d.), a candid treatment of the need for membership and money in order to reduce the electorate's information costs.

6. See North Dakota, Secretary of State, *1919 Legislative Manual* (Bismarck: n.d.), pp. 240–70.

7. Morlan, *Prairie Fire,* p. 126.

8. Quoted in William Millikan, "Defenders of Business: The Minneapolis Civic and Commerce Association versus Labor during W.W.I," *Minnesota History* 50 (Spring 1986): 4.

9. Cf. Theodore Blegen, *Minnesota: A History of the State* (St. Paul: Minnesota Historical Society, 1963); John R. Borchert and Donald P. Yaeger, *Atlas of Minnesota Resources and Settlement* (St. Paul: Minnesota State Planning Agency, 1969).

10. See U.S. Department of Commerce, Bureau of the Census, *Historical Statistics of the United States: Colonial Times to 1970* (Washington, D.C.: U.S. Department of Commerce, Bureau of the Census, 1975), 1:27–36, 129–30.

11. Political repression in Minnesota during World War I underscores the robustness of dual-sovereignty federalism despite war mobilization. The Nonpartisan League's experience with repression explains why Arthur Le Sueur, a Nonpartisan League attorney and the former Socialist mayor of Minot, North Dakota, played a role in the creation of the American Civil Liberties Union and served on its national board throughout the '20s. At least two other Minneapolis attorneys, Tom Latimer, later Farmer-Labor mayor of Minneapolis, and George Leonard, a close advisor of Minnesota's Farmer-Labor governor between 1930 and 1936, were also charter members of the ACLU. See American Civil Liberties Union, *A Year's Fight for Free Speech: The Work of the American Civil Liberties Union from Sept. 1921 to Jan. 1923* (New York: American Civil Liberties Union, 1923); idem, *The Fight for Civil Liberty* (New York: American Civil Liberties Union, 1929). For background on political repression in Minnesota during World War I, see Goldstein, *Political Repression in America,* pp. 103–35; Ora Almon Hilton, *The Minnesota Commission of Public Safety in World War One, 1917–1919* (Stillwater: Oklahoma Agricultural and Mechanical College, 1951); Carol Jenson, "Loyalty as a Political Weapon: The 1918 Campaign in Minnesota," *Minnesota History* 43 (Summer 1971): 43–57.

12. Millikan, "Defenders of Business."

13. For a useful description of the Home Guard and its activities, see Minnesota, Adjutant General, *Report of the Adjutant General of the State of Minnesota Covering the Thirtieth Biennial Period Ending December 31, 1918.*

14. La Follette said, "For my own part, I was not in favor of beginning the war. I don't mean to say that we had not suffered grievances, we had, at the hands of Germany." AP reported La Follette as saying, "We had no grievances against Germany." Bruce Larson, *Lindbergh of Minnesota: A Political Biography* (New York: Harcourt Brace Jovanovich, 1971), p. 219.

15. See Morlan, *Prairie Fire*, chap. 8, "The Reign of Terror."

16. Ibid., p. 165.

17. See National and State Executive Committees of the National Nonpartisan League, *Memorial to the Congress of the United States concerning Conditions in Minnesota, 1918* (n.p., n.d.), p. 1.

18. See Harry N. Scheiber, Harold G. Vatter, Harold Underwood Faulkner, *American Economic History*, 9th rev. ed. (New York: Harper & Row, 1976), a comprehensive revision of the earlier work by Harold Underwood Faulkner, p. 318. Between 1914 and 1916 unemployment dropped from about 2.2 million to about 220,000. Approximately simultaneously, the inflow of immigrants dropped from 1,218,480 in 1914 to 110,618 in 1918. U.S. Department of Commerce, Bureau of the Census, *Historical Statistics*, p. 105.

19. Cf. Valerie Jean Conner, *The National War Labor Board: Stability, Social Justice, and the Voluntary State in World War I,* supplementary volumes to the papers of Woodrow Wilson (Chapel Hill: University of North Carolina Press, 1983).

20. Secondary sources for this section are Millikan, "Defenders of Business"; Carl Chrislock, *The Progressive Era in Minnesota, 1899–1918* (St. Paul: Minnesota Historical Society, 1971), pp. 157–60; Conner, *National War Labor Board*, especially pp. 138–41; Loyola Brinckmann Thiltgen, "Relations of the Governor to the Settlement of Labor Disputes in the State of Minnesota prior to 1939," master's thesis, University of Minnesota, 1954, chaps. 1–4. Primary sources are National War Labor Board, record group 2, case 46, National Archives, Suitland, Md.; Minnesota State Federation of Labor, *Proceedings of the Thirty-sixth Convention, Virginia, Minn., July 15–17, 1918.*

21. Morlan, *Prairie Fire*, p. 191.

22. For Minneapolis socialism, see Chrislock, *Progressive Era in Minnesota;* David Paul Nord, "Hothouse Socialism: Minneapolis, 1910–1925," in Donald T. Critchlow, ed., *Socialism in the Heartland: The Midwestern Experience, 1900–1925* (Notre Dame: University of Notre Dame Press, 1986), pp. 133–66; idem, "Minneapolis and the Pragmatic Socialism of Thomas Van Lear," *Minnesota History* 45 (Spring 1976): 3–10; idem, "Socialism in One City: A Political Study of Minneapolis in the Progressive Era," master's thesis, University of Minnesota, 1972. On socialism in the IAM see John H. M. Laslett, *Labor and the Left: A Study of Socialist and Radical Influences in the American Labor Movement, 1881–1924*

(New York: Basic Books, 1970), pp. 144–92; David Montgomery, *Workers' Control in America: Studies in the History of Work, Technology, and Labor Struggles* (Cambridge: Cambridge University Press, 1979), pp. 48–90.

23. On conditions in the Twin Cities contract shops and their political consequences see Lewis Harthill, "St. Paul, Minn.," *Machinists Monthly Journal* 25 (1913): 1279–80.

24. See transcript of speech by Van Lear in Glencoe, Minn., 7 August 1917, in National Nonpartisan League Papers, microfilm edition, Minnesota Historical Society, St. Paul, roll 14.

25. See Minnesota State Federation of Labor, *Proceedings of the Thirty-fifth Convention, Faribault, Minn., July 16–18, 1917.*

26. Minnesota State Federation of Labor, *Proceedings of the Thirty-sixth Convention.*

27. See "Notes on the History of the Farmer-Labor Movement," 1 June 1939, typescript, in William Mahoney, Papers, Minnesota Historical Society, Division of Archives and Manuscripts, St. Paul. For a somewhat different memoir, see "History of the Farmer-Labor Party as Told by F. A. Pike to Ernest Lundeen, 5/16/33," pp. 4–5, based on an interview of F. A. Pike, a Nonpartisan League attorney and later chair of the Farmer-Labor party in the early 1920s, by Congressman Lundeen shortly before Pike's death. Ernest Lundeen, Papers, Hoover Institution Archives, Stanford, Calif., box 302, folder "Farmer-Labor Party, National Material 1." I thank Pruda Lood of the archives staff for locating this valuable memoir.

28. The story of Evans's selection is told in the transcript of Lundeen's interview with Pike, "History of Farmer-Labor Party," pp. 3–4.

29. Nord, "Socialism in One City," table 9, "Mayoral Election of 1918," p. 204; Bruce M. White et al., comps., *Minnesota Votes: Election Returns by County for Presidents, Senators, Congressmen, and Governors, 1857–1977* (St. Paul: Minnesota Historical Society, 1977), p. 183. Total voting in Hennepin County for governor was 61,995, while the total voting for mayor was 56,619. This is an 8.6 percent difference, but one has to remember that Minneapolis and Hennepin County in 1918 were not coextensive—a large part of the county was rural.

30. North Dakota, Secretary of State, *1919 Legislative Manual*, pp. 270–89.

31. Cf. Joseph H. Mader, "The North Dakota Press and the Nonpartisan League," *Journalism Quarterly* 14 (December 1937): 321–32.

32. See Blackorby, *Prairie Rebel*; Fred E. Haynes, *Social Politics in the United States* (1924; New York: AMS Press, 1970); Mader, "North Dakota Press."

Chapter Three

1. Cf. Maurice Duverger, *Political Parties: Their Organization and Activity in the Modern State*, trans. Barbara and Robert North (London: Methuen & Co., 1954; University Paperbacks, 1964), pp. 1–27.

2. See Nancy Hill Zingale, "Electoral Stability and Change: The Case of Min-

nesota, 1857–1966," Ph.D. dissertation, University of Minnesota, 1971, pp. 201–10.

3. Cf. Minnesota State Federation of Labor, *Proceedings of the Thirty-seventh Convention, New Ulm, Minn., July 21–23, 1919;* interview with Louis Reichel, 26 May 1983, Mankato, Minn.

4. Estimates of union membership figures for this period can be found in Minnesota, Department of Labor and Industries, *Sixteenth Biennial Report of the Depatment of Labor and Industries of the State of Minnesota, 1917–1918*, p. 150; idem *Seventeenth Biennial Report of the Department of Labor and Industries of the State of Minnesota, 1919–1920*, p. 172. The estimate in the second report is 89,410. According to census data the number of "production workers" in manufacturing in the state in 1919 was 113,800. See Donald B. Dodd and Wynelle S. Dood, *Historical Statistics of the United States, 1790–1970*, vol. 2, *The Midwest* (University: University of Alabama Press, 1976), p. 56. Using the former figure as the numerator and the latter as the denominator one gets the figure of 78 percent union density. This seems so high that I prefer to offer a safer estimate of density, namely 50 percent.

5. St. Paul, Board of Elections, *Votes Cast for City Officers from Year 1914 to Date*, available in St. Paul City Hall.

6. See "Declaration of Principles of the Working People's Nonpartisan Political League," Farmer-Labor Association Papers, Minnesota Historical Society, Archives and Research Center, St. Paul, box 1.

7. Minnesota, Secretary of State, *Legislative Manual of the State of Minnesota, Compiled for the Legislature of 1921*, pp. 100–101.

8. See *Minnesota Leader,* issues for May 1920; "Let Them Call Names," *Minnesota Leader,* 22 May 1920, p. 4; "Labor's Part in the Campaign," *Minnesota Leader,* 26 June 1920, p. 4.

9. Pike, "History of Farmer Labor Party," pp. 6–8.

10. Keller's Republican label should be seen in context. Formerly St. Paul's commissioner of public utilities, in 1919 he successfully ran as an independent in St. Paul's fourth district to fill the seat of an incumbent Democrat who died in office. In that contest he received labor backing because of his public support for the 1917–18 carmen's strike in the Twin Cities while he was St. Paul commissioner of public utilities. See U. S. Congress, Senate, *Biographical Directory of the American Congress, 1774–1971*, 92d Cong. lst sess., 1971, S. Doc. 92-8, s.v. "Oscar Keller," p. 1218; Chrislock, *Progressive Era in Minnesota*, p. 157.

11. See *Minnesota Leader,* January–April 1921, for discussion of the rule changes.

12. For a good account of the Leach–Van Lear contest, see "The Clash in Minneapolis," *Survey,* 25 June 1921, pp. 428–29.

13. Jessie McMillan Marcley, *The Minneapolis City Charter, 1856–1925*, Bureau for Research in Government, publication 5 (Minneapolis: University of Minnesota, 1925), p. 51.

14. Cf. Henry G. Teigan to D. C. Dorman, 8 February 1922, on Townley's "balance of power" plan, stating that labor was "overwhelming against it." National Nonpartisan League Papers, roll 10.

15. *Minnesota Leader,* 25 February 1922, p. 1, and 11 March 1922, p. 2. For a scholarly defense of Townley's position, see Samuel P. Huntington, "The Election Tactics of the Nonpartisan League," *Mississippi Valley Historical Review* 36 (March 1950): 613–52.

16. Stating that besides "the enrollment of members, the collection of old postdated checks is the most important problem facing the League at this time," the league's national manager recommended to state managers that they authorize local bankers to collect postdated checks by offering them up to 50 percent or more of the face value of the checks! He noted that local banks were able to collect the checks "much cheaper and quicker that we can by individual canvass." D. C. Dorman, national manager, to state managers, 7 July 1921, National Nonpartisan League Papers, Teigan Papers Supplement, roll 1.

17. On the name change, see Henry G. Teigan to H. O. Berve, 23 November 1922, National Nonpartisan League Papers, roll 11.

18. See ibid., rolls 1, 10, 11, and Teigan Papers Supplement, roll 2.

19. For some sense of the women's auxiliaries and their activities, see *Minnesota Daily Star,* 14 January 1921, p. 1; 2 March 1921, item re Eliza Evans Deming, p. 1; *Minnesota Leader,* 10 April 1920, item re Lily Anderson, p. 4; 31 July 1920, item re Victoria McAlmon, p. 2; 14 August 1920, item re Women's Nonpartisan Clubs, p. 2; 25 September 1920, item re auxiliaries of WPNPL, p. 1. The ideology of the women's auxiliaries is suggested in National Nonpartisan League, Women's Nonpartisan Clubs, *Minnesota: The Problems of Her People and Why the Farmers and the Workers Have Organized for Political Action* (Minneapolis: Women's Nonpartisan Clubs, National Nonpartisan League, [1920?]), which specifically rebuts charges that the league advocates free love and wishes to prevent upward mobility, ending by saying, "they [women] will not fail to see the cloven hoof under the disguise of society leaders . . . who implore them to fall down and worship the Beast [big business]."

20. What the size of the brotherhoods was is difficult to say, but some of them were large. The Brotherhood of Railway and Steamship Clerks had five thousand members in Minnesota at this time, for instance. State secretary of the Ohio State Federation of Brotherhood of Railway and Steamship Clerks to Henry G. Teigan, 2 July 1923, National Nonpartisan League Papers, Teigan Papers Supplement, roll 2.

21. Cf. letter of 5 December 1925 by chairman of the Minnesota Nonpartisan League, claiming a membership of forty-eight hundred paid-up members. National Nonpartisan League Papers, roll 11.

22. The *Minnesota Daily Star* for 1920–23, when it was sold to become the basis for the *Minneapolis Star,* is available on microfilm. The only secondary treatment of the newspaper is Harold L. Nelson, "The Political Reform Press: A

Case Study," *Journalism Quarterly* 29 (Summer 1952): 294–302, which presents valuable data on circulation and finances of the newspaper.

23. William Mahoney to Arnold E. Sevareid, 25 August 1937, Mahoney Papers, box 1.

24. Henry Teigan's postelection correspondence demonstrates that suspicion of fraud was widespread among farmer-labor activists. Even the Democratic gubernatorial candidate believed there was fraud, suspecting that local canvassing boards awarded Democratic votes to the Republican candidate since there were no opposition poll watchers, given the Democratic party's weakness and the Farmer-Labor party's newness.

25. Henry G. Teigan to C. M. Gislason, 6 July 1923, National Nonpartisan League Papers, Teigan Papers Supplement, roll 2.

26. *Minnesota Union Advocate*, 6 April 1922, p. 1; *Minnesota Union Advocate*, 28 February 1924, p. 5.

27. Mahoney to Sevareid, 25 August 1937.

28. *Minnesota Union Advocate*, 28 February 1924, p. 5.

29. William Mahoney to Henry G. Teigan, 18 December 1923, National Nonpartisan League Papers, roll 11.

30. *Minnesota Daily Star*, 11 September 1923, p. 6.

31. *Minnesota Union Advocate*, 10 January 1924, p. 4, and 17 January 1924, p. 1; *Farmer-Labor Leader*, letters to the editor, February 1931.

32. Murray E. King, "The Farmer-Labor Federation," *New Republic*, 2 April 1924, pp. 145–47. King once worked in the Nonpartisan League's publicity department.

33. See Arthur Naftalin, "A History of the Minnesota Farmer-Labor Party," Ph.D. dissertation, University of Minnesota, 1948, p. 119; Paul S. Holbo, "The Farmer-Labor Association: Minnesota's Party *within* a Party," *Minnesota History* 42 (Spring 1970): 301–9.

34. A fact that reveals much about the extent to which Communists were accepted within the Minnesota trade union movement is the selection of Julius Emme as the delegate of the St. Paul Trades and Labor Assembly to the 1924 Portland Convention of the American Federation of Labor. See *Minnesota Union Advocate*, 30 August 1924, p. 2.

35. For background, see Weinstein, *Decline of Socialism*, chaps. 4–8; Bert Cochran, *Labor and Communism: The Conflict That Shaped American Union* (Princeton: Princeton University Press, 1977), chaps. 1–2.

36. Cf. W. W. Royster to Henry G. Teigan, National Nonpartisan League Papers, Teigan Papers Supplement, roll 3: "There is much ironing out to be done, misunderstandings to be corrected. Mahoney, whose integrity I do not question is continualy [*sic*] stirring things up . . . He is not tactful nor diplomatic."

37. See William Mahoney to Henry G. Teigan, 29 May 1924, National Nonpartisan League Papers, roll 11.

38. Typical of this mindset was an editorial in the *Minneapolis Labor Review*

on the eve of the election: "You would fight to the last ditch to prevent some enemy from invading your home, enslaving you and impoverishing your family . . . Use your ballot Tuesday as though it were the last cartridge in your revolver." Otherwise, the *Review* told its working class readers, they would only have themselves to blame "when Coolidge and Dawes . . . enjoin your unions, send out the soldiers to shoot you down when you go on strike or conscript you to fight and die on foreign soil to protect the profits of Standard Oil and United States Steel." *Minneapolis Labor Review,* 31 October 1924, p. 3, in National Nonpartisan League Papers, roll 11.

39. For a sense of this crisis, see Mahoney to Teigan, 22 February 1924; Thomas Van Lear, "To the Stockholders of the Northwest Publishing Company," 6 March 1924, in National Nonpartisan League Papers, roll 11; Nelson, "Political Reform Press."

40. On aldermanic races, see Nord, "Socialism in One City," appendices B and C, to identify farmer-labor aldermen, and for decline in their strength, see, inter alia, Minneapolis, City Council, *Proceedings,* 1937–38, 63:7a. On the mayoral contests, see City Council, *Proceedings* 46:1380–81, 48:1400, 50:1454, 52:1328, 54:1444. From 1923 to 1929 there was no recognizably farmer-labor mayoral candidate in the general elections.

41. For a sense of the intellectual background to this challenge, see A. B. Gilbert, "Nonpartisan vs. Party Politics," *American Federationist,* November 1927, pp. 1350–53; Henry G. Teigan, "Independent Political Action in Minnesota," *American Federationist,* August 1928, pp. 966–68.

42. See John Beecher, *Tomorrow Is a Day: A Story of the People in Politics* (Chicago: Vanguard Books, 1980), pp. 223–26; Millard Gieske, *Minnesota Farmer-Laborism: The Third Party Alternative* (Minneapolis: University of Minnesota Press, 1979), pp. 110–19.

43. James R. Green, *Grass-Roots Socialism: Radical Movements in the Southwest, 1895–1943* (Baton Rouge: Louisiana State University Press, 1978), pp. 397–408, and Burbank, "Agrarian Radicals."

44. Ibid.

45. On the Farmer-Labor party of 1920, see Stanley Shapiro, "'Hand and Brain': The Farmer-Labor Party of 1920," *Labor History* 26 (Summer 1985): 405–22; Robert S. Gabriner, "The Farmer-Labor Party, 1918–1924: A Study in the Dynamics of Independent Political Action," master's thesis, University of Wisconsin, 1966.

46. Readers interested in the Washington Farmer-Labor party should consult Hamilton Cravens, "A History of the Washington Farmer-Labor Party, 1918–1924," master's thesis, University of Washington, 1962; Jonathan Dembo, *Unions and Politics in Washington State, 1885–1935* (New York: Garland Publishing, 1983), especially pp. 625, 627–28, data on decline in union membership; Robert Friedheim, *The Seattle General Strike* (Seattle: University of Washington Press,

1964); Earl Shimmons, "The Labor Dailies," *American Mercury,* 25 September 1928, pp. 85–93.

47. For data on the Idaho Progressive party, see Garrett O. Forbes, "Dynamics of Idaho Politics, 1920–1932," master's thesis, University of Idaho Graduate School, 1955; Hugh T. Lovin, "The Farmer Revolt in Idaho, 1914–1922," *Idaho Yesterdays: The Quarterly Journal of the Idaho Historical Society* 20 (Fall 1976): 2–15; Boyd A. Martin, *The Direct Primary in Idaho* (Stanford: Stanford University Press, 1947), pp. 67–75; Merle W. Wells, "Fred T. DuBois and the Nonpartisan League in the Idaho Election of 1918," *Pacific Northwest Quarterly* 56 (January 1965): 17–29.

48. See Minnesota State Federation of Labor, *Proceedings of the Forty-seventh Convention, Mankato, Minn., August 19–21, 1929,* p. 45.

Chapter Four

1. Background information for this section comes from Charles Adrian, "The Nonpartisan Legislature in Minnesota," Ph.D. dissertation, University of Minnesota, 1950; William Anderson, *Local Government and Finance in Minnesota* (Minneapolis: University of Minnesota Press, 1935), pp. 13, 15–16, 17–19, 29, 41, 82, 84, 87, 91, 98–99, 101, 331–38; idem, *Outline of the Government of Minnesota* (Minneapolis: Minnesota Republican Women's State Executive Committee, 1921); Esther Crandall, *Calendar of Minnesota Government, 1925,* Bureau for Research in Government of the University of Minnesota, no. 4 (Minneapolis: University of Minnesota Press, 1924); Arthur Naftalin, "The Failure of the Farmer-Labor Party to Capture Control of the Minnesota Legislature," *American Political Science Review* 38 (February 1944): 71–78.

2. Adrian, "Nonpartisan Legislature in Minnesota," p. 209.

3. Cf. McConnell, *Private Power and American Democracy,* chap. 6, "The States."

4. See Keillor, *Petersen,* pp. 98–99.

5. I. C. Strout, Papers, 1–11 February 1931, 17–30 April 1931, Minnesota Historical Society, Division of Archives and Manuscripts, St. Paul, box 2 correspondence.

6. Gieske, *Minnesota Farmer-Laborism,* p. 178.

7. Cf. Martin Shefter, "Party and Patronage: Germany, England, and Italy," *Politics & Society* 7 (1977): 403–51.

8. See Lloyd M. Short and Carl W. Tiller, *The Minnesota Commission of Administration and Finance, 1925–1939: An Administrative History,* University of Minnesota Public Administration Training Center, Studies in Administration, no. 1 (Minneapolis: University of Minnesota Press, 1942).

9. W. Anderson, *Local Government,* table 9, "Number of Public Officers and Employees in Various Governmental Units of Minnesota, 1934," p. 98.

10. See ibid., chap. 15, "Highways, Roads, and Streets," pp. 286–301; Arthur

Borak, "Highway Finance," chap. 13 in Roy Blakey and Associates, *Taxation in Minnesota,* University of Minnesota Studies in Economics and Business, no. 4 (Minneapolis: University of Minnesota Press, 1932), pp. 368–418. Also see Minnesota, Commissioner of Highways, *Biennial Report of the Commissioner of Highways of Minnesota,* 1930–38.

11. See Minnesota, Commissioner of Highways, *Biennial Report,* 31 December 1932, p. 9.

12. I am grateful to a confidential informant, to Mr. Arnold Lindquist of St. Paul, and to Mr. A. R. Rathert of San Francisco for helping me to understand the psychology and career of I. C. Strout. See also *Minnesota Union Advocate,* 16 June 1938, p. 6.

13. Carl Zappfe, *"75": Brainerd, Minnesota, 1871–1946* (Minneapolis: Colwell Press, for the Brainerd Civic Association, 1946), p. 130.

14. Memorandum from ARR (Albert R. Rathert) to I. C. Strout, 24 January 1935, Strout Papers, box 8, Correspondence, 17–31 January 1935.

15. See Minnesota, Commission of Administration and Finance, Director of Personnel, *Classes, Grades, and Titles of State Employees with Class Specifications, as Determined by the Commission of Administration and Finance, Director of Personnel* (January 1935); idem *Salary Scales for State Employees as Classified by the Commission of Administration and Finance, Director of Personnel* (January, 1935).

16. Memorandum from I. C. Strout to investigator 6, Strout Papers, box 8, Correspondence, 17–31 January 1935.

17. George Mayer, *The Political Career of Floyd B. Olson* (Minneapolis: University of Minnesota Press, 1951), p. 262.

18. Cf. Raymond Louis Koch, "The Development of Public Relief Programs in Minnesota, 1929–1941," Ph.D. dissertation, University of Minnesota, 1967, pp. 48–56.

19. See Minnesota, Legislature, Senate, *Report of the Investigating Committee of the Senate Created under Resolution No. 2, for the Purpose of Investigating All Departments of the State Government of Minnesota* (1935), pp. 38–39. See also Short and Tiller, *Minnesota Commission,* p. 36 n. 47.

20. *Third Ward Leader,* 18 September 1936, Newspaper Collection, Minnesota Historical Society, St. Paul. I am grateful to Mr. Sam Bellman of Minneapolis, a two-term Farmer-Labor legislator who represented the Third Ward in the 1935 and 1937 legislatures, for helping me to understand Third Ward politics better. Interview with Sam Bellman, 25 May 1983, Minneapolis.

21. Elmer C. Davis, "Minnesota Worry-Go-Round," *Collier's Weekly,* 26 June 1937, pp. 14–15, 41–42; membership figures, 1937, 1938; Farmer-Labor Association Papers; Holbo, "Minnesota's Party *within* a Party"; interview with Warren Creel, 6 August 1983, Albany, N.Y.

22. Interview with Warreb Creel; interview with Arnold Lindquist, 24 May

1983, St. Paul; confidential interview with former bureau staffer. See also Strout Papers, box 11, correspondence of the Farmer-Labor Educational Bureau.

23. I use the term "partial incorporation" for the sake of precision: not all of the unemployed could be given work relief by the Farmer-Labor party.

24. See Minnesota, Commissioner of Highway, *Biennial Report*, for the years 1931–38; summary of federal aid appropriations to Minnesota in *Biennial Report* for 1936–38 (submitted 1 March 1939 because of housecleaning in the Highway Department by the incoming Republican administration of Harold Stassen), pp. 105–6; Lorena Hickok to Harry L. Hopkins, 12 December 1933, in Richard Lowitt and Maurine Beasley, eds., *One Third of a Nation: Lorena Hickok Reports on the Great Depression* (Urbana: University of Illinois Press, 1981), pp. 134–35; Minnesota, Department of Highways, *History and Organization of the Department of Highways, State of Minnesota,* prepared in connection with Minnesota Highway Planning Survey conducted by the Department of Highways in cooperation with the Public Roads Administration of the Federal Works Agency (March 1942), pp. 69–70.

25. Cf. Minnesota, Commissioner of Highways, *Biennial Report,* 31 December 1934, pp. 7–9.

26. Charles Coy to George Griffith, 15 January 1935, copy in Strout Papers, box 8, Correspondence, 17–31 January 1935.

27. See Mayer, *Olson,* pp. 26–66; Adrian, "Nonpartisan Legislature in Minnesota," pp. 99–100, 287.

28. Sander Genis, Papers, folder "Miscellaneous Papers, 1934–1954," Minnesota Historical Society, St. Paul.

29. Cf. James Q. Wilson, *Political Organizations* (New York: Basic Books, 1973), chap. 3.

30. Frank J. Sorauf, "State Patronage in a Rural Country," *American Political Science Review* 50 (December 1956): 1054.

31. See Minnesota State Federation of Labor, *Proceedings of the Fifty-fifth Convention, Hibbing, Minn., September 20–22, 1937,* pp. 25–27, 33, 37–40, 44–45, 55–56.

32. *The Gallup Poll, Public Opinion, 1935–1971,* 1st ed., vol. 1, *1935–1948* (New York: Random House, 1971), p. 102.

33. Cf. Keillor's well-researched presentation in *Petersen,* pp. 104–31.

34. Bill 1514 of the forty-eighth session of the Minnesota legislature: see *Journal of the Forty-eighth Session of House of Representatives of Minnesota,* topical index, pp. 2383–2419; Keillor, *Petersen,* p. 104; A. R. Rathert to Vince Day, and A. R. Rathert to I. C. Strout, 3 October 1934, photocopies provided by A. R. Rathert, available in Strout Papers, box 8; Minnesota, Governor, *Third Inaugural Message of Olson,* p. 26; Minnesota, Department of Education, Educational Materials Project, *A Merit System for Minnesota,* Social Science Series, no. 1 (1937).

35. Adrian, "Nonpartisan Legislature in Minnesota," p. 190; Mayer, *Olson*, p. 257; Keillor, *Petersen*, p. 131.

Chapter Five

1. Hirschman, *Essays in Trespassing*, pp. 123–34.

2. John D. Hicks, *Republican Ascendancy, 1921–1933*, New American Nation series (New York: Harper & Row, 1960), chaps. 3, 5; Sidney Ratner, *Taxation and Democracy in America* (New York: John Wiley & Sons, 1967), chaps. 19–20.

3. David A. Lake, "International Economic Structures and American Foreign Economic Policy, 1887–1934," and Benjamin J. Cohen, "A Brief History of International Monetary Relations," in Jeffrey A. Frieden and David A. Lake, *International Political Economy: Perspectives on Global Power and Wealth* (New York: St. Martin's Press, 1987), pp. 145–66, 245–68.

4. Scheiber, Vatter, and Faulkner, *American Economic History*, chap. 21. Steffens is quoted in William E. Leuchtenberg, *The Perils of Prosperity, 1914–1932*, Chicago History of American Civilization (Chicago: University of Chicago Press, 1958), p. 202.

5. W. D. Burnham, "System of 1896," pp. 147–202; cf. Richard A. Easterlin, "Regional Income Trends, 1840–1950," in Seymour E. Harris, ed., *American Economic History* (New York: McGraw-Hill Book Co., 1961), pp. 525–47.

6. *Labor World*, Duluth, 13 November 1926, p. 6.

7. James. H. Shideler, *Farm Crisis: 1919–1923* (Berkeley: University of California Press, 1957), pp. vii, 282–95; Kenneth Finegold, "From Agrarianism to Adjustment: The Political Origins of New Deal Agricultural Policy," *Politics & Society* 11 (1981): 1–27; Gilbert C. Fite, "The Farmers' Dilemma, 1919–1929," in John Braeman, Robert H. Bremner, and David Brody, eds., *Change and Continuity in Twentieth Century America: The 1920s* (Columbus: Ohio State University Press, 1968), pp. 67–101.

8. U.S. Department of Commerce, Bureau of the Census, *Historical Statistics of the United States, Colonial Times to 1970* (Washington, D.C.: Bureau of the Census, 1975), series K17-81, 1:463. See also Scheiber, Vatter, Faulkner, *American Economic History*, table 21-4, "Index Numbers of Farm Prices, Prices Paid by Farmers, Farm Wages, Taxes, and Gross Income, 1910–1933," p. 346.

9. For a discussion of war demobilization, see Burt Noggle, *Into the Twenties: The United States from Armistice to Normalcy* (Urbana: University of Illinois Press, 1974), chaps. 3–4; Ellis W. Hawley, *The Great War and the Search for a Modern Order: A History of the American People and Their Institutions, 1917–1933* (New York: St. Martin's Press, 1979), chap. 3; David Burner, "1919: Prelude to Normalcy," in John Braeman, Robert H. Bremner, and David Brody, eds., *Change and Continuity in Twentieth Century America: The 1920s* (Columbus: Ohio State University Press, 1968), pp. 3–31.

10. B. M. Gile and J. D. Black, *The Agricultural Credit Situation in Minnesota*,

Technical Bulletin 55 (St. Paul: University Farm, Division of Agricultural Economics, University of Minnesota Agricultural Experiment Station, 1928), p. 79.

11. Hawley, *Search for a Modern Order,* pp. 53–54, 67–68; Gile and Black, *Agricultural Credit,* p. 79; Minnesota Institute of Governmental Research, *Minnesota and the Agricultural Situation,* State Governmental Research Bulletin 10 (St. Paul: n.p., 1939), pp. 17–22.

12. My discussion of McNary-Haugenism relies primarily on Gilbert C. Fite's classic work, *George N. Peek and the Fight for Farm Parity* (Norman: University of Oklahoma Press, 1954). I also rely on Richard Bensel, *Sectionalism,* pp. 139–47; John D. Black, "The McNary-Haugen Movement," *American Economic Review* 18 (September 1928): 405–27; Darwin N. Kelley, "The McNary-Haugen Bills, 1924–1928: An Attempt to Make the Tariff Effective for Farm Products," *Agricultural History* 14 (October 1940): 170–82; Rexford Guy Tugwell, "Reflections on Farm Relief," *Political Science Quarterly* 43 (December 1928): 481–97.

13. "Coolidge's Veto of the McNary-Haugen Bill, February 25, 1927," in Ross M. Robertson and James L. Pate, eds., *Readings in United States Economic and Business History* (Boston: Houghton Mifflin Co., 1966), pp. 438–39.

14. *Labor World,* 22 May 1926, p. 4.

15. Fite, *Fight for Farm Parity,* p. 122.

16. Cf. David Montgomery, "'Liberty and Union': Workers and Government in America, 1900–1940," in Robert Weible, Oliver Ford, and Paul Marion, eds., *Essays from the Lowell Conference on Industrial History, 1980 and 1981* (Lowell, Mass.: Lowell Conference on Industrial History, 1981), pp. 145–57; Mark Perlman, "Labor in Eclipse," in John Braeman, Robert H. Bremner, and David Brody, eds., *Change and Continuity in Twentieth Century America: The 1920s* (Columbus: Ohio State University Press, 1968), pp. 103–45.

17. For a sophisticated contemporary treatment of this moment in American industrial relations, written from a perspective sympathetic to employers, see Clarence E. Bonnett, *Employers' Associations in the United States: A Study of Typical Associations* (New York: Macmillan Co., 1922), chap. 1. See also Irving Bernstein, *The Lean Years: A History of the American Worker, 1920–1933* (Boston: Houghton Mifflin Co., 1960), pp. 146–57; Noggle, *Into the Twenties,* chap. 6; Andrew Tauber, "Alternative Visions of Economic Regulation, 1918–1930," second year paper, Ph.D. program, Department of Political Science, MIT, 1988; Allen M. Wakstein, "The Origins of the Open Shop Movement, 1919–1920," *Journal of American History* 51 (December 1964): 460–75; Robert H. Zeiger, *Republicans and Labor, 1919–1929* (Lexington: University of Kentucky Press, 1969), chap. 4.

18. Montgomery, *Workers' Control in America,* pp. 49–63; Nord, "Socialism in One City," chap. 3; Charles Rumford Walker, *American City: A Rank-and-File History* (New York: Farrar & Rinehard, 1937), pp. 185–92.

19. See Thiltgen, "Relations of the Governor," pp. 90–106; *Labor World,* 12 June 1926, p. 1, and 19 June 1926, p. 1; Minnesota, Adjutant General, *Report of*

the *Adjutant General of the State of Minnesota Covering the Thirty-second Biennial Period Ending December 31, 1922,* pp. 13–14.

20. David H. Chalmers, *Hooded Americanism: The First Century of the Ku Klux Klan, 1865–1965* (Garden City, N.Y.: Doubleday & Co., 1965), pp. 149–51; Jean E. Spielman, *The Stool Pigeon and the Open Shop Movement* (Minneapolis: American Publishing Co., 1923); Thiltgen, "Relations of the Governor," chap. 5.

21. Bernstein, *Lean Years,* pp. 190–243; Ernest C. Carman, "The Outlook from the Present Legal Status of Employers and Employees in Industrial Disputes," *Minnesota Law Review* 6 (June 1922): 533–59; Ben Chernov, "The Labor Injunction in Minnesota," *Minnesota Law Review* 24 (May 1940): 757–86; Felix Frankfurter and Nathan Green, *The Labor Injunction* (New York: Macmillan Co., 1930); Thiltgen, "Relations of the Governor," p. 98.

22. See Jean E. Spielman, *The Open Shop via the Injunction Route* (Minneapolis: Flour, Cereal, Mill, Grain Elevator, and Linseed Oil Workers Local Union No. 92, 1920; Pamphlets in American History Series, Sanford, N. C.: Microfilming Corporation of America, 1979), L2924, pp. 16, 19. Cf. also Minnesota State Federation of Labor, *Proceedings of the Thirty-ninth Convention, Brainerd, Minn., July 18–20, 1921,* Secretary's report, pp. 19–22. Governor Floyd B. Olson later appointed Jean Spielman the Minnesota state printer.

23. Cf. Keyssar, *Out of Work:* Frank Stricker, "Affluence for Whom? Another Look at Prosperity and the Working Classes in the 1920s," *Labor History* 24 (Winter 1983): 5–33.

24. Minnesota State Federation of Labor, *Proceedings of the Forty-fifth Convention, International Falls, Minn., August 15–17, 1927,* pp. 15–16; William H. Stead and Dreng Bjornaraa, *Employment Trends in St. Paul, Minneapolis, and Duluth,* Bulletins of the University of Minnesota Employment Stabilization Research Institute, vol. 1, no. 2 (Minneapolis: University of Minnesota Press, 1931), p. 33. Cf. also *Minnesota Union Advocate,* 1 March 1928, p. 1.

25. Cf. Arnold R. Alanen, "The 'Locations': Company Communities on Minnesota's Iron Ranges," *Minnesota History* 48 (Fall 1982): 94–107; Donald G. Sofchalk, "Organized Labor and the Iron Ore Miners of Northern Minnesota, 1907–1936," *Labor History* 12 (Spring 1971): 214–42.

26. Cf. Michael Goldfield, *The Decline of Organized Labor in the United States* (Chicago: University of Chicago Press, 1987), pp. 8–9.

27. *Farmer-Labor Leader,* 15 April 1930; Minnesota State Federation of Labor, *Proceedings of the Forty-fourth Convention, Hibbing, Minn., August 16–18, 1926,* pp. 33–34, and *Proceedings of the Forty-second Convention, Faribault, Minn., July 21–23, 1924,* pp. 27–34; Thiltgen, "Relations of the Governor," pp. 90–106.

28. Mayer, *Olson,* p. 33. Cf. William J. Barber, *From New Era to New Deal: Herbert Hoover, the Economists, and American Economic Policy, 1921–1933,* Historical Perspectives on Modern Economics (Cambridge: Cambridge University

Press, 1985), pp. 15–22; Vernon Arthur Mund, "Prosperity Reserves of Public Works," *Annals of the American Academy of Political and Social Science* 149, part 2 (May 1930): 1–49.

29. Frankfurter and Green, *Labor Injunction,* p. 207; Bernstein, *Lean Years,* chap. 11; Martin Ross, *Shipstead of Minnesota,* assisted by Katherine Ferguson Chalkley (Chicago: Packard & Co., 1940), pp. 73, 93–94.

30. Scheiber, Vatter, and Faulkner, *American Economic History,* pp. 279–338; Roland S. Vaile, "Report of a Conference on Problems of the Small City and Town," and "Integration and the Small Town," in Vaile, ed., *The Small City and Town; A Conference on Community Relations: The Report of a Conference on Problems of the Small City and Town, Held at the University of Minnesota, June 24–28, 1929* (Minneapolis: University of Minnesota Press, 1930), pp. 1–23, 38–42. See also H. Bruce Price and C. R. Hoffer, *Services of Rural Trade Centers in Distribution of Farm Supplies,* Minnesota Bulletin 249 (St. Paul: University Farm, University of Minnesota Agricultural Experiment Station, 1928), pp. 47–50. For contemporary commentary on national trends, see J. George Frederick, "Big Business and the Little Man," *North American Review,* October 1928, pp. 440–44; Merryle Stanley Rukeyser, "Chain Stores: The Revolution in Retailing," *Nation,* 28 November 1928, pp. 568–70; George Soule, "Farewell to the Shopkeeper," *New Republic,* 4 April 1928, pp. 210–12. Berle's comment is quoted in McConnell, *Private Power and American Democracy,* p. 250.

31. This discussion based on Ray Chase, Papers, Minnesota Historical Society, Archives and Manuscripts Division, St. Paul, folder "Bank Guarantee Law, 1924–1927," and folder "Banking, 1924–33"; Ben DuBois, Papers, Minnesota Historical Society, Archives and Manuscripts Division, St. Paul, folder 4, "History of the Independent Bankers Association"; Gile and Black, *Agricultural Credit,* pp. 73–79, 84–86; Russell A. Stevenson, ed., *A Type Study of American Banking: Non-Metropolitan Banks in Minnesota,* Bulletins of the Employment Stabilization Research Institute of the University of Minnesota, vol. 4, no. 1 (Minneapolis: University of Minnesota Press, 1934); C. S. Popple, *Development of Two Bank Groups in the Central Northwest: A Study in Bank Policy and Reorganization,* Harvard Studies in Business History, no. 9 (Cambridge: Harvard University Press, 1944), chap. 4; Scheiber, Vatter, and Faulkner, *American Economic History,* p. 338; Eugene Nelson White, "The Political Economy of Banking Regulation, 1864–1933," *Journal of Economic History* 42 (March 1982): 33–40. I am grateful to Mr. Patrick DuBois, president, First State Bank, Sauk Centre, for helping me to understand rural banking better. Interview, 29 July 1980, Sauk Centre, Minn.

32. DuBois Papers, "History of the Independent Bankers Association"; Robert J. Riordan, "A Tale of Two Towns," *Independent Banker,* July 1964, in DuBois Papers, folder 4.

33. *Labor World,* 13 February 1926, pp. 1, 4; 24 July 1926, p. 4; 14 August 1926, p. 4; 8 May 1926, p. 4.

Chapter Six

1. For this discussion I have relied on Barry D. Karl, *The Uneasy State: The United States from 1915 to 1945* (Chicago: University of Chicago Press, 1983); Thomas J. Ladenburg and Samuel Hugh Brockunier, *The Prosperity and Depression Decades* (New York: Hayden Book Company, 1971), chaps. 5–7; Frances Fox Piven and Richard Cloward, *Regulating the Poor: The Functions of Public Welfare* (New York: Vintage Books, 1971), chap. 2; Scheiber, Vatter, and Faulkner, *American Economic History,* chap. 22; Herbert Stein, *The Fiscal Revolution in America* (Chicago: University of Chicago Press, 1969), chap. 2; Tauber, "Alternative Visions."

2. From Herbert Hoover, "We Have Not Feared Boldly to Adopt Unprecedented Measures," address accepting the Republican renomination for president, 11 August 1932, in Frank Freidel and Norman Pollack, eds., *American Issues in the Twentieth Century* (Chicago: Rand McNally & Co., 1966), p. 162.

3. From Herbert Hoover, "I Am Opposed to Any Dole," annual message to the Congress, 8 December 1931, in ibid., pp. 165–66.

4. See Ladenburg and Brockunier, *Prosperity and Depression Decades,* pp. 58–60.

5. For this discussion I have relied on Peter Gourevitch, *Politics in Hard Times,* chap. 4; Karl, *Uneasy State;* Piven and Cloward, *Regulating the Poor,* chaps. 2–3; Albert U. Romasco, *The Politics of Recovery* (New York: Oxford University Press, 1983); Scheiber, Vatter, and Faulkner, *American Economic History,* chap. 23; Stein, *Fiscal Revolution in America,* chap. 3.

6. Roger Baldwin, "American Ideals (2): The Coming Struggle for Liberty," *Common Sense,* January 1935, p. 7.

7. The phrase is from Elmer Eric Schattschneider, *The Semisovereign People: A Realist's View of Democracy in America* (Hinsdale, Ill.: Dryden Press, 1975), p. 11.

8. The basic source for the discussion of the Farmers Holiday Association is John L. Shover, *Cornbelt Rebellion: The Farmers' Holiday Association* (Urbana: University of Illinois Press, 1965).

9. Roland A. White, *Milo Reno: Farmers Union Pioneer: The Story of a Man and a Movement* (Iowa City: Athens Press, for the Iowa Farmers Union, 1941; reprint New York: Arno Press, 1975), p. 151.

10. R. A. White, *Milo Reno,* pp. 41, 193, and "Reno-isms," pp. 193–207, passim.

11. H. C. M. Case, "Farm Debt Adjustment during the Early 1930s," *Agricultural History* 34 (October 1960): 173–81.

12. Everett E. Luoma, *The Farmer Takes a Holiday: The Story of the National Farmers' Holiday Association and the Farmers' Strike of 1932–1933* (New York: Exposition Press, 1967), pp. 62–66.

13. Luoma, *Farmer Takes a Holiday,* pp. 47–49.

14. For a vivid treatment of farm protest in one county, see D. Jerome Tweton,

The New Deal at the Grass Roots: Programs for the People in Otter Tail County, Minnesota (St. Paul: Minnesota Historical Society Press, 1988), chap. 2.

15. Interviews with Harry H. Peterson helped me understand him better, 27 and 28 August 1980, Minneapolis.

16. Interview with Roy Frank, 24 March 1981, Bethesda, Md.

17. Minnesota, Attorney General, *Biennial Report of the Attorney General to the Governor of the State of Minnesota for the Period Ending December 31, 1934,* p. 10.

18. Cf. Lee J. Alston, "Farm Foreclosure Moratorium Legislation: A Lesson from the Past," *American Economic Review* 74 (June 1984): 445–57.

19. A clear, concise description of cost-of-production can be found in Van Perkins, *Crisis in Agriculture: The Agricultural Adjustment Administration and the New Deal, 1933,* University of California Publications in History, vol. 81 (Berkeley and Los Angeles: University of California Press, 1969), pp. 62–63.

20. Cf. Richard S. Kirkendall, *Social Scientists and Farm Politics in the Age of Roosevelt* (Columbia: University of Missouri Press, 1966), pp. 1–60.

21. Quoted in Perkins, *Crisis in Agriculture,* p. 54.

22. Ibid., pp. 168–77.

23. Ibid., pp. 177–79.

24. Cf. Mark Hansen, "The Political Economy of Group Membership," *American Political Science Review* 79 (March 1985): 79–96.

25. Cf. Christiana McFayden Campbell, *The Farm Bureau and the New Deal: A Study of the Making of National Farm Policy, 1933–1940* (Urbana: University of Illinois, 1962); Murray R. Benedict, *Farm Policies of the United States, 1790–1950: A Study of Their Origins and Development* (New York: Twentieth Century Fund, 1953), pp. 119, 152–54, 162, 171, 176–78.

26. Campbell, *Farm Bureau,* pp. 13, 50, 63–64, 85–87; Hansen, "Political Economy of Group Membership," pp. 79–96, passim.

27. Gladys Baker, *The County Agent,* Studies in Public Administration, vol. 11 (Chicago: University of Chicago Press, 1939), p. 73.

28. See Tweton, *New Deal at the Grass Roots,* chap. 8.

29. *Minnesota Farm Bureau News* (South Central Edition), 1 February 1929, p. 1; 1 August 1928, p. 1.

30. Ibid., 1 May 1933, p. 1.

31. Joseph Stancliffe Davis, *Wheat and the AAA,* Institute of Economics Publication 61 (Washington, D.C.: Brookings Institution, 1935), p. 448; D. A. Fitzgerald, *Livestock under the AAA,* Institute of Economics Publication 65 (Washington, D.C.: Brookings Institution, 1935), pp. 368–71. For a description of the implementation of the corn-hog reduction program, see ibid., appendix B, "Details of the 1934 Corn-Hog Reduction Campaign," pp. 326–59. A clear description of its implementation in Minnesota is in Tweton, *New Deal at the Grass Roots,* chap. 8.

32. There are two membership estimates; I adopt the second. See Ralph Russell,

"Membership of the American Farm Bureau Federation, 1926–1935," *Rural Sociology* 2 (March 1937): 29–35; Robert L. Tontz, "Membership of General Farmers' Organizations, United States, 1874–1960," *Agricultural History* 38 (July 1964): appendix table C, p. 156. Tontz does not give figures for all years between 1926 and 1935, but his estimate for 1933 may be more reliable, given quirks in membership reporting procedures inside the bureau. *Minnesota Farm Bureau News* (South Central Edition), 1 October 1935, p. 1, and 1 December 1935, p. 1.

33. Tontz, "Membership of Farmers' Organizations," appendix table B, p. 155. See also Tweton, *New Deal at the Grass Roots,* chap. 1. On the difficulty of county-level reconstruction of the New Deal's impact, see Tweton, Acknowledgments.

34. Minnesota, Governor, *Inaugural Message of Governor Elmer A. Benson to the Legislature of Minnesota,* St. Paul, 5 January 1937, p. 30.

35. The best treatments of Olson are Mayer, *Olson,* and Beecher, *Tomorrow is a Day,* pp. 189–305. I also thank Elmer Benson, Orlin Folwick, Kenneth Haycraft, and Harry Peterson for deepening my understanding of Olson's personality.

36. See Mayer, *Olson,* pp. 128–30; and James M. Shields, *Mr. Progressive: A Biography of Elmer Austin Benson* (Minneapolis: T. S. Denison & Co., 1971), pp. 29–30, 44, for background on the Farmer-Labor party's banking politics and policy during the 1930s. Primary sources are the DuBois Papers and the transcript of an interview with John Newton Peyton, Olson's first superintendant of banks, interviewed by Lila M. Johnson, 9 October 1967, both at the Minnesota Historical Society. See also *Minnesota Leader,* 4 January 1936. I thank Mr. Patrick DuBois for helping me to understand banking politics and policy in the 1930s better. Interview with P. DuBois.

37. For general background, see Joseph Cornwall Palamountain, Jr., *The Politics of Distribution,* Harvard Political Studies, Department of Government, Harvard University (Cambridge: Harvard University Press, 1955), pp. 159–234. See also Shields, *Mr. Progressive,* p. 58; Harold M. Haas, *Social and Economic Aspects of the Chain Store Movement* (1939; New York: Arno Press, 1979), table 1, p. 210.

Chapter Seven

1. Irving Bernstein, *The New Deal Collective Bargaining Policy* (Berkeley and Los Angeles: University of California Press, 1950), chap. 3, and pp. 37–38.

2. Data on the 1933–34 strike wave can be found in P. K. Edwards, *Strikes in the United States, 1881–1974* (New York: St. Martin's Press, for the Social Science Research Council, 1981), pp. 134–40, and table 5.1, "Annual Strike Indices, 1927–46," p. 138, and table A.4, "'Strike Waves,' 1886–1970," p. 258.

3. This aspect of the open-shop movement in Minneapolis is captured in testimony given in 1929 before the Minnesota Temporary Board of Mediation and

Arbitration. An organizer for the Amalgamated Clothing Workers recollected a telling exchange with a local clothing manufacturer: "He told me, he says, 'Now we belong to the Citizens Alliance,' and he says, 'I can't do anything without the Citizens Alliance and they are against the organized labor, and if I do something my credit may be stopped.'" Transcript of testimony taken before the Divison of Mediation and Arbitration of the Minnesota Industrial Commission, p. 139, located in "Garment Workers Strike, 1929," Arthur Le Sueur, Papers, Legal Files, Minnesota Historical Society, St. Paul.

4. A bibliographical note is in order here. My understanding of the Dunne brothers, who led the Minneapolis strikes, has been helped by Dale Kramer's laconic and moving account, "The Dunne Boys of Minneapolis," *Harper's,* March 1942, pp. 388–98. I am grateful, also, to V. Raymond Dunne of Minneapolis for discussing with me the career of his father, Vincent Dunne, and for kindly granting me permission to listen to the only recorded interview of his father, on file at the Minnesota Historical Society, which helped in understanding his charisma. I also thank Mr. Harry DeBoer of Minneapolis, one of the top picket captains of the strike, for helping to bring many of the strike's military aspects alive. Finally, Mr. Carlos Hudson of Union City, Michigan, who edited the strike daily during the July–August strike, the first strike daily in American history, gave very generously of his time, both in correspondence and interviews, in helping me to understand the leadership of the strikes. As for the larger complex of events in which the Dunne brothers and their colleagues moved, I have relied on Charles Rumford Walker's *American City.* Mrs. Adelaide Walker kindly discussed the composition of the book with me and also lent me the materials that were used for its composition, which I catalogued and which are hereafter referred to as the Walker Papers. I also rely on a fascinating memoir of the strikes, Farrell Dobbs's *Teamster Rebellion* (New York: Monad Press, for the Anchor Foundation, 1972). Finally, Thomas Blantz, C. S. C., has written an admirably clear account of the federal government's role in the strikes and their origins, in *A Priest in Public Service: Francis J. Haas and the New Deal* Notre Dame Studies in American Catholicism, vol. 5 (Notre Dame: University of Notre Dame Press, 1982), especially chapters 4–6. His research changes what we know about this aspect of the strikes. Other sources are referred to as necessary; certain details are also referenced.

5. Larry D. Engelmann, "'We Were the Poor People': The Hormel Strike of 1933," *Labor History* 15 (Fall 1974): 483–510.

6. Edwards, *Strikes in the United States,* table A.8a, "Per Cent of Workers Involved in Strikes with Given Issue, 1881–1974," p. 263; Leverett S. Lyon et al., *The National Recovery Administration: An Analysis and Appraisal,* Institute of Economics Publication 60, (Washington, D.C.: Brookings Institution, 1935), part 4, and pp. 488–526.

7. Day had been William Lemke's assistant when Lemke and A. C. Townley wrote much of the reform legislation enacted by the North Dakota Nonpartisan League.

8. Dobbs, *Teamster Rebellion*, p. 65.

9. Quoted from *Minneapolis Tribune* in Carlos Hudson, "Chains Wear Thin in Minneapolis: Notes and Sketches on the Recent Strikes," undated manuscript [fall, 1934?], p. 7 Walker Papers, box 1, temporarily in possession of author.

10. C. R. Walker, *American City*, pp. 127–28.

11. Hudson, "Chains Wear Thin," p. 10.

12. Ibid., pp. 11–12.

13. I am grateful to Deputy Chief of Minneapolis Police Robert Lutz for helping me to understand better the career of the then Chief of Police Michael Johannes. Deputy Chief Lutz permitted me to inspect Johannes's personnel card and interpreted what it means for understanding Johannes's career.

14. "Speech by William Brown, President of 574," undated typescript, Walker Papers, box 1.

15. C. R. Walker, *American City*, pp. 176–78.

16. See Lois Quam and Peter J. Rachleff, "Keeping Minneapolis an Open-Shop Town: The Citizens' Alliance in the 1930s," *Minnesota History* 50 (Fall 1986): 105–17.

17. Goldstein, *Political Repression in America*, pp. 183–91.

18. As for the National Guard raid on Local 574's headquarters, this action may have been intended, in part, to preempt a police raid, for Olson had been told that the Employers Advisory Committee planned a radio broadcast charging the strikers with concealing arms. Cf. Selden Rodman, "Letter from Minnesota," *New Republic*, 15 August 1934, pp. 10–12. The raid may also have had the collateral effect of permitting Olson to argue to Roosevelt that he had done all he could to control the union.

19. The inner circle consisted of Ed Hudson and I. G. Scott. Scott, a former Socialist, was a founder of the Farmer-Labor party and was active in Minneapolis and Hennepin County politics as an elected official from the 1920s to the 1960s. Floyd B. Scott to author, 4 August 1933, and personal discussion with Floyd B. Scott.

20. See Gieske, *Minnesota Farmer-Laborism*, pp. 112, 115; *Northwest Organizer*, 29 April 1937, p. 2; Minnesota, Legislature, Senate, *Report of Investigating Committee*, pp. 17–37.

21. Carlos Hudson to author, 14 September 1983; interview with Gilbert and Grace Carlson, 19 May 1983, St. Paul.

22. Cf. Naftalin, "History of Farmer-Labor Party," pp. 258, 268–75.

23. For an opposite, but not—with respect to the Farmer-Labor party—a persuasive view, see Seymour Martin Lipset, "Roosevelt and the Protest of the 1930s," *Minnesota Law Review* 68 (1983): 273–98.

24. See James T. Patterson, *Congressional Conservatism and the New Deal: The Growth of the Conservative Coalition in Congress, 1933–1939* (Lexington: University of Kentucky Press, 1967).

Chapter Eight

1. In 1923 Magnus Johnson was elected to fill out a term, giving the Farmer-Labor party control of the Senate delegation until the 1924 elections. Governor Olson appointed Elmer Benson to the Senate in 1935.

2. See Adrian, "Nonpartisan Legislature in Minnesota," pp. 150–51.

3. Sources for this discussion are Irving Bernstein, *The Turbulent Years: A History of the American Worker, 1933–1941* (Boston: Houghton Mifflin Co., 1970); D. O. Bowman, *Public Control of Labor Relations: A Study of the National Labor Relations Board* (New York: Macmillan Co., 1942); Murray Edelman, "New Deal Sensitivity to Labor Interests," and R. W. Fleming, "The Significance of the Wagner Act," in Milton Derber and Edwin Young, eds., *Labor and the New Deal* (Madison: University of Wisconsin Press, 1959), pp. 157–92, 121–56; "The G—— D—— Labor Board," *Fortune*, October 1938, pp. 52–57, 115–23; Gilbert J. Gall, "Heber Blankenhorn, the La Follette Committee, and the Irony of Industrial Repression," *Labor History* 23 (Spring 1982): 246–53; James A. Gross, *The Making of the National Labor Relations Board: A Study in Economics, Politics, and the Law* (Albany: State University of New York Press, 1974); idem, *The Reshaping of the National Labor Relations Board: National Labor Policy in Transition, 1937–1947* (Albany: State University of New York Press, 1981); Peter Irons, *The New Deal Lawyers* (Princeton: Princeton University Press, 1982), part 3. I thank Leon Keyserling, Senator Wagner's legislative assistant in 1935 (interview, 30 December 1981, Washington, D.C.), and two former members of the NLRB's legal staff, who prefer anonymity, for helping me to understand the board better. I am grateful, too, to Mr. Luke Wilson, who worked for the La Follette Civil Liberties Committee as an investigator, for helping me to understand the links between the committee's work and the board's work. Interview, 27 December 1982, Bethesda, Md.

4. In reaction to liberal analyses of the Wagner Act that emphasized its liberating character, recent revisionist scholarship pictures the Wagner Act as harmful to the long-run interests of American workers. For a discussion and critique of this revisionist literature, see Howell Harris, "Snares of Liberalism? Politicians, Bureaucrats, and the Shaping of Federal Labor Policy, ca. 1915–1947," in Steven Tolliday and Jonathan Zeitlin, eds., *Shop Floor Bargaining and the State: Historical and Comparative Perspectives* (Cambridge: Cambridge University Press, 1985), pp. 148–91.

5. Sources for this section are Walter Galenson, *Rival Unionism in the United States* (New York: American Council on Public Affairs, 1940); Herbert Harris, *Labor's Civil War* (New York: Alfred A. Knopf, 1940); Edwin Young, "The Split in the Labor Movement," in Milton Derber and Edwin Young, eds., *Labor and the New Deal* (Madison: University of Wisconsin Press, 1959), pp. 45–76.

6. See Committee for Industrial Organization, *The Case for Industrial Organization* (Washington, D.C.: Committee for Industrial Organization, [1936?]);

Christopher L. Tomlins, "AFL Unions in the 1930s: Their Performance in Historical Perspective," *Journal of American History* 65 (March 1979): 1021–42.

7. *Gallup Poll* 1:71.

8. Minnesota State Federation of Labor, *Proceedings of the Fifty-fourth Convention, Cloquet, Minn., September 21–23, 1936*, pp. 71–72.

9. See Emily Marks and Mary Bartlett, "Employee Elections Conducted by National Labor Relations Board," *Monthly Labor Review* 47 (July 1938): 37.

10. Emily Clark Brown, "The New Collective Bargaining in Mass Production: Methods, Results, Problems," *Journal of Political Economy* 47 (February 1939): 30–66; U.S. National Labor Relations Board, Division of Economic Research, *Written Trade Agreements in Collective Bargaining*, Bulletin 4 (Washington, D.C.: Government Printing Office, 1939).

11. Estimates for the period between April and December 1937 are based on multiplying the pre–*Jones & Laughlin* number of elections by the average number of workers for union-affiliated type of election cited by Marks and Bartlett, "Employee Elections," p. 36, and subtracting it from totals presented in table 4 of their article.

12. Mark Perlman, *The Machinists: A New Study in American Trade Unionism*, Wertheim Publications in Industrial Relations (Cambridge: Harvard University Press, 1961), p. 229, and, generally, "The Meaning of Jurisdiction," chap. 9. See also Committee for Industrial Organization, *Case for Industrial Organization; Galenson, Rival Unionism*, introduction; *Encyclopaedia of the Social Sciences*, s.v. "Dual Unionism," by David Saposs; Tomlins, "AFL Unions in the 1930s."

13. On "private government," see McConnell, *Private Power and American Democracy*, chap. 5.

14. While Tomlins seeks to correct standard views concerning the extent of competition between the AFL and the CIO, his own data on interunion representation battles supervised by the NLRB, even though they begin in 1938 and they drop over the entire 1938–46 period he covers, suggest a mounting problem in 1937 and 1938. It was not until 1938 that the NLRB allowed itself to be dragged into interunion disputes. A quarter of the NLRB's supervision of representation contests between 1938 and 1940 involved rivalry. This was a significant level of rivalry, and suggests a growing problem in 1937 and 1938. The data may understate the extent of rivalry as well, since we do not know how many cases were not brought to the point of both sides requesting government umpirage. See Tomlins, "AFL Unions in the 1930s," p. 1040 n. 47.

15. See William Green, *Labor and Democracy* (Princeton: Princeton University Press, 1939), pp. 173–84. Among other primary sources, see *Machinists Monthly Journal* 141 (March 1936): 140, 141–42, 143. These arguments appeared in Minnesota in June 1937. See *Minnesota Federationist*, 15 July 1937, p. 1, reprint of 18 June 1937 article in *Minneapolis Labor Review*.

16. Was this an outcome intended by Communist and pro-Communist mem-

bers of the NLRB staff? See Earl Latham, *The Communist Controversy in Washington: From the New Deal to McCarthy* (Cambridge: Harvard University Press, 1966), pp. 124–50, for an affirmative answer and, for a negative, Bernard Karsh and Phillips Garman, "The Impact of the Political Left," in Milton Derber and Edwin Young, eds., *Labor and the New Deal* (Madison: University of Wisconsin Press, 1959), pp. 77–120.

17. Cf. American Federation of Labor, *Proceedings of the Twenty-ninth Annual Convention of the Metal Trades Department of the American Federation of Labor, Denver, Colorado, September 27, 1937*, pp. 26–29.

18. See John Earl Haynes, "Communism and Anti-Communism in the Northern Minnesota CIO," *Upper Midwest History* 1 (Fall 1981): 55–73.

19. *CIO News,* 22 December 1937, p. 4.

20. United Electrical, Radio, and Machine Workers of America, *Proceedings of the Second Annual Convention of the United Electrical, Radio, and Machine Workers of America, Philadelphia, September 3–6, 1937,* p. 4, and passim; idem *Proceedings of the Third Annual Convention of the United Electrical, Radio, and Machine Workers of America, St. Louis, September 5–9, 1938,* pp. 21–25, 90. Cf. *Union News Service,* 17 September 1937.

21. Minnesota State Federation of Labor, *Proceedings of the Fifty-fifth Convention,* passim, and pp. 62–63.

22. Cf. Leo Troy, *Distribution of Union Membership among the States, 1939 and 1953,* Occasional Paper 56 (New York: National Bureau of Economic Research, 1957), p. 4.

23. See *Timberworker* Duluth, 21 May 1937, item re funeral eulogy given by Nat Ross, state secretary, Minnesota Communist party, p. 4. *Timberworker* later became the official newspaper of the Minnesota Industrial Union Council. It is available in microfilm at the Minnesota Historical Society Newspaper Collection in St. Paul.

24. When the International Brotherhood of Teamsters became reconciled with the Trotskyist leaders of Local 574 not long after the 1934 strikes, a truce that lasted until the early '40s, Local 574 became Local 544.

25. See Ralph C. James and Estelle Dinnerstein James, *Hoffa and the Teamsters: A Study of Union Power* (Princeton: D. Van Nostrand Co., 1965), chap. 5; Tomlins, "AFL Unions in the 1930s," which places Dobbs's innovation in comparative perspective.

26. The phrase, "honor of socialism," is taken from Irving Howe, "Sad Events of Long Ago," *Dissent,* Summer 1988, p. 373.

27. See, inter alia, James Burnham, *The People's Front: The New Betrayal* (New York: Pioneer Publishers, 1937); James P. Cannon, *The History of American Trotskyism: From Its Origins (1928) to the Founding of the Socialist Workers Party (1938): Report of a Participant* (New York: Pathfinder Press, 1972), pp. 239–47; James Hawthorne, "Trotsky's Agents in Spain," *New Masses,* 13 July 1937, pp. 15–17; William Herrick, "Who Killed Andreu Nin?" *New Leader,* 27

June 1983, pp. 10–12; George Orwell, *Homage to Catalonia* (New York: Harcourt, Brace & World, Harvest Book, 1952); Edwin Rolfe, "Trotskyites on Trial: Spain's Tribunal of High Treason Hears the Evidence," *New Masses*, 25 October 1938, pp. 7–9.

28. This discussion is based on Karl, *Uneasy State;* Mark H. Leff, *The Limits of Symbolic Reform: The New Deal and Taxation, 1933–1939* (New York: Cambridge University Press, 1984); Stein, *Fiscal Revolution in America;* Romasco, *Politics of Recovery.*

29. Cited in Lipset, "Roosevelt," p. 289.

30. On the Wagner Act's social significance, see Karl E. Klare, "Judicial Deradicalization of the Wagner Act and the Origins of Modern Legal Consciousness, 1937–1941," *Minnesota Law Review* 62 (1978): 265–339.

31. See Edwards, *Strikes in the United States*, pp. 141–43, 258.

32. Cf. *Gallup Poll* 1:116.

33. In addition to Gross, *National Labor Relations Board,* cf. Leo Huberman, "The Attack on the NLRB," *New Republic,* 19 January 1938, pp. 298–300; "NLRB Maintains Its Batting Average in Highest Court," *Labor,* Washington, D.C., 7 June 1938, p. 3.

34. American Federation of State, County, and Municipal Employees, *Proceedings of the Second Convention of the American Federation of State, County, and Municipal Employees, Milwaukee, September 13–15, 1937,* pp. 36–37. For background, see E. B. McNatt, "The 'Appropriate Bargaining Unit' Problem," *Quarterly Journal of Economics* 56 (November 1941): 93–107; Tomlins, "AFL Unions in the 1930s," pp. 1040–42.

35. Cf. Robert Cantwell, "The Communists and the CIO," *New Republic,* 23 February 1938, p. 63.

36. For a subtle discussion of the long-run attitudinal and institutional sources of this issue, see Karl, *Uneasy State,* especially chap. 8. For a superb discussion of the political economy of the issue, see Romasco, *Politics of Recovery.* On public opinion regarding one aspect of the issue see Gregory Caldeira, "Public Opinion and the U.S. Supreme Court: FDR's Court-Packing Plan," *American Political Science Review* 81 (December 1987): 1139–53.

37 *Gallup Poll* 1:30–31.

38. See U.S. Department of Commerce, Bureau of Economic Analysis, *State Personal Incomes: Estimates for 1929–82 and a Statement of Sources and Methods* (Washington, D.C.: Department of Commerce, 1984), p. 31.

39. On the disarray in the implementation of old-age assistance and unemployment insurance, see Arthur J. Altmeyer, *The Formative Years of Social Security* (Madison: University of Wisconsin Press, 1966), chap. 3. On the anti-WPA backlash, see Lawrence Westbrook, "Error and Remedy in WPA Publicity," *Public Opinion Quarterly* 1 (July 1937): 94–98. On the concept of mass discontent with the welfare state, see Albert O. Hirschman, *Shifting Involvements: Private Interest and Public Action,* Eliot Janeway Lectures on Historical Economics in Honor of

Joseph Schumpeter, Princeton University, 1979 (Princeton: Princeton University Press, 1982), pp. 39–43.

40. *Gallup Poll* 1:89, 95, 99.

41. Ibid., p. 97.

42. Ibid., pp. 48–49, 52, 55, 120.

43. Ibid., p. 114.

44. "American Institute of Public Opinion: Surveys, 1938–1939," *Public Opinion Quarterly* 3 (October 1939): 594.

45. *Gallup Poll* 1:109.

46. Ibid., pp. 92, 111, 123, 125.

47. Ibid., p. 101.

48. Congress of Industrial Organizations,*Proceedings of the First Constitutional Convention of the Congress of Industrial Organizations, Pittsburgh, November 14–18, 1938,* pp. 60–63.

Chapter Nine

1. For a brief description of the Hotelling-Downs model, see Albert O. Hirschman, *Exit, Voice, and Loyalty: Responses to Decline in Firms, Organizations, and States* (Cambridge: Harvard University Press, 1970), chap. 6.

2. Cf. Douglas Yates, "The Roots of American Leadership: Political Style and Policy Consequences," in Walter Dean Burnham and Martha Wagner Weinberg, eds., *American Politics and Public Policy* (Cambridge: MIT Press, 1979), pp. 140–68.

3. The interlocutor between Floyd Olson and the Communist party was Clarence Hathaway, editor of the *Daily Worker*. A native Minnesotan, he once was in St. Paul Machinists Local 459 and in 1923 nearly became a member of the Executive Council of the Minnesota State Federation of Labor.

4. Harvey Klehr, *The Heyday of American Communism: The Depression Decade* (New York: Basic Books, 1984), pp. 257–65; Clarence Hathaway, "Problems in Our Farmer-Labor Party Activities," *Communist* 15 (May 1936): 427–433, especially pp. 431–33; Allen and Violet Sollie, Papers, Minnesota Historical Society, St. Paul, box 3, folder "Farmer-Labor Party Internal Struggles." Interviews with Nat Ross (20 January 1986, New York) and Lillian Schwartz Gates (8 November 1985, Glen Cove, N.Y.) helped me enormously in understanding this period in Minnesota politics. Mr. Ross was head of the Communist party in Minnesota during the Benson administration; Ms. Gates worked for the Hennepin County Farmer-Labor Association between 1936 and 1938. Also useful were (1) an interview with Harold Rutchick (23 July 1985, St. Paul), who helped me better to understand his brother, Roger Rutchick, Benson's executive secretary; (2) telephone interviews I conducted with Orville Olson, director of personnel in the Highway Department during the Benson administration (2 April and 3 August 1983); (3) excerpts from the transcript of an oral history of Orville Olson made by John Highkin and provided to me courtesy of Mr. Highkin; (4) an oral history of

Chester Watson (21 August 1968), president of the Workers Alliance in Minnesota and Farmer-Labor candidate for Congress from the first district in 1936, in the Audio-Visual Collection of the Minnesota Historical Society; and (5) a video documentary of the career of John Bernard, *A Common Man's Courage,* also in the society's Audio-Visual Collection. See also Barbara Stuhler, "The One Man Who Voted 'Nay': The Story of John T. Bernard's Quarrel with American Foreign Policy, 1937–1939," *Minnesota History* 43 (Fall 1972): 83–92. Bernard's interest in Communist foreign policy predated his congressional career. See *United Action,* organ of the Communist party, Minnesota District, 1 May 1936, p. 2, in Walker Papers.

5. Minnesota, Governor, *Inaugural Message of Benson,* p. 26.

6. Roy G. Blakey and Gladys C. Blakey, *Taxation in Minnesota, 1939 Supplement* (Minneapolis: University of Minnesota Press, 1939), pp. 20–25; B. U. Ratchford, *American State Debts* (Durham, N.C.: Duke University Press, 1941), pp. 353–57; Minnesota, Legislature, Senate, *Journal of the Senate of the Forty-seventh Session of the Legislature of Minnesota* (1931), pp. 1205–9.

7. See Adrian, "Nonpartisan Legislature in Minnesota," p. 151.

8. Clarence Hathaway, "The Minnesota Farmer-Labor Victory," *Communist* 15 (December 1936): 1112–24, especially p. 1120.

9. E. C. Davis, "Minnesota Worry-Go-Round"; Nat Ross, "The People's Mandate in Minnesota," *Communist* 16 (June 1937): 534–44.

10. A basic source for understanding the 1937 split in the Minneapolis Farmer-Labor party is the Sollie Papers, box 3.

11. *Northwest Organizer,* 18 March 1937, editorial, p. 4.

12. Haycraft had the distinction of leading the National Guard into Citizens Alliance headquarters in August 1934. In 1937 he administered the state's old-age pension system.

13. *Northwest Organizer,* 6 May 1937, editorial, p. 4, and item noting Vincent Dunne's radio address attacking Haycraft, p. 3.

14. Interview with Kenneth Haycraft, 1 June 1981, North Branford, Conn.; confidential interview with Benson speechwriter.

15. For additional background, see Dobbs, *Teamster Politics,* pp. 100–106.

16. *Northwest Organizer,* Special Edition, 1 October 1937, p. 1.

17. *Minnesota Leader,* 9 October 1937, editorial, p. 4; *Northwest Organizer,* 14 October 1937, editorial, p. 4.

18. I thank O. R. Votaw for discussing his career with me. Interview 23 May 1983, St. Paul.

19. O. R. Votaw, "The Communist Party's Rhumba Dance and the Farmer-Labor Party," *Minnesota Union Advocate,* 9 December 1937, p. 4.

20. O. R. Votaw, "Communists Working Overtime to 'Capture' Working Class," *Minnesota Union Advocate,* 16 December 1937, p. 4.

21. *Minnesota Union Advocate,* 9 December 1937, p. 7.

22. O. R. Votaw, "The Mildew of Communism," *Minnesota Union Advocate,* 2 December 1937, p. 5.

23. For background, see Dobbs, *Teamster Power,* pp. 157–68. I thank also a former Communist trade unionist in Minneapolis who knew the politics described here very well, for talking about these events with me. He prefers to remain anonymous.

24. *Minnesota Union Advocate,* 25 November 1937, p. 4.

25. James P. Cannon, "Who Killed Pat Corcoran and Why?" broadside in Sollie Papers, box 3, folder "Farmer-Labor Party Internal Struggles."

26. Shields, *Mr. Progressive,* pp. 164–65.

27. Dobbs, *Teamster Power,* p. 161; "Benson at Funeral of Slain Union Chief," *New York Times,* 21 November 1937, section 2, p. 8; "CIO Says Gangs Rule Minneapolis," *New York Times,* 22 November 1937, p. 4; "Asks Federal Aid in Twin-City Case," *New York Times,* 25 November 1937, p. 32.

28. For an indication of concern within the Benson administration over this development, see *Advance,* January 1937, article by Abe Harris, editor of the *Minnesota Leader,* p. 30.

29. See Keillor, *Petersen,* chaps. 8–9; idem, "A Country Editor in Politics: Hjalmar Petersen, Minnesota Governor," *Minnesota History* 48 (Fall 1983): 283–94. I am grateful to both Medora Petersen and Evelyn Petersen Metzger, Petersen's wife and daughter respectively, for helping me to understand Petersen. Medora Petersen to author, 7 August 1983; interview with Evelyn Petersen Metzger, 26 December 1983, McLean, Va.

30. E. C. Davis, "Minnesota Worry-Go-Round," p. 42.

31. *Northwest Organizer,* 27 January 1938, editorial, p. 4.

32. See "Labor Unions and Ulterior Motives," 20 January 1938, p. 3; "Should Unions Play Second Fiddle?" 3 February 1938, p. 4; "Remote Control," 10 February 1938, p. 4; "Plain Talk," 17 February 1938, p. 4; "More Plain Talk," 24 February 1938, p. 5; all editorials by O. R. Votaw in *Minnesota Union Advocate.*

33. For an account of the Duluth convention, see Keillor, *Petersen,* pp. 151–54.

34. For a treatment of political anti-Semitism in Minnesota in the 1930s, see Hyman Berman, "Political Antisemitism in Minnesota during the Great Depression," *Jewish Social Studies* 38 (Summer-Fall 1976): 247–64. See also Keillor, *Petersen,* pp. 154–58, 160, 162, 165–69.

35. Shields, *Mr. Progressive,* pp. 177–78; interview with Evelyn Petersen Metzger.

36. Nat Ross, "The Election Campaign in Minnesota," *Communist* 17 (October 1938): 941.

37. Cf. *St. Paul Pioneer Press,* 27 May 1938, p. 10.

38. Walter Beirce, "A Party without a Program," *New International,* March 1939, pp. 74–78; *Northwest Organizer,* 31 March 1938, p. 2. Walter Beirce was

the nom de plume of a Trotskyist staffer of the Farmer-Labor Educational Bureau, described in chapter 4.

39. *Minnesota Union Advocate,* 16 June 1983, p. 4; 7 July 1938, p. 4.

40. Berman, "Political Antisemitism in Minnesota"; Robert C. Emery, *Thirty Years from Now* (St. Paul: n.p., 1934), an anti-Semitic, anti-Communist pamphlet written by a Twin Cities journalist; Minnesota, Legislature, Senate, *Journal of the Forty-ninth Session of the Legislature of Minnesota,* pp. 923–25.

41. Medora Petersen to author.

42. *St. Paul Pioneer Press,* 23 May 1938, p. 1.

43. Medora Petersen to author.

44. *Minnesota Union Advocate,* 23 June 1938, p. 4.

45. I thank Harold Stassen for discussing the 1938 campaign with me. Although we stuck to generalities, I still learned a great deal, especially as I listened to him on a radio talk show while waiting for him at a Manchester, N.H., radio station. Interview, 23 February 1984, Manchester, N.H.

46. Here Stassen profited from the detailed reportage of splits inside the Farmer-Labor party that appeared in the *St. Paul Pioneer Press* under the byline of its political reporter, Joseph Ball, later a United States senator who played an important role in the passage of the Taft-Hartley Act. Interview with Joseph Ball, 3 June 1981, Front Royal, Va.

47. Keillor, *Petersen,* p. 145.

48. Ivan Hinderaker, "Harold Stassen and Developments in the Republican Party in Minnesota, 1937–1943," Ph.D. dissertation, University of Minnesota, 1949, pp. 63–64, 80–81, 89, 92–94, 100, 126–28.

49. *Minnesota Union Advocate,* 10 November 1938, p. 1.

50. Hinderaker, "Harold Stassen," pp. 22–23, 81, 89, 100, 237; Minnesota, Department of Conciliation, *First Annual Report of the Division of Conciliation* (1940), pp. 21–24; *Minnesota Union Advocate,* 9 December 1937, p. 8.

51. Ray P. Chase, *Are They Communists or Catspaws? A Red Baiting Article* (Anoka, Minn.: n.p., 1938). See also Berman, "Political Antisemitism in Minnesota"; Hinderaker, "Harold Stassen," pp. 242–43, 259–60, 272–75, 363; Keillor, *Petersen,* pp. 163–64.

52. Paul Y. Anderson, "Behind the Dies Intrigue," *Nation,* 12 November 1938, pp. 499–500; Hinderaker, "Harold Stassen,: pp. 357–58; U.S. Congress, House, Special Committee on Un-American Activities, *Hearings before a Special Committee on Un-American Activities on H. R. 282,* 75th Cong., 3d sess., 1938, pp. 1360–82, 1410–17, 1420–22, 1464–66. A Gallup poll showed that by mid-November 1938, 60 percent of respondents had heard of the Dies Committee, and of these 74 percent thought that its work was important. *Gallup Poll* 1:128.

53. See *Minneapolis Journal,* 2 June 1938, p. 3; Hinderaker, "Harold Stassen," pp. 259–60; *Minnesota Union Advocate,* 21 July 1938, p. 4; *Willmar Tribune,* Minnesota, 6 June 1938, p. 8. Cf. Charles C. Killingsworth, *State Labor Relations*

Acts: A Study of Public Policy (Chicago: University of Chicago Press, 1948), pp. 16–23.

54. George Gallup and Claude Robinson, "American Institute of Public Opinion: Surveys, 1935–38," *Public Opinion Quarterly* 2 (July 1938): 379.

55. Hinderaker, "Harold Stassen," p. 81.

56. Ibid., p. 240.

57. See *Catholic Bulletin* (Official Publication of St. Paul Archdiocese), 12 February 1938, 12 March 1938, 16 April 1938, 21 May 1938, 4 June 1938, 27 August 1938, 3 September 1938, 10 September 1938, 15 October 1938.

58. Keillor, *Petersen,* pp. 159–60.

59. "American Institute of Public Opinion," p. 593.

60. See Searle Charles, *Minister of Relief: Harry Hopkins and the Depression* (Syracuse: Syracuse University Press, 1963), pp. 167–205, passim. In addition to poll data previously cited, cf. "Relief Standards," 28 pp., address given at the Minnesota State Conference on Social Work, 25 May 1938, by Karl A. Lundberg, deputy administrator of the State Relief Agency, in Chase Papers, box 16.

61. Forrest A. Walker, *The Civil Works Administration: An Experiment in Federal Work Relief, 1933–1934* (New York: Garland Publishing Co., 1979), pp. 144–47; Harold R. Kerbo and Richard A. Shaffer, "Unemployment and Protest in the United States, 1890–1940: A Methodological Critique and Research Note," *Social Forces* 64 (June 1986): 1046–57.

62. Keillor, *Petersen,* p. 164.

63. Cf. Zingale, "Electoral Stability and Change," pp. 154–55, and chap. 1.

64. In two of those rural counties where turnout dropped, there were growing urban centers, Austin and Albert Lea. If these counties are not counted, rural turnout jumped in 83 percent of the counties. Also, in the rest of the counties that did not experience a jump in turnout the Republican party historically had been much stronger than the Farmer-Labor party.

65. See Zingale, "Electoral Stability and Change," pp. 205, 214. Other data for calculations are in *Minnesota Votes.*

66. Source of calculations is the *Legislative Manual of Minnesota* for the relevant years.

67. Samuel T. McSeveney, "The Michigan Gubernatorial Campaign of 1938," *Michigan History* 45 (June 1961): 97–127; Richard C. Keller, "Pennsylvania's Little New Deal," in John Braeman, Robert H. Bremner, and David Brody, eds., *The New Deal,* vol. 2, *The State and Local Levels* (Columbus: Ohio State University Press, 1975), pp. 45–76. Cf. also Milton Plesur, "The Republican Congressional Comeback of 1938," *Review of Politics* 24 (October 1962): 525–62.

68. Hugh T. Lovin, "The Fall of Farmer-Labor Parties, 1936–1938," *Pacific Northwest Quarterly* 62 (January 1971): 16–26; Gieske, *Minnesota Farmer-Laborism,* pp. 274–75.

69. Gieske, *Minnesota Farmer-Laborism,* pp. 276–332. An authoritative study

of factionalism in the Farmer-Labor party and the Democratic Farmer-Labor Party, 1939–48, is John Earl Haynes, *Dubious Alliance: The Making of Minnesota's DFL Party* (Minneapolis: University of Minnesota Press, 1984). See also Labor's Non-partisan League Papers, box 2, folder "Hennepin County Farmer-Labor Association," State Historical Society of Wisconsin, Madison.

Chapter Ten

1. Cf. also David Brody, "On the Failure of U.S. Radical Politics: A Farmer-Labor Analysis," *Industrial Relations* 22 (Spring 1983): 141–63.

2. M. J. Coldwell, a famous M. P. elected from Saskatchewan by the Cooperative Commonwealth Federation, once stressed the similarity of CCF and Minnesota Farmer-Labor politics: "One of my happiest recollections is that of the cordial welcome the late Floyd Olsen [sic] gave me in 1935, when I was accorded the opportunity of addressing your State Legislature regarding the principles and policies of our Co-operative Commonwealth Federation . . . We would greatly appreciate a message of greeting from your Farmer-Labor Association . . . as a symbol of the unity of spirit between our two organizations which will inspire us to carry forward the work of building a better world." M. J. Coldwell to Vienna P. Johnson, 18 June 1942, Farmer-Labor Association Papers, box 7. Ms. Vienna Johnson was then secretary-treasurer of the Minnesota Farmer-Labor Association.

3. See, inter alia, John F. Burns, "A Leftist Leader Surging in Canada," *New York Times*, 8 November 1987, pp. 1, 16; Thomas S. Axworthy, "Left Turn in Canada?" *Public Opinion*, September-October 1987, pp. 52–54.

4. J. R. Mallory, *The Structure of Canadian Government* (New York: St. Martin's Press, 1971), pp. 326–27, 332–34, 356.

5. Garth Stevenson, *Unfulfilled Union: Canadian Federalism and National Unity* (Toronto: Gage Publishing, 1979), chaps. 4–5; J. Harvey Perry, *Taxation in Canada* (Toronto: University of Toronto Press, 1951), chaps. 8–13; Kenneth McNaught, *The Pelican History of Canada* (London: Penguin Books, 1976), p. 246. An indicator of the shift in the federal distribution of power was the drop in the number of provincial statutes disallowed by the federal government. Between 1867 and 1906 the Dominion disallowed, on average, twenty-two pieces of provincial legislation per decade, for a total of eighty-seven. Between 1907 and 1926 the Dominion disallowed only an average of seven per decade, for a total of fourteen. See series Y271-281, "Number of Provincial Statues Disallowed by the Federal Government, by Province and Decade, 1867 to 1976," in Canada, Statistics Canada, *Historical Statistics of Canada*, 2nd ed., ed. F. H. Leacy (Ottawa, 1983).

6. Michiel Horn, *The Great Depression of the 1930s in Canada*, Historical Booklet 39 (Ottawa: Canadian Historical Association, 1984), pp. 3–5; McNaught, *History of Canada*, p. 246.

7. Horn, *Great Depression in Canada*, pp. 7–13; McNaught, *History of Canada*, pp. 247–48.

8. See Alvin Finkel, *Business and Social Reform in the Thirties* (Toronto: James

Lorimer & Co., 1979), chap. 5; C. A. Curtis, "Dominion Legislation of 1935: An Economist's Review," *Canadian Journal of Economics and Political Science* 1 (November 1935): 599–608.

9. McNaught, *History of Canada,* pp. 251–55; F. R. Scott, "The Privy Council and Mr. Bennett's 'New Deal' Legislation," *Canadian Journal of Economics and Political Science* 3 (May 1937): 234–40. Electoral data are from Y75-198, "Votes Polled in Federal Elections, by Party and Province, 1896 to 1974," Canada, Statistics Canada, *Historical Statistics of Canada.* On the Judicial Committee of the Privy Council, see Mallory, *Structure of Canadian Government,* pp. 335–48.

10. For a somewhat different account of why Canada did not have a New Deal (but one that could be assimilated into the account given here), see Peter G. Bruce, "Political Parties and the Evolution of Labor Law in Canada and the United States," Ph.D. dissertation, MIT, 1988, pp. 250–58.

11. Horn, *Great Depression in Canada,* p. 21.

12. On the tax rentals, see Mallory, *Structure of Canadian Government,* pp. 362–66. Dominion assumption of unemployment insurance policy is sketched in Finkel, *Business and Social Reform,* p. 96. Dominion-provincial diplomacy as a site for the expansion of the Canadian welfare state is discussed perceptively in Christopher Leman, "Patterns of Policy Development: Social Security in the U.S. and Canada," *Public Policy* 25 (Spring 1977): 261–91.

13. This discussion is based on Seymour Martin Lipset, *Agrarian Socialism: The Cooperative Commonwealth Federation in Saskatchewan: A Study in Political Sociology,* rev. and exp. ed. (Berkeley: University of California Press, 1971), chap. 11; Dean E. McHenry, *The Third Force in Canada: The Cooperative Commonwealth Federation, 1932–1948* (Berkeley and Los Angeles: University of California Press, 1950), chap. 7.

14. Lipset, *Agrarian Socialism,* p. 279.

15. See Bruce, "Political Parties." On the relationship between law and union strength see chapters 2–3; on the diffusion of the Saskatchewan model, see pages 440–53; on "contagion from the left" in general, see pages 170–84, and in the case of Ontario politics, see chapters 5–7.

16. This discussion is based on Charles Herbert Backstrom, "The Progressive Party of Wisconsin, 1934–1946," Ph.D. dissertation, University of Wisconsin, 1956; John E. Miller, *Governor Philip F. La Follette: The Wisconsin Progressives and the New Deal* (Columbia: University of Missouri Press, 1982); Harold F. Gosnell and Morris H. Cohen, "Progressive Politics: Wisconsin an Example," *American Political Science Review* 34 (October 1940): 920–35. For electoral data I used *Congressional Quarterly's Guide to U.S. Elections.*

17. Keillor, *Petersen,* p. 112.

18. Mayer, *Olson,* p. 281.

19. Primary sources are John T. Bernard, "Give Us a Program" *New Masses,* 31 August 1937, pp. 3–5; Jerry J. O'Connell, "The Challenge of the Special Session," *New Masses,* 23 November 1937, pp. 3–5; Henry G. Teigan, "Rolling

Our Own Logs," *New Masses,* 21 December 1937, pp. 3–4. For a perceptive critique of the bloc, see M. R. Bendiner, "Dim Dawn over the Capitol,"*New Masses,* 9 February 1937, pp. 7–9. A secondary source is Stuart L. Weiss, "Maury Maverick and the Liberal Bloc," *Journal of American History* 57 (March 1971): 880–95. The best study to date is James J. Lorence, "Community Spirit and Welfare: Gerald J. Boileau and the Progressive-Farmer-Labor Alliance in the Interwar Era," manuscript.

20. Altmeyer, *Formative Years of Social Security,* pp. 30–31; folder "Social Insurance File, Unemployment Insurance Subcommittee, Hon. Matthew A. Dunn, Chmn," Lundeen Papers; Skocpol and Ikenberry, "American Welfare State," pp. 122–23; Edwin F. Witte, *The Development of the Social Security Act* (Madison: University of Wisconsin Press, 1963), pp. 80, 85, 86, 99, 130.

21. Roger H. Davidson and Walter J. Oleszek, *Congress and Its Members* (Washington, D.C.: Congressional Quarterly Press, 1981), p. 277; E. Pendleton Herring, "First Session of the Seventy-fourth Congress," *American Political Science Review* 29 (December 1935): 985–1005, especially pp. 986–87; O. R. Altman, "First Session of the Seventy-fifth Congress," *American Political Science Review* 31 (December 1937): 1071–93, especially pp. 1073–76. For an analysis of the cohesion of the Democrats, see Barbara Sinclair, *Congressional Realignment, 1925–1978* (Austin: University of Texas Press, 1982), pp. 3–36.

22. Cf. Malcolm Moos and E. W. Kenworthy, "Dr. Shipstead Comes to Judgment," *Harper's,* July 1946, pp. 21–27.

23. See, inter alia, Floyd B. Olson, "My Political Creed: Why a New Party Must Challenge Capitalism," *Common Sense,* April 1935, pp. 6–7; idem, "Why a New National Party?" *Common Sense,* January 1936, pp. 6–8. On the 1934 platform, see Keillor, *Petersen,* p. 105.

24. Donald R. McCoy, *Angry Voices: Left-of-Center Politics in the New Deal Era* (Lawrence: University of Kansas Press, 1958), pp. 88–114; idem, "The Progressive National Committee of 1936," *Western Political Quarterly* 9 (June 1956): 454–69.

25. Arthur Schlesinger, quoted in Lipset, "Roosevelt." See also Lipset's entire discussion of the campaign and its origins, which is very clear and perceptive.

26. E. L. Oliver, executive vice-president, Labor's Non-Partisan League, to Sidney Hillman, treasurer, LNPL, 30 September 1938; Roger Rutchick to Sidney Hillman, 30 September 1938, Amalgamated Clothing Workers of America Archives, Cornell University, Ithaca, N.Y., Sidney Hillman Correspondence, 1930–46. I thank Peter Bruce for providing me with a photocopy of these documents.

27. Lipset, "Roosevelt," pp. 285–87.

28. Rutchick to Hillman, 30 September 1938; Shields, *Mr. Progressive,* pp. 184–85, 208–10; Arthur Krock, "Roosevelt Seen Veering to Farmer-Labor Left," *New York Times,* 11 September 1938, section 4, p. 3.

29. Shields, *Mr. Progressive,* pp. 150–53; but see Henry G. Teigan, "Why the Farmer-Labor Party Is Still Local," *Common Sense,* November 1937, pp. 13–14.

30. *Gallup Poll* 1:104; Lipset, "Roosevelt," p. 278.

31. Seymour Martin Lipset, "North American Labor Movements: A Comparative Perspective," in Lipset, ed., *Unions in Transition: Entering the Second Century* (San Francisco: Institute for Contemporary Studies Press, 1986), pp. 421–52, especially pp. 445–46.

32. Cf. Mayhew, *Placing Parties,* part 2, especially chap. 11.

Afterword

1. See Michael Walzer, "Socializing the Welfare State: Democracy in the Distributive Sector," in Amy Gutmann, ed., *Democracy and the Welfare State* (Princeton: Princeton University Press, 1988), reprinted in *Dissent,* Summer 1988, pp. 292–300.

2. See Cass R. Sunstein, "Constitutionalism after the New Deal," *Harvard Law Review* 101 (December 1987): 421–510.

3. Thomas Ferguson and Joel Rogers, *Right Turn: The Decline of the Democrats and the Future of American Politics* (New York: Hill & Wang, 1987); Frances Fox Piven and Richard Cloward, *Why Americans Don't Vote* (New York: Pantheon Books, 1988).

Bibliography

Additional citations of materials on the Minnesota Farmer-Labor party can be found in Richard M. Valelly, "State-Level Radicalism and the Nationalization of American Politics: The Case of the Minnesota Farmer-Labor Party," Ph.D. dissertation, Harvard University, 1984.

Secondary Sources

Books and Pamphlets

Altmeyer, Arthur J. *The Formative Years of Social Security*. Madison: University of Wisconsin Press, 1966.

Anderson, William, *City Charter Making in Minnesota*. Bureau for Research in Government of the University of Minnesota, no. 1. Minneapolis: University of Minnesota Press, 1922.

———. *Local Government and Finance in Minnesota*. Minneapolis: University of Minnesota Press, 1935.

———. *Outline of the Government of Minnesota*. Minneapolis: Minnesota Republican Women's State Executive Committee, 1921.

Badie, Bertrand, and Birnbaum, Pierre. *The Sociology of the State*. Translated by Arthur Goldhammer. Chicago: University of Chicago Press, 1983.

Baker, Gladys. *The County Agent*. Studies in Public Administration, vol. 11. Chicago: University of Chicago Press, 1939.

Baldwin, Sidney. *Poverty and Politics: The Rise and Decline of the Farm Security Administration*. Chapel Hill: University of North Carolina Press, 1968.

Barber, William J. *From New Era to New Deal: Herbert Hoover, the Economists, and American Economic Policy, 1921–1933*. Historical Perspectives on Modern Economics. Cambridge: Cambridge University Press, 1985.

Beecher, John. *Tomorrow Is a Day: A Story of the People in Politics*. Chicago: Vanguard Books, 1980.

Bell, Daniel. "Marxian Socialism in the United States." In *Socialism and American Life,* edited by Donald Drew Egbert and Stow Persons. Princeton: Princeton University Press, 1952. Reprinted separately. Princeton: Princeton University Press, 1967.

Benedict, Murray R. *Farm Policies of the United States 1790–1950. A Study of Their Origins and Development*. New York: Twentieth Century Fund, 1953.

Bensel, Richard. *Sectionalism and American Political Development, 1880–1980*. Madison: University of Wisconsin Press, 1984.

Bernstein, Irving. *The Lean Years: A History of the American Worker, 1920–1933*. Boston: Houghton Mifflin Co., 1960.

———. *The New Deal Collective Bargaining Policy*. Berkeley and Los Angeles:

University of California Press, for the Institute of Industrial Relations, University of California, 1950.

————. *The Turbulent Years: A History of the American Worker, 1933–1941.* Boston: Houghton Mifflin Co., 1970.

Blackorby, Edward. *Prairie Rebel: The Public Life of William Lemke.* Lincoln: University of Nebraska Press, 1963.

Blakey, Gladys. *History of Taxation in Minnesota.* University of Minnesota Studies in Economics and Business, no. 9. Minneapolis: University of Minnesota Press, 1934.

Blakey, Roy, and Associates. *Taxation in Minnesota.* University of Minnesota Studies in Economics and Business, no. 4. Minneapolis: University of Minnesota Press, 1932.

Blakey, Roy, and Blakey, Gladys. *Taxation in Minnesota: 1939 Supplement.* Minneapolis: University of Minnesota Press, 1939.

Blantz, Thomas. *A Priest in Public Service: Francis J. Haas and the New Deal.* Notre Dame Studies in American Catholicism, vol. 5. Notre Dame: University of Notre Dame Press, 1982.

Blegen, Theodore. *Minnesota: A History of the State.* St. Paul: Minnesota Historical Society, 1963.

Bonnett, Clarence E. *Employers' Associations in the United States: A Study of Typical Associations.* New York: Macmillan Co., 1922.

Borchert, John R., and Yaeger, Donald P. *Atlas of Minnesota Resources and Settlement.* St. Paul: Minnesota State Planning Agency, 1969.

Bowman, D. O. *Public Control of Labor Relations: A Study of the National Labor Relations Board.* New York: Macmillan Co., 1942.

Campbell, Christiana McFayden. *The Farm Bureau and the New Deal: A Study of the Making of National Farm Policy, 1933–1940.* Urbana: University of Illinois Press, 1962.

Cannon, James P. *The History of American Trotskyism: From Its Origins (1928) to the Founding of the Socialist Workers Party (1938): Report of a Participant.* New York: Pathfinder Press, 1972.

Chalmers, David H. *Hooded Americanism: The First Century of the Ku Klux Klan, 1865–1965.* Garden City, N.Y.: Doubleday & Co., 1965.

Charles, Searle. *Minister of Relief: Harry Hopkins and the Depression.* Syracuse: Syracuse University Press, 1963.

Chrislock, Carl. *The Progressive Era in Minnesota, 1899–1918.* St. Paul: Minnesota Historical Society, 1971.

Cochran, Bert. *Labor and Communism: The Conflict That Shaped American Unions.* Princeton: Princeton University Press, for the Columbia University Research Institute on International Change, 1977.

Congressional Quarterly's Guide to U.S. Elections. 2d ed. Washington, D.C.: Congressional Quarterly Press, 1985.

Conner, Valerie Jean. *The National War Labor Board: Stability, Social Justice, and the Voluntary State in World War I.* Supplementary volumes to the Papers of Woodrow Wilson. Chapel Hill: University of North Carolina Press, 1983.

Crandall, Esther. *Calendar of Minnesota Government, 1925.* Bureau for Research in Government of the University of Minnesota, no. 4. Minneapolis: University of Minnesota Press, 1924.

Davidson, Roger H., and Oleszek, Walter, J. *Congress and Its Members*. Washington, D.C.: Congressional Quarterly Press, 1981.
Davis, Joseph Stancliffe. *Wheat and the AAA*. Institute of Economics Publication 61. Washington, D.C.: Brookings Institution, 1935.
Dembo, Jonathan. *Unions and Politics in Washington State, 1885–1935*. New York: Garland Publishing, 1983.
Derber, Milton, and Young, Edwin, eds. *Labor and the New Deal*. Madison: University of Wisconsin Press, 1959.
Dobbs, Farrell. *Teamster Politics*. New York: Monad Press, for the Anchor Foundation, 1975.
———. *Teamster Rebellion*. New York: Monad Press, for the Anchor Foundation, 1972.
Dodd, Donald B., and Dodd, Wynelle S. *Historical Statistics of the United States, 1790–1970*. Vol. 2, *The Midwest*. University: University of Alabama Press, 1976.
Downs, Anthony. *An Economic Theory of Democracy*. New York: Harper & Row, 1957.
Duverger, Maurice. *Political Parties: Their Organization and Activity in the Modern State*. Translated by Barbara and Robert North. London: Methuen & Co., 1954; University Paperbacks, 1964.
Edwards, P. K. *Strikes in the United States, 1881–1974*. New York: St. Martin's Press, for the Social Science Research Council, 1981.
Ferguson, Thomas, and Rogers, Joel. *Right Turn: The Decline of the Democrats and the Future of American Politics*. New York: Hill & Wang, 1987.
Finkel, Alvin. *Business and Social Reform in the Thirties*. Toronto: James Lorimer & Co., 1979.
Fite, Gilbert C. *George N. Peek and the Fight for Farm Parity*. Norman: University of Oklahoma Press, 1954.
Fitzgerald, D. A. *Livestock under the AAA*. Institute of Economics Publication 65. Washington, D.C.: Brookings Institution, 1935.
Frankfurter, Felix, and Green, Nathan. *The Labor Injunction*. New York: Macmillan Co., 1930.
Friedheim, Robert. *The Seattle General Strike*. Seattle: University of Washington Press, 1964.
Galenson, Walter. *Rival Unionism in the United States*. New York: American Council on Public Affairs, 1940.
The Gallup Poll, Public Opinion, 1935–1971. 1st ed. Vol. 1, *1935–1948*. New York: Random House, 1971.
Gieske, Millard. *Minnesota Farmer-Laborism: The Third Party Alternative*. Minneapolis: University of Minnesota Press, 1979.
Gile, B. M., and Black, J. D. *The Agricultural Credit Situation in Minnesota*. Technical Bulletin 55. St. Paul: University Farm, Division of Agricultural Economics, University of Minnesota Agricultural Experiment Station, 1928.
Goldfield, Michael. *The Decline of Organized Labor in the United States*. Chicago: University of Chicago Press, 1987.
Goldstein, Robert Justin. *Political Repression in Modern America, 1870 to the Present*. Cambridge, Mass: Schenkman Publishing Co.; New York: Two Continents Publishing Group, 1978.

Gourevitch, Peter. *Politics in Hard Times: Comparative Responses to International Economic Crises*. Cornell Studies in Political Economy. Ithaca, N.Y.: Cornell University Press, 1986.

Green, James R. *Grass-Roots Socialism: Radical Movements in the Southwest, 1895–1943*. Baton Rouge: Louisiana State University Press, 1978.

Green, William. *Labor and Democracy*. Princeton: Princeton University Press, 1939.

Gross, James A. *The Making of the National Labor Relations Board: A Study in Economics, Politics, and the Law*. Albany: State University of New York Press, 1974.

———. *The Reshaping of the National Labor Relations Board: National Labor Policy in Transition, 1937–1947*. Albany: State University of New York Press, 1981.

Grubbs, Frank L., Jr. *The Struggle for Labor Loyalty: Gompers, the A.F.L., and the Pacifists, 1917–1920*. Durham, N.C.: Duke University Press, 1968.

Haas, Harold M. *Social and Economic Aspects of the Chain Store Movement*. 1939. New York: Arno Press, 1979.

Harris, Herbert. *Labor's Civil War*. New York: Alfred A. Knopf, 1940.

Hartz, Louis. *The Liberal Tradition in America: An Interpretation of American Political Thought since the Revolution*. New York: Harcourt, Brace & Co., 1955.

Hawley, Ellis W. *The Great War and the Search for a Modern Order: A History of the American People and Their Institutions, 1917–1933*. New York: St. Martin's Press, 1979.

Haynes, Fred E. *Social Politics in the United States*. 1924. Reprint. New York: AMS Press, 1970.

Haynes, John Earl. *Dubious Alliance: The Making of Minnesota's DFL Party*. Minneapolis: University of Minnesota Press, 1984.

Hicks, John D. *Republican Ascendancy, 1921–1933*. New American Nation Series. New York: Harper & Row, 1960.

Hilton, Ora Almon. *The Minnesota Commission of Public Safety in World War One, 1917–1919*. Stillwater: Oklahoma Agricultural and Mechanical College, 1951.

Hirschman, Albert O. *Essays in Trespassing: Economics to Politics and Beyond*. Cambridge: Cambridge University Press, 1981.

———. *Exit, Voice, and Loyalty: Responses to Decline in Firms, Organizations, and States*. Cambridge: Harvard University Press, 1970.

———. *Shifting Involvements: Private Interest and Public Action*. Eliot Janeway Lectures on Historical Economics in Honor of Joseph Schumpeter, Princeton University, 1979. Princeton: Princeton University Press, 1982.

Horn, Michiel. *The Great Depression of the 1930s in Canada*. Historical Booklet 39. Ottawa: Canadian Historical Association, 1984.

Irons, Peter. *The New Deal Lawyers*. Princeton: Princeton University Press, 1982.

James, Ralph C., and James, Estelle Dinnerstein. *Hoffa and the Teamsters: A Study of Union Power*. Princeton: D. Van Nostrand Co., 1965.

Karl, Barry D. *The Uneasy State: The United States from 1915 to 1945*. Chicago: University of Chicago Press, 1983.

Keillor, Steven J. *Hjalmar Petersen of Minnesota: The Politics of Provincial Independence*. St. Paul: Minnesota Historical Society Press, 1987.

Key, V. O., Jr. *American State Politics: An Introduction*. New York: Alfred A. Knopf, 1956. Reprinted. Westport, Conn.: Greenwood Press, 1983.

Keyssar, Alexander. *Out of Work: The First Century of Unemployment in Massachusetts*. Interdisciplinary Perspectives on Modern History. Cambridge: Cambridge University Press, 1986.

Killingsworth, Charles C. *State Labor Relations Acts: A Study of Public Policy*. Chicago: University of Chicago Press, 1948.

Kirkendall, Richard S. *Social Scientists and Farm Politics in the Age of Roosevelt*. Columbia: University of Missouri Press, 1966.

Klehr, Harvey. *The Heyday of American Communism: The Depression Decade*. New York: Basic Books, 1984.

Ladenburg, Thomas J., and Brockunier, Samuel Hugh. *The Prosperity and Depression Decades*. Hayden Twentieth Century Issues Series. New York: Hayden Book Co., 1971.

Larson, Bruce. *Lindbergh of Minnesota: A Political Biography*. New York: Harcourt Brace Jovanovich, 1971.

Laslett, John H. M. *Labor and the Left: A Study of Socialist and Radical Influences in the American Labor Movement. 1881–1924*. New York: Basic Books, 1970.

Latham, Earl. *The Communist Controversy in Washington: From the New Deal to McCarthy*. Cambridge: Harvard University Press, 1966.

Lee, Susan Previant, and Passell, Peter. *A New Economic View of American History*. New York: W. W. Norton & Co., 1979.

Leff, Mark H. *The Limits of Symbolic Reform: The New Deal and Taxation, 1933–1939*. New York: Cambridge University Press, 1984.

Leuchtenburg, William E. *The Perils of Prosperity, 1914–1932*. Chicago History of American Civilization. Chicago: University of Chicago Press, 1958.

Lipset, Seymour Martin. *Agrarian Socialism: The Cooperative Commonwealth Federation in Saskatchewan: A Study in Political Sociology*. Rev. and exp. ed. Berkeley: University of California Press, 1971.

Lowitt, Richard, and Beasley, Maurine, eds. *One Third of a Nation: Lorena Hickok Reports on the Great Depression*. Urbana: University of Illinois Press, 1981.

Luoma, Everett E. *The Farmer Takes a Holiday: The Story of the National Farmers' Holiday Association and the Farmers' Strike of 1932–1933*. Foreword by Elmer A. Benson. New York: Exposition Press, 1967.

Lyon, Leverett S., et al. *The National Recovery Administration: An Analysis and Appraisal*. Institute of Economics, publication 60. Washington, D.C.: Brookings Institution, 1935.

McConnell, Grant. *Private Power and American Democracy*. New York: Alfred A. Knopf, 1966; Vintage Books, 1970.

McCoy, Donald R. *Angry Voices: Left-of-Center Politics in the New Deal Era*. Lawrence: University of Kansas Press, 1958.

McHenry, Dean E. *The Third Force in Canada: The Cooperative Commonwealth Federation, 1932–1948*. Berkeley and Los Angeles: University of California Press, 1950.

McNaught, Kenneth. *The Pelican History of Canada.* London: Penguin Books, 1976.

Mallory, J. R. *The Structure of Canadian Government.* New York: St. Martin's Press, 1971.

Marcley, Jessie McMillan. *The Minneapolis City Charter, 1856–1925.* Bureau for Research in Government, publication 5. Minneapolis: University of Minnesota, 1925.

Martin, Boyd A. *The Direct Primary in Idaho.* Stanford: Stanford University Press, 1947.

Mayer, George. *The Political Career of Floyd B. Olson.* Minneapolis: University of Minnesota Press, 1951.

Mayhew, David R. *Placing Parties in American Politics: Organization, Electoral Settings, and Government Activity in the Twentieth Century.* Princeton: Princeton University Press, 1986.

Miller, John E. *Governor Philip F. La Follette: The Wisconsin Progressives and the New Deal.* Columbia: University of Missouri Press, 1982.

Montgomery, David. *Workers' Control in America: Studies in the History of Work, Technology, and Labor Struggles.* Cambridge: Cambridge University Press, 1979.

Moore, Barrington, Jr. *The Social Origins of Dictatorship and Democracy: Lord and Peasant in the Making of the Modern World.* Boston: Beacon Press, 1966.

Morlan, Robert. *Political Prairie Fire: The Nonpartisan League, 1915–1922.* Minneapolis: University of Minnesota Press, 1955. Reprint, with a new introduction by Larry Remele. St. Paul: Minnesota Historical Society Press, 1985.

Noggle, Burt. *Into the Twenties: The United States from Armistice to Normalcy.* Urbana: University of Illinois Press, 1974.

Nye, Russell B. *Midwestern Progressive Politics.* East Lansing: Michigan State College Press, 1951.

Ogden, Daniel, Jr., and Bone, Hugh A. *Washington Politics.* New York: New York University Press, 1960.

Orwell, George. *Homage to Catalonia.* New York: Harcourt, Brace and World, Harvest Book. 1952.

Page, Benjamin. *Who Gets What from Government.* Berkeley: University of California Press, 1983.

Palamountain, Joseph Cornwall, Jr. *The Politics of Distribution.* Harvard Political Studies, Department of Government, Harvard University. Cambridge: Harvard University Press, 1955.

Patterson, James T. *Congressional Conservatism and the New Deal: The Growth of the Conservative Coalition in Congress, 1933–1939.* Lexington: University of Kentucky Press, 1967.

Perkins, Van. *Crisis in Agriculture: The Agricultural Adjustment Administration and the New Deal, 1933.* University of California Publications in History, vol. 81. Berkeley and Los Angeles: University of California Press, 1969.

Perlman, Mark. *The Machinists: A New Study in American Trade Unionism.* Wertheim Publications in Industrial Relations. Cambridge: Harvard University Press, 1961.

Perry, J. Harvey. *Taxation in Canada.* Toronto: University of Toronto Press, 1951.

Peterson, Paul. *City Limits*. Chicago: University of Chicago Press, 1981.

Piven, Frances Fox, and Cloward, Richard. *Regulating the Poor: The Functions of Public Welfare*. New York: Vintage Books, 1971.

————.*Why Americans Don't Vote*. New York: Pantheon Books, 1988.

Popple, C. S. *Development of Two Bank Groups in the Central Northwest: A Study in Bank Policy and Reorganization*. Harvard Studies in Business History, no. 9. Cambridge: Harvard University Press, 1944.

Price, H. Bruce, and Hoffer, C. R. *Services of Rural Trade Centers in Distribution of Farm Supplies*. Minnesota Bulletin 249. St. Paul: University Farm, University of Minnesota Agricultural Experiment Station, 1928.

Ratchford, B. U. *American State Debts*. Durham, N.C.: Duke University Press, 1941.

Ratner, Sidney. *Taxation and Democracy in America*. New York: John Wiley & Sons, 1967.

Robinson, Elwyn B. *History of North Dakota*. Lincoln: University of Nebraska Press, 1966.

Rogin, Michael Paul. *The Intellectuals and McCarthy: The Radical Specter*. Cambridge: MIT Press, 1967.

Romasco, Albert U. *The Politics of Recovery*. New York: Oxford University Press, 1983.

Ross, Martin. *Shipstead of Minnesota*. Assisted by Katherine Ferguson Chalkley. Chicago: Packard & Co., 1940.

Schattschneider, Elmer Eric. *The Semisovereign People: A Realist's View of Democracy in America*. Hinsdale, Ill.: Dryden Press, 1975.

Scheiber, Harry N.; Vatter, Harold G.; Faulkner, Harold Underwood. *American Economic History*. 9th rev. ed. New York: Harper & Row, 1976.

Shideler, James H. *Farm Crisis: 1919–1923*. Berkeley: University of California Press, 1957.

Shields, James M. *Mr. Progressive: A Biography of Elmer Austin Benson*. Minneapolis: T. S. Denison & Co., 1971.

Short, Lloyd M., and Tiller, Carl W. *The Minnesota Commission of Administration and Finance, 1925–1939: An Administrative History*. University of Minnesota Public Administration Training Center, Studies in Administration, no. 1. Minneapolis: University of Minnesota Press, 1942.

Shover, John L. *Cornbelt Rebellion: The Farmers' Holiday Association*. Urbana: University of Illinois Press, 1965.

Sinclair, Barbara. *Congressional Realignment, 1925–1978*. Austin: University of Texas Press, 1982.

Skowronek, Stephen. *Building a New American State: The Expansion of National Administrative Capacities, 1877–1920*. Cambridge: Cambridge University Press, 1982.

Stead, William H., and Bjornaraa, Dreng. *Employment Trends in St. Paul, Minneapolis, and Duluth*. Bulletins of the University of Minnesota Employment Stabilization Research Institute, vol. 1, no. 2. Minneapolis: University of Minnesota Press, 1931.

Stein, Herbert. *The Fiscal Revolution in America*. Studies in Business and Society, Graduate School of Business, University of Chicago. Chicago: University of Chicago Press, 1969.

Stevenson, Garth. *Unfulfilled Union: Canadian Federalism and National Unity.* Canadian Controversies Series. Toronto: Gage Publishing, 1979.

Stevenson, Russell A., ed. *A Type Study of American Banking: Non-Metropolitan Banks in Minnesota.* Bulletins of the Employment Stabilization Research Institute of the University of Minnesota, vol. 4, no. 1. Minneapolis: University of Minnesota Press, 1934.

Troy, Leo. *Distribution of Union Membership among the States, 1939 and 1953.* Occasional Paper 56. New York: National Bureau of Economic Research, 1957.

———. *Trade Union Membership, 1897–1962.* Occasional Paper 92. New York: National Bureau of Economic Research, 1965.

Tweton, D. Jerome. *The New Deal at the Grass Roots: Programs for the People in Otter Tail County, Minnesota.* St. Paul: Minnesota Historical Society Press, 1988.

Vaile, Roland S., ed. *The Small City and Town; a Conference on Community Relations: The Report of a Conference on Problems of the Small City and Town, Held at the University of Minnesota, June 24–28, 1929.* Minneapolis: University of Minnesota Press, 1930.

Walker, Charles Rumford. *American City: A Rank-and-File History.* New York: Farrar & Rinehart, 1937.

Walker, Forrest A. *The Civil Works Administration: An Experiment in Federal Work Relief, 1933–1934.* New York: Garland Publishing Co., 1979.

Weinstein, James. *The Decline of Socialism in America, 1912–1925.* New York: Vintage Books, 1969. Reprint. New Brunswick, N.J.: Rutgers University Press, 1984.

White, Bruce M., et al., comps. *Minnesota Votes: Election Returns by County for Presidents, Senators, Congressmen, and Governors, 1857–1977.* St. Paul: Minnesota Historical Society, 1977.

White, Roland A. *Milo Reno: Farmers Union Pioneer: The Story of a Man and a Movement.* Iowa City: Athens Press, for the Iowa Farmers Union, 1941. Reprint. New York: Arno Press, 1975.

Wilson, James Q. *Political Organizations.* New York: Basic Books, 1973.

Witte, Edwin F. *The Development of the Social Security Act.* Madison: University of Wisconsin Press, 1963.

Zeiger, Robert H. *Republicans and Labor, 1919–1929.* Lexington: University of Kentucky Press, 1969.

Articles

Alanen, Arnold R. "The 'Locations': Company Communities on Minnesota's Iron Ranges." *Minnesota History* 48 (Fall 1982): 94–107.

Alston, Lee, J. "Farm Foreclosure Moratorium Legislation: A Lesson from the Past." *American Economic Review* 74 (June 1984): 445–57.

Altman, O. R. "First Session of the Seventy-fifth Congress." *American Political Science Review* 31 (December 1937): 1071–93.

"American Institute of Public Opinion: Surveys, 1938–1939." *Public Opinion Quarterly* 3 (October 1939): 581–607.

Axworthy, Thomas S. "Left Turn in Canada?" *Public Opinion,* September-October 1987, 52–54.

Berman, Hyman. "Political Antisemitism in Minnesota during the Great Depression." *Jewish Social Studies* 38 (Summer-Fall 1976): 247–64.

Black, John D. "The McNary-Haugen Movement." *American Economic Review* 18 (September 1928): 405–27.

Brody, David. "On the Failure of U.S. Radical Politics: A Farmer-Labor Analysis." *Industrial Relations* 22 (Spring 1983): 141–63.

Brown, Emily Clark. "The New Collective Bargaining in Mass Production: Methods, Results, Problems." *Journal of Political Economy* 47 (February 1939): 30–66.

Burbank, Garin. "Agrarian Radicals and Their Opponents: Political Conflict in Southern Oklahoma, 1910–1924." *Journal of American History* 58 (June 1971): 5–23.

Burner, David. "1919: Prelude to Normalcy." In *Change and Continuity in Twentieth Century America: The 1920s,* edited by John Braeman, Robert H. Bremner, and David Brody, 3–31. Columbus: Ohio State University Press, 1968.

Burnham, Walter Dean. "The System of 1896: An Analysis." In *The Evolution of American Electoral Systems,* Paul Kleppner, Walter Dean Burnham, Ronald P. Formisano, Samuel P. Hays, Richard Jensen, and William G. Shade, 147–202. Contributions in American History, no. 95. Westport, Conn.: Greenwood Press, 1981.

Burns, John F. "A Leftist Leader Surging in Canada." *New York Times,* 8 November 1987, 1, 16.

Caldeira, Gregory. "Public Opinion and the U.S. Supreme Court: FDR's Court-Packing Plan." *American Political Science Review* 81 (December 1987): 1139–53.

Carman, Ernest C. "The Outlook from the Present Legal Status of Employers and Employees in Industrial Disputes." *Minnesota Law Review* 6 (June 1922): 533–59.

Case, H. C. M. "Farm Debt Adjustment during the Early 1930s." *Agricultural History* 34 (October 1960): 173–81.

Chernov, Ben. "The Labor Injunction in Minnesota." *Minnesota Law Review* 24 (May 1940): 757–804.

Cohen, Benjamin J. "A Brief History of International Monetary Relations." In *International Political Economy: Perspectives on Global Power and Wealth,* edited by Jeffrey A. Frieden and David A. Lake, 245–68. New York: St. Martin's Press, 1987.

Easterlin, Richard A. "Regional Income Trends, 1840–1950." In *American Economic History,* edited by Seymour E. Harris, 525–47. New York: McGraw-Hill Book Co., 1961.

Edelman, Murray. "New Deal Sensitivity to Labor Interests." In *Labor and the New Deal,* edited by Milton Derber and Edwin Young, 157–92. Madison: University of Wisconsin Press, 1959.

Engelmann, Larry D. "'We Were the Poor People': The Hormel Strike of 1933." *Labor History* 15 (Fall 1974): 483–510.

Ferguson, Thomas. "Party Realignment and American Industrial Structure: The Investment Theory of Political Parties in Historical Perspective." In *Research in Political Economy: A Research Annual,* edited by Paul Zarembka, 6:1–82. Greenwich, Conn.: JAI Press, 1983.

Finegold, Kenneth. "From Agrarianism to Adjustment: The Political Origins of New Deal Agriculture Policy." *Politics & Society* 11 (1981): 1–27.

Fite, Gilbert C. "The Farmers' Dilemma, 1919–1929." In *Change and Continuity in Twentieth Century America: The 1920s,* edited by John Braeman, Robert H. Bremner, and David Brody, 67–101. Columbus: Ohio State University Press, 1968.

Fleming, R. W. "The Significance of the Wagner Act." In *Labor and the New Deal,* edited by Milton Derber and Edwin Young, 121–56. University of Wisconsin Press, 1959.

Freyer, Tony. "The Federal Courts, Localism, and the National Economy, 1865–1900." *Business History Review* 53 (1979): 344–63.

Fusfeld, Daniel R. "Government and the Suppression of Radical Labor, 1877–1918." In *Statemaking and Social Movements: Essays in History and Theory,* edited by Charles Bright and Susan Harding, 159–92. Ann Arbor: University of Michigan Press, 1984.

Gall, Gilbert J. "Heber Blankenhorn, the La Follette Committee, and the Irony of Industrial Repression." *Labor History* 23 (Spring 1982): 246–53.

Gallup, George, and Robinson, Claude. "American Institute of Public Opinion—Surveys, 1935–38." *Public Opinion Quarterly* 2 (July 1938): 373–98.

Gitelman, Howard M. "Perspectives on American Industrial Violence." *Business History Review* 47 (1973): 1–23.

Gosnell, Harold F., and Cohen, Morris H. "Progressive Politics: Wisconsin an Example." *American Political Science Review* 34 (October 1940): 920–35.

Hansen, Mark. "The Political Economy of Group Membership." *American Political Science Review* 79 (March 1985): 79–96.

Harris, Howell, "Snares of Liberalism? Politicians, Bureaucrats, and the Shaping of Federal Labor Policy, ca. 1915–1947." In *Shop Floor Bargaining and the State: Historical and Comparative Perspectives,* edited by Steven Tolliday and Jonathan Zeitlin, 148–91. Cambridge: Cambridge University Press, 1985.

Haynes, John Earl. "Communism and Anti-Communism in the Northern Minnesota CIO." *Upper Midwest History* 1 (Fall 1981): 55–73.

Herrick, William. "Who Killed Andreu Nin?" *New Leader,* 27 June 1983, 10–12.

Herring, E. Pendleton. "First Session of the Seventy-fourth Congress." *American Political Science Review* 29 (December 1935): 985–1005.

Holbo, Paul S. "The Farmer-Labor Association: Minnesota's Party *within* a Party." *Minnesota History* 42 (Spring 1970): 301–9.

Howe, Irving. "Sad Events of Long Ago." *Dissent,* Summer 1988, 373–75.

Huntington, Samuel P. "The Election Tactics of the Nonpartisan League." *Mississippi Valley Historical Review* 36 (March 1950): 613–52.

Jenson, Carol. "Loyalty as a Political Weapon: The 1918 Campaign in Minnesota." *Minnesota History* 43 (Summer 1971): 43–57.

Karsh, Bernard, and Garman, Phillips. "The Impact of the Political Left." In *Labor and the New Deal,* edited by Milton Derber and Edwin Young, 77–120. Madison: University of Wisconsin Press, 1959.

Keillor, Steven J. "A Country Editor in Politics: Hjalmar Peterson, Minnesota Governor." *Minnesota History* 48 (Fall 1983): 283–94.

Keller, Richard C. "Pennsylvania's Little New Deal." In *The New Deal,* vol. 2, *The*

State and Local Levels, edited by John Braeman, Robert H. Bremner, and David Brody, 45–76. Columbus: Ohio State University Press, 1975.

Kelley, Darwin N. "The McNary-Haugen Bills, 1924–1928: An Attempt to Make the Tariff Effective for Farm Products." *Agricultural History* 14 (October 1940): 170–82.

Kerbo, Harold R., and Shaffer, Richard A. "Unemployment and Protest in the United States, 1890–1940: A Methodological Critique and Research Note." *Social Forces* 64 (June 1986): 1046–57.

Klare, Karl E. "Judicial Deradicalization of the Wagner Act and the Origins of Modern Legal Consciousness, 1937–1941." *Minnesota Law Review* 62 (1978): 265–339.

Kramer, Dale. "The Dunne Boys of Minneapolis." *Harper's,* March 1942, 388–98.

Lake, David A. "International Economic Structures and American Foreign Economic Policy, 1887–1934." In *International Political Economy: Perspectives on Global Power and Wealth,* edited by Jeffrey A. Frieden and David A. Lake, 145–66. New York: St. Martin's Press, 1987.

Leman, Christopher. "Patterns of Policy Development: Social Security in the U.S. and Canada." *Public Policy* 25 (Spring 1977): 261–91.

Levinson, Sanford. "Clashes of Taste in Constitutional Interpretation." *Dissent,* Summer 1988, 301–12.

Lipset, Seymour Martin. "North American Labor Movements: A Comparative Perspective." In *Unions in Transition: Entering the Second Century,* edited by Seymour Martin Lipset, 421–52. San Francisco: Institute for Contemporary Studies Press, 1986.

———. "Roosevelt and the Protest of the 1930s." *Minnesota Law Review* 68 (1983): 273–98.

Lovin, Hugh T. "The Fall of Farmer-Labor Parties, 1936–1938." *Pacific Northwest Quarterly* 62 (January 1971): 16–26.

———. "The Farmer Revolt in Idaho, 1914–1922." *Idaho Yesterdays: The Quarterly Journal of the Idaho Historical Society* 20 (Fall 1976): 2–15.

McCoy, Donald R. "The Progressive National Committee of 1936." *Western Political Quarterly* 9 (June 1956): 454–69.

McCurdy, Charles W. "American Law and the Marketing Structure of the Large Corporation, 1875–1890." *Journal of Economic History* 38 (September 1978): 631–49.

McNatt, E. B. "The 'Appropriate Bargaining Unit' Problem." *Quarterly Journal of Economics* 56 (November 1941): 93–107.

McSeveney, Samuel T. "The Michigan Gubernatorial Campaign of 1938." *Michigan History* 45 (June 1961): 97–127.

Mader, Joseph H. "The North Dakota Press and the Nonpartisan League." *Journalism Quarterly* 14 (December 1937): 321–32.

Marks, Emily, and Bartlett, Mary. "Employee Elections Conducted by National Labor Relations Board." *Monthly Labor Review* 47 (July 1938): 31–38.

Millikan, William. "Defenders of Business: The Minneapolis Civic and Commerce Association *versus* Labor during W. W. I." *Minnesota History* 50 (Spring 1986): 2–17.

Montgomery, David. "'Liberty and Union': Workers and Government in America, 1900–1940." In *Essays from the Lowell Conference on Industrial History, 1980 and 1981,* edited by Robert Weible, Oliver Ford, and Paul Marion, 145–57. Lowell, Mass.: Lowell Conference on Industrial History, 1981.

Naftalin, Arthur. "The Failure of the Farmer-Labor Party to Capture Control of the Minnesota Legislature." *American Political Science Review* 38 (February 1944): 71–78.

Nelson, Harold L. "The Political Reform Press: A Case Study." *Journalism Quarterly* 29 (Summer 1952): 294–302.

Nord, David Paul. "Hothouse Socialism: Minneapolis, 1910–1925." In *Socialism in the Heartland: The Midwestern Experience, 1900–1925,* edited by Donald T. Critchlow, 133–66. Notre Dame: University of Notre Dame Press, 1986.

———. "Minneapolis and the Pragmatic Socialism of Thomas Van Lear." *Minnesota History* 45 (Spring 1976): 3–10.

Perlman, Mark. "Labor in Eclipse." In *Change and Continuity in Twentieth Century America: The 1920s,* edited by John Braeman, Robert H. Bremner, and David Brody, 103–45. Columbus: Ohio State University Press, 1968.

Plesur, Milton. "The Republican Congressional Comeback of 1938." *Review of Politics* 24 (October 1962): 525–62.

Quam, Lois, and Rachleff, Peter J. "Keeping Minneapolis an Open-Shop Town: The Citizens' Alliance in the 1930s." *Minnesota History* 50 (Fall 1986): 105–17.

Russell, Ralph. "Membership of the American Farm Bureau Federation, 1926–1935." *Rural Sociology* 2 (March 1937): 29–35.

Schattschneider, Elmer Eric. "United States: The Functional Approach to Party Government." In *Modern Political Parties: Approaches to Comparative Politics,* edited by Sigmund Neumann, 194–215. Chicago: University of Chicago Press, 1956.

Scheiber, Harry N. "American Federalism and the Diffusion of Power: Historical and Contemporary Perspectives." *University of Toledo Law Review* 9 (Summer 1978): 619–90.

———. "Federalism and Legal Process: Historical and Contemporary Analysis of the American System." *Law and Society Review* 14 (Spring 1980): 663–722.

———. "Government and the American Economy: Three Stages of Historical Change, 1790–1941." In *Essays from the Lowell Conference on Industrial History, 1980 and 1981,* edited by Robert Weible, Oliver Ford, and Paul Marion, 129–44. Lowell, Mass. Lowell Conference on Industrial History, 1981.

———. "Law and American Agricultural Development." *Agricultural History* 52 (October 1978): 439–57.

Scott, F. R. "The Privy Council and Mr. Bennett's 'New Deal' Legislation." *Canadian Journal of Economics and Political Science* 3 (May 1937): 234–40.

Shapiro, Stanley, "'Hand and Brain': The Farmer-Labor Party of 1920." *Labor History* 26 (Summer 1985): 405–22.

Shefter, Martin. "Party and Patronage: Germany, England, and Italy." *Politics & Society* 7 (1977): 403–51.

———. "Regional Receptivity to Reform: The Legacy of the Progressive Era." *Political Science Quarterly* 98 (Fall 1983): 459–84.

Skocpol, Theda, and Finegold, Kenneth. "State Capacity and Economic Intervention in the Early New Deal." *Political Science Quarterly* 97 (Summer 1982): 255–78.

Skocpol, Theda, and Ikenberry, John. "The Political Formation of the American Welfare State in Historical and Comparative Perspective." In *Comparative Social Research,* edited by Richard F. Tomasson, 6:87–148. Greenwich, Conn.: JAI Press, 1983.

Sofchalk, Donald G. "Organized Labor and the Iron Ore Miners of Northern Minnesota, 1907–1936." *Labor History* 12 (Spring 1971): 214–42.

Sorauf, Frank J. "State Patronage in a Rural County." *American Political Science Review* 50 (December 1956): 1046–56.

Stricker, Frank. "Affluence for Whom? Another Look at Prosperity and the Working Classes in the 1920s." *Labor History* 24 (Winter 1983): 5–33.

Stuhler, Barbara. "The One Man Who Voted 'Nay'. The Story of John T. Bernard's Quarrel with American Foreign Policy, 1937–1939." *Minnesota History* 43 (Fall 1972): 83–92.

Sunstein, Cass R. "Constitutionalism after the New Deal." *Harvard Law Review* 101 (December 1987): 421–510.

Tomlins, Christopher L. "AFL Unions in the 1930s: Their Performance in Historical Perspective." *Journal of American History* 65 (March 1979): 1021–42.

Tontz, Robert L. "Membership of General Farmers' Organizations, United States, 1874–1960." *Agricultural History* 38 (July 1964): 143–56.

Tugwell, Rexford Guy. "Reflections on Farm Relief." *Political Science Quarterly* 43 (December 1928): 481–97.

Vogel, David. "Why American Businessmen Distrust Their State: The Political Consciousness of American Corporate Executives." *British Journal of Political Science* 8 (January 1978): 45–78.

Wakstein, Allen M. "The Origins of the Open Shop Movement, 1919–1920." *Journal of American History* 51 (December 1964): 460–75.

Walzer, Michael. "Socializing the Welfare State: Democracy in the Distributive Sector." In *Democracy and the Welfare State,* edited by Amy Gutmann. Princeton: Princeton University Press, 1988. Reprint. *Dissent,* Summer 1988, 292–300.

Weiss, Stuart L. "Maury Maverick and the Liberal Bloc." *Journal of American History* 57 (March 1971): 880–895.

Wells, Merle W. "Fred T. DuBois and the Nonpartisan League in the Idaho Election of 1918." *Pacific Northwest Quarterly* 56 (January 1965): 17–29.

White, Eugene Nelson. "The Political Economy of Banking Regulation, 1864–1933." *Journal of Economic History* 42 (March 1982): 33–40.

Wiecek, William. "The Reconstruction of Federal Judicial Power, 1863–1876." Reprinted and abridged from *American Journal of Legal History* 13 (1969): 333–59. In *American Law and the Constitutional Order,* edited by Lawrence Friedman and Harry N. Scheiber. Cambridge: Harvard University Press, 1978.

Yates, Douglas. "The Roots of American Leadership: Political Style and Policy Consequences." In *American Politics and Public Policy,* edited by Walter Dean Burnham and Martha Wagner Weinberg, 140–68. Cambridge: MIT Press, 1979.

Young, Edwin. "The Split in the Labor Movement." In *Labor and the New Deal,* edited by Milton Derber and Edwin Young, 45–76. Madison: University of Wisconsin Press, 1959.

Manuscripts

Adrian, Charles. "The Nonpartisan Legislature in Minnesota." Ph.D. dissertation, University of Minnesota, 1950.

Backstrom, Charles Herbert. "The Progressive Party of Wisconsin, 1934–1946." Ph.D. dissertation, University of Wisconsin, 1956.

Bruce, Peter G. "Political Parties and the Evolution of Labor Law in Canada and the United States." Ph.D. dissertation, MIT, 1988.

Cravens, Hamilton. "A History of the Washington Farmer-Labor Party, 1918–1924." Master's thesis, University of Washington, 1962.

Forbes, Garrett O. "Dynamics of Idaho Politics, 1920–1932." Master's thesis, University of Idaho Graduate School, 1955.

Gabriner, Robert S. "The Farmer-Labor Party, 1918–1924: A Study in the Dynamics of Independent Political Action." Master's thesis, University of Wisconsin, 1966.

Hinderaker, Ivan. "Harold Stassen and Developments in the Republican Party in Minnesota, 1937–1943." Ph.D. dissertation, University of Minnesota, 1949.

Koch, Raymond Louis. "The Development of Public Relief Programs in Minnesota, 1929–1941." Ph.D. dissertation, University of Minnesota, 1967.

Lorence, James J. "Community Spirit and Welfare: Gerald J. Boileau and the Progressive-Farmer-Labor Alliance in the Interwar Era." Manuscript.

Naftalin, Arthur. "A History of the Minnesota Farmer-Labor Party." Ph.D. dissertation, University of Minnesota, 1948.

Nord, David Paul. "Socialism in One City: A Political Study of Minneapolis in the Progressive Era." Master's thesis, University of Minnesota, 1972.

Tauber, Andrew. "Alternative Visions of Economic Regulation, 1918–1930." Second year paper, Ph.D. program, Department of Political Science, MIT, 1988.

Thiltgen, Loyola Brinckmann. "Relations of the Governor to the Settlement of Labor Disputes in the State of Minnesota prior to 1939." Master's thesis, University of Minnesota, 1954.

Zingale, Nancy Hill. "Electoral Stability and Change: The Case of Minnesota, 1857–1966." Ph.D. dissertation, University of Minnesota, 1971.

Primary Sources

Articles

Anderson, Paul Y. "Behind the Dies Intrigue." *Nation,* 12 November 1938, 449–500.

Baldwin, Roger. "American Ideals (2): The Coming Struggle for Liberty." *Common Sense,* January 1935, 6–7.

Beard, Charles A. "Mines Eyes May Behold." *New Republic,* 19 January 1938, 306.

Beirce, Walter. "A Party without a Program." *New International,* March 1939, 74–78.

Bendiner, M. R. "Dim Dawn over the Capitol." *New Masses,* 9 February 1937, 7–9.

Bernard, John T. "Give Us a Program!" *New Masses,* 31 August 1937, 3–5.

Cantwell, Robert. "The Communists and the CIO." *New Republic,* 23 February 1938, 63–66.

"The Clash in Minneapolis," *Survey,* 25 June 1921, 428–29.

Curtis, C. A. "Dominion Legislation of 1935: An Economist's Review." *Canadian Journal of Economics and Political Science* 1 (November 1935): 599–608.

Davis, Elmer C. "Minnesota Worry-Go-Round." *Collier's Weekly,* 26 June 1937, 14–15, 41–42.

Frederick, J. George. "Big Business and the Little Man." *North American Review,* October 1928, 440–44.

"The G—— D—— Labor Board." *Fortune,* October 1938, 52–57, 115–23.

Gilbert, A. B. "Nonpartisan vs. Party Politics." *American Federationist,* November 1927, 1350–53.

Hathaway, Clarence. "The Minnesota Farmer-Labor Victory." *Communist* 15 (December 1936): 1112–24.

———. "Problems in Our Farmer-Labor Party Activities." *Communist* 15 (May 1936): 427–33.

Hawthorne, James. "Trotsky's Agents in Spain." *New Masses,* 13 July 1937, 15–17.

Herrick, William. "Who Killed Andreu Nin?" *New Leader,* 27 June 1983, 10–12.

Huberman, Leo. "The Attack on the NLRB." *New Republic,* 19 January 1938, 298–300.

King, Murray E. "The Farmer-Labor Federation." *New Republic,* 2 April 1924, 145–47.

Kramer, Dale. "The Dunne Boys of Minneapolis." *Harper's,* March 1942, 388–98.

Krock, Arthur. "Roosevelt Seen Veering to Farmer-Labor Left." *New York Times,* 11 September 1938, section 4, 3.

Lundeen, Ernest. "A Farmer-Labor Party for the Nation." *Common Sense,* June 1935, 6–8.

Moos, Malcolm, and Kenworthy, E. W. "Dr. Shipstead Comes to Judgment." *Harper's,* July 1946, 21–27.

Mund, Vernon Arthur. "Prosperity Reserves of Public Works." *Annals of the American Academy of Political and Social Science* 149, part 2 (May 1930): 1–49.

O'Connell, Jerry J. "The Challenge of the Special Session." *New Masses,* 23 November 1937, 3–5.

Olson, Floyd B. "My Political Creed: Why a New Party Must Challenge Capitalism." *Common Sense,* April 1935, 6–7.

———. "Why a New National Party?" *Common Sense,* January 1936, 6–8.

Rodman, Selden. "Letter from Minnesota." *New Republic,* 15 August 1934, 10–12.

Rolfe, Edwin. "Trotskyites on Trial: Spain's Tribunal of High Treason Hears the Evidence." *New Masses,* 25 October 1938, 7–9.

Ross, Nat. "The Election Campaign in Minnesota." *Communist* 17 (October 1938): 937–44.

———. "The People's Mandate in Minnesota." *Communist* 16 (June 1937): 534–44.

Rukeyser, Merryle Stanley. "Chain Stores: The Revolution in Retailing." *Nation,* 28 November 1928, 569–70.
Shimmons, Earl. "The Labor Dailies." *American Mercury,* 25 September 1928, 85–93.
Soule, George. "Farewell to the Shopkeeper." *New Republic,* 4 April 1928, 210–12.
Teigan, Henry G. "Independent Political Action in Minnesota." *American Federationist,* August 1928, 966–68.
———. "Rolling Our Own Logs." *New Masses,* 21 December 1937, 3–4.
———. "Why the Farmer-Labor Party Is Still Local." *Common Sense,* November 1937, 13–14.
Votaw, O. R. "The Communist Party's Rhumba Dance and the Farmer-Labor Party." *Minnesota Union Advocate,* 9 December 1937, 4.
———. "Communists Working Overtime to 'Capture' Working Class." *Minnesota Union Advocate,* 16 December 1937, 4.
———. "The Mildew of Communism." *Minnesota Union Advocate,* 2 December 1937, 5.
Westbrook, Lawrence. "Error and Remedy in WPA Publicity." *Public Opinion Quarterly* 1 (July 1937): 94–98.

Books and Pamphlets
American Civil Liberties Union. *The Fight for Civil Liberty.* New York: American Civil Liberties Union, 1929.
———. *A Year's Fight for Free Speech: The Work of the American Civil Liberties Union from Sept. 1921 to Jan. 1923.* New York: American Civil Liberties Union, 1923.
Burnham, James. *The People's Front: The New Betrayal.* New York: Pioneer Publishers, 1937.
Chase, Ray P. *Are They Communists or Catspaws? A Red Baiting Article.* Anoka, Minn.: n.p., 1938.
Committee for Industrial Organization. *The Case for Industrial Organization.* Washington, D.C.: Committee for Industrial Organization, [1936?].
Emery, Robert C. *Thirty Years from Now.* St. Paul: n.p., 1934.
Minnesota Institute of Governmental Research. *Minnesota and the Agricultural Situation.* State Governmental Research Bulletin 10. St. Paul: n.p., 1939.
National and State Executive Committees of the National Nonpartisan League. *Memorial to the Congress of the United States concerning Conditions in Minnesota, 1918.* N.p., n.d.
National Nonpartisan League. *Why Should Farmers Pay Dues?* N.p., n.d.
———. Women's Nonpartisan Clubs. *Minnesota: The Problems of Her People and Why the Farmers and the Workers Have Organized for Political Action.* Minneapolis: Women's Nonpartisan Clubs, National Nonpartisan League, [1920?].
Spielman, Jean E. *The Open Shop via the Injunction Route.* Minneapolis: Flour, Cereal, Mill, Grain Elevator, and Linseed Oil Workers Local Union No. 92, 1920. Pamphlets in American History Series. Sanford, N.C.: Microfilming Corporation of America, 1979.

————. *The Stool Pigeon and the Open Shop Movement.* Minneapolis: American Publishing Co., 1923.
Zapffe, Carl. *"75": Brainerd, Minnesota, 1871–1946.* Minneapolis: Colwell Press, for the Brainerd Civic Association, 1946.

Correspondence

Hudson, Carlos. Editor, *The Organizer,* Minneapolis, 1934. To author, 14 September 1983.
Peterson, Medora. Newspaper publisher; widow of Hjalmar Petersen, former governor of Minnesota. To author, 7 August 1983.
Scott, Floyd B. Son of I. G. Scott, a founder of Farmer-Labor party. To author, 4 August 1983.

Interviews (with the author, unless otherwise stated)

Ball, Joseph. Retired businessman; former political editor, *St. Paul Pioneer Press;* U.S. senator from Minnesota, 1940–49. Front Royal, Va., 3 June 1981.
Bellman, Sam. Lawyer; former state legislator and activist in Farmer-Labor party. Minneapolis, 25 May 1983.
Benson, Elmer A. Retired businessman; former governor of Minnesota. Appleton, Minn., 10 August 1979, and Lutsen, Minn., 9 August 1980.
Bingham, Alfred. Editor of *Common Sense* and national third-party activist during the early and mid-30s. Salem, Conn., 19 September 1981.
Carlson, Gilbert. Former attorney for teamsters Local 544. St. Paul, 19 May 1983.
Carlson, Grace. Former activist in Socialist Workers party; first woman in America to be a vice-presidential candidate. St. Paul, 19 May 1983.
Confidential interview. Former Communist labor leader in Minneapolis; named before Dies Committee, October 1938.
Confidential interview. Former member, staff, Farmer-Labor Educational Bureau.
Confidential interview. Former speechwriter for Farmer-Labor governor Elmer Benson.
Confidential interview. Former state legislator affiliated with conservative caucus, House of Representatives, Minnesota legislature, 1930s.
Confidential interviews. Former members of legal staff, National Labor Relations Board, 1937–38.
Creel, Warren. Former member, staff, Farmer-Labor Educational Bureau; candidate for Congress from third district, Minn., 1946. Albany, N.Y., 6 August 1983.
DeBoer, Harry. Retired labor leader; picket captain, 1934 strikes. Minneapolis, 26 May 1983.
DuBois, Patrick. Banker; former state bank regulator; activist in Farmer-Labor party. Sauk Centre, Minn., 29 July 1980.
Dunne, Vincent. Trotskyist leader of teamsters Local 574 (later Local 544), Minneapolis, 1934–41. Interviewed by Lila M. Johnson, 28 April 1969. In Audio-Visual Collection, Minnesota Historical Society, St. Paul.
Fiterman, Harry. Tax analyst; former adviser to Governor Floyd B. Olson. Minneapolis, 1 September 1980.
Folwick, Orlin. Retired newspaper reporter; reporter for *Minnesota Daily Star* during its Farmer-Labor period. Minneapolis, 28 May 1983.

Frank, Roy. Retired government lawyer; Farmer-Labor assistant attorney general, 1933–39. Bethesda, Md., 24 March 1981.

Freeman, Orville. Businessman; former activist, Democratic Farmer-Labor party. New York, 2 April 1980.

Gadler, Steve. Environmentalist; active in Hjalmar Petersen's campaign, Farmer-Labor gubernatorial primary, 1938. St. Paul, 20 May 1983.

Gates, Lillian Schwartz. Art gallery director; employee of Hennepin County Farmer-Labor Association, 1936–38. Glenn Cove, N.Y., 8 November 1985.

Genis, Sander. Retired labor leader; former vice-president, Amalgamated Clothing Workers of America; activist in Farmer-Labor party. St. Paul, 16 August 1979 and 20 August 1980.

Greenberg, Morris. Labor lawyer and Farmer-Labor activist, 1930s. Interviewed by Irene Paull, September 1968. In Audio-Visual Collection, Minnesota Historical Society, St. Paul.

Haycraft, Kenneth. Retired businessman; Farmer-Labor candidate for mayor of Minneapolis, 1937. North Branford, Conn., 1 June 1981.

Hudson, Carlos. Retired writer and journalist; editor and writer for *The Organizer* (strike daily of Local 574, July-August 1934) and for its successor, *Northwest Organizer*. Union City, Mich., 16 November 1985.

Keyserling, Leon. Economist; former legislative assistant to Senator Robert Wagner. Washington, D.C., 30 December 1981.

Lindquist, Arnold. Retired health professional; former member, staff, Farmer-Labor Educational Bureau. St. Paul, 24 May 1983.

Mendow, Hyman. Retired lawyer; legal and childhood acquaintance of Floyd B. Olson. Minneapolis, 22 July 1985.

Metzger, Evelyn Petersen. Publisher; daughter of Farmer-Labor governor Hjalmar Petersen. McLean, Va., 26 December 1983.

Morrow, Felix. Literary agent; former activist in Socialist Workers party. New York, 22 April 1982.

Olson, Orville. Former director of personnel, Minnesota Department of Highways, 1936–38. By telephone, 2 April and 3 August 1983.

———. Excerpts of interviews conducted by John Highkin in Los Angeles, 30 May and 13 June 1982. In possession of author.

Peterson, Harry H. Retired lawyer; Farmer-Labor attorney general, 1933–36; appointed to Minnesota Supreme Court by Farmer-Labor governor Hjalmar Petersen. Minneapolis, 27 and 28 August 1980.

Peyton, John Newton. Commissioner of Banks, Minnesota, 1931–33. Interviewed by Lila M. Johnson, 9 October 1967. Transcript at Minnesota Historical Society, St. Paul.

Rathert, Albert R. Former assistant to I. C. Strout, budget director for Governor Floyd B. Olson. Minneapolis, 27 May 1983.

Reichel, Louis. Retired labor leader; former vice-president of the Minnesota State Federation of Labor. Mankato, Minn., 26 May 1983.

Ross, Nat. Businessman; head of Communist party of Minnesota, 1937–39. New York, 20 January 1986.

Russel, Al. Activist in and organizer for Minneapolis teamsters Local 574, middle and late '30s. New York, 20 January 1986.

Rutchick, Harold. Attorney; brother of Roger Rutchick, executive secretary to Minnesota governor Elmer A. Benson, 1937–39. St. Paul, 23 July 1985.

Stassen, Harold. Lawyer; former governor of Minnesota. Manchester, N.H., 23 February 1984.

Tauer, Jerome. Retired manager, Buildings and Grounds Department of the University of Minnesota at Minneapolis; former staffer of a St. Paul Farmer-Labor ward club, 1930s. St. Paul, 23 July 1985.

Votaw, O. R. Retired labor leader; founder of Farmer-Labor party; former secretary-treasurer, District 77, International Association of Machinists. St. Paul, 23 May 1983.

Watson, Chester. President of the Workers Alliance in Minnesota, 1936–38; Farmer-Labor candidate for Congress from Minnesota first district in 1936. Interview conducted by Irene Paull, 21 August 1968. In Audio-Visual Collection of Minnesota Historical Society, St. Paul.

Wilson, Luke. Former member, staff, La Follette Civil Liberties Committee. Bethesda, Md., 27 December 1982.

Manuscripts and Archives

Chase, Ray. Papers. Minnesota Historical Society, Archives and Manuscripts Division, St. Paul.

DuBois, Ben. Papers. Minnesota Historical Society, Archives and Manuscripts Division, St. Paul.

Farmer-Labor Association Papers. Minnesota Historical Society, Archives and Manuscripts Division, St. Paul.

Genis, Sander. Papers. Minnesota Historical Society, Archives and Manuscripts Division, St. Paul.

Hillman, Sidney. Correspondence, 1930–46. Amalgamated Clothing Workers of America Archives, Cornell University, Ithaca, N.Y.

Labor's Non-partisan League Papers. State Historical Society of Wisconsin, Madison.

Le Sueur, Arthur. Papers. Minnesota Historical Society, Archives and Manuscripts Division, St. Paul.

Lundeen Ernest. Papers. Hoover Institution Archives, Stanford, Calif.

Mahoney, William. Papers. Minnesota Historical Society, Archives and Manuscripts Division, St. Paul.

Minneapolis. Police Department. Personnel Records.

National Nonpartisan League Papers. Microfilm edition. Minnesota Historical Society, Archives and Manuscripts Division, St. Paul.

National War Labor Board. Record group 2, series 4. National Archives, Suitland, Md.

Sollie, Allen and Violet. Papers. Minnesota Historical Society, Archives and Manuscripts Division, St. Paul.

Strout, I. C. Papers. Minnesota Historical Society, Archives and Manuscripts Division, St. Paul.

Walker, Charles Rumford. Files of *American City*. On loan from Mrs. Adelaide Walker to author, Cambridge, Mass.

Newspapers and Proceedings

Advance (Amalgamated Clothing Workers of America). 1936–38.
American Federation of Labor. Metal Trades Department. *Proceedings of the Twenty-ninth Annual Convention of the Metal Trades Department of the American Federation of Labor, Denver, Colorado, September 27, 1937.*
American Federation of State, County, and Municipal Employees. *Proceedings of the First Annual Convention of the American Federation of State, County, and Municipal Employees, Detroit, September 17–19, 1936.*
———. *Proceedings of the Second Convention of the American Federation of State, County, and Municipal Employees, Milwaukee, September 13–15, 1937.*
Catholic Bulletin. Publication of St. Paul Archdiocese. 1936–38.
CIO News. 1936–38.
Congress of Industrial Organizations. *Proceedings of the First Constitutional Convention of the Congress of Industrial Organizations, Pittsburgh, November 14–18, 1938.*
Farmer-Labor Leader. 1930–34.
Labor. Washington, D.C., 1935–38.
Labor World. Duluth, 1918–26.
Machinists Monthly Journal. 1913, 1935–39.
Minneapolis Journal. 1938.
Minnesota Farm Bureau News (South Central Edition). 1925–38.
Minnesota Federationist. 1937–38.
Minnesota Leader. 1919–25, 1935–38.
Minnesota State Federation of Labor. *Proceedings of the Fifty-sixth Convention, Mankato, Minn., September 12–14, 1938.*
———. *Proceedings of the Fifty-fifth Convention, Hibbing, Minn., September 20–22, 1937.*
———. *Proceedings of the Fifty-fourth Convention, Cloquet, Minn., September 21–23, 1936.*
———. *Proceedings of the Fifty-third Convention, Red Wing, Minn., August 19–21, 1935.*
———. *Proceedings of the Forty-seventh Convention, Mankato, Minn., August 19–21, 1929.*
———. *Proceedings of the Forty-fifth Convention, International Falls, Minn., August 15–17, 1927.*
———. *Proceedings of the Forty-fourth Convention, Hibbing, Minn., August 16–18, 1926.*
———. *Proceedings of the Forty-third Convention, Austin, Minn., September 21–23, 1925.*
———. *Proceedings of the Forty-second Convention, Faribault, Minn., July 21–23, 1924.*
———. *Proceedings of the Forty-first Convention, Duluth, Minn., July 17–19, 1923.*
———. *Proceedings of the Thirty-ninth Convention, Brainerd, Minn., July 18–20, 1921.*
———. *Proceedings of the Thirty-eighth Convention, Rochester, Minn., July 19–21, 1920.*

———. *Proceedings of the Thirty-seventh Convention, New Ulm, Minn., July 21–23, 1919.*
———. *Proceedings of the Thirty-sixth Convention, Virginia, Minn., July 15–17, 1918.*
———. *Proceedings of the Thirty-fifth Convention, Faribault, Minn., July 16–18, 1917.*
Minnesota Union Advocate. St. Paul, 1922–24, 1928–30, 1934–38.
Northwest Organizer (Teamsters Local 574; Teamsters Local 544). Minneapolis, 1935–38.
St. Paul Pioneer Press. 1938.
Third Ward Leader. Minneapolis, 1936. Newspaper Collection, Minnesota Historical Society, St. Paul.
Timberworker. Duluth, 1937–38.
Union News Service (Committee for Industrial Organization). 1937–38.
United Electrical, Radio, and Machine Workers of America. *Proceedings of the Second Annual Convention of the United Electrical, Radio, and Machine Workers of America, Philadelphia, September 3–6, 1937.*
———. *Proceedings of the Third Annual Convention of the United Electrical, Radio, and Machine Workers of America, St. Louis, September 5–9, 1938.*
Willmar Tribune. Minnesota, 1936–38.

Newsreels and Videos

A Common Man's Courage. Video documentary of career of John T. Bernard, Farmer-Labor congressman, Minnesota eighth district, 1937–39. In Audio-Visual Collection, Minnesota Historical Society, St. Paul.
Paramount News. Newsreels. "Floyd Olson Speaking 1936 Farmer-Labor Convention." "Strike Outbreak: Scenes of Crowds in Minneapolis, and Violence between Strikers and Deputies." "Move for Labor Peace." "Political Pot Comes to Boil (Floyd B. Olson Calls for a National Third Party)," Film can D-51. In Audio-Visual Collection, Minnesota Historical Society, St. Paul.

Government Sources

Canada. Statistics Canada. *Historical Statistics of Canada.* 2d ed. Edited by F. H. Leacy. Ottawa, 1983.
Minneapolis. City Council. *Proceedings.* Vols. 42–63, 1916–38.
Minnesota. Adjutant General. *Report of the Adjutant General of the State of Minnesota Covering the Thirtieth Biennial Period Ending December 31, 1918.*
———. *Report of the Adjutant General of the State of Minnesota Covering the Thirty-second Biennial Period Ending December 31, 1922.*
Minnesota. Attorney General. *Biennial Report of the Attorney General to the Governor of the State of Minnesota for the Period Ending December 31, 1934.*
———. *Biennial Report of the Attorney General to the Governor of the State of Minnesota for the Period Ending December 31, 1936.*
———. *Biennial Report of the Attorney General to the Governor of the State of Minnesota for the Period Ending December 31, 1938.*
Minnesota. Commissioner of Highways. *Biennial Report of the Commissioner of Highways of Minnesota.* 1930–38.

Minnesota. Commission of Administration and Finance. Director of Personnel. *Classes, Grades, and Titles of State Employees with Class Specification, as Determined by the Commission of Administration and Finance, Director of Personnel.* January 1935.

———. *Salary Scales for State Employees as Classified by the Commission of Administration and Finance, Director of Personnel.* January 1935.

Minnesota. Department of Conciliation. *First Annual Report of the Division of Conciliation.* 1940.

Minnesota. Department of Education. Educational Materials Project. *A Merit System for Minnesota.* Social Science Series, no. 1. 1937.

Minnesota. Department of Highways. *History and Organization of the Department of Highways, State of Minnesota.* March 1942.

Minnesota. Department of Labor and Industries. *Seventeenth Biennial Report of the Department of Labor and Industries of the State of Minnesota, 1919–1920.*

———. *Sixteenth Biennial Report of the Department of Labor and Industries of the State of Minnesota, 1917–1918.*

Minnesota. Governor. *Inaugural Message of Governor Elmer A. Benson to the Legislature of Minnesota.* 5 January 1937.

———. *Inaugural Message of Governor Floyd B. Olson to the Legislature of Minnesota.* 7 January 1931.

———. *Second Inaugural Message of Governor Floyd B. Olson to the Legislature of Minnesota.* 4 January 1933.

———. *Third Inaugural Message of Governor Floyd B. Olson to the Legislature of Minnesota.* 9 January 1935.

Minnesota. Legislature. House. *Journals.* 1919–37.

Minnesota. Legislature. Senate. *Journals.* 1919, 1921, 1923, 1927, 1931, 1935.

———. *Report of the Investigating Committee of the Senate Created under Resolution No. 2, for the Purpose of Investigating All Departments of the State Government of Minnesota.* 1935.

Minnesota. Secretary of State. *Legislative Manual of the State of Minnesota.* 1919–39.

North Dakota. Secretary of State. *1919 Legislative Manual.* Bismarck: n.d.

St. Paul. Board of Elections. *Votes Cast for City Officers from Year 1914 to Date.* St. Paul City Hall.

U.S. Congress. House. Congressman Ernest R. Lundeen presenting material on the Minnesota Farmer-Labor party. *Congressional Record,* vol. 77. 73d Cong., 1st sess., 29 May 1933. *Congressional Record,* vol. 79. 74th Cong., 1st sess., 17 August 1935. *Congressional Record,* vol. 80. 74th Cong., 2d sess., 17 June 1936.

U.S. Congress. House. Committee on Roads. *Hearing on H.R. 8838, a Bill to Amend the Federal Aid Highway Act.* 75th Cong., 3d sess., 1938.

U.S. Congress. House. Special Committee on Un-American Activities. *Hearings before a Special Committee on Un-American Activities on H.R. 282.* 75th Cong., 3d sess., 1938.

U.S. Congress. Senate. *Biographical Directory of the American Congress, 1774–1971.* 92d Cong., 1st sess., 1971. S. Doc. 92–8.

U.S. Department of Commerce. Bureau of Economic Analysis. *State Personal*

Incomes: Estimates for 1929–82 and a Statement of Sources and Methods.
Washington, D.C.: Department of Commerce, 1984.
U.S. Department of Commerce. Bureau of the Census. *Historical Statistics of the
United States: Colonial Times to 1970.* 2 vols. Washington, D.C.: Bureau of the
Census, 1975.
U.S. National Labor Relations Board. Division of Economic Research. *Written
Trade Agreements in Collective Bargaining.* Bulletin 4. Washington, D.C.: Government Printing Office, 1939.

Miscellaneous

Coolidge, Calvin. "Coolidge's Veto of the McNary-Haugen Bill, February 25,
1927." In *Readings in United States Economic and Business History,* edited by
Ross M. Robertson and James L. Pate, 438–39. Boston: Houghton Mifflin Co.,
1966.
Hoover, Herbert. "I Am Opposed to Any Dole." Annual message of the president
to the Congress, 8 December 1931. In *American Issues in the Twentieth Century,* edited by Frank Freidel and Norman Pollack, 165–66. Chicago: Rand
McNally & Co., 1966.
———. "We Have Not Feared Boldly to Adopt Unprecedented Measures." Address accepting the Republican nomination for president, 11 August 1932. In
American Issues in the Twentieth Century, edited by Frank Freidel and Norman
Pollack, 158–64. Chicago: Rand McNally & Co., 1966.

Index

Accumulationist model (of political economy), 4, 10; balancing with reformist role, 69, 70, 82, 85; and farmers' interests, 76; in 19th century, 6; in 1920s, 70; risk of reestablishment of, 170; and state-level radicalism, 15

Agrarian discontent and protest, 6; in Canada, 158; and Farmers Holiday Association, 87–93; in Iowa, 87–90; in Minnesota, 23–25, 89–92, 142; in North Dakota, 17–18; and People's Lobby, 142; resurgence of, 96; in Wisconsin, 166. *See also* Agriculture; Farmers

Agricultural Adjustment Act (AAA; 1933), xi, 136, 166; and county extension agents, 98–99; and farm prices, 85–86, 96; implementation of, 97–100; invalidation of (1936), 101

Agricultural Marketing Act (1929), 84

Agricultural prices: and AAA, 85–86, 96; and "cost-of-production" legislation, 89–94, 96–97; declines in, 7, 72; and farm market withholding action, 92; and McNary-Haugen bill, 74–76; "parity" for, 95; production control proposals, 95–96; stabilization of, 161

Agriculture: attempts at collective solutions, 18–19, 74; and banking, 73, 81; in Canada, 160, 161, 163; cash crop production, 7, 71, 159; economic difficulties in, 7, 88–89; farm crisis (1920–23), 72–77; farm crisis (1933–34), 86–87, 94–100, 134, 166; in Minnesota, 21–22, 71–73; New Deal policy concerning, 93–102; in North Dakota, 18–19; and plan for price con l (McNary-Haugen bill), 74–

76; second-class status of, 82. *See also* Agrarian discontent and protest; Farmers

Alberta, 158

Amalgamated Clothing Workers, 122

American Farm Bureau Federation, 91; and credit for production control, 98–99

American Federation of Labor (AFL), 25–26, 48, 107; and Communism, 126, 143, 147; convention (1935), 121–22; and NLRB-run elections, 123; perception of support for Stassen, 152; rift with NLRB, 132; split with CIO, xi, 122–23, 126, 143, 155, 166; support for Petersen by, 147

"Americanism," portrayal of Communism as, 128

American Labor Party of New York, origin of in New Deal, not state-level radicalism, 170

American Society of Equity, 19

American Youth Congress, 128

Anti-semitism: and campaign of Petersen, 147, 149; and anti-Communism, 150; among conservative businessmen, 148

"Associationalism," 84

Atlantic City, AFL convention in, 122

Attorney general (Minnesota), 56; and institutional modernization, 59; Peterson as, 93; use of state highway patrol to disband farm picket lines, 92

Auditor (Minnesota), 56

Austin, Minn., 105, 155

Baker, Gladys, 99

"Balance of power," Townley plan for, 38

"Balancing" political economy, 69, 70, 82, 85, 120, 137
Baldwin, Roger, 86
Bank of North Dakota, 3, 31
Banks: closing of (1931), 89; crisis (1933), 102; and indebtedness of Minnesota, 141; in Minneapolis strikes, 113–14; proposals for public ownership of, 2, 171; rural, 18, 81–82; and union employers, 104, 115
Bellamy, Edward, 88
Bennett, R.B., 161
Bennett New Deal (Canada), 161, 162
Benson, Elmer, 115, 119, 130, 169; and Communism, 146, 148; deepening of labor disunity by, 146; election race against Stassen (1938), 149–55; leadership style of, 139; and People's Lobby, 142; and politics of Olson's succession, 66–67, 137; and Popular Front, 140–41; primary race against Petersen (1938), 146–49; progressive tax program of, 140–41; Roosevelt's endorsement of, 171; and split within machinists, 144
Berle, Adolph, 81
Berman, Hyman, x
Bernard, John, 127, 141
"Big Three," and Minnesota administrative reform, 59
Black, John D., 95
Blacklisting, of railroad shopmen, 60
Blacks, disenfranchisement of, 11
"Bloody Friday," 110, 111
Bonds, issued to raise money for highways, 63–64
Bosch, John, 105; and national Farmers Holiday Association, 89–90
Bosch, Richard, 90
Brainerd, Minn., 60
Bretton Woods system, 176
British North America Act (BNA Act), 159–60
Brown, Bill, 110, 112; murder of, 148
Bryan, William Jennings, 13
Bryant, Louise, 40
Buckler, R.T., 101

Budget (federal), attempts to balance, 85, 133, 134
Building Trades Council, 108
Bureau of Criminal Apprehension, 80
Bureau of Public Roads, 59
Burnquist, J.A.A., 24, 25, 154; election as governor (1918), 27, 28, 30; replacement by Preus, 35
"Business commonwealth," 71
Business interests: alliance with Farmer-Labor party, 81–82, 138; and collective bargaining, 86; and corporate support for Petersen, 147; and fascist movements, 148–49; government support of, 5, 6, 134; and Hoover, 83–84; intransigence to unions of, 26, 77–78, 113; in 19th century, 6; opposition of to New Deal, 130; policies encroaching on, 130. See also Capitalism; Economic elites; Regulatory agencies and powers

California: tax revolt in (1970s), 3; volatility of electorate in, 12
Canada: advantages of CCF vs. Minnesota Farmer-Labor party, 162–63; and Bennett New Deal, 161; emergence of CCF in, 158; federalism in, 159–60, 163–64; Great Depression in, 160–61; political elites in, 162; province-level radicalism in, 158–65; similarities to United States, 159
Candidates. See Political candidates
Cannon, James, 112, 145–46
Capitalism: attacks on, 2, 19; and backlash against changes in political economy, 137; distribution of rewards of, ix, x; effects of New Deal on, 172; government role in defense of, 4–5. See also Business interests; Class conflict; Economic inequality; Redistributive politics
Capital Times, 166
Carmen's union, threatened strike of, 26. See also Streetcar franchise
Cash crops, 7, 71, 159

Catholics: in St. Paul, 49, 152; and social justice movement, 111
Central Labor Union, 108
Central States Drivers Council, 129
Chain stores: protest against, 81, 102; proposed regulation of, 2; tax system used against, 140
Chase, Ray, 54, 150
Chicago, 173
Chicago Tribune, 146
Child labor, 6
Christensen, Parley Parker, 13
Christianson, Theodore, 58, 59
Citizens Alliance, 104; denunciation of Communist League, 113; and Employers Advisory Committee, 108, 112; and Minneapolis strikes, 108–9, 111–15; National Guard raid on, 112; and open-shop drive, 77–78; and Reconstruction Finance Corporation loans, 113–14
Civilian Conservation Corps (CCC), 86
Civil liberties: Senate committee investigating abuses of, 169; concerns for, 28
Civil servants: merit system proposals, 59, 66–68, 149; and regulatory agencies, 162; and welfare services, 174. *See also* Patronage
Civil War: and Canada, 160; pension system, 6
Civil Works Administration (CWA), 64, 86, 153
Class conflict: Communist League expectations of, 105; and drive for open primary ballots, 56; and ideology of Trotskyists, 116; and image of union domination, 43; Mahoney's view of, 44; New Deal success in damping, 173
Class interests, of middle class, 81–82
Cleveland, Grover, 6
"Closed-shop" agreement, 107–8. *See also* Open shop drive
Coal yards, truckers' strike in (Minneapolis, 1934), 105–7
Collective bargaining, 115; in Canada,

163; and Farmer-Labor party, 2; federal recognition of, 86, 103, 113; with IWW, 3, 31; Murray Hill agreement, 77; for railway labor, 70. *See also* Strikes; Union(ism)
Comintern: hostility to Farmer-Labor party, 48; and political direction of American communism, 47, 128. *See also* Communist party; Popular Front
Commerce, federalism in, 9
Commission of Administration and Finance (Minnesota), 59
Commission of Public Safety. *See* Minnesota Commission of Public Safety
Committee for Industrial Organization (CIO): Communists in, 125, 126–27, 144; and endorsement of Benson, 152; formation of, xi, 122; hostility to, 134; increasing legitimacy of, 123; and La Follette Committee, 169; radical organizing tactics of, 125; split with AFL, 122–23, 126, 143, 155, 166; state councils of, 126; use of NLRB-run elections, 123; and Wagner Act, 136
Committee on Industrial Relations, 146
Commodity options market, 95. *See also* Agricultural prices
Commons, John R., 90
Communist League of America, 116; denunciation by Citizens Alliance, 113; and Minneapolis strikes (1934), 105–7; and *The Organizer,* 114; and teamsters union, 107
Communist party: AFL's attitude to, 126; and CIO, 125–27; and Farmer-Labor party, 116, 145; and Minnesota politics, 128–30, 140–41, 148, 152; and People's Lobby, 142. *See also* Popular Front
Communists, 50; Benson's ties with, 146, 148, 152; and Federated Farmer-Labor party, 47; goals of in links to left-wing organizations, 128; influence on Mahoney, 43–44, 47; and Minneapolis' mayoral race, 143; and ten-

Communists (*continued*)
sion within Minnesota labor
movement, 136; in trade unions, 43–
44, 104, 109, 126–28, 144, 146; and
United Farmers League, 92. *See also*
Trotskyists
Company unions, 82, 86, 107, 121
Conference for Progressive Political Action, 47
"Consensus" view, of political development, 172–73
Conservative party (Canadian), 160–61
Constituency, size of: in politics of CCF
(Saskatchewan), 164; and relationship
to relative influence of interest groups
in Minnesota politics and elsewhere in
American politics, 101–2, 118, 137,
157–58
Conventions, preprimary endorsing, 36,
38
Coolidge, Calvin, and McNary-Haugen
plan, 75, 76
Coolidge administration, 70
Cooperative Commonwealth Federation
(CCF) of Saskatchewan, 16; accomplishments of, 163, 165; advantages
of vs. Minnesota Farmer-Labor party,
162–63; Canadian circumstances affecting, 164; emergence of, 158; and
state-level radicalism in U.S., 159, 162
Cooperatives: in Canada, 164; marketing, 19
Corcoran, Patrick, 144; assassination of,
145–46
Corn Belt Committee, 89
Corn loan program, 97
Corporate profits, tax on, 130
"Cost-of-production" legislation, 89–
94; Olson's plan for, 91; renewed
attempt for, 96–97
Counties: agricultural agents and extension service in, 98–99; Farmer-Labor
party committees in, 39, 40; subsidized newspapers in, 31–32
Court-packing plan, 133
Courts (federal): activism of, 9; and labor law, 78. *See also* Supreme Court
Courts (Minnesota): and institutional

modernization, 59; and judicial elections, 56–57; and labor law, 78
Crafts organizations, 125
Credit: crisis (1932), 85; and New Deal
programs for farmers, 99
Currency: government defense of, 4–5;
inflation of, 97

Day, Vince, 107
DeBoer, Harry, 106, 110
Debs, Eugene, 15
Debsian socialism, 1, 6, 14, 172; practical side of, 15
Decentralization, xi, 8; vs. centralization
of European political systems, 9; of
Minnesota's institutional structure,
57; of social services, 174; and state
militias, 10; of unemployment compensation, 168, 174. *See also*
Federalism
Deficit spending, 133–34
Deflation, 7, 72; postwar, 74. *See also*
Agricultural prices
Democracy: and capitalism, 2, 172; and
Popular Front theory of Communist
presence, 128
Democratic Farmer-Labor party, 156
Democratic leaders, in House of Representatives, 169
Democratic party: and balancing political economy, 70, 83, 102, 103; Farmer-Labor party merging with, 156;
gain of strength in off-year election
(1934), 135; middle-class focus of,
175; in Minnesota, 30, 42, 46, 156;
and New Deal watershed, 172, 173;
and political change, 102, 176, 177;
and Socialists, 15; in South, 11;
strength of (1930s), 157; weakness of,
173–75; in Wisconsin, 167. *See also*
New Deal; Presidential election
Democratic-Populist vote, in 1896 election, 14
Depression. *See* Great Depression, 159
Des Moines, Iowa, 89
Devold, Andrew, 59
Dies, Martin, 150–51
Dies Committee, 135, 150–51; 169

Dobbs, Farrell, 112, 129
Dominion (Canadian), inactivity of, 161–62
Dominion-Provincial Conference (1927), 160
"Dual sovereignty" federalism, 9–10, 175
Dubinsky, David, 122
DuBois, Ben, 82
Dukakis, Michael, 174, 175
Duluth, Minn., 28, 30, 35, 79, 155; Farmer-Labor convention in (1938), 147–48; farmer-labor newspaper in, 40
Duluth Federated Trades and Labor Assembly, 144
Duluth *Labor World*, 40, 82
"Dumping" (of farm surpluses): impossibility of, 94; McNary-Haugen plan for, 75–76
Dunne, Vincent, 104, 105, 112, 116, 144
Dunne brothers, 104, 112, 116, 144
Dunnigan, E.H., 111–13

Economic elites: and balance between capital and labor, 137; and desire to amend Wagner Act. *See also* Business interests; Political elites
Economic inequality: and institutional biases, 18–19; and McNary-Haugen bill, 76; in 1920s, 71; worsening of, 175. *See also* Redistributive politics
Economic protest, 8; political effects of, 14–15
Economy: effect of World War I on, 19; expanded role of government in, 74–75; and interstate competition, 9; and monetarist policy instruments, 176; in 1920s, 71–73; shift from rural to industrial, 7; theories about government intervention in, 4–5, 16, 74–75. *See also* Great Depression; Recession
Economy Act (1933), 87
Educational Bureau, Farmer-Labor, 62, 63
Elections. *See* Farmer-Labor party, in elections; Presidential elections; Primaries
Electoral politics: access to, 10, 14–15, 21, 68; labor influence on, 136–37; and mobilization of voters, 170, 175; and North Dakota Nonpartisan League, 2–3, 17–19; and regional voting patterns, 10–13, 117–18, 154–55. *See also* Political education
Electoral realignment: toward Democratic party, 135, 157; in development of balancing political economy, 135, 157; toward Republican party in Minnesota in 1938, and long-run consequence, 154, 156
Electoral rules: changes in Minneapolis, 37, 38; Republican-engineered changes in Minnesota, 35–36
Elites. *See* Business interests; Economic elites; Political elites
Emme, Julius F., 35, 45
Employers Advisory Committee, 108, 112, 114
Employment and Social Insurance Act, 161
"Equalization fee," and dumping of farm surpluses, 75, 76
Erath, Peter, 108
Ervin, William, 146
Esch-Cummins Act (1920), 73, 74
Europe: as agricultural market, 72; centralized political systems in, 9
Executive branch conferences, and Hoover, 83, 84
Exports: agricultural, 72, 75–76, 94; Canada's dependence on, 160
Extension service, of U.S. Department of Agriculture, 98–99
Extremism, in opposition to Nonpartisan League, 24–25

Factionalism (in Farmer-Labor party), 137; and Benson's policy, 139, 141; and Dies hearing, 150–51; early freedom from, 33; and Minneapolis mayoral race (1937), 142–43; and patronage, 65–66, 68, 120; and splits in labor movement, 145; and Stassen's

Factionalism (*continued*)
candidacy, 149; in Washington Farmer-Labor party, 50
Factionalism (in Nonpartisan League), 32
Fair trade practice, legislation for, 102
Farley, James, 170
Farm Bureau. *See* American Farm Bureau Federation; Minnesota Farm Bureau
Farm credit programs, 99
Farm crisis (1920–23), 72–77; (1933–34), 86–87, 94–100, 166
Farmer-Labor Advocate, 43
Farmer-labor alliances: cooperation of leaders in, 33–34; in electoral realignment (1890s), 6; enthusiasm for, 45; and Minnesota Commission of Public Safety, 25; in Minnesota election (1920), 36; and Minnesota Farm Conference, 140; and Nonpartisan League, 32. *See also* Farmer-Labor party
Farmer-Labor Association: and decline of political action in Twin Cities, 48–49; and Educational Bureau, 63; exclusion of Communists from, 48; increases in membership of, 62; and legislative vs. patronage strategy, 67–68
Farmer-Labor clubs, 62–63, 65
Farmer-Labor Educational Bureau, 62, 63
Farmer-Labor Federation: and La Follette's presidential candidacy, 46–47; in Minnesota election (1924), 45–46; origin in WPNPL, 45; renaming of as Farmer-Labor Association, 48
Farmer-Labor Leader, 61, 66, 67
Farmer-Labor party, 156; in Minneapolis, 142–43; in national campaigns, 13, 50; in other states, 50–51; platform of (1934), 1–2, 170; public opinion about, 171; in U.S. Senate, 169. *See also* Third parties
Farmer-Labor party (Minnesota), 1, 16, 173; and alliance of farmers and labor, ix, 29; changes in interest group environment of, 115–16, 136–37; changes in labor base of, 126; and Communists, 44, 138, 143; cooperation of leaders of, 33–34; death of (1944); disarray of leadership (1937–38), 130, 141; in elections (1918), 29–30; (1920), 36, 41; (1922), 39, 41, 42; (1924), 45–47, 51, 54; (1926), 49; (1928), 49, 51, 59; (1930), 53–54, 57, 117, 120, 154; (1932), 57, 117–18, 120, 154; (1934), 67, 68, 117–18, 120, 154; (1936), 119–20, 154, 170; (1938), 120, 146–56, 171; and Farm Bureau, 98, 101–2; and farm crisis (1920s), 74–76; and Farmers Holiday Association, 91–93; hostility of teamsters to, 116; increased moderation of (1936–38), 2; international comparisons, xii, 158–65; leadership limitations, 118, 137, 168; and Mahoney's plan for consolidation, 42–43, 47; and middle-class interests, 81–82; and Minnesota bureaucracy, 57–58; naming of, 29; New Deal effect on, 102, 118, 120, 135–38, 155, 171; and nonpartisan elections, 54–55; and Nonpartisan League, 17, 21; organizational problems (1930s), 53; and problems of labor, 80; programs and goals of, x, 33, 82; and realignment toward Republican party, 154; and split of AFL and CIO, 126–27; and State Federation of Labor, 128–29, 150; support in rural vs. urban areas, 117–18, 136, 154–55; use of patronage by, 57–66, 68, 120; weakness of, 51; and Wisconsin Progressive Party, 165; zenith of (1936), 119–20, 170. *See also* Factionalism (in Farmer-Labor party)
Farmer-Labor Progressive Federation (Wisconsin), 166–67, 171
Farmer-Labor Reconstruction League (Oklahoma), 50
Farmer-Labor State Central Committee, 43
Farmer-labor tensions, ix; and agri-

cultural vs. industrial interests, 76; in Canada, 164; deepening of by La Follette Committee, 169; after Minneapolis strikes (1934), 117–18; and Petersen's candidacy, 147; Stassen's exploitation of, 149–51; and Wagner Act, 136

Farmer-Labor youth clubs, 168

Farmer-Labour party (Saskatchewan), 158

Farmers, 6; educational programs for, 98–99; financial burdens on, 73; and industrialism, 7; insurance for, 18, 74; New Deal help for, 85–86; picketing by, 90; and state purchasing agencies, 2. *See also* Agriculture; Farmer-labor alliances; Mortgages

Farmers' Creditors Arrangement Act, 161

Farmers Equity Union, 166

Farmers Holiday Association, 136; background of, 87–89; collapse of, 102; and cost-of-production proposals, 96–98; and Farmer-Labor party, 91-93; ideology of, 101; initial actions of, 90; and mortgage foreclosures, 92–93; parade with Local 574, 109; in Wisconsin, 166

Farmers Union (Minnesota), 89, 94, 136; and cost-of-production prices, 91, 98; and Farmers Holiday Association, 88; membership decline in, 100

Farm Loan Act, 161

Farm market withholding action, 92

Farm prices. *See* Agricultural prices

Farm protest. *See* Agrarian discontent and protest

Farm Relief and Inflation Act (1933), 85

Farms, foreclosure of. *See* Mortgages (farm and chattel)

Farm security legislation, in Canada, 161, 163, 164

Farm surpluses: McNary-Haugen plan for, 75–76; and production control proposals, 95–96; production expansion causing, 72–73

Fascist movements: National Progressives of America, 171; Silver Shirts, 148

Federal Emergency Relief Administration (FERA), 86

Federal Farm Board, 84, 88, 95

Federal government: checks and balances in, 175; expanded role of in economy, 74–75; and funding for highway construction, 63; theories about intervention in economy, 4–5, 16. *See also* Government activism; New Deal

Federal Highway Act (1916), 9

Federalism: in Canada, 159–60, 163–64; "dual-sovereignty," 9–10, 175; and goals of politicians, 6; reinvigoration of, 175; and state-level radicalism, 8–10, 15; theory of, 80. *See also* Decentralization

Federal Reserve system, 74

Federal Trade Commission, 70

Federated Farmer-Labor party, 47

Fite, Gilbert, 76

Flint, Mich., sit-down strike in, 117

Foster, William Z., 47

Fraser, Don, 2

Gallup poll, 66, 134

Gehan, Mark, 151

General strikes: in San Francisco (1934), 103; in Seattle (1919), 103; threat of (Twin Cities, 1917–18), 26

Genis, Sander, 122; and division in Farmer-Labor party, 65–66

Georgists, 15

Gieske, Millard, x

Gifford, Walter, 85

Gold purchases, by Reconstruction Finance Corporation, 97

Gold standard, 6, 85; removal from (1933), 87; return to (1920s), 70–71

"Good government" issues, 58; and election of Stassen, 151; and patronage, 68

Government. *See* Federal government; State government(s)

Government activism: in Canada, 161; and economic intervention, 4–5, 16, 74–75; Farmer-Labor views of, 82; of state governments, 3–4, 175; of US

Government activism (*continued*)
  government, 74–75; and Wagner Act,
  121. *See also* State-level radicalism
Governmental capacities: in changing
  political economy, 83, 118, 136, 157;
  and growth of Farm Bureau, 99–100;
  in implementation of AAA (1933),
  97–99; in implementation of NIRA
  Section 7(a), 106, 111, 113; in implementation of Wagner Act (1935), 121;
  lack of in implementation of welfare-
  state services, 134; in passage of Soil
  Conservation and Domestic Allotment
  Act, 101; as stimulus to change in
  group organization, 116, 118, 136
Grain: AAA contracts for acreage, 100;
  corn loan program, 97; falling demand for, 72; government inspection
  of, 74; increased freight costs for, 73.
  See also Agricultural prices
Grain mills and elevators, 18, 74
Great Depression: approach of incoming
  Roosevelt administration to, 85–87;
  in Canada, 159, 160; and farm crisis,
  86–87, 94–100; onset of, 83–85; rea-
  sons for, 84. *See also* New Deal
Great Lakes–St. Lawrence seaway, 74,
  82
"Great Society," 173
Green, William, 103, 150
Greenbackers, 88
Gross national product, in Canada, 160

Haas, Father Francis, 111–13
Haas-Dunnigan plan, 111–13
Harding administration, 70, 74, 76, 77
Harris, Abe, 149
Hartz, Louis, 173
Haugen, Gilbert, 75
Haugland, Harry, 92
Haycraft, Kenneth, 112, 143
Hayden-Cartwright Act (1934), 63
Heil, Julius, 167
Highway construction, 9, 59–60, 63–64
Highway Department (Minnesota): link
  with teamsters, 116; and patronage,
  59–60, 63–64, 66
Hillman, Sidney, 122, 171

Home Building Association, 3, 31
Home Building and Loan Association v.
  Blaisdell, 93
Home Guard (Minnesota), 24, 27
Homestead exemption legislation, 135,
  140
Hoover, Herbert, 157; and Great De-
  pression, 84; and unemployment, 60,
  80, 85
Hoover administration, 115; contrast
  with Roosevelt administration, 84–85;
  political economy of, 83–84
Hormel strike, 105
Hotelling-Downs model, of party pol-
  itics, 139
House Labor Committee, 168, 169
Housing, public, 3
Hudson, Carlos, 116
Humphrey, Hubert, 2, 156
"Hundred Days," 83, 86
Hutcheson, Bill, 124

Idaho Nonpartisan League, 50
Idaho Progressive party, 1, 51
Immigrants, x, 11
Independent Bankers Association (IBA),
  82, 102
Industrial Commission (Minnesota), 3,
  31, 55
Industrialization, 7–8
Industrial policy, state-level, 3, 175
Industry: effect of Depression on, 160;
  and farm machinery, 73; and Wagner
  Act, 120
Insurance: for farmers, 18, 74; unem-
  ployment, 18, 134, 163, 168, 174
Interest groups: agricultural vs. indus-
  trial, 76, 136; in CCF, 164; and
  Farmer-Labor party, 115–16, 164;
  and New Deal policies, 157; and
  state-level parties vs. presidential par-
  ties, 101–2, 118, 136–37
International Association of Machinists
  (IAM), 28, 47, 127; and Murray Hill
  agreement, 77
International Brotherhood of Electrical
  Workers, 124

International Ladies' Garment Workers, 122
International politics, and domestic politics, 176–177
International Workers of the World (IWW), 3, 21; and Floyd Olson's membership in, 100
Iowa: farmers' protests in, 87–90; and mortgage moratorium law, 92–93
Iron ore shipping, taxation of, 74, 141–42
Iron Range, Minn., 126; Communist union power in, 126; economic problems in, 79

Jackson, Jesse, 175
Japan, 176
Johannes, Michael, 108
Johnson, Hugh, 97
Johnson, Magnus, 71; Farmer-Labor support for, 43; gubernatorial race (1922), 41, 46; senatorial campaigns (1923, 1924), 41–42, 45, 54
Jones, Jesse, 114, 115
Jones & Laughlin, 121–23, 131
Judiciary. *See* Courts; U.S. Supreme Court

Keillor, Steven, x
Keller, Oscar, 36
Kellogg, Frank, 24; senatorial race (1922), 41
Kennedy, E.F., 90
Keynesianism, 95, 133, 140; and unemployment rates, 86
King, Mackenzie, 161, 164
Ku Klux Klan, 50, 78

Labor: federal policy toward, 26; political influence of, 136–37, 173; shift in division of, 7; war-induced scarcity of, 25–26. *See also* Farmer-Labor party; Labor movement; Union(ism)
Labor courts, 121
Labor law: in Canada vs. U.S., 165; changes in facilitating attacks on unions, 78
Labor movement: coalition of with Non-

partisan League, 27; left- and right-wing divisions of, 136; in Minnesota, 28, 34, 49, 126–30, 136; and NIRA, 103; in North Dakota, 3, 31; and open-shop drive, 77, 80; and Roosevelt campaign, 170; and split of AFL and CIO, 122–23, 126, 143, 155, 166; Stassen's appeal to, 151–52; weakness of in 1920s, 79–80; in Wisconsin, 166. *See also* Strikes; Union(ism)
Labor Municipal Nonpartisan League, 28
Labor policy: and administrative labor courts, 121; and Wagner Act, 120. *See also* National Labor Relations Board (NLRB)
"Labor racketeering," charges of, 146
Labor Review, 40
Labor World (Duluth), 40, 82
La Follette, Philip: and dictatorship issue, 166–67; and national third party (1938), 171
La Follette, Robert, Jr., 169
La Follette, Robert, Sr.: defeat and death of (1924–25), 48, 74; and national third party (1924), 13, 46–47, 49, 170, 172; as reputed German sympathizer, 24
La Follette Committee, 169
La Follette family, 165–67
Langer, William, 32
Latimer, Thomas, 143
Lawson, George, 144
Leach, Colonel George, 37, 48, 143
League Against War and Fascism, 128
League of Women Voters, 58
Legislature: nonpartisan, 11, 55; in Wisconsin, 167
Legislature (in Minnesota), 54–55; and Benson's tax proposals, 140–42; Farmer-Labor party domination of (1937), 119; and mortgage moratorium, 92, 93; proposed strategy of Farmer-Labor Association toward, 67–68; Republican domination of (1939), 154
Lemke, William, 29, 31, 32

Le Sueur, Arthur, 29
Lewis, John L., 103, 122, 136, 145; attitude to AFL, 124; and Communist organizers, 125
Liberalism, 173
Liberal party (Canadian), 160, 161
Liberal Tradition in America, The (Louis Hartz), 173
Lilly, Richard, 146
Limitation of Hours of Work Act, 161
Lindbergh, Charles, Sr., 27, 30
Lipset, Seymour Martin, 163
"Little Steel" strikes, 131
Livestock, and agricultural crisis of Depression, 88
Local 544 (teamsters), 128–30
Local 574 (teamsters), 105–6
Long, Huey, 3, 29
Looking Backward (Edward Bellamy), 88
Loomis, Orland, 167
Lorence, James, 168
Lundeen, Ernest, 116, 119, 156, 168, 169
Lundeen Bill, 168–69, 174
Lyman, Arthur, 108

Machinists: Communist influence in, 43, 127, 144; split in, 144–45; in Twin Cities, 28, 77
Macroeconomic management, 158
Mahoney, William, 52, 105, 129; Communist influence on, 43–44, 47; and Farmer-Labor Federation, 44–45, 48, 166; and naming of Farmer-Labor party, 29; and national third party (1924), 46–47, 170; plan of for single partisan infrastructure, 42–43; and State Federation of Labor, 28, 35; and WPNPL, 42
Manahan, James, 29
Manitoba, 158
Mankato, Minn., 81
Market, self-correcting, 4
Mayer, George, x
Mayhew, David, 12
McCarthy, Eugene, 156
McEwen, William, 82

McGee, John, 24, 25, 28
McNary, Charles, 75
McNary-Haugen bill (1924–28), 74–76; and New Deal agricultural policy, 94–95
Meatpackers' strike (1933), 105
Merchants, independent vs. chain stores, 81
"Metropole," agricultural, 71
"Metropolitan" states, 13. *See also* "Nonmetropolitan" areas
Michigan Democratic party, and collapse of Governor Murphy's coalition, 155–56
Middle class: and Democratic party, 175; and party control of bureaucracy, 58; problems of, 81–82
Milk production control, 166
Miller, Glen, 89
Milwaukee, socialists in, 15, 166
Minimum Wage Act, 161
Minneapolis: decline of labor's political action in, 48; electoral rules change in, 37, 48–49; mayoral elections in (1921), 37; (1937), 142–43; realignment away from Farmer-Labor party, 155; Socialist party in, 15, 28; truckers' strikes in (1934), 80, 86, 103–15, 143; WPNPL power in, 37; *See also* Twin Cities
Minneapolis Central Labor Union, 48; and AFL insistence on expulsion of CIO delegates, 144
Minneapolis Journal, 40
Minneapolis Labor Review, 40
Minneapolis Trades and Labor Assembly, 48
Minneapolis Tribune, 40
Minnesota: agricultural problems in, 72–73; indebtedness of, 141; institutional structure of, 53–58; labor movement in, 28, 34, 49, 126–30; middle class and independent businesses in, 81–82; Nonpartisan League in, 20–21, 27–28; radical delegation in U.S. Senate, 41; regulatory agencies and commissions, 55–56; response to tensions in national labor movement,

126–30; union strength in, 34, 126; volatility of electorate in, 12. *See also* Farmer-Labor party (Minnesota); Legislature (in Minnesota); Minneapolis; St. Paul

Minnesota Commission of Public Safety, 23, 24, 28, 29; as antilabor agency, 25–26; and Farmer-Labor party, 80

Minnesota Daily Star, 40, 44; bankruptcy of, 48

Minnesota Department of Agriculture, 55

Minnesota Employers Association, 26

Minnesota Farm Bureau, xi, 155; and agricultural extension service, 99, 100; and Farmer-Labor party, 98, 101–2; membership of, 100

Minnesota Farm Conference, 140

Minnesota Farmer-Labor Party. *See* Farmer-Labor Party (Minnesota)

Minnesota Highway Department: and patronage, 59–60, 63–64, 66; and work relief, 80

Minnesota Industrial Union Council, 126

Minnesota Leader, 61, 144, 149

Minnesota Mortgage Moratorium Act, 93

Minnesota Nonpartisan League. *See* Nonpartisan League

Minnesota Railroad and Warehouse Commission, 37

Minnesota State Federation of Labor, 26, 28, 146; anti-Communism of, 116, 126, 127; civil service bill, 149–50; commitment to political action (1919), 34; convention (1936), 122; and debate over establishing permanent third party, 36–37; disbanding of political action committee, 52; and Farmer-Labor party, 150; and state printing plant, 80; and unemployment problem, 79

Minnesota State Highway Patrol, 80; presence of CIO organizer in offices of, 145; use of to disband farm picket lines, 92

Minnesota Union Advocate, 40, 144, 145, 147, 149

Mob disturbances: during Minneapolis strikes, 108–10, 112; by People's Lobby (1937), 142. *See also* Agrarian discontent and protest

Mondale, Walter, 2

Money supply, restriction of, 7

Montana, 7; state-level radicalism in, 50

Mortgages (farm and chattel): foreclosures on, 89; increased ratio of debt to valuation, 73; mob action to prevent foreclosures, 91, 92; moratorium legislation, 2, 90, 92–93, 135; and Rural Credits Bureau, 141

Murphy, Frank, 155–56

Murray, Philip, 117

Murray Hill agreement, 77

Muscle Shoals, 82

Naftalin, Arthur, x

National Civic Federation, 77

National Grange, 91

National Guard, 24, 135; Benson's use on labor's behalf, 139; Farmer-Labor pledge never to use in strike, 80; in Minneapolis strike (1934), 111–13, 115, 143; in packinghouse strike (1921), 78; Stassen's promise never to use in strike, 149

National Industrial Recovery Act (NIRA; 1933): provisions of, 85, 86, 103; section 7(a), and collective bargaining, 103, 113, 114; and Wagner Act, 120

National Labor Board (NLB), 120; abolition of, 111; limited power of, 109; referral of dispute to in Minneapolis strike, 106

National Labor Relations Board (NLRB), 25, 111; activism of, 123–24, 131–32; and Communist party, 125; election machinery of, and AFL and CIO, 123; functioning of, 121; public perception of, 134; and Wagner Act, 120, 132

National Nonpartisan League, 3, 32; financial difficulties of, 38

National Pacific Railroad, 60

National politics: vs. state level, 8; and world political economy, 176

National Progressives of America, 166, 171
National Recovery Administration (NRA), 96
National War Labor Board (NWLB), 25; and state labor policy, 27
Natural Products Marketing Act, 161
Nelson, Knute, 41
Ness, Henry, 110, 111
"New Day" (North Dakota), 3, 31–32
New Deal: agricultural policy of, 93–102; as break from political-economic orthodoxy, 87; counterattack on, 130–35; effect on American politics, 120; and Farmer-Labor party, 102, 118, 120, 135–38, 155, 171; and federalism, 10; initial relief and recovery programs, 85–87; and interest groups, 157; policies of, xi, 172–73; and political change, 135–36; and political elites, 162; reconsideration of, 174–75; and relief cutbacks, 153; and Republican politicians, 158; ruling on constitutionality of, 157; as watershed, 172–73. *See also* Democratic party
"New Deal constitutionalism," 175
New Democratic Party (NDP), 158, 165
Newspapers. *See* Press
New York Times, 167
NLRB vs. Jones & Laughlin, 121–23; effect of on union strength, 131
"Nonmetropolitan" areas, 12–13, 17; and postwar farm crisis, 72; protest politics in, 172; Socialists in, 13–15. *See also* Regionalism
Nonpartisanism: and Communist issue, 47; vs. third parties, 30, 38; and voter education, 54–55
Nonpartisan Leader, 32
Nonpartisan League, 1, 2, 16, 170, 173; allegations against, 21; comparison with other farmers' organizations, 87, 98, 101; decline and collapse of, 32, 34, 38; factionalism in, 32; in Idaho, 50–51; and Mahoney's proposal for coalition with Farmer-Labor party, 42, 45; in Minnesota, 20–21, 27–28,

43, 62; and National Nonpartisan League, 3, 32, 38; and "New Day" in North Dakota, 31–32; and North Dakota Republican primary (1916), 18–20; opposition to permanent third party, 36–37; origins in North Dakota, 17–18; as policy laboratory, 3; and recall election (1921), 32, 38; tactics of, 30, 39
Norris, George, 49, 81, 96, 169
Norris-LaGuardia Act, 80
North central states, party politics in, 11
North Dakota, 3; and economic institutions in Twin Cities, 21; farmer discontent in, 17–18; "New Day" in, 31–32; Republican primary (1916), 18–20. *See also* Nonpartisan League
North Dakota Agricultural College, 18, 19
North Dakota Mill and Elevator Association, 3, 31
North Dakota Nonpartisan League. *See* Nonpartisan League
North Dakota Socialist Party, 17
Northwestern states, party politics in, 11
Northwest Organizer, 144, 147
Nye, Gerald, 169

Oklahoma Farmer-Labor Reconstruction League, 1, 50; socialism in, 15
Old-age assistance, 134; in Canada, 163; and Civil War pension system, 6, 11; in Minnesota, 135
Olson, Floyd B., 62, 82, 100–1, 146; and alliance with Popular Front, 140; and control of state agencies, 58; and cost-of-production legislation, 90–91, 96–97; death of (1936), 119; and Farmer-Labor party, 49; and Farmers Holiday Association, 90–93; gubernatorial races, 45–46, 53–54, 57, 92, 117–18; intervention in Minneapolis strikes (1934), 108–14, 129; and legislative strategy, 67–68; and brief membership in IWW, 100; and Minnesota's institutional structure, 54–55; need for successor to, 66–67, 137, 168; and picketing by farmers (1932),

91–92; and politics of patronage, 57–
61, 67–68; and Republicans, 64–65;
strength of in rural areas, 117–18,
136; and Trotskyists, 116; use of National Guard by, 111–13, 115
Olson, Robert, 144
Ontario, 158, 160
Open-shop drive, 50, 104; and Citizens
Alliance, 77–79; and Farmer-Labor
party, 80; in Minneapolis, 114, 115
The Organizer (strike newspaper), 110,
112, 114, 116
Ottawa, 162

Padway, Joseph, 132
"Parity" concept, 95, 96
Park Region Echo, 64
Parliament (Canadian), 160, 161
Party-building: and debate over permanent party, 37–38; and partisan infrastructure, 38–41; patterns of, 10–
15; strategies of Farmer-Labor Association, 68, 69
Party platform(s): Farmer-Labor (1934),
1–2, 170; value of, 19
Party politics: antiparty feeling, 16, 51;
and Farmer-Labor party, 33; Hotelling-Downs model of, 139; Mahoney's
view of, 44; and Minnesota electoral
rules changes, 38; and Minnesota's
resistance to partisan control, 53–58;
in nonmetropolitan states, 14; one-
partyism, 11, 18, 19; and political
economy, 16; and political entrepreneurs, 157; and preprimary endorsing conventions, 36; regional
patterns of, xi, 6, 10–15, 17; types of,
1, 16, 173; value of competition in,
19–20; and volatility of electorate,
11–12, 44. *See also* Political education; Political parties; Third parties
Patronage: advantages of, 53; and civil
service merit system, 59, 66–68; and
control of Minnesota state bureaucracy, 57–58; cost of reorganizing,
64–67; and factionalism, 65–66, 68,
120; and Farmer-Labor Party, 65–66,
68, 120; vs. legislative strategy, 67–

68; and Minnesota Highway Depart-
ment, 59–60, 63–64, 66; partisan
control of, 59; resentment of, 66;
strategy of, 60–64
Peek, George N., 75, 95
Pennsylvania, collapse of Governor
Earle's coalition in, 155, 156
"Penny sales," 92
Pension system, Civil War, 6, 11. *See
also* Old-age assistance
People's Lobby, 142, 153
People's party, 13, 88
People's Voice, The, 36
Petersen, Hjalmar, 66–67, 115; cam-
paign against Benson, 146–47, 149
Peterson, Harry H., 57; and mortgage
moratorium act, 93
Picketing: and Farmers Holiday Association (1932), 90–92; in Minneapolis
strikes, 106, 108, 110; use of highway
patrol to disrupt, 93; violence involv-
ing, 108, 110
Pike, Frederick, 29, 93; and Mahoney's
plan for single partisan infrastructure,
43–44
Poirier, Joseph, 116
Police, clash with picketers in Minneapolis (1934), 108, 110
Political candidates: differentiation
among, 19–20; recruitment of, 33, 44
Political change: adaptation to, 163,
167–68; in Canada, 159; effects of,
xii; electoral change, 157; New Deal
as watershed, 172–73; and state-level
radicalism, 69, 177
Political culture, U.S. vs. Canada, 159
Political development, "consensus" view
of, 172–73
Political economy: balancing vs. accumulationist, 69, 70, 82, 85, 120,
135, 137; and effects of industrialization, 7–8; Farmer-Labor party, 82; of
Hoover administration, 83–85; national vs. regional, xi; neo-orthodox,
71; of 1920s, 70; NIRA as attempt to
balance, 103; and party politics, 16;
power to shape, 157; radical approach
in North Dakota, 2–3; redefinition at

Political economy (*continued*)
start of New Deal, 85–87; reform of, 8; and state governments generally, 3–4; transition in types of, 172; world, 176–77. *See also* Accumulationist model

Political education: and creation of party's infrastructure, 39; and Farmer-Labor Educational Bureau, 62–63; and Farmer-Labor party, 33, 42, 49; in nonpartisan elections, 54–55; and Nonpartisan League, 20. *See also* Propaganda; Voter registration

Political elites: and accumulationist model of economy, 6; and autonomy of state bureaucracy, 58; in Canada vs. U.S., 159, 162; and changing political economy, 69; and farmer-labor coalition, 146; in Minnesota Farmer-Labor party, 27, 30, 33–34, 48, 51; and permeability of party politics, 21; and political economy of 1920s, 71

Political entrepreneurs: Canadian, 163; disunity among, xii; in Farmers Holiday Association, 87; and interest groups, 157; limits of, and Nonpartisan League, 32; Mahoney as, 44; and Minnesota farmer-labor movement, 33–34, 42, 51–52; and Minnesota Republican primary (1918), 27–28; national focus of, 176; organization-building skills, 39; Republican, 139; responses of toward new public policies, 157; role of, 14; and state-level radicalism, 8; and type of political economy, 4, 172

Political entrepreneurs (radical): as builders of strong party organization in Minnesota, 33; constrained in Minnesota by antiparty environment, 51–52, 69; cooperation of in maintaining farmer-labor politics, 34; as counterelites, 16; creativity of, 172; as creators of Minnesota farmer-labor coalition, 27–28; as developers of Farmers Holiday Association, 87, 88; as developers of North Dakota Non-

partisan League, 17; as developers of state-level radicalism, 14–15; as organizers of Minneapolis strikes (1934), 105

Political indicators: of electoral receptivity in "nonmetropolitan" states to economic protest candidates, 11–14; of electoral strength of Minnesota farmer-labor coalition (1919–21), 34–37; of Farmer-Labor collapse (1938), 153–55; of Farmer-Labor success (1930s), 120; of Olson's success (1930), 53–54; of performance of Minnesota Farmer-Labor Federation (1924), 45–46; of Republican crossover voting in Farmer-Labor primary (1938), 148; of rural-urban tensions in Minnesota (1930–34), 117–18; of relative stability of Minnesota Farmer-Labor party (1926–1928), 49

Political leadership, and values of people, x

Political parties: effect of New Deal on, 170; features of, ix, xi, 10–11; national vs. state-level, 8, 101–2, 118, 136–37; traditional organizations of, 12, 173; in U.S. vs. Canada, 159. *See also* Democratic party; Party politics; Republican party; Third parties

Political thought, effect of New Deal on, 172

Politics, restructuring of, 176; and consolidation of Farmer-Labor party infrastructure, 44–45; Mahoney's plan for, 46–47. *See also* National politics; Party politics; Political economy; State-level radicalism

Popular Front, 148, 171; and Benson administration in Minnesota, 140–41, 147; as stage of Communist party, 128; and teamsters Local 544, 129–30. *See also* Comintern; Communist party

Populism, 1, 8, 34, 172; and John Bosch, 89

Populist party, vote in 1892 election, 13

Poverty, in less developed areas, 7

Prairie Farm Rehabilitation Act, 161
Presidency: expanded power of, 133, 175; and reformist focus, 176
Presidential elections: (1892, 1896), 8, 14; (1912), 15; (1920, 1924), 13, 50; (1928), 49; (1932), 90–91; (1936), 135, 157, 170, 171; (1984, 1988), 173–75. *See also* Electoral politics
Presidential politics: Mahoney's plan to reshape, 46–47; vs. state-level politics, 101–2, 118, 137
President's Mediation Commission, 26
President's Re-Employment Agreement (PRA), 85, 96
Press: attack of on NLRB, 132; county newspapers in North Dakota, 31–32; network of supporting farmer-labor coalition, 40; and Nonpartisan League, 20, 24; strike newspaper, *The Organizer,* 110
Preus, J.A.O.: and antisorehead legislation, 36; election as governor, 35, 77; and packinghouse strike, 78; senatorial campaign of, 41
Price deflation, and agriculture, 7
Primaries: diffusion of, 176; direct, 11; open ballots for, 56, 135; and preprimary endorsements, 166. *See also* Elections; Presidential elections
Primaries (Republican): Minnesota (1918), 27–28; (1920), 35–36; North Dakota (1916), 18–20; (1918), 31
Printing plant, state, 80
Privy Council, Judicial Committee of, 162
Producers and Consumers Convention, 24
Production control: credit for to Farm Bureau, 98–99; and farm prices, 94–96
Progressive, 166
Progressive movement, 8; in Canada, 158; regional successes of, 11
Progressive party. *See* Idaho Progressive party; National Progressives of America; Wisconsin Progressive party
Propaganda: anti-semitic and anti-Communist, 148; and county presses in North Dakota, 31–32; and WPNPL, 36, 39. *See also* Political education
Property tax, in Minnesota, 135, 139, 141
Province-level radicalism (in Canada), 158–65; and political change, 159
Provincial governments (Canadian), and shift of power, 160
Public health, and Sheppard-Towner Act (1921), 70
Public opinion polls, 134–35, 137, 151, 171
Public ownership: in Canada, 163, 164; of grain mills and elevators, 18, 74; support for, 2, 171
Public policies, implementation of, 157
Public Utilities Holding Company Act (1935), 130
Public works: labor control of in Twin Cities, 37–38; programs, 2; and work relief, 80
Public Works Administration (PWA), 86

Quebec, 160

Radicalism: in Farmer-Labor party, x, 2; investigation of by Dies Committee, 135, 169; and origin of American Labor Party of New York, 170. *See also* Communist party; Socialism; State-level radicalism
Railroad(s), 159, 160; return to private ownership of, 73; shopmen's strike, 60
Railroad brotherhoods, 54; and Conference for Progressive Political Action, 47; and WPNPL, 39–40
Railroad and Warehouse Commission, 56
Railway Labor Act (1926), 70, 132
"Ratio-price" concept, 95
Reagan, Ronald, 173, 174, 175
Recall: establishment of, 11; in North Dakota (1919), 32
Recessions (1920s), 79, 84; (1929–30), Hoover's attitude toward, 84; (1937:

Recessions (*continued*)
  Roosevelt Recession), xi, 133–34,
    140, 152, 158, 167; (1982–83), 175.
    See also Great Depression
Reconstruction, 11; after World War I,
    and farm crisis, 72–73
Reconstruction Finance Corporation, 85,
    114, 157; inflation of currency by, 97;
    and Minneapolis strikes, 113–14
Redistributive politics: and Farmer-
    Labor party, x, 140; as federal re-
    sponsibility, 176; and goals of Wagner
    Act, 131; role of state government in,
    4, 16. *See also* Economic inequality
Referendum, 11
Reform model, 4–5. *See also*
    Accumulationist model
Regionalism: in Canada and U.S., 159;
    patterns of economic and social de-
    pendency, 71; patterns of party build-
    ing, 10–15. *See also* "Nonmetropoli-
    tan" areas
Regulatory agencies and powers
    (federal), 175; curbing of (1920s), 70;
    and economic regulation, 9; and gov-
    ernment activism, 121; as national
    center of power, 162; and political
    change, 157
Regulatory agencies and powers (state),
    10; and Farmer-Labor goals, 82; in
    Minnesota, 55–56
Reno, Milo, 105; and Farmers Holiday
    Association, 88–90; and farm strike,
    96, 97
Republican party, 6, 11; and accumula-
    tionist policy (1920s), 70–71; and dis-
    array of Farmer-Labor leadership,
    139; increased intention to vote for
    (1938), 135; investigations of, by
    Olson, 64–65; and North Dakota
    Nonpartisan League, 32; and patron-
    age issue, 65; and political change,
    137, 177; and regional voting pat-
    terns, 12–13; and Socialists, 15; and
    state constabulary, 80; in Wisconsin,
    166–67. *See also* Party politics; Politi-
    cal parties; Primaries (Republican)
Republican party (in Minnesota), 41,

    118; boring from within, 30, 35–36;
    conservative domination of state legis-
    lature, 55; and election of Stassen,
    151–53; extremism of hardliners in,
    24; and Farmer-Labor party, 18, 35–
    36, 46, 119; hegemony of, 21, 57,
    156; and Minneapolis streetcar com-
    pany, 37; and Nonpartisan League,
    23; and open-shop movement, 77; re-
    alignment toward, 154; victory of in
    1938 election, 153–56
Republicans: adaptation to New Deal,
    158; civil servants, replacement of by
    Farmer-Labor appointees, 61; and
    push to amend Wagner Act, 132
Revenue Act of 1936, 130
Robinson-Patman Fair Trade Practice
    Bill, 102
Rockwell, John, 116
Roosevelt, Franklin D.: aim at budget
    balancing, 168; farm policy of, 90–
    91, 95–97; leftward movement of,
    130–32; and Minnesota strikes, 113,
    115; movement beyond party of
    (1936), 170; and NIRA, 103; presi-
    dential campaigns, 90–91, 135, 157;
    and Recession (1937–38), xi, 133;
    view of as would-be dictator, 133,
    166–67. *See also* New Deal
Roosevelt, Theodore, 29
Roosevelt Recession (1937–38), xi,
    133–34, 140, 152, 158, 167
Rural Credits Bureau, 141
Ryan, Father John, 111

St. Lawrence seaway, 74, 82
St. Paul, Minn., 35; Farmer-Labor party
    in, 155; labor movement in, 38, 39;
    population mix of, 152; strikes in, 78.
    See also Twin Cities
St. Paul convention (1924): Communist
    domination of, 47; and nomination of
    La Follette, 46;
St. Paul Trades and Labor Assembly, 28,
    35
Salaries. *See* Wages and salaries
San Francisco general strike (1934), 86,
    103

Saskatchewan Farmer-Labour Party, 158
Schachtman, Max, 112
Schall, Tom, 45, 54, 66
Schaper, William, 139
Sears, Roebuck, and Company, 81
"Sears-Roebuck sales," 92
Seattle general strike (1919), 103
Sheppard-Towner Act (1921), 70
Shipstead, Henrik, 119, 169; business
   support for, 43; conversion to Re-
   publican party (1940), 156; guber-
   natorial candidacy of (1920), 35, 36;
   and McNary-Haugenism, 76; and pol-
   icy on labor injunctions, 80; senatorial
   races (1922, 1928), 41, 42, 49
Silver Shirts, 148
Simpson, John, 91, 94, 96
Sioux City, Iowa, governors' meeting in,
   90, 91
Sit-down strikes, 117, 131, 150; meatpackers' (1933), 105; public hostility
   to, 134
Skoglund, Karl, 105, 107, 116
Smith, Al, 49, 89
Smith-Lever Act (1914), 98
Socialism: damage of Stalinism to, 129;
   and independent businessmen, 82; influence of on Milo Reno, 88; and
   political entrepreneurs, 14. See also
   Communists; Debsian socialism;
   Trotskyists
Socialist party, 8, 104; in Minnesota,
   27–28; and nonmetropolitan electo-
   rates, 13–15; in North Dakota, 17,
   18; in Oklahoma, 50; and union lead-
   ers, 28; working with other activists,
   15
Social Security Act (1935), 130, 169
Soil Conservation and Domestic Allot-
   ment Act (1936), 101
Sorauf, Frank, 66
"Sorehead" tactics, 36
South, 71; party politics in, 10–11
South Dakota, state-level radicalism in,
   50
Southwestern states, party politics in, 11
Soviet Union, 128, 176; reporting of
   events in, 40. See also Comintern

Spillman, W.J., 95
Stalinism, 129, 143
Stassen, Harold, 139; and Communist
   issue, 150; election as governor, 152–
   55; and Farmer-Labor factionalism,
   149–51; and Republican domination
   of Minnesota, 156; and revolt of
   "reasonable middle," 151–52
"State-building" processes, 157
State Federation of Labor. See
   Minnesota State Federation of Labor
State government(s): accumulationist vs.
   reform models of, 4–5; changes in
   sovereignty of, 9; and interstate competition, 9; political climate generally,
   3; regulatory powers of, 10
State-level radicalism: Canadian perspective on, 158–65; conditions for, 5–6,
   157; crisis of, 135–38; and different
   views of government, 4, 172; diffusion
   of, 20–21; effect of New Deal on,
   170, 172–73; and federalism, 8–10,
   15; limits of, 69, 101–2; as model in
   current political economy, 176; and
   national forces, xi, 8, 170; North Dakota's "New Deal" as model, 32; organizations exemplifying, 1; in other
   states, 50–51; and political change,
   157–58, 167–71; and political entrepreneurs, 14; possibility of today,
   174, 175; regional differences in, 10–
   13; and social stress, 6–8; as type of
   politics, 16. See also specific party or
   organization, e.g., Farmer-Labor Party; Nonpartisan League
State militia (in strikes), 10; Olson's refusal to use, 92. See also Police; National Guard
States, nonmetropolitan. See
   "Nonmetropolitan" areas
Steffens, Lincoln, 71
Stevenson, Adlai, 139
Stock market, 1929 crash of, 83
Streetcar franchise: and carmen's union,
   26; in Minneapolis, 37, 48
Strikes: farm strike, 89, 96, 97; general
   strikes, 26, 103; Hormel strike (1933),
   105; "Little Steel" strike, 131; in

Strikes (*continued*)
Minneapolis (1920–21), 78; (1934),
80, 86, 103–15; public opinion about,
151; of St. Paul printers and pack-
inghouse workers (1920–21), 78; sit-
down strikes, 105, 117, 131, 134,
150; and state militias, 10; use of
National Guard in, 78, 80, 111–13,
115; waves of (1932–34), 86, 103,
106; (1937), 131, 134, 155. *See also*
Picketing
Strong, A.W., 77, 114
Strout, I.C. "Dutch," 60; and Farmer-
Labor party infrastructure, 62–63; as
state director of personnel, 61–62
Supreme Court, Canadian, 161. *See also*
Courts (Minnesota); U.S. Supreme
Court
Surpluses. *See* Farm surpluses
"System of 1896," 6, 8

Tariffs, 4–5, 6; in Canada, 159; and
McNary-Haugen bill, 75
Taxation: burden of on farmers, 73; in
Canada, 160; exemption from on
farm improvements, 18; and goal of
balanced budget, 85, 134; and government policy, 4–5; of iron ore shipping, 74, 141–42; in Minnesota, 74,
135, 140; motor vehicle and gasoline,
59; reductions in, 70. *See also*
Property tax
Tax codes, regulation of, 10
Tax measures, Revenue Act of 1936,
130
Tax reforms, in Minnesota, 2, 135,
139–40
"Tax rental" agreements, 163
Teamsters union, 103; and assassination
of Corcoran, 145–46; and development of network of locals by, 129
Teamsters union (Local 544): links with
Farmer-Labor party, 129; and murder
of Bill Brown, 148; and political
changes in Communist party, 129–
130; Trotskyist leadership of, 128
Teamsters union (Local 574): and Min-

neapolis strikes (1934), 105–10, 115;
organization of by Trotskyists, 104–5;
"red-baiting" of, 116; reorganization
as Local 544, 128
Teigan, Henry, 42, 67
Texas, state-level radicalism in, 50
Third parties: and anti-sorehead legislation, 36; collapse of, 170, 172; labor
preference for, 38; and nonmetropolitan electorates, 13; vs. nonpartisan tactics, 30; obstacles to, 33;
opposition to, 38; origins in Minnesota, 29–30; and Philip La Follette
(1938), 166, 171; and Robert La Follette (1924), 46–47; and state-level
radicalism, ix, 1. *See also* Farmer-Labor Party; Nonpartisan League
Third Ward Club (Minneapolis), 62
Tobin, Daniel, 103, 116, 129
Toledo strikes (1934), 86, 103, 111
Tonnage tax proposal, 74
Townley, Arthur Claude, 105, 147; and
Nonpartisan League, 18, 20; and
North Dakota legislature, 17, 31; op-
position of to third party, 38; organi-
zational skills of, 17–18; prosecution
of, 24; and Republican primaries, 18,
35
Townsend Plan, 168
Tracy, Dan, 124
Trades and Labor Assemblies, 34; in
Minneapolis, 48; in St. Paul, 28, 35
Trade unions, in Canada, 158
Tri-County Council of Defense, 92
Trotskyists, 103, 143, 145; and changes
in Communist party, 129, 130; and
Farmer-Labor leaders, 116, 148; relations with Benson, 144; support for
Petersen by, 147; and teamsters union,
104, 115, 116, 128–29; and tension
within Minnesota labor movement,
136
Truckers' strikes (Minneapolis, 1934),
80, 86; beginning of, 105–6; and Citizens Alliance, 109–15; and Communist League, 105–7; and employer
recognition of unions, 103, 104, 106–

7, 111; Haas-Dunnigan plan for ending, 111–12; Olson's use of National Guard in, 112–13, 143; violent confrontations in, 108, 110

Twin Cities (Minneapolis and St. Paul, Minn.), 30, 43; economic institutions in, 21; farmer-labor newspapers in, 40; farmer protests in, 90, 91; importance of to Farmer-Labor party, 138; labor movement in, 26, 37–38, 48; relocation of Nonpartisan League to, 20–21; socialist strength in, 28; unemployment in, 79. *See also* Minneapolis; St. Paul

Twin Cities Ladies' Garment Workers, 122

Unemployed Councils, 128

Unemployment, 7, 79, 134; and Benson's use of WPA, 152–53; in Canada, 160; and Farmer-Labor party, 64; Hoover's nonintervention in, 85; in 1920s, 71, 79; protest involving, 153; public works programs to relieve, 2, 63–64, 80, 86

Unemployment insurance, 134; in Canada, 163; and Lundeen Bill, 168, 174; in North Dakota, 18

Union(ism): business attitudes toward, 26, 77; in Canada, 161, 163, 165; and charges of gangsterism, 146; collective bargaining, 2, 3, 31, 70, 77, 86, 113, 115, 163; Communists in, 43–44, 104–7, 146; company, 82, 86, 121; employer recognition of, 103, 104, 106–7, 111, 123; government-supervised elections in, 111; injunctions against union tactics, 78, 80; jurisdictional disputes, 124; membership decline (1920s), 39, 49; membership growth (1900–40), 125; in Minnesota, 28, 34, 49, 126; percentages of membership, 125; public attitude toward, 134; and Socialist party, 28; split between AFL and CIO, 122–23, 126, 143, 155, 166;

use of force against, 10, 78, 80, 161; and Wagner Act, 121. *See also* Labor movement; Strikes

Union Advocate, 40, 44

United Electrical, Radio, and Machine Workers (UE), 127, 144

United Farmers League, 92

United Mine Workers, 103, 122

U.S. Congress: approaches to agricultural crisis, 94–100; centralization of power in, 169; Democratic strength in (1930s), 157; Farmer-Labor politicians in, 36, 41, 45, 46, 119, 156, 169; liberal bloc in, 168; special session of (1933), 83, 133. *See also* New Deal

U.S. Department of Agriculture: extension service and county agents of, 98–99; and loans on stored corn, 97

U.S. House of Representatives, and Lundeen Bill, 168–69

U.S. Senate: Committee on Forestry and Agriculture, 89; motion to expel La Follette from, 24

U.S. Steel, 142

U.S. Supreme Court, 6; and constitutionality of New Deal, 157; and *Home Building and Loan Association v. Blaisdell*, 93; invalidation of AAA by, 101; and labor law, 78; and *NLRB vs. Jones & Laughlin*, 121–23, 131; Roosevelt's plan to pack, 133; validation of Wagner Act, 120, 121

University of Minnesota, 58, 139

Utilities, public ownership of, 171

Van Lear, Thomas, 143; fear of Communist influence, 44; and Nonpartisan League, 28, 37; opposition of A.W. Strong to, 114; races for mayor of Minneapolis, 28, 30–31; retirement to Florida, 48; and WPNPL, 35, 42

Veterans, and loyalty to Republican party, 11

Volatility, of electorate, 12

Votaw, O.R., 144–45, 147

Voter registration, 175; Farmer-Labor efforts in, 42

Voting patterns: in nonmetropolitan states, 12–13; regional differences in, 10–12, 117–18, 154–55. *See also* Electoral politics

Wages and salaries: cuts in 1921 vs. 1930, 84; federal, slashing of, 87; inequality of, 175

Wagner (Senator), 131

Wagner Act (1935), xi, 120, 136; and administrative activism, 121; campaign to revise, 132, 134; redistributive goals of, 131

Wallace, Henry, 96

Walsh, General Ellard, 108

Washington (D.C.): as power center, xi, 157

Washington (state) Farmer-Labor party, 1, 50

Wealth, distribution of. *See* Economic inequality; Redistributive politics

Weaver, General, 13

Weekly Rest in Industrial Undertakings Act, 161

Wefald, Knud, 91

Welfare services: in Canada, 165; involvement of recipients in, 174; state-run, 2

Welfare state: basis of in Minnesota mortgage moratorium act, 93; constitutional foundations of, 2; discontent with, xi, 134, 137, 174

Western states, party politics in, 11

Wharton, Arthur, 124

Wheat Board, 161

Wheat farming, 18–19; and decreasing prices and demand, 72. *See also* Grain

White supremacists, 11

Wilson, Milburn L., 95

Wilson, Woodrow, 72, 122, 139

Wisconsin, political economy of, 166–71

Wisconsin Agriculture Council, 166

Wisconsin Farmer-Labor Progressive Federation, 166–67, 171

Wisconsin Farmers Holiday Association, 166

Wisconsin Progressive Party, 1, 16, 156, 172, 173; collapse of, 166; formation of, 165; in U.S. Senate, 169

Wisconsin State Federation of Labor, 166

Wobblies, 15, 104

Women's auxiliaries (of political leagues), 39, 40

Workers, and new industrialism, 7. *See also* Farmers and workers; Labor; Union(ism)

Workers Alliance, 149

Workers' Bill for Unemployment and Social Insurance, 168

Working People's Nonpartisan Political League (WPNPL), 60; change of name to Farmer-Labor Federation, 45; decline of, 39; leafletting by, 36, 39; and Mahoney's plan for consolidation, 42–43; membership in, 62; origin of in Working People's Political League, 35; strength of, 39–40. *See also* Farmer-Labor Federation

Working People's Political League, 29, 35

Work relief: Minnesota Highway Department as, 59–60, 63–64; New Deal programs for, 86; protests involving, 153. *See also* Public Works; Unemployment

Works Progress Administration (WPA), 130; Benson's use of for electoral purposes, 152

World War I: Canadian involvement in, 160, 162; economic impact of, 19, 70, 79; farm crisis in aftermath of, 72–73; labor advances in, 25; socialist attitude toward, 28

World War II, Canadian involvement in, 163

WPA, 171

Wright, William F., 144

Young Communist League, 152

Zingale, Nancy Hill, 154–55